Git

Rheinwerk Computing

The Rheinwerk Computing series from Rheinwerk Publishing offers new and established professionals comprehensive guidance to enrich their skillsets and enhance their career prospects. Our publications are written by leading experts in the fields of programming, administration, security, analytics, and more. Each book is detailed and hands-on to help readers develop essential, practical skills that they can apply to their daily work. For further information, please visit our website: *www.rheinwerk-computing.com*.

Philip Ackermann
JavaScript: The Comprehensive Guide
2022, 982 pages, paperback and e-book
www.rheinwerk-computing.com/5554

Sebastian Springer
Node.js: The Comprehensive Guide
2022, 834 pages, paperback and e-book
www.rheinwerk-computing.com/5556

Johannes Ernesti, Peter Kaiser
Python 3: The Comprehensive Guide
2022, 1036 pages, paperback and e-book
www.rheinwerk-computing.com/5566

Christian Ullenboom
Java: The Comprehensive Guide
2023, 1128 pages, paperback and e-book
www.rheinwerk-computing.com/5557

Bernd Öggl, Michael Kofler
Docker: Practical Guide for Developers and DevOps Teams
2023, approx. 496 pp., paperback and e-book
www.rheinwerk-computing.com/5650

Bernd Öggl, Michael Kofler

Git

Project Management for Developers and DevOps Teams

Editor Megan Fuerst
Acquisitions Editor Hareem Shafi
German Edition Editors Christoph Meister, Anne Scheibe
Translation Winema Language Services, Inc.
Copyeditor Yvette Chin
Cover Design Graham Geary
Photo Credit Shutterstock: 80373751/© tovovana; iStockphoto: 157567712/© grandriver
Layout Design Vera Brauner
Production Graham Geary
Typesetting III-satz, Germany
Printed and bound in Canada, on paper from sustainable sources

ISBN 978-1-4932-2289-6
© 2023 by Rheinwerk Publishing, Inc., Boston (MA)
1st edition 2023
2nd German edition published 2022 by Rheinwerk Verlag, Bonn, Germany

Library of Congress Cataloging-in-Publication Control Number: 2022035131

Contents at a Glance

Dear Reader,

Never have I felt a greater need for version control than when I played a game of pool with five children under 10.

On a recent family vacation to a cabin in Colorado, the basement pool table was a big hit. When I joined my nieces and nephews for a game, I quickly realized that the rules would be *nontraditional*, to say the least. There were spontaneous guidelines for using hands (offensive) versus pool cues (defensive), guarding pockets, and scoring combos. Learning the rules was hard enough; tracking them as they changed minute-by-minute was harder.

And then there was mediating the different versions of the game between the five kids. One niece's arrangement of stripes and solids was one nephew's target for impact. Despite my best efforts, fingers were pinched in the chaotic flurry of ideas.

Working together in an organized (and peaceful) way has its challenges, regardless of age or subject. In the programming world, collaboration is essential. Developers need to write, test, and iterate on code in tandem with other team members, and the different versions need to be controlled to maintain organized, traceable changes and avoid loss of work. That's where Git comes in—and this book.

What did you think about *Git: Project Management for Developers and DevOps Teams*? Your comments and suggestions are the most useful tools to help us make our books the best they can be. Please feel free to contact me and share any praise or criticism you may have.

Thank you for purchasing a book from Rheinwerk Publishing!

Megan Fuerst
Editor, Rheinwerk Publishing

meganf@rheinwerk-publishing.com
www.rheinwerk-computing.com
Rheinwerk Publishing · Boston, MA

Contents

3   Basic Principles of Git

6   GitLab

7   Azure DevOps, Bitbucket, Gitea, and Gitolite

8   Workflows

9 Working Techniques 283

10   Git in Real Life

11   Git Problems and Their Solutions

Preface

Whenever several people work together on a software project, a system is needed to store all the changes made in a traceable way. Such a version control system must also give all developers access to the entire project. Each programmer knows what the others have done recently; developers can try out the code of the others and test the code's interaction with their own changes.

In the past, many version control systems were used, such as Concurrent Versions System (CVS), Apache Subversion (SVN), or Microsoft Visual SourceSafe (VSS). In the last decade, however, Git has become the de facto standard.

The GitHub web platform played a significant role in this success, making learning and using Git much easier. Countless open-source projects use the free GitHub offering for project hosting. Commercial customers who didn't want to publish their source code pay for this service. GitHub is not the only Git platform, of course: Major competitors include GitLab, Azure DevOps Services, and Bitbucket. Microsoft bought GitHub in 2018 for $7.5 billion. Unlike other acquisitions, this development hasn't hurt GitHub's popularity so far.

The Story of Git

Git came into being because Linus Torvalds needed a new version management system for the further development of the Linux kernel. The developer community had previously used the BitKeeper program. Torvalds was basically satisfied with the program, but a license change necessitated a switch. Of the open-source programs available at the time, none met his high standards.

So, the Linux chief developer briefly stopped his main work and created the basic framework for Git in just two weeks. The name *Git* stands for *stupid* or *moron*, and the help page man git also refers to the program as the *stupid content tracker*.

That this definition was an understatement became clear only gradually, long after Torvalds had given up on further development of Git and put it out of his hands. Not only did kernel developers quickly and easily switch their work to Git, but in the years that followed, more and more software projects outside the open-source world switched to Git as well.

Git made its final breakthrough when web platforms such as GitHub and GitLab became established. These websites simplify the hosting of Git projects enormously and have become an indispensable part of everyday Git life. (Even the Linux kernel is now on GitHub!)

Ironically, Torvalds' main goal in designing Git was to create a decentralized version control system. But the centralized approach of GitHub and others made Git attractive for developers outside the guru league.

Some rate the importance of Git as highly as that of Linux. Torvalds has thus twice succeeded in completely turning the software universe on its head.

Everyone Uses It, but No One Understands It

With all the enthusiasm, Git was clearly designed by professionals for professionals. We don't want to give you the impression in this book that Git is easy because it isn't. You'll need to keep in mind the following considerations:

- Often, more than one way exists to reach a goal. For readers already familiar with Git, this idea is useful, but if you're just learning Git, this diversity can be confusing.
- Many open-source projects are accused of being poorly documented. You really can't say that about Git. On the contrary, every git command and every possible application is explained in man pages as well as on the website (*https://git-scm.com/docs*) in such granularity and with so many conceivable special cases that you can get lost in the details.
- Complicating matters further, some terms carry many different meanings, and easily confused subcommands might perform widely divergent tasks. Some terms have different meanings depending on their context or are used inconsistently in the documentation.

We have a confession: Despite years of using Git, we still learned a lot while writing this book!

About This Book

Of course, you can use Git in a minimalistic way. However, small deviations from the daily routine can then lead to surprising and often incomprehensible side effects or errors.

Every Git beginner knows that feeling when a git command returns an incomprehensible error message: In a cold sweat, you wonder whether you've just permanently destroyed a repository for all your developers and try to find someone to persuade Git to continue working after all with the right commands.

Thus, describing Git without going into depth isn't useful. Only a good understanding of how Git works gives you the confidence you'll need to cleanly fix merge conflicts or other problems.

At the same time, however, we knew that this book could only work if we gave priority to the essential functions. Despite its over 400 pages, this book is *not* the all-encompassing guide to Git. We cannot consider every single special case or introduce every Git sub-command, no matter how exotic. We've therefore tried to separate the wheat from the chaff in this book.

This book is divided into manageable chapters that you can read as needed, like building blocks:

- After a short introduction in **Chapter 1**, we'll introduce the use of Git in **Chapter 2** through **Chapter 4**. We'll focus on the use of Git at the command level and only marginally discuss platforms such as GitHub or other user interfaces (UIs).

  For Git beginners, we recommend starting with these first four chapters. Even if you have some Git experience, you should definitely take a few hours to read **Chapter 3** and try out some of the techniques we present (merging, rebasing, etc.) in a test repository.

- The next three chapters introduce the most important Git platforms. Especially for complex projects, these platforms provide useful additional functions, for instance, to perform automatic tests or to implement continuous integration (CI).

  Of course, we also show you how to host your own Git repository. With GitLab, Gitea, or Gitolite, this goal can be realized relatively easily.

- Then, we'll turn from the basics to the practical:

  - In **Chapter 8**, we'll describe popular patterns for guiding the work of numerous developers into orderly paths (*branches*) with Git.

  - **Chapter 9** focuses on advanced Git features, such as hooks, submodules, subtrees, and two-factor authentication, which are all supported by major Git platforms.

  - **Chapter 10** shows how you can use version configuration files (*dotfiles*) or the entire */etc* directory with Git on Linux systems, how to switch a project from SVN to Git, and how to realize a simple website quickly and easily with Git and Hugo.

  - **Chapter 11** helps you break the deadlock on hard-to-understand error messages. In this chapter, you'll also find instructions on implementing special requests, for example, removing large files from a Git repository or performing a merge operation on a selected file only.

- To close the book, **Chapter 12** briefly summarizes the most important git commands and their options. In this chapter, we followed the motto "Less is more." Our goal was not a complete reference, but rather a guide to the "essence of Git".

Sample Repositories

Some examples from this book are available on GitHub at the following link:

https://github.com/git-compendium

A Note to Readers

We realize that you may not begin reading this book with great enthusiasm: Perhaps you need to use Git for a project. Your goal might not be Git as such—you want to produce code to drive your project. You may not really have the time or inclination to learn about Git; you just want to know enough to use Git without errors.

We understand that motivation. Nevertheless, we strongly recommend that you invest a few hours more than planned to get to know Git systematically.

We promise you: You'll win this time back later! Poor understanding of Git inevitably means that you'll need to keep searching the internet for solutions to problems you've already encountered (often under time pressure).

Although your current focus is primarily on your project, Git skills are a long-term core competency that you'll need as a developer in many future projects. With this need in mind, we wish you much success with Git!

Michael Kofler (*https://kofler.info*)
Bernd Öggl (*https://webman.at*)

Chapter 1
Git in Ten Minutes

In this mini chapter, we want to introduce you to Git without overwhelming you with too many details. We explain what Git is for and what you can do with it, even if you don't know the concepts behind Git yet.

The title of this chapter is admittedly a bit sensational: We've calculated the time quite optimistically, but "Git in ten minutes" definitely sounds better than "Git in 25 minutes," doesn't it?

1.1   What Is Git?

Git is a decentralized version control program. In software projects, Git remembers the changes made by various developers. Later, you can track who made which changes and when (and ultimately who was responsible for a catastrophic security bug discovered two years later....).

Basically, you can use Git for any kind of project where only you or a whole team repeatedly modify, add, or delete various files. We even managed the Markdown files and images for this book with Git.

Git works especially well when a project consists of many relatively small text files. Although Git can handle binary files, tracking changes *within* such files is difficult. In this respect, Git isn't ideal for tracking changes in Microsoft Office documents, in audio and video files, or in virtual machine (VM) images.

1.1.1   The git Command

In the terminal or in PowerShell, you can control Git by using the `git` command. Numerous options available with this command allow you to download Git projects from external repositories like GitHub, save changed files in a "commit" and upload them again, switch between different branches of a software project (e.g., `main` and `develop`), undo changes, and more. A *repository* is a collection of all the files that make up a project, containing not only the current version, but also all previous versions and all development branches.

> **"Git" or "git"?**
>
> In this book, we use both the term "Git" and the command git. In addition to upper-case and lowercase, the font also makes our meaning clear: "Git" refers to the version control system in its entirety, including its concepts and ideas. git, on the other hand, stands for the command to use these functions.
>
> This distinction is important because some of Git's features are available to you without the git command—for example, in integrated development environments (IDEs), editors, or web interfaces. So, you can use Git in many ways. The git command is only one way (but for special functions, it's the most important one!).

1.1.2   Git User Interfaces

Many chapters in this book focus on the git command. However, you can also use at least a subset of the Git functions via convenient interfaces. All popular IDEs (Microsoft Visual Studio, Xcode, IntelliJ IDEA, Android Studio, etc.) and many editors (Atom, Sublime Text, Visual Studio Code [VS Code], etc.) provide menu commands for performing elementary Git operations in a straightforward manner. Web interfaces include GitHub or GitLab. Not only do these user interfaces (UIs) enable you to manage Git projects and, for example, track the changes made in a file, but you can also use various additional functions for issue/bug management, automated tests, and more.

In this book, we'll introduce you to Git functions through some editors or IDEs as examples in Chapter 2. However, for all the charm that comes from comfortable Git graphical user interfaces (GUIs), one thing must be clear: If you don't understand Git, you'll hit a dead end sooner or later (more likely sooner) when using even the most wonderful tools.

1.1.3   Git versus GitHub versus GitLab

Basically, Git is a standalone tool that doesn't rely on central repositories. In practice, however, external Git repositories such as GitHub or GitLab are ubiquitous. Modern web interfaces facilitate both the entry and the administration of projects. These platforms greatly simplify data exchange between members of a development team, serve as an additional backup, and provide various additional functions (documentation, bug tracker, quality assurance [QA], etc.). For public projects, these repositories also act as an information and download page for anyone interested in the project.

Among Git hosting providers, *GitHub*, which was acquired by Microsoft in 2018, currently has the largest market share. You could always set up open-source projects at GitHub for free. In April 2020, many restrictions also fell on private projects due to competitive pressure. (In a private project, the source code is only visible to selected people.) As a result, even relatively large projects can be stored on GitHub for free.

1

GitHub offers commercial users many additional features for a fee—that's its business model.

Many alternatives to GitHub are available. The best known is the company *GitLab*, which offers rather similar functions—also either for free or commercially, depending on requirements. As with GitHub, the free features are quite generous. The real special feature of GitLab is that the source code of the program is freely available. Thus, you can set up GitLab on its own server—a great advantage for organizations or companies uncomfortable with handing over all their intellectual property. In addition, running your own Git server can reduce ongoing costs. But don't forget your own costs for administration, server operation, network traffic, and backups!

Other providers for Git hosting or for corresponding software include *Azure Repos*, *Bitbucket*, *Gitea*, and *Gitolite* (the last two for running on a custom server). In this book, we assume that you have a (free) account with GitHub, GitLab, or another Git provider. Some basic functions of GitHub are described in introductory chapters. Separate chapters are then devoted to features for advanced users and for setting up GitLab on your own server.

Git Hosts Aren't an Alternative to Git, but a Supplement

We'd like to clarify one point especially for beginners to Git: Providers like GitHub or GitLab don't replace basic Git concepts or the `git` command. Rather, these providers have built upon the ideas provided by Git to offer additional functions that have proven enormously useful in practice, *while also* lowering the barriers to entry. A free account with a Git provider and the `git` command on your computer form the ideal playground for learning how Git works.

1.2   Downloading Software from GitHub

The first time you encountered Git, perhaps you landed on the GitHub portal while searching for a program. There you can choose between several download options: For beginners, the easiest option is to download the whole project as a ZIP file. However, if you want to learn Git or use its features, you should get familiar with `git` commands. With the `git clone` command, you can download a copy of the Git project to your own computer, thus creating a "clone" of the project, so to speak.

Requirements

In the following sections, we assume that the `git` command is already installed on your computer. If not the case, refer to Chapter 2, Section 2.1.

For this first example, on the other hand, registering with GitHub isn't necessary. `git clone` works for public projects without any registration.

In the GitHub download dialog box, the **Clone** with **HTTPS** variant is active by default. (The **SSH** option shown in Figure 1.1 is only available if you have a GitHub account and are logged on. We'll discuss communication via SSH in Chapter 2, Section 2.4.) Now, copy the URL to the clipboard by clicking the button and paste the URL into the terminal, Git Bash, or PowerShell after `git clone`:

```
git clone https://github.com/<author>/<project>.git
```

Figure 1.1 Download Dialog Box on GitHub

`git clone` creates a new project directory in the current directory and unpacks all files for the Git project in that project directory. Not as simple as downloading the project, you now need to get it up and running: Depending on the project, you may now need to compile the code, load it into an IDE, or run it with other tools. The decisive factor in this step is that all the requirements are met on your computer that are usually summarized in the documentation for the project (i.e., that you've installed the necessary programming languages, compilers, libraries, etc. in their correct versions).

1.2.1   Example: Hello World!

On the *https://github.com/git-compendium* page, we've compiled some examples for this book. The simplest example is named `hello-world`. You can download it to your computer with the following command:

```
git clone https://github.com/git-compendium/hello-world.git
```

If you then go to the local project directory via `cd`, you'll find four files: `README.md`, `index.html`, `style.css`, and `git.jpg`. You can view the resulting web page in your web browser:

```
cd hello-world
```

```
ls/dir
  git.jpg  index.html  README.md  style.css
```

1.2.2 Example: Python Game

Recently, one of the authors was looking for a simple game implemented in Python—not to pass the time, but as inspiration for his son who is just learning to program with Python. In the process, he came across this repository:

https://github.com/Seitoh63/PySpaceInvaders

To ensure that this repository will still work even if the original developer deletes it, we created a copy (in GitHub language, a *fork*) available at the following address:

https://github.com/git-compendium/PySpaceInvaders

The game is a variant of the *Space Invaders* game popular in the 1980s. With about 1,200 lines, the codebase is not tiny, but it is still manageable. Provided that Python 3 and git are already installed on your computer, three commands are enough to download and try the game:

```
git clone https://github.com/git-compendium/PySpaceInvaders.git
cd PySpaceInvaders
python3 main.py
```

The game requires the Pygame library in a current version. If the error *No module named pygame* arises when starting the game, you'll need to install the missing library. The pip3 (macOS, Linux) or pip (Windows) command supplied with Python can help in this context:

```
pip3 install pygame          (macOS, Linux)
pip  install pygame          (Windows)
```

1.3   Learning to Program with Git Support

Imagine you want to learn Python (or any other language). Over the course of a few weeks, you try out new functions and create various small sample programs. And as always when learning something new, you make a lot of mistakes. Suddenly, an example that was already working no longer runs.

Now, you see to why you should put your sample programs under version control and sync them with GitHub. Doing so will allow you to reconstruct all the changes you've made over time. At the same time, you'll now have an external backup.

1.3.1   Preparation Tasks

Again, we assume that you already have `git` installed (see Chapter 2, Section 2.1). In a terminal or `cmd.exe`, you need to run two commands so that Git knows your name and email address. This data is stored in each commit. (You don't have to provide real data now if you don't want to.)

```
git config --global user.name "Henry Hollow"
git config --global user.email "hollow@my-company.com"
```

You'll also set up a free account at *https://github.com* along with the new, private repository, `hello-python`. ("Private" means that only you have access to the files it contains. If you encounter any problems while getting started on GitHub, refer to Chapter 2, Section 2.2.)

Now, you still need an editor. We suggest using the free program *Visual Studio Code (VS Code)*, which has particularly good Git support. After installation, press F1 to open the command palette and run **Git • Clone**. In the small dialog box, you must enter the URL of your repository in the following format:

https://github.com/<accountname>/hello-python.git

Don't forget the `.git` extension when copying the URL from the web browser. If you're accessing GitHub for the first time in VS Code, you'll need to authenticate. VS Code redirects you to the GitHub website for this purpose. The process is a little bit tricky and doesn't always succeed on the first try. As soon as everything works, VS Code remembers the identification token acquired in this way and can use it to access your account in the future.

Reauthenticating

If you've previously used VS Code for another GitHub account, you'll only have access to that account's repositories as well as to public repositories. Before you can access another account's private repository, you must delete the previously stored authentication credentials.

On Linux, you can execute the **Sign Out** command in VS Code via the **Accounts** icon (usually the second-to-last icon in the sidebar). On Windows, you must start the *Windows Credential Management* program, go to the **Windows Credentials** dialog box, and delete the `git:https://github.com` entry. This step will cause VS Code to ask you to authenticate again the next time you connect.

Generally, Git and VS Code work best if you always use the same account. More details on the many authentication options available with Git follow in Chapter 2, Section 2.4.

VS Code finally asks you for the directory where you want to store the files of the repository locally. For example, select the *Documents* folder on Windows. VS Code creates a new subdirectory and uses it as the project directory.

1.3.2   Programming and Synchronizing

The **EXPLORER** view in the VS Code sidebar now shows the project directory, which is empty for now except for a README file. Now, you can add the first file (e.g., *hello-world.py*) via the context menu, enter the first lines of code, and try out the program. (This example assumes you've installed Python on your computer and the Python extension in VS Code.)

When the first program is running to your satisfaction, now is the right time for your first *commit*. With this action, you'll save the current state of all files of the project.

Before committing, you must explicitly mark for commit all files that have been changed or newly added to the project. For this step, open the **SOURCE CONTROL** sidebar by pressing Ctrl+Shift+G or by clicking on the **Source Control** menu icon (see Figure 1.2 ❶). In the **SOURCE CONTROL** sidebar, click the plus button (**Stage Changes**), as shown in Figure 1.2 ❷, for all files that should be part of the commit.

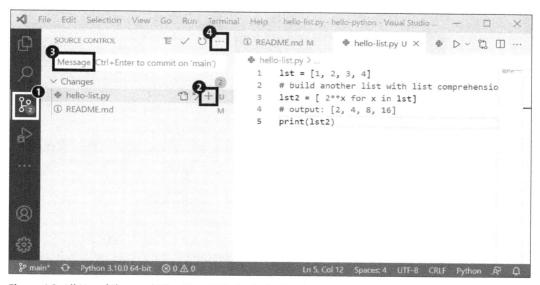

Figure 1.2 All New/Changed Files Should Be Included in the Commit

Then, in the **Message** field, enter a short text summarizing the most recent changes made to the code ❸. Pressing Ctrl+Enter executes the commit. If you forget to mark files for commit, VS Code will ask if it should simply include all new and changed files in the commit.

With the commit, VS Code has simply created a *local* snapshot of all your files. If you want your commits to be backed up to the external Git repository as well (i.e., GitHub in our case), click the three dots (...) menu button in the **SOURCE CONTROL** sidebar ❹ and execute the **Pull, Push • Sync** command. Behind the scenes, this step runs both git pull and git push. So, any changes occurred in the external repository that haven't yet been downloaded to your machine will be downloaded at the same time. What the `git pull` and `git push` commands mean in detail will be described in Chapter 3.

1.3.3 The Git Time Machine

The advantages of Git become clear when you want to test an example again after some time and problems arise. You can't exactly tell when the error happened. In VS Code **EXPLORER** view, execute the **Open Timeline** context menu command on the affected file. VS Code not only shows all commits where the affected file has been changed; clicking on the commit also immediately makes clear what changes have been made.

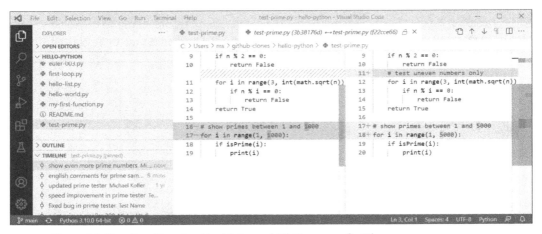

Figure 1.3 Timeline Showing the History of All Changes of a File

However, VS Code doesn't give you an immediate way to restore an old version of a file. The *GitLens* extension provides this function, however. Alternatively, you could also familiarize yourself with the `git restore` command (outside of VS Code). But we're already getting ahead of ourselves for this first chapter!

Chapter 2
Learning by Doing

This chapter continues what we started in the previous chapter: Through concrete examples, we'll show you the practical application of Git. In contrast to the introductory chapter, however, we'll now dive a bit deeper and introduce you to a whole range of tools. In detail, we'll cover the following topics:

- Installing Git
- Setting up a GitHub account
- Applying the `git` command
- Authentication (HTTPS versus SSH, credential caching)
- Git graphical user interfaces (GUIs)
- Collaboration on third-party GitHub projects (pull requests)
- Synchronization and backup policies

Before we get started, we'll whet your appetite for Chapter 3 where we explain the basic concepts behind Git. To understand how Git *really* works (and that's what you're reading this book for, right?), there's no way around these basics. While this chapter still talks a lot about graphical tools, the next chapter focuses entirely on using the `git` command in a terminal window.

2.1 Installing the git Command

This entire book is based on the assumption that you have a sufficiently up-to-date version of the `git` command. Also, many of the editors and integrated development environments (IDEs) presented in this book will draw on this command. This section summarizes how you can install `git`.

Download links and additional installation tips can be found at the following link:

https://git-scm.com/downloads

Git without Installation

Some IDEs (e.g., Microsoft Visual Studio or Xcode) include Git libraries or the `git` command directly. As long as you work exclusively with these IDEs, you don't need to explicitly install the `git` command.

Furthermore, you can also try out basic Git functions directly on some web platforms such as *https://github.com* or *https://gitlab.com*. (All files remain in the repositories of the Git host, so they do not reside on your computer.)

However, for using this book, you should definitely have the ability to add git as a standalone command. Test in a terminal or in PowerShell whether git --version works. If it doesn't, install git!

2.1.1 Linux

On Linux, you can install git using the relevant package management tool:

```
apt install git        # Debian, Raspbian, Ubuntu
dnf install git        # Fedora/RHEL and clones
zypper install git     # SUSE/openSUSE
```

Instead of git, you can also install git-all on some distributions (e.g., Debian, Ubuntu). This option provides you with various additional tools besides the git command (e.g., the GUI git-gui) as well as tools that graphically compare two versions of a file or visualize the branches of a repository. However, an additional 50 packages are associated with git-all. For this reason, we recommend starting with the basic git package first and then installing other packages only when needed.

git --version enables you to determine whether git is working and in which version:

```
git --version
  git version 2.32.0
```

2.1.2 macOS

On macOS, you have access to git as part of Xcode, provided you install its *command-line tool*. If necessary, you can initiate the installation of these tools using the following command:

```
xcode-select --install
```

If you do not want to install Xcode, you should set up *Homebrew* on your Mac (see *https://brew.sh*). Then, install the git command in the following way:

```
brew install git
```

2.1.3 Windows

On Windows, things are (as always) a bit more complicated: The setup program, which you can download from *https://git-scm.com/downloads*, not only sets up the git command, but also installs a terminal environment (*Git Bash*) with the most important components known from the Linux world, including the bash shell and commands such as ls, find, grep, tar, gzip, etc. Also included is the *Git GUI*, a simple user interface (UI) of rather dubious utility.

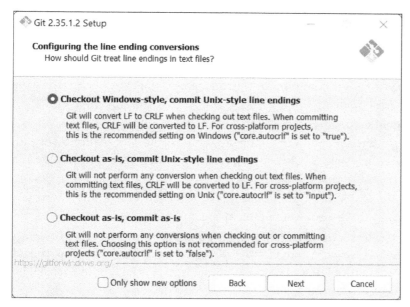

Figure 2.1 One of the Countless Configuration Dialog Boxes of the Git Setup Program for Windows

During the setup process, you must answer all possible questions and select from several options right from the start. You won't go wrong if you simply accept the preset options except for the editor. Nevertheless, we've taken the trouble to document the dialog boxes in this chapter, which are often difficult to understand for beginners:

- **Installation location**
  By default, the git command and associated tools are installed in the *C:\Program Files\Git* directory. If necessary, you can select another directory.

- **Installation scope**
  In the next dialog box, select the components to install in addition to the actual git command. By default, these components include Git Bash, the Git GUI, and the large-file support (LFS) extension (see Chapter 10, Section 10.5). You also specify whether and where icons should be set up and which links to file extensions should be created.

- **Editor**
  When executing some git commands, an editor starts automatically where you can, for example, enter an explanation for a merge operation or edit a configuration file. By default, git on Windows uses the Git Bash editor, namely, vim. However, only Linux veterans will appreciate its charm. If you aren't familiar with this editor, you

should definitely set another editor in this dialog box. Choices include *Notepad++* and *Visual Studio Code (VS Code)* (or VS Code's open-source variant *VSCodium*).

Note that this setting isn't about the editor you use to edit the code of your software projects—no restrictions in that regard exist. This setting is exclusively about if the git command itself wants to start an editor.

- **Default branch name**
  In the past, the branch master was automatically set up along with each new Git repository. Today, main is common. In this dialog box, you can freely define the name of the default branch.

- **PATH environment variable**
  The next dialog box is about how the setup program sets the PATH environment variable. This variable determines in which directories cmd.exe or PowerShell will search for programs:
  - The **Use Git from Git Bash only** option leaves PATH unchanged. For this reason, you can run git only in Git Bash, but not in cmd.exe or PowerShell.
  - The default setting **Git from the command line and also from 3rd-party software** is recommended. This option extends PATH by the path to the git command. The git command can then be invoked in cmd.exe, in PowerShell, and in Git Bash, and it can also be used by external tools.
  - The final option is **Use Git and optional Unix tools from the Command Prompt**. In this case, the directory with all Linux tools of the Git Bash is also added to PATH. This choice has an advantage in that you can use Linux commands like ls, tar, and more in cmd.exe, PowerShell, or the terminal. However, one disadvantage is that standard Windows commands, such as find or sort, will no longer work as usual because their incompatible Linux variants are used instead.

- **SSH**
  Many git commands require an interaction with SSH. In this dialog box, you'll define which SSH client git should use. By default, git uses the SSH client provided as part of Git Bash (*C:\Program Files\Git\usr\bin\ssh.exe*).

  If PuTTY is installed on the computer, you may prefer this program.

  Finally, you can use any preinstalled SSH client, provided that the program has the name ssh.exe and is located in a directory enumerated in PATH. In this way, you can use the proprietary SSH client in Windows (i.e., *C:\Windows\System32\OpenSSH\ ssh.exe*, which you can install via the system settings module **Apps & Features**).

- **HTTPS**
  Unless SSH is involved, git communicates via HTTPS. In the corresponding dialog box, you can set which encryption library should be used. By default, git uses the supplied OpenSSL library, which in turn uses certificates from the *C:\Program Files\ Git\etc\pki* directory. Alternatively, git can also use libraries provided by Windows. This feature is especially useful in a corporate environment so that git can access

the certificate authority (CA) certificates that are distributed to all of your company's machines via Active Directory.

- **End of line**

  Windows and macOS/Linux use different characters in text files to indicate the end of a line: A combination of *carriage return (CR)* plus *line feed (LF)* on Windows, (i.e., CRLF); LF only on MacOS/Linux.

  By default, Git on Windows is configured to adapt text files to Windows conventions when downloading and back to macOS/Linux conventions when uploading (setting `core.autocrlf = true`). Keep this option if you want your projects to work across different platforms. You can find the relevant background information on this topic at the following link:

  https://docs.github.com/en/github/using-git/configuring-git-to-handle-line-endings

- **Terminal for Git Bash**

  By default, Git Bash uses the *MinTTY* program to display the window where you enter commands. This program is called a *terminal emulator* and provides more functions than the Windows program `cmd.exe`, which you can use as an alternative. The option is only relevant if you use Git Bash.

- **Git pull behavior**

  The `git pull` command is used to pull changes stored in the external repository into the local repository. When merging files (via the merge process), different procedures are possible. By default, fast-forward is used in simple cases; if that option isn't possible, you must confirm a merge commit. Alternatively, you can choose the rebase procedure or **Only ever fast-forward** in this configuration dialog box. (With this third option, `git pull` will result in an error if fast-forward isn't possible.)

  You're probably out of your depth with this decision point simply because you lack the necessary background knowledge. We'll cover this topic in greater detail in the next chapter (starting with Chapter 3, Section 3.6). Leave the option as the default setting **Fast-forward or merge** for the time being.

- **Additional options**

  In the final step, you can set some special options:

  - **Enable Git Credential Manager** is set by default. This setting is absolutely necessary so that you can log in to GitHub with a token. This setting corresponds to the `credential.helper=manager-core` entry by `git config`.

    Why this setting is optional at all is a mystery. In the past, a separate *Git Credential Manager for Windows* served as an alternative to the *Git Credential Manager*. However, this software is obsolete and isn't even included with current Git versions.

  - **Enable file system caching** is set by default and accelerates Git.

  - **Enable symbolic links** allows symbolic cross-references between files. On Linux and macOS, such links are a basic feature of the file system. Windows also has a similar function, which is disabled by default. For more information, refer to the following link:

https://github.com/git-for-windows/git/wiki/Symbolic-Links

2.1.4   Changing Options Later and Performing Updates

Of course, you're not bound eternally to the initial settings you've made. One way to change these options is to simply run the setup program again. However, this approach will perform a complete reinstallation of Git.

Internally, your global settings are stored in *C:\Program Files\Git\etc\gitconfig*. Instead of performing a new installation, you can also change the settings stored in that directory using the `git config` command (which we'll describe next). More information about where Git settings are stored and how they can be changed is summarized in Chapter 12, Section 12.3. To update Git, you must download the latest version of the setup program and repeat the installation steps. In this case, you can access all the configuration dialogs again (unless you select the **Only show new options** option).

2.1.5   Changing the Default Editor

Git starts the Vim editor by default when you need to enter some text or modify a configuration file. If you're familiar with this editor, all is well. Otherwise, you should set another editor. On macOS or Linux, you can change this setting by running the following command, replacing /usr/bin/nano with the path to your favorite editor:

```
git config --global core.editor "/usr/bin/nano"
```

On Windows, the command for the VS Code editor is slightly different. Thanks to the --wait option, git waits until you have closed the file in question in the editor before it continues to process the command:

```
git config --global core.editor "code --wait"
```

To test the setting, you must change to a repository directory and run `git config --edit`. This command should start the editor you just set. Tips for configuring other editors (e.g., Notepad++ or Sublime Text) can be found at the following link:

https://docs.github.com/en/get-started/getting-started-with-git/associating-text-editors-with-git.

Exiting Vim

Maybe you landed on this page only when it was already too late, so Git shows you a text in the program Vim and you have no idea how to leave the editor. Press `Esc`. Then, enter ":q!" and press `Enter` again to exit the program without saving changes to the file. You can replace :q! with :wq! if you want to save the changes you've made.

2.1.6   Git Bash, cmd.exe, PowerShell, or Windows Terminal?

On Linux and macOS, the matter is clear: If you're command oriented, you can open a terminal window and run `git` in that window. On Windows, on the other hand, up to four variants are available:

- **cmd.exe**

  Traditionally, the `cmd.exe` program (i.e., the *command prompt*) provides the option to execute single text commands on Windows. `cmd.exe` exudes all the charm of Microsoft Disk Operating System (MS-DOS).

- **PowerShell**

  In PowerShell, Microsoft has implemented contemporary techniques for executing commands. However, the efficient operation of PowerShell requires you to learn its peculiarities. Some tips on configuring PowerShell for optimal `git` command integration can be found in the official Git documentation:

  https://git-scm.com/book/en/v2/Appendix-A%3A-Git-in-Other-Environments-Git-in-PowerShell.

- **Windows Terminal**

  Meanwhile, Microsoft provides its developers with a "real" terminal. In Windows 11, the program is even installed by default. Note that Windows Terminal is only a graphical interface within which the traditional command interpreter (`cmd.exe`) or the PowerShell is still executed.

- **Git Bash**

  Git Bash, installed together with the `git` command, is especially useful for developers who have already worked with Linux. A brief description of Git Bash follows in the next section.

  Since the authors of this book have a Linux background, we've mostly worked in Git Bash on Windows, but you don't have to do the same.

2.1.7   Git Bash

Git Bash is a shell environment that's usually installed with Git on Windows. The window doesn't look any more visually appealing than `cmd.exe` but does provides you with all the elementary Linux commands.

To list the files in the current directory, you must use `ls` instead of `dir`. To quickly scroll through a text file, you should call `less` instead of bothering with `more`. (As long as no Linux commands of the same name exist, you can continue to use MS-DOS commands.) The biggest advantage of Git Bash is the integration of the `ssh` command, which you'll often need when interacting with Git.

Unfortunately, however, one shortcoming is quite serious: The ubiquitous `man` command to read the online documentation is missing. However, with `git clone --help`, for example, you can open the man page for git-clone. Of course, this approach works the same for all other Git subcommands.

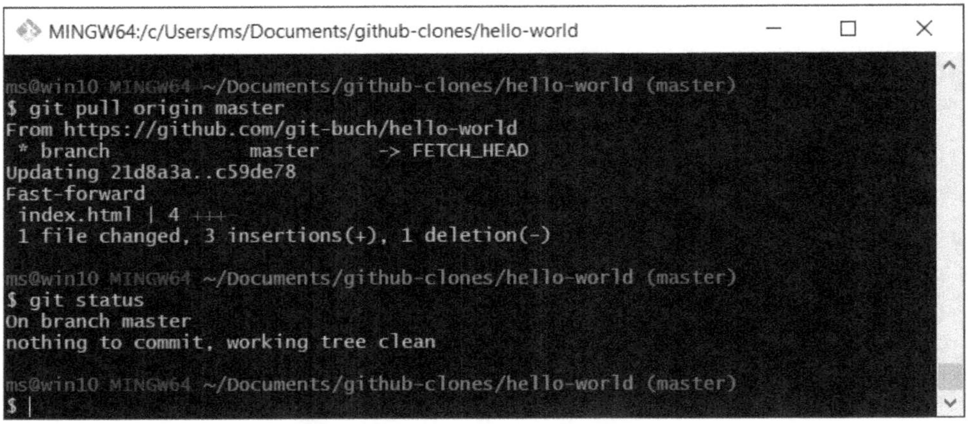

Figure 2.2 Running Git Commands in Git Bash

Compared to cmd.exe, other keyboard shortcuts also work: Ctrl+A moves the cursor to the beginning of the line, Ctrl+E to the end, etc. The middle mouse button function adopted from Linux is extremely useful: This button inserts the current clipboard contents at the cursor position.

Of course, Git Bash is Unicode compatible, using UTF-8 encoding by default. This encoding makes editing text files in projects where developers work on different platforms easier.

2.1.8   Git in the Windows Subsystem for Linux

An alternative way to use the git command is with the *Windows Subsystem for Linux (WSL)*. This tool allows you to install Linux first and then install the git command in it. However, this approach is only useful if you want to edit the projects downloaded with git primarily in a Linux environment (and not with Windows programs).

2.2   Setting Up a GitHub Account and Repositories

Basically, the git command can be used without an external hub. But the ability to synchronize files between your own computer and an external repository for initial testing can make your first steps and later understanding of Git much better. Also, the web interface helps visually track changes to files and switch between different versions and branches of your project.

2

Git beyond GitHub

Don't worry, this book is not a GitHub book! We'll also discuss other Git platforms in later chapters and describe the use of `git` without the use of a commercial host entirely. But for your first steps, learning elementary working techniques in the currently most popular environment is useful.

If for some reason you have an aversion to GitHub, you can just as easily reproduce the examples in this chapter using GitLab or another platform of your choice. The examples in this chapter use only the most basic functions of Git. All the additional features provided by GitHub, GitLab, Bitbucket, and others don't matter at all for the time being.

2.2.1   Setting Up a GitHub Account

To set up a free GitHub account, you must complete the signup form at *https://github.com*. Only three data points are required: an account name (user name), an email address, and a sufficiently long/secure password. The account name will be visible later in all your GitHub links. So, try to find a name that makes as much sense as possible and will last for a long time. Apart from letters and numbers, the only special character allowed is a hyphen.

Subsequently, you must solve a simple puzzle (to make sure that you aren't a bot), and you can provide some voluntary information about your professional background and programming experience. Finally, your email address will be verified. You can also personalize your account with a photo or avatar, a link to your website, etc. later on—but all this data is optional. (At a minimum, when applying for a job, "dressing up" your GitHub account might be worthwhile. In the IT world, your GitHub page is almost like a business card.)

2.2.2   Setting Up Repositories

In simple terms, a *repository* (literally, "warehouse") is the collection of all the files that make up a project including old/changed versions of those files. Along with a repository, you can also manage additional data in GitHub (issues, documentation in wiki format, etc.), but this additional data represents GitHub-specific extensions and have nothing to do with Git in any strict sense. The most important option when setting up a new repository concerns public access:

- With **Public**, the repository is visible to everyone. Anyone can read its files or download them using `git clone` (but cannot modify them).
- **Private** indicates repositories that only you and developers selected by you have access (see the next section). In the past, you needed a paid GitHub account for private repositories. Gradually, GitHub has dropped this restriction, and as of April

2020, even private repositories allow any number of collaborators (i.e., people with write permissions).

Of course, you can change the visibility of a repository later. But be careful never to store confidential data (e.g., passwords) in a public repository.

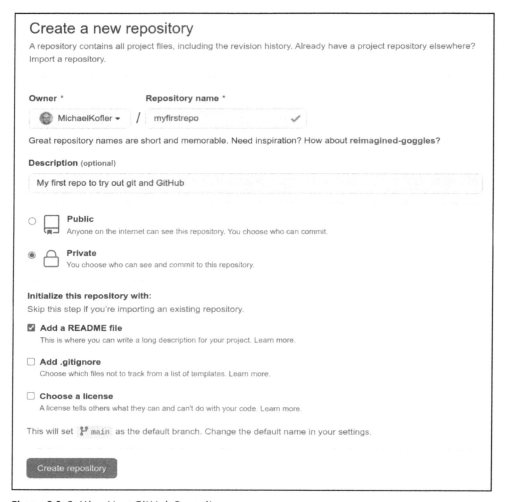

Figure 2.3 Setting Up a GitHub Repository

A common practice is to create a README file in Markdown format in the new repository right away. Then, the repository immediately contains at least one file, and as a result, you can try out git clone immediately.

The address of the repository is a combination of *https://github.com*, the account name, and the project name, for example:

https://github.com/<accountname>/<reponame>

2.2.3   Giving Access to a Repository

Whether a repository is private or public, only you can change its content at the beginning. Of course, if you want multiple people to work together on your project, they first need their own GitHub accounts. You must also invite them to collaborate, and they must agree. To issue invitations, first select the repository in question and then open the **Settings • Collaborators** page. There, clicking **Add people** leads to a dialog box where you can enter the email addresses of the target collaborators.

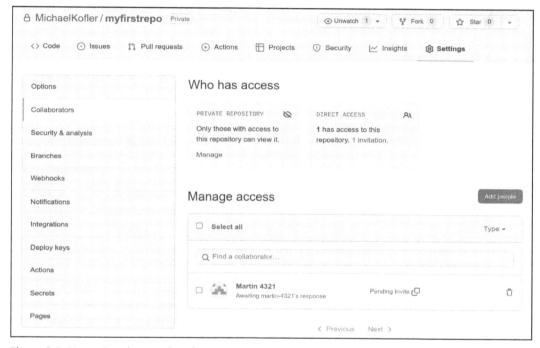

Figure 2.4 Managing the People Who Have Access to a Repository

---

Collaboration without Access Rights

The approach outlined so far is not the only way to contribute to a GitHub project. An alternative is to set up a copy of a third-party project in your own account (called a *fork*), make changes in that fork, and then offer these changes to the external project in the form of what's called a *pull request*. Especially for repositories of large, public projects, this approach makes more sense than adding more and more people to a repository. We'll describe this approach in detail in Section 2.7.

2.2.4   GitHub Organizations

In GitHub, an *organization* refers to an account to which multiple people have access. GitHub provides the option to form an organization via **Settings • Organizations**.

Within an organization, you can then set up repositories again (to which all members of the organization automatically have access). The repository name within an organization is accessible via the following link:

https://github.com/<organizationname>/<reponame>

Organizations are a simple yet effective mechanism for collaborating on multiple repositories. At the same time, organizations provide an easy way to obtain "nice" GitHub URLs without setting up your own account. As a logical consequence, you can only use names for organizations that don't match active account names.

2.2.5   Setting Up Personal Access Tokens

To log on to the GitHub website, you must enter your account name or email address and a password. (If you've enabled two-factor authentication, another code will be required at logon; see Chapter 9, Section 9.5.)

In the past, the combination of name/email plus password was also sufficient to authenticate Git operations, whether they were performed in an editor, in an IDE, or manually using the git command. For security reasons, since 2020, this option no longer works.

Now, Git operations require a different type of authentication, with various variants to choose from: tokens, OAuth, or SSH keys (see Section 2.4). Which method you should use depends on which operating system you're running, how you invoke Git (at the command level or in a GUI), and which protocol you use (HTTPS or SSH).

In this section, we'll show you how to set up *personal access tokens*. These tokens are particularly suitable for your first experiments with the git command on Linux or macOS. Once set up, tokens can be applied instead of passwords. However, tokens often have expiration dates or can authorize only a subset of operations. A safety gain results from these restrictions: If the GitHub password gets into the wrong hands, the entire account is compromised. If, on the other hand, the incident only affects one token, then the possible damage is limited; in addition, the token can be deleted quickly if necessary.

Personal access tokens can be managed in the GitHub web interface via **Settings • Developer settings**. To create a new token for executing git commands, go to **Settings • Developer settings • Personal access tokens** in the GitHub web interface. In this dialog box, click the **Generate new token** button, assign a name to the token, set its validity period, and define its scope. If the token is only for basic Git operations, selecting the action scope **repo** is sufficient.

When you click **Generate token**, the token code is displayed only once. You can copy this code and save it for further use. In the GitHub web interface, you have no way to view the token's code again later. You can then only delete the token. After all, you'll be reminded by mail before a token expires, and then you can extend its validity period. (The token can then be reused without any changes.)

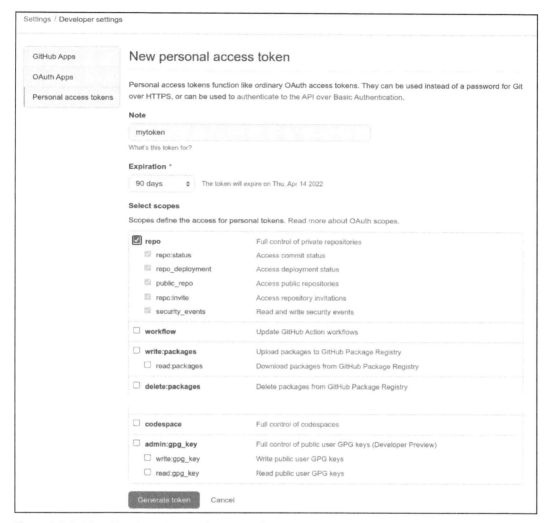

Figure 2.5 Setting Up a New Personal Access Token

2.3   Using the git Command

You can try using the git command only locally, without using any external Git server like GitHub or GitLab. However, we suggest that, for your first experiments, you should first set up an account on a Git platform as well as create a private repository including an initial README file (as described in the previous section).

The reason for this approach is that many of Git's features become obvious only when you have at least *two* repositories: a local one and an external one. (Remember: A *repository* is the collection of all files of your project including old versions, backups of deleted files, etc.)

2.3.1   Setting the Name and Email Address (git config)

Before you can get started, `git` needs to know your name and email address. This data will later be stored along with each commit. The email address should (but doesn't have to) be the same as the address you specified on your Git platform.

```
git config --global user.name "Henry Hollow"
git config --global user.email "hollow@a-company.com"
```

The data specified using `git config --global` applies as the default setting for all Git repositories on your machine. This data is stored in *.gitconfig* in your home directory.

If necessary, you can adjust the settings in each of your repositories to be different from the default data. For this task, use `cd` to change to the directory in question and run `git config` again, but this time without the `--global` option.

> **Hiding the Email Address**
>
> GitHub (as well as various other Git platforms) provides the option of hiding your email address. You must select the option **Keep my email addresses private** under **Settings • Emails**. In this case, you should use `git config` to set the following email address locally:
>
> ```
> git config --global user.email "<accountname>@users.noreply.github.com"
> ```

2.3.2   Downloading a Repository (git clone)

As a basis for the following examples, you'll need to set up a new repository in your GitHub account. The repository initially exists only there, not yet on your computer. To create a local copy of the repository, you must open a terminal window, change to any directory, and run `git clone`, specifying the URL of your repository as a parameter. Thus, replace *https://github.com/MichaelKofler/first-test.git* with the address of your own repository.

For your experiments, use a local directory that is *not* synchronized between multiple computers via the cloud or with other tools! Synchronization tools can upset Git (see Section 2.8).

```
cd my-work-directory

git clone https://github.com/MichaelKofler/first-test.git
  Clone after 'first-test' ...
  Username for 'https://github.com':          <account-name>
```

```
Password for 'https://user-name@github.com':   <token-code>
remote: Enumerating objects: 3, done.
remote: Counting objects: 100% (3/3), done.
remote: Compressing objects: 100% (2/2), done.
remote: Total 3 (delta 0), reused 0 (delta 0), pack-reused 0
Unpack objects: 100% (3/3), done.

cd first-test

ls (or dir in cmd.exe)
   README.md
```

During the initial execution of git clone to access a private repository, you must authenticate yourself. On macOS and Linux, you would enter the account name (or, if you have defined a GitHub organization in your account, the name of the organization) and the previously generated code of your personal access token.

On Windows, on the other hand, a window appears with three authentication variants to choose from. We recommend you use the **Sign in with your browser** option. A web browser window will then appear to log on to your GitHub account. (If you're currently logged on, this step can be omitted.) Then, using the OAuth process, GitHub provides an authentication code that is stored by the Windows Credential Manager. This approach has an advantage in that later git commands (e.g., git push) won't require repeated authentication.

After successful authentication, git clone creates a new directory with the same name as the repository, downloads all files from the external repository to it, and creates the *.git/config* file. The local configuration settings are stored in that file (see Chapter 12, Section 12.3).

Figure 2.6 GitHub Authentication on Windows

> **Don't Forget "cd"!**
>
> git clone creates a new directory. All further git commands are to be executed *in* this directory. So, don't forget cd directory; otherwise, git will complain that it doesn't recognize a Git repository in the current directory.

2.3.3   Adding Files (git add)

Your repository is still empty except for the README file. Using any editor (that doesn't need any Git functions), you can now add files to your project. For this example, we assume that you want to develop a Java program that consists of several classes. You start with the Main class, which for now contains only the main method and outputs Hello World!. (We haven't included the code here; it is not important. You can use any programming language you're familiar with to construct as simple a project as possible, consisting of several files.)

For Git, having the *Main.java* file stored in the directory of your Git project isn't enough. You must explicitly add the file to the repository or subsequently mark the changed state for inclusion in the next commit. For this step, run git add in the following way:

```
git add Main.java
```

2.3.4   Saving an Intermediate State (git commit)

When you've completed a work step or a new feature in your project, you should save the entire state of the project. This step is what git commit is for. A *commit* is a kind of snapshot you can restore later if needed.

For each commit, you must use -m 'message' to specify a message that briefly summarizes all the changes. The commit message should be short but meaningful, containing especially valuable information for other developers and that can serve as the basis for a targeted search. (We provide tips on formulating concise commit messages in Chapter 9, Section 9.2.)

```
git commit -m 'initial commit, hello world'
  [main 3cd6219] inital commit
  1 file changed, 5 insertions(+)
```

> **Many Small Commits Are Better Than One Big One**
>
> A golden rule when dealing with Git: Several small commits are better than a few big ones! This advice is even more true when several developers are working on a project.

Of course, you can exaggerate everything. A few commits per day may be reasonable for projects you're actively working on; however, performing a commit every 5 minutes rarely makes sense.

2.3.5 Adding and Changing Files, More Commits

You can now gradually add more files to your project or modify existing files, as in the following example:

```
git add Main.java Rectangle.java

git commit -m 'added Rectangle class'
  [main 0d2f90d] added Rectangle class
  2 files changed, 18 insertions(+)
```

Remember that, before each commit, you must add not only the new files, but also modified ones. Instead of git add, you can also use the perfectly equivalent git stage command.

You can omit git add/stage if you pass the additional -a option to commit. This approach will automatically take into account any files already under Git control that have changed since the last commit. (If you've added new files, however, they won't be included in the commit. In this case, you still need git add.)

```
git commit -a -m 'implemented getPerimeter for Rectangle class'
  [main 7c87e9c] implemented getPerimeter for Rectangle class
  1 file changed, 4 insertions(+)
```

Caution, "git commit" Only Works Locally

If you've worked with other version control programs, especially Apache Subversion (SVN), you may have mentally associated a commit with an upload to an external repository. But Git behaves differently in this respect.

git commit performs the commit only in the local repository. No data is transferred to an external repository. The git push and git pull commands are responsible for synchronization with external repositories, which we'll introduce in Section 2.3.8 and Section 2.3.9.

2.3.6 Status (git status)

If you've lost track of which files are under Git control, which ones have been changed since the last commit, etc., you should run git status. This command provides a good overview of the state of your repository, as shown in the following example:

```
git status
```

```
On branch main
Your branch is ahead of 'origin/main' by 2 commits.
(use "git push" to publish your local commits)

Untracked files:
(use "git add <file>..." to include in what will be committed)

    Circle.java
    Main.class
    Main.java~
    Rectangle.class

nothing added to commit but untracked files present
(use "git add" to track)
```

In plain language, this output means the following statements are true:

- The active branch is main. (We'll come to branches in Section 2.3.11.)
- You've made two commits in your local repository that aren't yet known in the remote repository (i.e., on GitHub in this example).
- Four files aren't under the control of Git. Concerning the *Circle.java* file, you've probably forgotten about git add so far. The remaining three files are compilations or backups.

Status Messages

If you use Git on Windows, English-language messages are the default. On Linux or macOS, the messages may be in a different language. Not using English is OK unless you specifically need to search for an error message on the internet. In this case, you should re-execute the command but prefix it with LANGUAGE=en:

LANGUAGE=en git status

Alternatively, you can change the language to English for the entire course of the session with export LANGUAGE=en. The export command remains valid until you close the terminal window.

2.3.7 Excluding Files from Git Management (.gitignore file)

Often, a useful approach is to explicitly place certain files or file types outside of Git. This choice applies, for example, to all files generated by the compiler, backup files of the respective editor, files containing confidential information (passwords), and so on.

Using the *.gitignore* file, you can avoid mistakenly placing these files under version control or having irrelevant output get in the way of clarity in git status. For this task, specify names or patterns line-by-line in *.gitignore* for files to indicate which files you want the git command to simply ignore. For a sample project, a *.gitignore* file might include the following lines:

```
# .gitignore file in the repository directory
*.class
*~
```

We'll cover the syntax of *.gitignore* in more detail in Chapter 12, Section 12.3. The easiest way to verify that the file is working is to run git status again. Don't forget to add the *.gitignore* file itself to the repository via git add!

2.3.8   Transferring the Repository to a Remote Server (git push)

The git push command transfers commits in the local repository to an external repository, thus "pushing" local updates to the server (remote). Ideally, the command simply works in the following way:

```
git push
  Username for 'https://github.com':            <account-name>
  Password for 'https://user-name@github.com':  <token-code>
  Enumerating objects: 3, done.
  Counting objects: 100% (3/3), done.
  Delta compression using up to 12 threads
  Compressing objects: 100% (2/2), done.
  Writing objects: 100% (2/2), 269 bytes | 269.00 KiB/s, done.
  Total 2 (delta 1), reused 0 (delta 0)
  remote: Resolving deltas: 100% (1/1), completed with 1 local
    object.
  To github.com:<account>/<repo>
   8360a94..7bb8255  main -> main
```

Depending on the operating system you're working on and how you authenticated with git clone, git pull will again ask for the GitHub account name and the corresponding password or token. Windows provides more comfort in this respect: By default, Git's built-in credential manager communicates with Windows Credential Manager and obtains stored authentication data from it. You can learn how to prevent the annoying password query on Linux and macOS in Section 2.4.

For git push to work, the command must know which branch of the repository to process and to which external server to transfer the data. The required information has been stored by git clone in the *.git/config* file. If you want to use other data, you'll need to pass appropriate parameters to git push. The following command sends the changes in the main branch to the server that was used in the initial git clone command (i.e., to origin). If you followed this example, git push and git push origin main are equivalent.

```
git push origin main
```

> **"git pull" before "git push"**
>
> In this example, we excluded the possibility that someone else has made changes that may be in the remote repository but are not yet in your local repository.
>
> In practice, however, several developers often work on one project. Thus, another programmer can easily make changes to the code in the meantime. If git push detects this case, the whole thing will fail. For this reason, you should get in the habit of always running the git pull command, as described in the following section, before typing git push.

2.3.9   Updating the Local Repository (git pull)

The counterpart to git push is git pull. This command downloads changes known in the external repository to your local machine. To try out the command, you can log on to the GitHub website, visit your test repository, modify a file there, and complete the process with a commit. Then, run git pull on your local machine, as shown in the following example:

```
git pull
  Username for 'https://github.com':        <account-name>
  Password for 'https://user-name@github.com':  <token-code>
  remote: Enumerating objects: 5, done.
  remote: Counting objects: 100% (5/5), done.
  remote: Compressing objects: 100% (3/3), done.
  remote: Total 3 (delta 2), reused 0 (delta 0), pack-reused 0
  Unpack objects: 100% (3/3), done.
  From https://github.com/<account>/<repo>
     750ab9a..a6e075b  main      -> origin/main
  Updating 750ab9a..a6e075b
  Fast-forward
   Main.java | 1 +
   1 file changed, 1 insertion(+)
```

> **Merge Conflicts**
>
> What happens when two developers edit a file at the same time? In this case, when you merge the changes, a conflict will occur that needs to be resolved. The execution of git pull aborts, and you'll need to resolve the conflict manually. In Chapter 3, Section 3.9, we'll describe how you can resolve this conflict and which tools can help you.

2.3.10   Uploading a Local Repository to GitHub/GitLab

In this section so far, we've assumed that you have first set up a repository on GitHub or another Git platform, have downloaded the (still almost empty) repository to your local machine using git clone, and gradually have filled it with files—all while uploading all changes back to GitHub (via git push). Especially for Git beginners, this approach is the easiest.

In practice, however, the other way around is often required: You already have a directory of code and want to upload it to a Git platform in its current state and subsequently synchronize it regularly. We'll cover this process next.

First, make the local directory a Git repository by simply running git init. This command will create a *.git* directory. However, the repository is still empty.

```
cd project directory
git init
  Initialized empty Git repository in
  /home/kofler/project-directory/.git/
```

In the next step, add the desired files to the repository using git add and then perform a first commit:

```
git add file1 file2 file3 ...
git commit -m 'initial commit'
```

You can continue to use Git without restrictions (i.e., make additional commits, create and reassemble branches, etc.). Git isn't at all dependent on synchronization with an external repository.

However, you can't put team projects into practice in this way. If solo work is your intention, or if you just want to use GitHub as a project backup, you should set up a new repository on the Git platform. (This action can't be performed via the git command.)

The name of the repository doesn't need to be the same as your project directory. Under no circumstances should you activate the **Initialize this repository with a README** option. If you do, the merging of the external and local repositories will fail.

Depending on whether you want to communicate via HTTPS or SSH (see Section 2.4), you must now run git remote add origin and specify the URL or SSH address of the external repository. With git remote -v, you can verify whether or not this command worked:

```
git remote add origin https://github.com:<account>/<repo>.git
git remote add origin git@github.com:<account>/<repo>.git

git remote -v
  origin https://github.com:<account>/<repo>.git (fetch)
  origin https://github.com:<account>/<repo>.git (push)
```

`git branch -M main` gives the current branch the name `main`. With current `git` versions, this command is redundant because new repositories automatically use the branch name `main`. In older `git` versions, however, the default name is `master`, which is now uncommon.

`git push -u` uploads the local repository for the first time, with the -u option causing the external repository to become the default upstream for the current branch. So, in the future, you can simply run `git pull` or `git push` to synchronize the main branch with the external repository.

```
git branch -M main

git push -u origin main
  ...
  To github.com:<account>/<repo>.git
   * [new branch]  main -> main
  Branch main set up to track remote branch main from origin.
```

2.3.11 Branches (git checkout and git merge)

Repository *branches* come into play when you want to work on two (or more) versions of your software at the same time. Imagine that the program developed up to this point is now running stably and goes into production use. Now, you want to develop the program further without endangering the stability of the production version. For this task, you must separate the code into two branches:

- In the production branch, you perform only tiny bug fixes should the need arise.
- The developer or feature branch, on the other hand, is the playground for further development. Only when the new version is more stable (after many tests) should you merge it with the main version again and deliver it to your customers (e.g., as a web service).

In Git, `git checkout <name>` enables you to switch to a branch. Initially, only one branch exists: the *main branch*. (In older versions of Git, the *master* branch was used instead, but that word has fallen out of favor.) To create a new branch and activate it at the same time, you must use `git checkout` with the -b option. If changes without a commit already exist at this point, then these changes will automatically be applied to the new branch.

```
git checkout -b newfeature
  Switched to a new branch 'newfeature'
```

This step now makes the `newfeature` branch (or whatever you want to call it) active. You can work in this branch as before; that is, you can modify files, add new ones, and run `git commit` after each major change. However, these changes now only affect the new branch.

```
git add ...
git commit -m 'implemented xy'
```

The attempt to simply upload the changes to the feature branch with `git push` fails:

```
git push
  fatal: The current branch newfeature has no upstream branch.
  To push the current branch and set the remote as upstream, use

  git push --set-upstream origin newfeature
```

The error message indicates the correct procedure: You must use the `--set-upstream` option or `-u` to specify that the already known origin repository (i.e., `origin`) should also be used for the new branch:

```
git push --set-upstream origin newfeature
  ...
  remote: Resolving deltas: 100% (3/3), completed with 3 local
  objects. To https://github.com/<account>/<repo>:
   * [new branch]      newfeature -> newfeature
  Branch 'newfeature' set up to track remote branch 'newfeature'
  from 'origin'.
```

Even before you're done with the new feature, a security gap appears in the production branch that needs to be resolved immediately. After a commit in the feature branch, you switch back to the main branch:

```
git checkout main
```

In the local directory, all new files of the feature branch now disappear. At the same time, the remaining code files jump back to the previous state (i.e., before the work on the new feature was started). Now, let's fix the problem and activate the bugfix:

```
git commit -a -m 'bugfix for bug nnn, check for negative numbers'
  [main 0fc361d] bugfix for bug nnn, check for negative numbers
  1 file changed, 2 insertions(+)
git push
```

Using `git checkout newfeature`, you can return to the developer branch. If the bug you just fixed also affects this branch and should be fixed immediately as well, you must apply the changes made in the course of the previous commit to the developer branch as well. Git provides the `cherry-pick` subcommand for this purpose, to which you must pass the first digits of the commit's hash code (see also the `git commit` output shown earlier). Provided that the changes are incorporated without collisions, the command can be executed without any queries. Otherwise, you must resolve the conflicts manually (see Chapter 3, Section 3.9).

```
git checkout newfeature
git cherry-pick 0fc361d
  [newfeature a7edbe8] bugfix for bug nnn, check for negative numbers
  Date: Wed Apr 22 17:55:42 2020 +0200
  1 file changed, 2 insertions(+)
```

"git cherry-pick" Is Optional

What would happen if you forgot git cherry-pick? If the bug also affected the feature branch, the error would of course continue to occur there for the time being. However, if you then later merge the feature branch with the main branch using git merge, the bugfix remains active. As the word *merge* implies, the feature branch doesn't replace the main branch, but instead, changes made in both branches are combined. To put it another way, you don't need to worry that a bug fixed in the main branch will suddenly reappear once work on a new feature has been completed.

At some point, work on the new feature will be completed, and then, we'll execute the following commit:

```
git commit -a -m 'final tests for new feature done'
git push
  ...
  To https://github.com/<account>/<repo>
     df21773..d89873f  newfeature -> newfeature
```

Now, let's resolve the newfeature branch and integrate the changes it contains into main. For this task, you must first switch to the main branch and run git merge there. With a little luck, the function will work right away. However, as with git pull and git cherry-pick, Git may detect a merge conflict that you must resolve manually.

```
git checkout main
git merge newfeature
  CONFLICT (add/add): Merge conflict in Rectangle.java
  Auto-merging Rectangle.java
  Automatic merge failed; fix conflicts and then commit the
  result.
```

A list of files in conflict can be accessed via git status, if required. The files contain both code variants, with the affected passages located between >>>, ===, and <<<:

```
less Rectangle.java
  ...
  <<<<<<< HEAD
  throw new IllegalArgumentException("error message");
```

```
=======
    throw new IllegalArgumentException("better error message");
>>>>>>> newfeature
```

Thus, in this example, the error message (IllegalArgumentException) has changed, and Git doesn't know whether to stay with the old version or use the text of the new version. Open the file in an editor, decide which solution you want, and remove the conflict markers. Then, save the change with git commit, as in the following example:

```
git commit -a -m 'resolved merge conflict in Rectangle class'
```

The feature branch (newfeature, in this example) is preserved despite the merge process. You can continue to use this branch to develop a new function, or you can delete the branch with the following command:

```
git branch -d newfeature
  Deleted branch newfeature (was c5cf7f1).
```

Branches for Professionals

Dealing with branches is full of pitfalls. We'll provide more detail about the basics of branches in Chapter 3, Section 3.5. Also, in Chapter 8, we've compiled some established best practices on how you can establish well-functioning workflows in large software projects.

2.3.12   Logging (git log)

git log returns a list of all commits, with the most recent commit displayed first. If the output has more lines than the terminal and you're working on macOS, on Linux, or in Git Bash, Git redirects the output to less. This option allows you to scroll through the output page by page or to prematurely end the logging output by pressing Q.

```
git log
```

```
  commit acdb7bcd752ebc975a2a1734bdd4dbeaf4de55c8
  Merge: 0fc361d d89873f
  Author: Michael Kofler
  Date:    Wed Jan 19 18:29:40 2020 +0200
      resolved merge conflict in Rectangle class

  commit d89873f3e73c8c3af9e7e17e3637cc7f9a5b4661
  Author: Michael Kofler
  Date:    Wed Jan 19 18:13:47 2020 +0200
      final tests for new feature done
```

To see all the changes made in the commits, you must pass the -p option as well. As a rule, git log then provides more information than you can process. The additional -1 option shows only the details of the last commit (-3 for the last three commits, etc.).

A more detailed description of git log, as well as various other commands that specifically extract information from a Git repository, is available in Chapter 4.

2.3.13 More Git Commands, Options, Special Cases, and Basics

The last few pages were just a crash course on the git command—nothing more! Many more git commands are available, and with all those commands, you can control their behaviors via countless options. Various problems can occur when executing the commands, such as merge conflicts between local and external repositories. In short, with the knowledge you've now acquired, you're only at the beginning.

Where to go next and how?

- The following section explains how to authenticate to external repositories in different ways, thus eliminating the hassle of entering passwords.

- Chapter 3 describes the internals of Git and Git repositories while deepening your knowledge of git commands and options.

- Chapter 9 describes various advanced working techniques.

- Chapter 12 summarizes the most important git commands and their options and describes the function and syntax of git configuration files.

2.4 Authentication

Before you're allowed to download a repository from a non-public Git server (git clone) or synchronize your local repository with an external one (git fetch/pull/push), you must authenticate yourself. Whether and how this authentication is performed depends on many boundary conditions, such as the following:

- What operating system do you use?

- Do you use HTTPS or SSH protocol to communicate with the Git server?

- Have you additionally enabled two-factor authentication on the external server?

- Do you use different accounts in different projects?

- What does the local Git configuration look like (git config --list)?

- What's your company's network configuration (firewalls and proxies)?

- Which program do you work with? Some editors or IDEs use their own authentication procedures and are thus independent of the system-wide authentication mechanisms.

With authentication, meeting all requirements can be difficult: On one hand, authentication should be secure; otherwise, you could do without it right away. On the other hand, the solution must be sufficiently convenient and shouldn't drive your development team to despair with continuous logon prompts.

In the following pages, we'll explain the practical application of the most important authentication variants and give you some tips on how to track down the causes of authentication problems. We'll describe the topic of two-factor authentication separately in Chapter 9, Section 9.5.

We've deliberately refrained from an encyclopedic description of all variants in this book. This topic could have filled an entire chapter without contributing much information relevant to practice.

2.4.1 Windows Credential Manager

A prime example of a well-functioning authentication model is the interaction of the *Git Credential Manager* with the *Windows Credential Manager*, where Windows can securely store logon data. You can get an overview of all logons by starting the *Login Information Management* program and switching to the **Windows Login Information** dialog box.

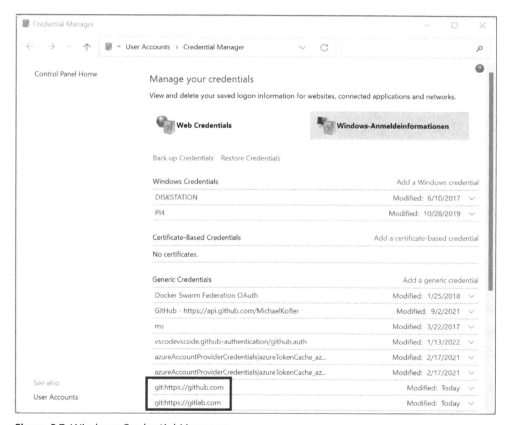

Figure 2.7 Windows Credential Manager

On the first `git` command that requires authentication with an external Git host and communicates via HTTPS, a logon dialog box appears on the screen. The design of the dialog box and the provided logon variants vary depending on the Git host, but the functionality is uniform: After a successful logon, an authentication code (a token) is transferred to the computer via the OAuth procedure and stored by Windows Credential Manager. Subsequently, Git can draw on this data so that further authentication is performed automatically without prompting.

More details about the interaction between Git and Windows Credential Manager are available on the project website at the following link:

https://github.com/GitCredentialManager/git-credential-manager.

An overview of how OAuth works can be found at the following link:

https://en.wikipedia.org/wiki/OAuth.

As Linux fans, we like to take every opportunity to complain a bit about Windows (of course, with all respect for peaceful cooperation across all platforms....). But even we must admit that Windows Credential Manager works fantastically well—if it works!

Two problems, however, have come to our attention:

- If you make a mistake on your first logon attempt, you won't get a second chance. The logon window doesn't reappear, the `git` command just complains (without giving any reason) that authentication fails.

  Remedy: Start the *Credentials Management* program; switch to the **Windows Credentials** dialog box; look for the entry of your Git host (GitHub, GitLab, Microsoft Azure, etc.); and delete the entry. At the next `git` command, the logon dialog box will appear again.

- Interaction with Windows Credential Manager fails if you have multiple accounts on a Git server. Windows Credential Manager can store only *one* token per website (e.g., *github.com*).

  In such cases, several variants for setting up other authentication methods for the repository in question are available using `git config` (see also *https://git-scm.com/docs/gitcredentials*). In our experience, however, these approaches are either error-prone or insecure (i.e., involving the storage of plaintext passwords).

The Git server website memorizes all tokens. You also have the option to revoke (delete) individual tokens at that website. Where you find the authentication data in the nested websites depends on the respective Git host. On GitHub, navigate to **Applications • Settings • Authorized OAuth Apps** in the settings. For the Git Credential Manager, its entry can be revoked.

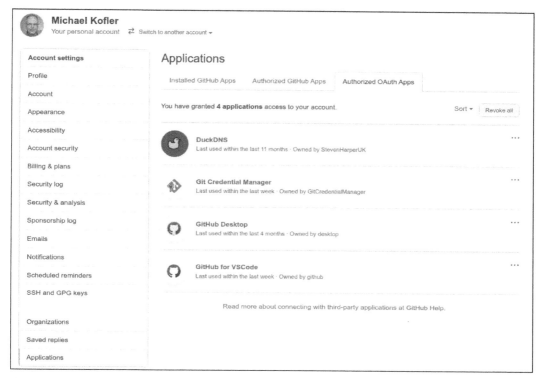

Figure 2.8 Managing OAuth Programs Associated with a GitHub Account

2.4.2 macOS Keychain

For HTTPS authentication, the helper mechanism osxkeychain is active on macOS. You can use the standard configuration via git config --get or, if necessary, make the setting yourself using git config --global, as in the following example:

```
git config --get credential.helper
  osxkeychain
git config --global credential.helper osxkeychain
```

Git asks for an account name and password at the first HTTPS logon and passes this data to the macOS *Keychain Management* application. This application memorizes the data and can pass it on to Git for further commands.

Note that most Git hosts (most notably GitHub) no longer accept the password intended for the web interface to authenticate git commands, for security reasons. Therefore, instead of the password, you must specify a personal access token generated in advance in the Git host's web interface.

If authentication doesn't work, for example, because you want to use a different account or because you've changed your GitHub password, start the Keychain Management application on macOS, search for the key there, and remove it. The next time you authenticate yourself, you'll be asked for the account name and password again. (Don't confuse the *Keychain Management* with the *Keywords* module in macOS preferences. The *Keychain Management* is a purely local program, while the *Keywords* module from System Preferences is used to share keywords across multiple devices connected via iCloud.)

2.4.3   libsecret (Linux)

On Linux, the situation looks bleak: By default, no authentication support exists for the manual execution of git commands via HTTPS. Every time you run git pull, git push, or a similar command, you must specify the account name of your Git host again, as well as the almost endless token code.

You can get out of this dilemma in several ways: A best practice is to use SSH keys for authentication. (Details follow in Section 2.4.4.) Alternatively, you can forgo running git commands directly and use an editor or IDE that takes care of authentication.

But Linux wouldn't be Linux if a hack didn't exist. With the libsecret program, Linux can remember the strings necessary for Git authentication. Along with git, the code for libsecret is already provided. However, you must compile the program yourself and set it up as a credential helper. In Ubuntu, you would use the following commands:

```
sudo apt install libsecret-1-0 libsecret-1-dev

cd /usr/share/doc/git/contrib/credential/libsecret

sudo make

git config --global credential.helper /usr/share/doc/\
   git/contrib/credential/libsecret/git-credential-libsecret
```

An important step is that you specify /usr/share/...-libsecret as a contiguous string without the \ separator and without spaces. Subsequently, Git passes passwords or tokens to the secrets library, which takes care of storing them. You can read more details about installing libsecret at the following link:

https://stackoverflow.com/questions/36585496

Behind the scenes, the passwords end up in the binary file *.local/share/keyrings/login.keystore*. You can read or delete the data using the secret-tool command or via the GNOME program *Seahorse*.

2.4.4   SSH instead of HTTPS

Up to now, we've assumed that you're communicating with the external Git server via HTTPS. This option is safe and suitable for your first experiments. As long as you're working on Windows and aren't affected by the restrictions of Windows Credential Manager, you can certainly stick with the HTTPS option.

On Linux, SSH provides the easiest and best way to put an end to constant logon prompts—and there's absolutely nothing wrong with using the SSH variant on Windows and macOS either. (All the information in this section also applies without restriction to Windows, where SSH has been installed as part of Git Bash.)

With SSH, you first upload the public part of one of your SSH keys to GitHub, GitLab, or another platform. When you run `git pull`, you must specify the SSH address of your repository instead of the HTTPS URL. Git then uses the SSH public key stored on the Git server and matches the public part of the key with the private part of the key on your machine.

Now for the details: First, you must have an SSH key on your local computer. On Linux and macOS, this key probably already exists. It's located in the *.ssh* directory in your home directory and is usually named `id_rsa` (private part) and `id_rsa.pub` (public part).

```
cd
ls -l .ssh/
   2602 Jan 18    id_rsa
    566 Jan 18    id_rsa.pub
   ...
```

> **The ".ssh" Directory**
>
> On macOS and Linux, files and directories whose name begins with a period (.) are considered hidden. Configuration settings are often located in these files, which are called *dotfiles*.
>
> Windows also permits file or directory names starting with a period. However, these files or directories aren't treated in any special way.
>
> The *.ssh* directory is always located in the home directory: on Linux usually in */home/ <name>*, on macOS in */Users/<name>*, and on Windows in *C:\Users\<name>*.

If no pair of files exists where one file has the *.pub* identifier, you must generate the key. For this task, execute the command `ssh-keygen`. During execution, you can choose any name. Also, you can secure the key itself with a password, which has both advantages and disadvantages. If a key without password gets into foreign hands, the thief will immediately have access to all (Git) servers where you've deposited the public part of the key. You pay for the additional security gained by a password when you use it: Every time you (or `git`) need the key, you must type the password.

---

ssh-agent

No problem exists without a solution: To avoid typing SSH passwords repeatedly, you can set up an *SSH agent*. Thus, you'll only specify the password once per session (when you use it for the first time).

On Linux and macOS, the SSH agent runs by default but must be configured. On Windows, the preparation work is somewhat more complex, as described at the following links:

- *https://www.ssh.com/academy/ssh/agent*
- *https://stackoverflow.com/questions/18683092*

We believe that, at least for use in Git authentication, a SSH key without a password is sufficient. However, we assume that the SSD of your notebook is encrypted. (This encryption keeps the key file inaccessible to a perpetrator if your computer is stolen.)

```
cd .ssh
ssh-keygen -b 4096 -C "name@somehost.de"
  Enter file in which to save the key
          (/home/kofler/.ssh/id_rsa): <Return>
  Enter passphrase (empty for no passphrase):  <Return>
  Enter same passphrase again:  <Return>
  Your identification has been saved in id_rsa.
  Your public key has been saved in id_rsa.pub.
```

Then, you must upload the public key with the identifier *.pub* to your Git platform. In GitHub, you'll find the corresponding page under **Settings • SSH and GPG keys**; in GitLab, under **Settings • SSH Keys**. The easiest approach is to output the SSH key in the terminal with cat or less, copy the text (only about 10 lines), and paste it into the web form via the clipboard.

To download and set up a new local repository with git clone, you can now use the SSH address that GitHub/GitLab optionally displays once you have set up a SSH key (**Clone with SSH**):

```
git clone git@github.com:<account>/<repo>.git
```

When running git clone for the first time, you must accept the key from GitHub. The warning appears in the terminal: *The authenticity of host github.com can't be established*. Press Enter to confirm that you want to communicate with *github.com*.

To switch an existing local repository from HTTPS to SSH, you must change the line in the [remote "origin"] section of the repository's *.git/config* file:

```
# .git/config file
# previous configuration (HTTPS)
```

```
[remote "origin"]
    url = https://github.com/MichaelKofler/first-test.git
    ...

# switch to SSH
[remote "origin"]
    url = git@github.com:MichaelKofler/first-test.git
```

You can launch the editor easily via git config --edit. The logic for the switch is simple: Simply replace https://<git-host> with git@<git-host>. Instead of modifying the file in an editor, you can also run the following command:

```
git remote set-url origin git@github.com:<account>/<repo>.git
```

> **"git@github.com," not "account@github.com"**
> Make sure that the SSH address at GitHub/GitLab always starts with git@.... You might be tempted to specify your account name instead of git, but doing so is incorrect.

Git uses SSH, which only considers the .ssh/id_rsa key by default. You can store multiple keys in the *.ssh* directory, perhaps earmarking one specifically for use with GitHub. But you'll need to set up another *.ssh/config* file in this case, specifying which key to use for which site, in the following way:

```
# .ssh/config file
Host github.com
  IdentityFile ~/.ssh/my_git_key_for_github

Host gitlab.com
  IdentityFile ~/.ssh/my_git_key_for_gitlab
...
```

Be sure to use the correct spelling: The keyword is IdentityFile with two ts, not IdentifyFile!

> **Working with Multiple Computers**
> If you work alternately on different computers, you must deposit the public part of the key from *each* computer on the Git platform.
>
> Alternatively, you can also store the same SSH key on all your computers. However, you must ensure that Git always uses the correct key (see also *https://serverfault.com/questions/170682*). Also, you must ensure that only you have read and write permissions to the key (chmod 600 key on macOS/Linux); otherwise, SSH will ignore the key files.

2.4.5   Different SSH Keys for Multiple GitHub/GitLab Accounts

If you have multiple accounts on a Git platform, you might run into problems during an authentication process with Windows Credential Manager. Unfortunately, the situation isn't different with SSH: You must not store the same SSH key in two different GitHub accounts. (The web interface displays the error message *key is already in use*.)

Now, you can easily generate another key with ssh-keygen. But how do you tell Git, or SSH to be precise, which key to use for which account?

Let's assume you already have a GitHub account, and in the course of a company change, you're assigned a second account. In your notebook, you create a new SSH key for the company account in the following way:

```
cd ~/.ssh
```

```
ssh-keygen -b 4096 -C "name@a-company.com"
  Generating public/private rsa key pair.
  Enter file in which to save the key
    (/home/kofler/.ssh/id_rsa): git_a-company
  ...
```

You deposit the public part of this key on GitHub. Now comes the trick: In the *.ssh/config* file, add the following lines:

```
# in .ssh/config
Host github-work.com
  Host name github.com
  IdentityFile  ~/.ssh/git_a-company
```

Thus, any SSH command that uses the host *github-work.com* should actually apply to *github.com*, using the key git_a-company. When you use git-clone for the first time, you must replace *github.com* with *github-work.com*:

```
git clone git@github-work.com:<name>/<repo>.git
```

As a result, commands (like git pull, git push, etc.) will work without any problem. If you want your commits in this repository to have a different name or email address from the default settings, you must also run git config:

```
cd repo
git config user.name  "other name"
git config user.email "other.name@a-company.com"
```

Only a Hack

Note that, while the approach outlined in this section works well in simple cases, it's ultimately just a hack. The local *.git/config* file (intentionally) contains an incorrect remote URL, which will cause errors in complex setups.

An alternative approach, but equally imperfect, is described in the following blog: *https://dev.to/arnellebalane/setting-up-multiple-github-accounts-the-nicer-way-1m5m*.

2.4.6   If It Doesn't Work

As we've hinted in the introduction to this section, an almost infinite number of authentication variants exist, and it's correspondingly difficult to formulate universally applicable rules for troubleshooting.

Some `git` commands that are useful in the context of troubleshooting you must run in a Git repository. You can summarize all currently valid Git settings and specify in which file the options are set system-wide, user-specific, or repository-specific. The following listing, shortened for space reasons, was created on Windows in a repository with HTTPS communication. The crucial lines are `credential.helper` and `remote.origin.url`.

```
cd <directory-with-git-repo>

git config --list --show-origin
  [... heavily abridged]
  file:C:/Program Files/Git/etc/gitconfig
     diff.astextplain.textconv=astextplain
     http.sslbackend=openssl
     http.sslcainfo=C:/Program Files/.../certs/ca-bundle.crt
     credential.helper=manager-core
  file:C:/Users/ms/.gitconfig
     user.name=Michael Kofler
     user.email=MichaelKofler@users.noreply.github.com
  file:.git/config
     remote.origin.url=
       https://github.com/git-compendium/hello-world
     remote.origin.fetch=+refs/heads/*:refs/remotes/origin/*
```

If the authentication fails without giving any reasons, you can try to delete the data stored in Windows Credential Manager for your Git host. This approach will give you the option to reauthenticate on the next `git` command. If you use personal access tokens for authentication, you should check the web interface of your Git host to see if perhaps their validity period has expired.

To debug Git authentication via SSH, a best practice is to use the command `ssh -vT git@github.com`. This command checks whether a SSH connection to the GitHub server is possible and displays a lot of debugging information (including which SSH key is used). If the connection succeeds, one of the last lines reads `You've successfully authenticated`, as in the following example:

```
ssh -vT git@github.com
  OpenSSH_8.4p1 Ubuntu-6ubuntu2.1, OpenSSL 1.1.1l  24 Aug 2021
  [... heavily abridged]
  Reading configuration data /home/kofler/.ssh/config
  /home/kofler/.ssh/config: Applying options for github.com
  Reading configuration data /etc/ssh/ssh_config
  Will attempt key: mk@kofler.info RSA SHA256:j7I6...
  Will attempt key: mk@p1 RSA SHA256:ACiO...
  Will attempt key: my-git-key  explicit
  Offering public key: mk@kofler.info RSA SHA256:j7I6...
  Server accepts key:  mk@kofler.info RSA SHA256:j7I6...
  Hi! You've successfully authenticated, but GitHub does not
    provide shell access.
```

If you've made changes to the SSH keys, you should restart the SSH agent; otherwise, old keys may be stored in the cache. On macOS and Linux, you must run the following command for this task:

```
killall ssh-agent; eval `ssh-agent`
```

The following GitHub page offers more troubleshooting tips:

https://docs.github.com/en/authentication/troubleshooting-ssh.

2.5   Learning Git in a Playful Way (Githug)

The Ruby program *Githug* (*https://github.com/Gazler/githug*) is a great, playful way to learn Git. Every time you execute the githug command, the program gives you a task. You then try to solve this task via git commands. Afterwards, you must run githug again to check. The command checks whether you've completed the last task correctly and then assigns you the next task.

2.5.1   Requirements

To play Githug, the Ruby programming language must be installed on your computer. You can check this using ruby --version. Githug requires at least version 1.8.7. If Ruby isn't available, you can find installation instructions at the following link:

https://www.ruby-lang.org/en/documentation/installation.

In Debian and Ubuntu, you can easily install Ruby via sudo apt install ruby-full. Githug is a Ruby extension package, which you can install with the Ruby package management command gem:

```
sudo gem install githug
```

2.5.2   Game Structure

When first started, GitHub asks whether it can create the git_hug subdirectory in the
current directory. After that step, the first task starts immediately:

```
githug
  No githug directory found, do you wish to create one? [yn]  y
  Welcome to Githug!
  --
  Name: init
  Level: 1
  Difficulty: *
  --
  A new directory, `git_hug`, has been created; initialize an
  empty repository in it.
```

The first task is simple: You can change to the new directory and run git init there.

```
cd git_hug
git init
githug
  Congratulations, you have solved the level!
  --
  Name: config
  Level: 2
  Difficulty: *
  --
  Set up your git name and email, this is important so that your
  commits can be identified.
```

Nothing is required for the second task. You must have already run git config --global
for user.name and user.email. Thus, you can execute githug again right away. As a check,
the program asks for your name and email address and checks if the information
matches the Git configuration.

```
githug
  What is your name?  > Michael
  What is your email? > michael@somehost.com
  Your config has the following name: Michael
  Your config has the following email: michael@somehost.com
  Congratulations, you have solved the level!
  --
  Name: add
  Level: 3
  Difficulty: *
  --
```

> There is a file in your folder called `README`, you should add
> it to your staging area. Note: You start each level with a new
> repo. Don't look for files from the previous one.

Continue with task 3, but we'll leave the solution to you. If you fail at a task, you should continue reading parts of Chapter 3 where we systematically introduce you to the logic of Git and to many more commands and terms.

2.6   IDEs and Editors

In this section, we'll briefly discuss the Git-related features of some selected IDEs, editors, and other tools. In this context, we'll look at *Git GUI*, *GitHub Desktop*, *IntelliJ IDEA*, *TortoiseGit*, *VS Code*, and *Xcode* (in alphabetical order). Note that most editors/IDEs don't use internal Git libraries but instead draw on a separately installed git command.

For reasons of space, presenting all established programs is neither useful nor possible. We'd rather show you, by way of examples, how you can use elementary Git features from within development environments and thus make you confident to take your first steps.

You probably chose your editor or IDE according to your personal preferences or depending on your project. Its Git functionality is rather a subordinate criterion, especially since you can assume its presence in every contemporary program. But if you haven't made up your mind yet and are looking for a versatile editor, we have a clear recommendation: VS Code! We know of no other program that integrates Git functions as intuitively.

> **Back to Square One**
>
> We explicitly warn against skipping the previous sections and entering the chapter at this point. For almost all IDEs/editors the following applies: Using Git features is easy and convenient, *provided* you understand Git. Otherwise, you'll soon stare helplessly at the second or third incomprehensible error message and ask the internet for advice. You're really investing your time much better if you spend an hour or two getting to know and understand Git at the command level. Go back to reading Section 2.3, if you've skipped it!

2.6.1   Git GUI

Git GUI is a plain program that's installed by default along with Git for Windows, which is why it ends up on many Windows machines. But you can also install it in Debian/ Ubuntu, for example, with apt install git-gui gitk.

The easiest way to start the program is to run the git gui command in Git Bash. The interface then opens the repository in the current directory. For the first test, after opening a repository, you must first use **Edit • Options** to change the **Default File Contents Encoding** setting to utf-8; otherwise, all non-ASCII characters will be displayed incorrectly.

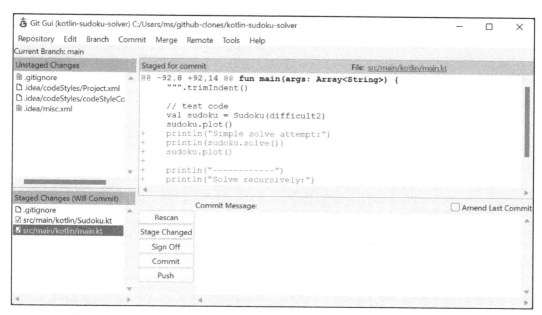

Figure 2.9 Git GUI's Antiquated Interface

In the default view, the program provides an overview of modified files of the project directory. The changes made within a file are displayed in a different view.

Going to **Repository • Visualize History** launches gitk, a second program that complements the Git GUI but must be installed as a separate package on Linux. This graphical alternative to the git log command is good for viewing the commits of a repository with a mouse click.

The Git GUI and gitk owe their popularity to the fact that this program was one of the first GUIs for Git. Meanwhile, many development environments or web interfaces have integrated similar functions in more modern ways. In addition, an almost unmanageable number of programs combine similar functions with a contemporary interface for free or for a fee—for example, *GitKraken*, *GitUp*, *SmartGit*, *SourceTree*, or *Tower*. (Some of these programs run only on Windows or only on macOS.)

2.6.2   GitHub Desktop

GitHub Desktop (*https://desktop.github.com*) is a free program available for Windows and macOS for managing Git repositories hosted on GitHub. Unlike "pure" Git tools such as the `git` command, GitHub Desktop also supports GitHub-specific functions. Some operations that can typically only be performed on the GitHub website are thus also accessible in a desktop program.

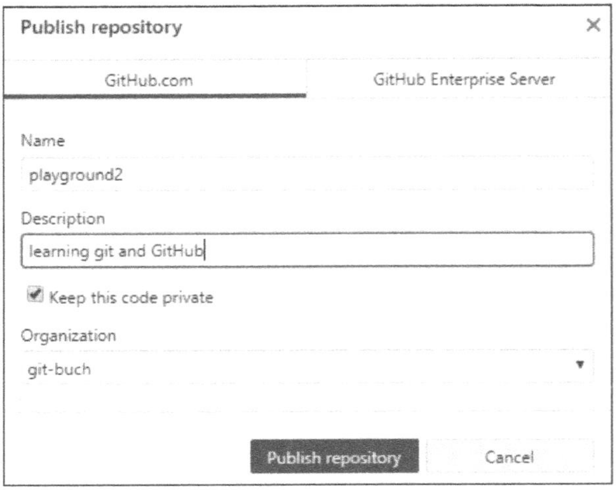

Figure 2.10 Setting Up a New Repository on GitHub

The main advantage of the GitHub Desktop is its ease of use: Once you've authenticated, you can create a local repository using **File • New Repository**, for example. You can add a *.gitignore* file for common programming languages, a license file, and a README file. In the next step, you can then click **Publish repository** to upload the entire project to GitHub. While creating a new repository on GitHub, you can choose whether the repository should be private or public and which of your organizations it should be associated with.

Basically, GitHub Desktop doesn't provide any functions that aren't also available in other tools or via the GitHub web interface. Nevertheless, we've come to appreciate the convenience associated with the program. Setting up a local repository, creating the corresponding `origin` on GitHub, and opening the project directory in VS Code—all this can be done within 30 seconds, which is unrivaled! GitHub Desktop doesn't shy away from advanced features and supports operations like stashing and rebasing. So, you can perform trivial actions in the GitHub Desktop without being forced back to a command window constantly.

The **History** sidebar allows you to view the commit history of any Git repositories. Whether the `origin` is located at GitLab or at another Git platform doesn't matter. If necessary, you must first add the project directory to the list of all repositories known to GitHub Desktop using **File • Add existing repository**.

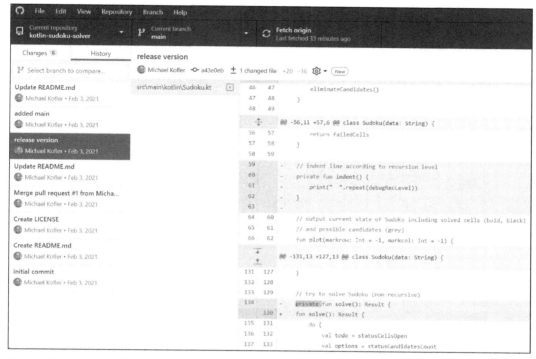

Figure 2.11 Commit with Changes to a Project in the Kotlin Programming Language

2.6.3   IntelliJ IDEA

The Java and Kotlin development environment *IntelliJ IDEA* can work with both Git and other version control programs. The functions are controlled via the central **VCS** menu. When Git is used for a project, **VCS** is replaced by a specific **Git** menu.

If your external repositories are on GitHub, the first step is to log on. First, switch to **Version Control • GitHub** in the settings dialog box. After logging on with your account name and password, IntelliJ IDEA requests an authentication token from GitHub. The stored token will be used for HTTPS authentication in the future. Alternatively, you can select an option to communicate via SSH.

Unfortunately, IntelliJ IDEA doesn't provide similarly good support for GitLab. Of course, you can store your IntelliJ IDEA projects on GitLab or on any other Git host; however, you must give up the convenience of authentication with tokens. (Better GitLab support is in the works, though without a concrete timeline: *https://youtrack.jetbrains.com/issue/IDEA-109294.*)

To open (*clone*) a project already on a Git platform in IntelliJ IDEA, run **File • New • Project from Version Control**, enter the project URL, and select an empty local directory. After git clone, IntelliJ IDEA asks if it should open the project.

If you have an existing project that's not yet under version control, run **VCS • Enable Version Control • Git**. Once you've marked the first source code file for a commit, the **Project configuration files can be added to Git** notice appears. Select the option **Always Add**. After all, you want the entire project to be backed up, not just the actual code.

You must add Gradle configuration files by yourself (e.g., *build.gradle*). However, you should *not* use Git to manage all directories and files with dynamically generated files, especially the *build* and *.gradle* directories. More tips on which IntelliJ IDEA-specific files you should usually not put under version control are summarized at the following link:

https://intellij-support.jetbrains.com/hc/en-us/articles/206544839.

A comprehensive sample *.gitignore* file for IntelliJ IDEA projects can be found at the following link:

https://github.com/github/gitignore/blob/main/Global/JetBrains.gitignore.

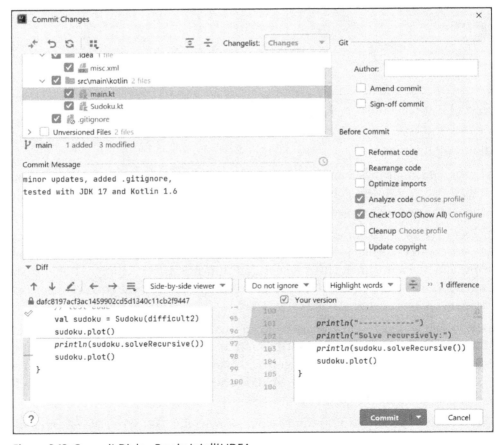

Figure 2.12 Commit Dialog Box in IntelliJ IDEA

On the first commit (menu command **Git • Commit**), IntelliJ IDEA asks if it may run `git config --global core.autocrlf`. If so, in the future, the line endings for all projects will be adapted to the respective operating system. This choice is appropriate for projects whose teams work on different operating systems, as described at the following link:

https://docs.github.com/en/get-started/getting-started-with-git/configuring-git-to-handle-line-endings.

The commit dialog box is displayed as a modal box dialog by default, so it blocks other functions until it's finished. Alternatively, you can integrate the dialog box into the interface as a non-modal pane. For this step, search for **Version Control • Commit** in the settings and activate the option **Use non-modal commit interface**.

Going to **Git • Push** enables you to upload your commits to an external repository. The first time, you'll need to click the **origin** link in the push dialog box and use **Define Remote** to specify the URL of the external repository. For detailed documentation on other Git features in IntelliJ IDEA, refer to the manual at the following link:

https://www.jetbrains.com/help/idea/using-git-integration.html.

For numerous other IDEs by JetBrains, Git functions are implemented in an identical or similar way.

2.6.4   TortoiseGit

TortoiseGit is an extension for Windows Explorer. After installation, you can execute all important `git` commands in the Explorer via the context menu command **Show more options • TortoiseGit**—provided, of course, that the current directory is a Git repository.

At first glance, this feature doesn't sound particularly spectacular. However, depending on the other tools you use, these additional Explorer commands can be quite useful. This usefulness is especially true if you have many Git repositories on your machine whose contents you don't usually edit with a development environment.

2.6.5   Visual Studio Code

As mentioned in Chapter 1, Section 1.1.2, we don't know of any program that integrates Git features as convincingly as VS Code. This belief holds true both from a beginner's perspective (i.e., the features are easy to use) and for professionals (i.e., the feature set is comprehensive). Current versions of VS Code use tokens for authentication on Linux and macOS. On Windows, VS Code uses Windows Credential Manager.

Since we've already introduced elementary Git functions in VS Code in Chapter 1, Section 1.3, in the context of an example, we'll be brief. Now, we'll introduce two extensions you can install via **File • Preferences • Extensions**:

- **GitLens**

  Once activated, this extension displays a lot of helpful information and offers buttons in the Git sidebar, status bar, and directly in the code. This extension allows you to see the latest commits, quickly browse through the latest versions of a file, and more. In addition, GitLens discreetly fades into the currently active file in light gray text, in which commit the current line was last changed and by whom. Thus, GitLens constantly provides a lot of contextual information without having to explicitly search for it.

- **Copilot**

  The Copilot supports you during your programming work. When you start developing a new function or method, Copilot looks in the public GitHub repositories to see if comparable code can be found there. (Artificial intelligence is supposedly involved in the search.) If the extension finds comparable code, it will suggest that you apply this code. You must then decide for yourself whether you can accept the code as is or whether specific changes are required for your application.

  Since VS Code isn't clairvoyant, the Copilot extension requires that you use meaningful English names for your functions and variables and document in advance (and clearly express) what tasks a function is supposed to perform.

  At the time of writing, Copilot wasn't publicly available yet. Before you can try the extension, you'll need to register with *https://copilot.github.com*, and then you'll receive access data. Unfortunately, we weren't part of the elite test circle, so we can't report from our own experience how well Copilot works. A broad mix of enthusiasm and skepticism exists currently within the developer community.

  Two main criticisms are that Copilot pulls code from obsolete, unmaintained projects and that some copyright issues are unresolved: Can you take 10 or 20 lines of code from a project that is subject to the *GNU Public License (GPL)* if your own code uses a completely different license?

  One final note: Copilot isn't a VS Code project, but a GitHub development. (VS Code and GitHub are, of course, both under the care of Microsoft, so a clear separation is difficult.) In any case, Copilot will be available for other development environments and editors.

2.6.6   Xcode

In Apple's *Xcode* development environment, Git has long been the preferred version control program. Before you get started, navigate to **Preferences • Accounts**. Click the plus button to add your account. Xcode supports multiple platforms (i.e., GitHub, GitLab, and Bitbucket). In any case, you'll need to provide your account name as well as a token. To generate this token in advance, for example, on the GitHub website, navigate to **Settings • Developer settings • Personal access tokens**. The token must allow relatively many actions.

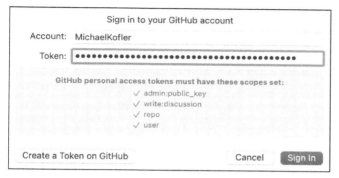

Figure 2.13 Adding an External Git Account Once Requires a Personal Access Token

When you set up a new project, you can enable the **Create Git repository on my Mac** option in the final step of the wizard, when selecting the project directory. This setting will activate Git for the project. All files relevant when setting up the project are automatically added to the local repository in an initial commit. To retroactively place an existing project under Git control, you must run **Source Control • Create Git Repositories**.

Commits must be executed via **Source Control • Commit**. Changed files that are already part of the repository are automatically marked for the commit. If you want to put new files under version control, you must select them explicitly.

```
pacman ⟩ shared ⟩ Maze ⟩ No Selection
Hierarchical  Flat      108 for x in 0..<w {                                  110 for y in 0..<h {
                        109   for y in 0..<h {                                111   let mazeId = walls[x][y]
⟶ ios-pacman           110     let mazeId = walls[x][y]                      112   if mazeId == Tileset.wall {
  ⟶ ios-pacman         111     if mazeId == Tileset.wall {                   113     // walls
       Maze.swift  M   112       // walls                                    114     let wall = SKSpriteNode(imageNamed: "wall")
                        113       let wall = SKSpriteNode(imageNamed: "wall") 115     wall.zPosition   = 0
                        115       wall.position   = CGPoint(x: x * iUnit, y: y * iUnit) 116     wall.position   = CGPoint(x: x * iUnit, y: y * iUnit)
                        116       wall.size       = blocksize                117     wall.size       = blocksize
                        117       wall.zPosition  = 0                        118     scene.addChild(wall)
                        118       scene.addChild(wall)                       119   } else if mazeId == Tileset.floor {
                        119     } else if mazeId == Tileset.floor {          120     // background
                        120       // background                              121     let floor = SKSpriteNode(imageNamed: "floor")
                        121       let floor = SKSpriteNode(imageNamed: "floor") 122   floor.zPosition  = 0
                        122       floor.position  = CGPoint(x: x * iUnit, y: y * iUnit) 123   floor.position  = CGPoint(x: x * iUnit, y: y * iUnit)
                        123       floor.size      = blocksize                124     floor.size      = blocksize
                        124       floor.zPosition = 0                        125     scene.addChild(floor)
                        125       scene.addChild(floor)                      126   }
                        126     }                                            127 }
Floor
minor refactoring       ios-pacman ⟩ main ⟩ Local Revision          1/4 ⟩  ios-pacman ⟩ main ⟩ 19.01.22 Michael Kofler 9a7b0f7 (HEAD)

Push to remote   No Remote                                                    Cancel    Commit 1 File
```

Figure 2.14 Commit Dialog Box Visualizes the Implemented Changes

To compare a code file with an older version, click the **Enable Code Review** button in the Xcode window bar. If necessary, you can undo individual changes by clicking **Discard Changes**.

Whether you enable Git when creating the project or later, for now there is only one local Git repository. Before you can synchronize the project with an external repository, you must add it. First, switch to the **Source Control Navigator** in the sidebar, select

Repositories • Remotes, and execute the context menu command **New remote** or **Add to existing remote**. Then, you can synchronize your local and external repositories using **Source Control** • **Push** and **Source Control** • **Pull**.

Of course, you can also create a new local project from an existing external repository. For this approach, you must run **Source Control** • **Clone** and either specify the URL of a third-party repository or select a repository from your own GitHub, GitLab, or Bitbucket account. In the second step, Xcode asks for the local directory in which the project should be set up.

2.7 Contributing to a Third-Party GitHub Project

Many large open-source projects have a public GitHub repository. As a result, you can easily run git clone, download the code, and run or compile the program. But you're out of luck if you try to change the code and upload it again after a commit via git push: After all, you aren't a member of the development team and therefore can't make any changes. Consequently, git push will fail with an error message.

Now, of course, you could contact the development team and ask to join the team and request collaboration rights to the repository. If you haven't already made a name for yourself in the community, however, the response will be cautious and skeptical. After all, how much expertise you have, whether your code has a convincing quality, and whether you comply with the guidelines of other developers are all unclear. In general, most projects limit the number of people allowed to make changes in the repository independently as much as possible.

2.7.1 Forks

For this reason, GitHub established a novel approach many years ago, now used by most other Git platforms in some manner: To contribute to someone else's project, you can visit its GitHub page and click the **Fork** button. You use this function to create a copy of the third-party repository in your own GitHub account.

In a subsequent step, you can then create a local repository on your machine from this copy using git clone. In the clone, you can make whatever changes you want, test the code, and make commits. Finally, when your changes are complete, you must commit them back to the GitHub fork, that is, your copy of the original repository, using git push.

2.7.2 Pull Requests

In the GitHub web interface, you can find the **New pull request** button in the **Pull requests** dialog box in your local fork. This button will redirect you to the page of the original project.

Figure 2.15 Pull Request Button Is Hidden in the Dialog Box of the Same Name

The GitHub interface first displays a summary of the changes made. In a further step, you must submit a message to the developers of the external repository, usually with information about what you've changed and possibly why. **Create pull request** completes the process.

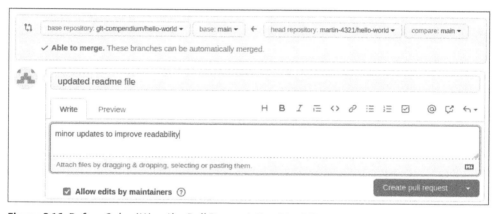

Figure 2.16 Before Submitting the Pull Request, You Must Document It

Next, the owners of the foreign repository will decide whether to accept your changes (**Merge pull request**), reject them, or make suggestions for improvement and request further changes from you (**Comment**).

Pull requests provide the only way to participate in GitHub projects without being a member of the team. However, pull requests are also often used internally in projects to prevent too many uncoordinated changes to the repository.

Outside the Git Standard

Note that *forks* and *pull requests* aren't Git techniques. Accordingly, no `git` subcommands for them are available. Instead, you must perform these operations in the web interface of your Git platform. The nomenclature can vary depending on the platform. In GitLab, for example, pull requests are sometimes called *merge requests*.

More details on pull requests will follow in Chapter 5, Section 5.1, and in Chapter 8, Section 8.4.

2.8 Synchronization and Backups

Many developers have cloud clients running on their machines (e.g., Dropbox or Next-cloud) to regularly transfer the contents of their file directories to the cloud. Motivations, on one hand, include having an external backup and having the ability synchronize your own files between several computers in an uncomplicated way.

Alternatively or in combination, some software also regularly synchronize selected directories between multiple computers or devices *without* resorting to cloud offerings. A popular program in this regard is *Syncthing*.

Finally, we always recommend making regular backups of the computer (e.g., on an external hard drive or on a NAS device). Traditional backups have an advantage over synchronization solutions in that they work even if you accidentally delete a directory. (With synchronization solutions, the directory is also deleted from the connected devices and is thus lost, unless you have additional backup mechanisms in place.)

2.8.1 Git Issues

Now, what does this discussion of synchronization have to do with Git? A high risk of conflict arises when using Git in synchronized directories or in directories reconstructed from a backup. Git memorizes when files were last modified. However, due to synchronization software, Git management information may not match the files (which have been modified separately from Git). This results in error messages that are difficult to understand, defective repositories, and trouble without end.

Without this information, the synchronization of Git repositories is mostly completely superfluous: Provided you regularly run `git pull` as well as `git commit` and `git push`, Git will take care of synchronizing your repositories between different locations (e.g., locally on machine 1 and machine 2 as well as on an external server from GitHub, Git-Lab, or another provider). Git handles this task for typical software projects more efficiently than any synchronization software.

2.8.2 Conclusion

There are a few key takeaways to keep in mind:

- Make sure that the directories with Git repositories on your computer are excluded from synchronization with the cloud or with other computers.
- Traditional backups pose much less risk to Git than constant synchronization. In addition, backups can be a stopgap if you accidentally destroy your repository by using `git` commands incorrectly.

  However, after a data loss, you should only draw on the backup if there really is no longer an external Git repository with current data available. Exercise the utmost caution when importing the backup and reactivating Git!

- If you don't update your Git repositories regularly anyway as part of your work (`git pull`, `git commit`, and `git push`), you can also use the `git` command specifically to create backups. `git clone --mirror` creates a copy of a Git repository. You can execute the command automatically (e.g., on Linux via Cron).

Chapter 3
Basic Principles of Git

In the first two chapters of this book, we aimed to provide a practical introduction to Git without confusing you with too many details. In fact, for many tasks, understanding git add, git commit, git push, and git pull (plus five or six more commands) is sufficient. With this basic knowledge, you can use Git in an elementary way. However, a true Git professional is required to control the project, work with Git, and help with problems. Our wish is that this book helps you understand Git so well that you become that Git professional yourself!

In this chapter, we'll therefore go into much more depth. We'll provide an overview of the terminology and then explain some advanced concepts like branches, tags, merge operations, and rebasing. You'll also learn, to some extent, how Git stores your data internally.

In this chapter, we're pursuing two goals in parallel:

- First, we want to show you the variety of ways Git can be used. So far, we've really only scratched the surface of Git. Unfortunately, the many commands, options, and variants are also associated with a high level of complexity, which we don't want to conceal.

- Second, we want to provide an understanding of how Git works behind the scenes by describing its internal mechanisms.

3.1 Terminology

Every man page on a git subcommand, every Stack Overflow article, and of course every section of this book uses technical terms, some of which may still be foreign to you. In this section, we want to explain the most important terms from the Git world briefly as an introduction. (Don't worry, more details on each term will be provided in this chapter.)

Instead of alphabetically, in this section, we'll go from the top down, that is, moving from the big picture to the details.

A *repository* is the collection (the archive) of all files of a project, including their change histories. Think of a repository as a database system that contains all the states of a project from its first file to its current state, along with information about who made what changes and when. In the repository, you can thus trace the steps through which each file has reached its current state. This information is referred to as the *history*.

Any number of branches can exist within the repository. Branches help you develop new features without tampering with the stability of the main version. Branches give multiple developers the ability to independently perform different tasks. Each branch has its own set of files or file versions.

The main branch plays a special role. When setting up a new repository, the main branch (the only one at that time) is automatically set up. This branch is considered the default branch—and most Git users leave it at that. Internally, the main branch is a branch like any other branch.

From "Master" to "Main"

As a result of protests in the U.S. following the death of George Floyd, discussion in the IT industry has considered how to avoid terms that can be construed as racist: master/ slave processes, whitelists and blacklists, etc.

In the Git environment, this discussion has affected the master branch: Until 2020, the default branch of new repositories was always referred to as the master. However, most Git tools have converted to main.

But this change only affects new repositories. Therefore, you'll probably encounter a master branch in older repositories for many years to come. From a technical perspective, what the main branch of a Git repository is called doesn't matter as long as no naming conflict with other branches exists. We'll explain how you can rename master to main in your own repositories if necessary in Section 3.5.

A Git repository consists of the files in the working directory, which reflect the current state of the currently active branch, and the repository database in the *.git* subdirectory. Instead of working directory, the term *workspace* is also common.

3.1.1   About Commits

Before you save anything permanently in the repository, you must specify *which* changes you want to include. Not all changes should always be saved: Maybe you've created three new files. Two files contain code and should become part of the project. However, the third file contains personal annotations that you don't want to include in the repository.

For this differentiation, Git provides the *staging area* (often abbreviated as *stage*). The staging area includes the entire active branch, including any changes that should be permanently saved on the next commit. To stage a file in its current state, you must run the git add <file> or the equivalent git stage <file> command.

> **Stage = Index = Cache!**
>
> Alternative names for "stage" are "index" and "cache." Although we prefer the term *staging area* in this book, all of the terms we've mentioned are in common use. We want to highlight that these terms are synonyms, not different things or functions. When a *directory cache index* is mentioned in man git-ls-files, again the staging area is being discussed.

With each commit, the changes marked in the staging area are permanently stored in the repository database. As soon as a commit occurs, the changes summarized in this way can later be transferred to another branch if required, or the changes can be revoked.

The last (most recent) commit in the current branch is called HEAD. Note that Git differentiates between *head* and *HEAD*. Each branch has a most recent commit (i.e., a *head*). The *HEAD* with all caps explicitly refers to the *active* branch you're currently editing.

To switch from one branch to another, you must perform a *checkout*. A checkout replaces the current files in the project directory with those of the branch. So, with a checkout, new files can be added, existing files can change, and other files can disappear. (Usually, a commit must occur before each checkout. Otherwise, you risk that the changes made most recently will be overwritten and thus lost.)

Sometimes, you may want to save unfinished changes *without* committing those changes. Maybe you're working on a new feature, but in the meantime, you need to fix a small bug in another branch. Now, on one hand, you don't want to commit (so that your co-workers don't have problems with your still unfinished code). On the other hand, you need a way to temporarily save your changes. This scenario is exactly where a *stash*, a kind of storage space for code that's not yet committable, comes in handy.

To merge branches, you must run a *merge*. The merge process is a delicate matter: What should Git do with files that have been modified in both branches since the code was separated into two branches? Git often finds solutions on its own, for instance, if changes have been made in different parts of a code file and don't affect each other. In more complicated cases, Git leaves the decision to you: You then see both code variants in an editor. Then, you must manually select one variant and save the change thus made in a separate commit. (We'll discuss this topic in more detail in Section 3.9.)

Merge processes also occur when you synchronize multiple repositories. Even if the merge process now has a different cause, technically, nothing changes from a Git perspective. Again, the process is about merging changes stored in commits.

Repeated merge operations often create a cluttered structure in the local repository, with branches constantly opening and closing. By *rebasing*, you can clean up the commit sequence (the history) and straighten it out, so to speak.

By default, commits are identified by a hexadecimal hash code. So that you don't lose the overview, you can identify or name commits by *tags*. Tags are commonly used to mark milestones or delivered versions.

3.1.2   Log and Logging

Git uses the terms *log* or *logging* in two different contexts:

- The git log command allows you to view the history of one or more branches, that is, the sequence of commits leading to the current state. This representation is called a *log*. The required information is located in the commits. (Each commit refers to its predecessor. For commits created by a merge process, there are multiple predecessors.) No custom logging files are used as a basis.

- The *reference log (reflog)* is the sequence of locally executed commands that change the head of a branch. This is local data that isn't synchronized between repositories. The reflog can in some cases help to undo erroneously or incorrectly executed commands.

3.1.3   Local and Remote Repositories

An irony of fate is that Git, unlike many other programs, was conceived as a decentralized version control system, but only made its big breakthroughs in conjunction with (centralized) platforms like GitHub, GitLab, and others.

For communications with remote repositories (i.e., non-local repositories), Git provides the HTTPS and SSH protocols. Relatively little effort is required to turn a typical web server into a Git server. Although the web interface familiar from GitHub and other platforms is then missing, this feature is sufficient for synchronizing repositories.

Regardless of whether the external peer is a minimal Git server or a full Git platform like GitLab, you can now synchronize your repository via the git command if you have the relevant access rights.

Subcommands of the same name exist in each platform for the three most important git commands:

- clone enables you to copy an external repository to your local machine.

- pull allows you to update your local repository and replicate the changes stored in the external repository since the last clone or pull action. This process downloads the new commits from the external repository for the currently active branch and merges them locally (merge including commit).

- push allows you to transfer locally executed commits back to the external repository. By default, this process is permitted only if you have previously performed a pull, so your local repository is up to date. Under this condition, the push action in the remote repository doesn't require a full merge process. Rather, your commits just need to be uploaded, and a pointer to the most recent commit of that branch needs to be updated. This simple variant of a merge process is referred to as a *fast-forward merge*.

Git provides many configuration options for push and pull operations with one or even multiple remote repositories. The *origin* repository plays a special role in this context. This repository is the external repository from which the project was originally cloned or which was explicitly configured as the external default repository. Push and pull operations where you do not explicitly specify another remote repository automatically affect the origin.

3.1.4   Hooks, Submodules, and Subtrees

Git can automatically run a script when certain events occur. The configuration of this feature is performed via *hooks*, which are script files in the *.git/hooks* directory (see Chapter 9, Section 9.1).

Some projects use subprojects (libraries, database drivers, etc.). To enable changes to the code of these subprojects in parallel with your project, but at the same time leave the project in its entirety in one directory, Git uses *submodules*. This feature allows directories of a Git repository to house additional Git repositories. Nevertheless, the commits of all repositories remain independent of each other.

A variant to submodules are *subtrees*. In this approach, an external repository is also integrated into your own repository. However, in this case, all files are managed in *one* Git database, which simplifies the handling a bit. Details on submodules and subtrees are provided in Chapter 9, Section 9.3.

3.2   The Git Database

When we conceived of this book, we wanted to include the internal details of Git at the end of this chapter. After all, you're reading this book because you want to use Git efficiently, not because you're interested in the mechanisms behind the scenes.

During the writing process, however, we realized that Git concepts are much easier to explain if you have at least a rudimentary understanding of how Git actually works. We thus decided on a compromise: This section provides some basic insights into what's going on in the *.git* directory. More details are provided in Section 3.13.

3.2.1   The .git Directory

Let's assume you're creating a new project directory, which is still completely empty. Now, you must run git init in that directory to make the directory a repository. If you work on Linux, the tree .git command immediately provides an overview of the newly set up Git database. This command isn't available on macOS or Windows. You can run the Finder, use the Explorer, or run the `ls -laR` or `dir /s` commands instead.

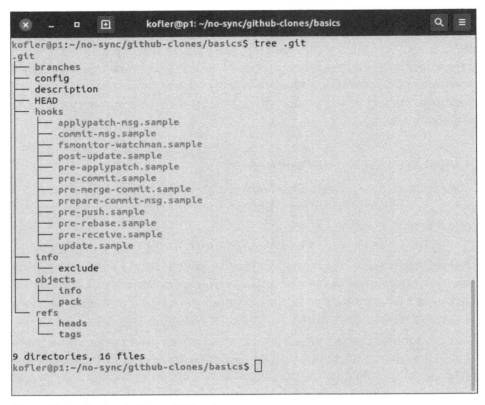

Figure 3.1 Contents of a New .git Directory

What's the purpose of these various subdirectories and files?

- The *branches* directory is usually empty. This directory provides the option to define URL shortcuts for the `git fetch`, `pull`, and `push` commands. However, this approach is uncommon and considered outdated.

- *config* is the repository-specific configuration file (see Chapter 12, Section 12.3).

- *description* contains a short description of the repository as text. Initially, this file contains sample text that you can replace with your own information.

- *HEAD* is a tiny text file that points to the current commit of the current branch. As long as *main* is the active branch, the file will contain the following line:

```
ref: refs/heads/main
```

- The *hooks* directory contains examples of scripts that should be executed automatically in certain situations. We'll describe hooks in more detail and show you how to use hooks in Chapter 9, Section 9.1.

- *info/exclude* is a repository-specific addition to the *.gitignore* file, which usually contains only a few sample lines. *info/exclude* can be used to exclude files locally from version control without touching the *.gitignore* file, which is shared with other team members as part of the repository (see also *https://stackoverflow.com/questions/22906851*).

- The *index* file is used for the internal storage of the staging area. The file is created when you run `git add` for the first time. The binary file contains references to changed files that were added to the staging area using `git add`.

- The *logs* directory for storing the *reflog* is missing if the repository is empty. This directory is set up with the first commit and then contains text files that summarize all actions that change the head of a branch. In addition to commits, checkouts and push and pull operations are also logged.

- The *objects* directory is initially empty except for two subdirectories, but this directory will later become the most extensive one. In this directory, Git stores all the data of the repository in binary files. Git objects not only include commits, but also trees, binary large objects (BLOBs), and tags (see Section 3.2.2).

  The object database is organized as a key-value storage, with the hash code of the objects serving as the access key. Because a lot of files end up in the *objects* directory, subdirectories are created for the first 2 digits of the hash code during operation. So, to store a file with the hash code `a23cd4352`, Git will store the `a2` directory (if one doesn't already exist) and, in it, store the file `3cd4352`. (Of course, the hash codes are longer than in this example.)

  For efficiency reasons, the individual files from the *objects* directory are often packed into larger archive files located in the `pack` subdirectory.

- The *refs* directory contains references to commits or objects. Among other things, these references point to the most recent commits (*heads*) of local and remote branches, as well as to commits named with a tag. To avoid too many tiny files, all references are regularly combined in the text file *packed-refs*.

Within the *.git* directory, additional files and subdirectories are gradually created when `git` commands are executed. A concise summary of their functions can be found at the following link:

https://schacon.github.io/git/gitrepository-layout.html

3.2.2   Git Object Types: Commits, BLOBs, Trees, and Tags

Git stores four types of objects in the *.git/objects* directory:

- **Commits**
  A commit object contains the metadata of a commit: When were the changes saved? By whom? With which commit message? With which signature, if any?

The commit object references two other objects using hash codes: a tree object that lists all versioned files on the branch and the predecessor commit on the same branch.

- **BLOBs**
  BLOB stands for *binary large object*. Git uses BLOBs to internally store all versioned files, whether large or small. To save space, Git can compress the files or store only the differences compared to other files (deltas).

- **Trees**
  A tree object contains a list of filenames with hash codes that point to the associated BLOBs.

- **Tags**
  Git uses different types of tags (see Section 3.11). The simplest form, called *lightweight tags*, are just references (i.e., tiny text files in the *.git/objects/tags* directory). In contrast, annotated and signed tags are stored as real Git objects, which contain various additional information in addition to the tag name.

3.2.3 References

References are tiny files that point to a specific object (most often a commit). For example, the *refs/heads/main* file contains the hash code of the most recent commit of the main branch.

References are used for two tasks:

- The *.git/ref/heads* and *.git/ref/remotes* directories contain files that point to the most recent commits of the branches in the local repository as well as in remote repositories.

- The *.git/refs/tags* directory contains cross-references to tagged commits.

Don't worry if the *.git/refs* directory is largely empty. Some references are placed in the *.git/packed-refs* file to save space. The command git show-ref lists all known references.

A special case is the *.git/HEAD* file. This file doesn't contain a hash code but, rather, the name of the head file for the current branch. So, this file is more or less a link to a link. If the develop branch is currently active, *.git/HEAD* has the following content:

```
cat .git/HEAD
  ref: refs/heads/develop
```

The *.git/refs/head/develop* file contains the hash code of the commit in question:

```
cat .git/refs/heads/develop
  f348eaa6f985875801ac2bb7a9a8543d972fb65b
```

You can use git show to view details about the commit. For this command, you must pass the first 4 digits of the hash code.

```
git show f348
  commit f348eaa6f985875801ac2bb7a9a854...65b (HEAD -> develop)
  Author: Michael Kofler <MichaelKofler@...>
  Date:   Thu Jan 20 07:32:24 2022 +0200
      added documentation
  ...
```

3.3   Commits

You already know (or think you know) what a commit is: A commit permanently saves the changes made to the project directory in the repository. If you've read the text carefully up to this point, you're already aware that `git commit` doesn't simply save all changes, but only those changes that were previously transferred to the staging area via `git add`.

This section explains what goes on in detail before and during a commit. Maybe you think the internal workings aren't that important—what matters is that it works. But the commit is a central operation of Git. If you want to understand how Git works, you'll also need to understand what a commit means internally.

The starting point for the following examples is an initially empty directory in which you create a repository using `git init` and then store two files in the default branch (i.e., main) in an initial commit:

```
mkdir test
cd test
git init
echo "lorem ipsum" > file1
echo "hello git"   > file2
git add file1 file2
git commit -m 'initial commit'
```

3.3.1   The Staging Area

In the next step, you'll make a change in `file2` and create the new file `file3`:

```
echo "more text" >> file2
echo "123" > file3
```

An attempt to simply save these changes via `git commit` fails, and `git` even reveals why, as shown in the following example:

```
git commit
  On branch main
  Changes not staged for commit: (use "git add <file>..."
```

```
to update what will be committed)
    modified:   file2
Untracked files: (use "git add <file>..." to include in
what will be committed)
    file3
no changes added to commit
```

Thus, git detects that something has changed but requires that you explicitly run git add for all changed and new files, as in the following command:

```
git add file2 file3
```

git add stores the current state of file2 and file3 in the staging area. If you were to run git commit now, the result would be clear: The modified file file2 and the new file file3 would be saved permanently.

To further emphasize the difference between the project directory (workspace), staging area, and repository, let's implement two more changes: echo adds a third line of text to file2, and rm deletes file3. Since we won't run git add again, these changes are *not* in the staging area.

```
echo "third line" >> file2
rm file3
```

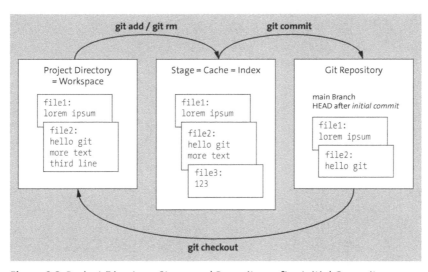

Figure 3.2 Project Directory, Stage, and Repository after Initial Commit

Currently, we have three different states for file2: cat file2 shows the current state in the project directory, git show :file2 shows the contents of the file as it exists in the staging area, and git show HEAD:file2 shows the file in its state at the last commit. (We'll explain the :<filename> and HEAD:<filename> notations in more detail in Section 3.12.)

```
cat file2                   (file in the workspace)
  hello git
  more text
  third line

git show :file2             (file in staging area)
  hello git
  more text

git show HEAD:file2         (file at last commit)
  hello git
```

In addition, git status indicates that file2 and file3 are in the staging area but that changes were implemented after that, as shown in the following example:

```
git status --long
  On branch main

  Changes to be committed:
    (use "git restore --staged <file>..." to unstage)
      modified:   file2
      new file:   file3
  Changes not staged for commit:
    (use "git add/rm <file>..." to update what will be committed)
    (use "git restore <file>..." to discard changes in working
    directory)
      modified:   file2
      deleted:    file3
```

Thus, from the perspective of the commit, a file can have three states at the same time:

- The current state in the project directory
- The state in the staging area (*staged*)
- The state in the repository (*committed*)

3.3.2   The Commit

If you now run git commit, then the current state of the staging area will be permanently stored in the repository:

```
git commit -m '2nd commit'
```

Because we still made changes to the project directory after git add, the last commit doesn't reflect the current project state. To save these changes permanently as well, we must run git add again, then git rm for file3, and git commit one more time.

```
git add file2
git rm file3
git commit -m '3rd commit'
```

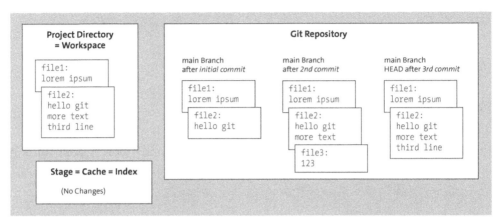

Figure 3.3 Project Directory, Stage, and Repository after the Third Commit

---

Stage versus Repository

Figure 3.2 and Figure 3.3 show the staging area represented as a separate data store located between the workspace and the repository. This concept is well within the tradition of many other Git articles and manuals, including the original documentation:

https://git-scm.com/book/en/v2/Getting-Started-What-is-Git%3F

Strictly speaking, however, the separation between stage and repository is misleading. The staging area is an integral part of the repository:

- Like all files of the repository, the *index* file, which is a kind of table of contents for the staging area, is located in the *.git* directory.
- Once you run git add, the file in question is immediately stored in a BLOB in *.git/objects*. So, the file even ends up in the repository before the commit!

3.3.3 More Details

Already, when you run git add file, the contents of the file are stored in a new BLOB file in the *.git/objects* directory. The easiest way to test this process is to first pool all object files into one package using git gc. Now, you can easily identify object files created later via tree or find and display them using git show.

In our examples, we always pass only 4 digits of the otherwise 40-digit hash codes to our git commands. This convention is sufficient for a clear identification of the few objects. Of course, when you reproduce these examples at home, different (much longer) hash codes will result.

```
git gc
echo "long text" > file4
git add file4

find .git/objects/ -type f
  .git/objects/9a/26ae2b65bf11943339cd025a84ea7157242302
  ...

git show 9a26
  long text
```

At the same time, git add updates the *.git/index* file. This file contains cross-references to the BLOBs with the changes represented in a binary format.

Two new objects are created using git commit: a commit object and a tree object. In addition, the *index* file is tidied up. The changes referenced in that file have now become part of the commit and are no longer needed in the staging area.

```
git commit -m '4th commit'
  [main 8dce80c] 4th commit
  1 file changed, 1 insertion(+)
```

Via find, you can determine the filenames of the new objects:

```
find .git/objects/ -type f
  .git/objects/9a/26ae2b65bf11943339cd025a84ea7157242302
  .git/objects/8d/ce80c0e4d9a9962998aae685ce389574863c4b
  .git/objects/6e/d4afc8ff4ed389f936052d4c065b51aa24c3c7
  .git/objects/pack/pack-b01430f33de5b1ff10248bf...c511.idx
  .git/objects/pack/pack-b01430f33de5b1ff10248bf...c511.pack
```

git cat-file -p reveals the details of the commit object. (git cat-file helps you look at Git objects in more detail. You can often use the more convenient git show command instead, but when committing, git show provides more detail than is useful in this context.)

```
git cat-file -p 8dce
  tree      6ed4afc8ff4ed389f936052d4c065b51aa24c3c7
  parent    a89f7b97fa7a12d527afe7eba62c748215a1a620
  author    Michael Kofler <MichaelKofler@...> 1642666315 +0100
  committer Michael Kofler <MichaelKofler@...> 1642666315 +0100

  4th commit
```

From the resulting output, notice that all the files captured in the current branch are listed in the tree object 6ed4. The previous commit in the same branch (main) had the hash code a89f.

A look into the tree object completes the picture:

```
git cat-file -p 6ed4
   100644  blob   01a59b011a48660bb3828ec72b2b08990b8cf56b   file1
   100644  blob   5ee9a0baef58bed383ef410689409f69cfe1ccaa   file2
   100644  blob   9a26ae2b65bf11943339cd025a84ea7157242302   file4
```

The current commit (the HEAD) of the main branch thus consists of the three files: file1, file2, and file4. Each of these files is located in a BLOB. The BLOB file with hash code 9a26 has already been created with git add and is now reused in the commit. The other two BLOBs were created as part of earlier git add commands. Because of git gc, no single files for each BLOB exist; rather, the BLOBs are contained in the *.git/objects/pack/pack-xxx* file.

In summary, a commit creates multiple objects in the Git database:

- The commit object summarizes the metadata (capturing who and when). The object contains the commit message, a reference to the previous commit in the same branch (*parent*), and a reference to a tree object.
- The tree object points to the BLOBs *of all* files of the active branch (and not only to new and changed files). The combination of commit and tree object enables you to easily access all versioned files of the branch in question. (The parent reference is only of interest if you're interested in historical information concerning *how* the current state came into being.)
- Each versioned file has a BLOB with the contents of the file.

If you've followed our example up to this point, the Git database contains four commits pointing to as many tree objects and six BLOBs with the different states of the four files.

You can also find this tiny Git repository on GitHub:

https://github.com/git-compendium/commit-internals.git

When you clone the archive, the *.git/objects* directory is empty except for a **.pack* file. This file contains the objects.

You can obtain the hash codes of all objects with the following command:

```
git show-index < .git/objects/pack/pack-<nnn>.idx
```

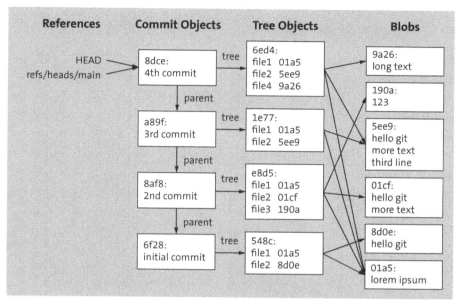

Figure 3.4 Internal Structure of the Repository after Four Commits, Each with the First Four Digits of the Hash Code

---

More Information

We think that's enough internal details for now. We wanted to give you an understanding of how Git works, but our goal is not to decipher all of Git's internal data structures to enable you to develop Git further.

However, we'd like to clarify that our description in this section is still highly abbreviated. In particular, Git includes various mechanisms to ensure that the Git database doesn't take up more space on your SSD than is absolutely necessary and that Git works as fast as possible, even with large repositories.

If you're interested in this topic, refer to the following pages or look directly into the C source code (the final link):

- *https://git-scm.com/book/en/v2/Git-Internals-Plumbing-and-Porcelain*
- *https://indepth.dev/posts/1168/becoming-a-git-pro-part-1-internal-git-architecture*
- *https://gist.github.com/matthewmccullough/2695758*
- *https://github.com/git/git*

3.3.4   Renaming, Moving, or Deleting Files from the Repository

git mv renames a file that's already in the repository. You can also use the command to move the file to another directory. The next time you commit, the file will be saved in the new location.

```
git mv <oldfilename> <newfilename>
git mv <file> <into-another-directory>/
```

No comparable command exists for copying a file to a new location. Instead, you should copy the file using cp and then add the copy to the repository via git add.

git rm deletes a file from both the working directory and the repository. If the file has been modified since the last commit, you must pass the --force option. Caution: The changes made since then can't be restored.

```
git rm <file>
```

> **Removing Files Permanently from the Repository**
>
> The file deleted using git rm remains in the repository. Otherwise, restoring an old commit together with the deleted file at a later time would be impossible.
>
> Sometimes, however, it's desirable to *really* delete a file, for instance, because it takes up a lot of space or because it contains sensitive data (passwords or keys). We've described the required procedure in Chapter 11, Section 11.4.

3.4   Commit-Undo

Developers make mistakes, and Git makes things right—right? This section provides some examples of how to undo unwanted actions in the context of a commit. But be careful not to do more damage! The rather similar sounding commands git reset, git revert, git restore, and git checkout may have rather different effects than their names suggest.

3.4.1   Not Saving a Change Permanently after All (git reset)

Let's say you've added a file to the staging area via git add, but now, you don't want to include the file in the next commit. git reset removes the file from the staging area *without* changing the file in the project directory:

```
git reset <file>
```

If you want to exclude all files in the project directory from the commit, you must run git reset without any other parameters.

3.4.2   Restoring Changes Made since the Last Commit (git restore)

Perhaps, since the last commit, you've made changes to a file under version control that turned out to be unfavorable. You want to restore the file to the state it was in when you last committed it. `git restore` restores the state of `file`. (The command overrides the changes made since then without any queries and without the option of undoing.)

```
git restore <file>
```

To restore all files in the project directory, you must pass a period (.) to `git restore` as a placeholder for the current directory. (The period is—unlike with `git reset`—absolutely necessary!)

```
git restore .
```

`git restore` has only been available since Git version 2.23 (since August 2019). If you use an older version of Git (check with `git --version`), you should upgrade. Alternatively, you can run `git checkout -- <file>`, with at least one space before and after the two hyphens.

> **Stashing**
>
> An alternative to `git restore` is `git stash`. This command also restores files to their original state. At the same time, however, the last changes made are cached in a separate area and can be restored later. You can find more detailed instructions about `git stash` in Section 3.7.

3.4.3   Viewing a File in an Old Version (git show)

If you want to see what state a file had at an earlier time, `git show` can help you. You pass the hash code of the commit, a tag (see Section 3.11), or the desired *revision* in a notation relative to a fixed point.

```
git show HEAD~3:<file>          (third-last commit)
```

> **References to Commits**
>
> For example, `HEAD~3` denotes the third-to-last commit. Alternatively, you can specify, for example, the name of a branch or a tag to refer to the corresponding commit. We'll explain this option and many other syntax variants in Section 3.12.
>
> The syntax is inconsistent if you want to specify a filename in addition to the revision, as in this case. For many commands, including `git show`, you must separate the revision specification and the filename with a colon. However, for several other commands, including `git checkout`, `git restore`, and `git diff` (see the following examples), you must pass the filename as a separate parameter.

3.4.4   Viewing Changes Compared to an Old Version (git diff)

Instead of viewing the whole file in its old state, you may want to see only the changes made since then. No problem—just use `git diff`. The following command shows the changes between the current state and the previous commit:

```
git diff HEAD~ <file>          (previous commit)
```

Note that the revision and filename are passed as separate parameters with this command. You can also look at the difference between the third-last commit and the last commit. The following command ignores the changes you've made since the last commit:

```
git diff HEAD~3 HEAD <file>
```

> **Searching the Git Repository**
>
> More procedures to search for information in the Git repository (who, when, and why?) are described in Chapter 4.

3.4.5   Restoring a File to an Old Version (git restore)

Once you've found the version of the file you want via `git show` or `git diff`, you can restore it to its old state. For this task, pass the desired revision to `git restore` with the `-s` option:

```
git restore -s HEAD   <file>   (last commit)
git restore -s HEAD~  <file>   (second to last commit)
git restore -s HEAD~2 <file>   (third to last commit)
```

As mentioned earlier, the `git restore` command has been available since August 2019 (Git version 2.23). In older versions of Git, you must run `git checkout` instead, but you must include two hyphens between the revision and the filename. (Notice how, for each command, the syntax looks a little different. In the case of `git checkout`, these differences are due to the many functions this command is overloaded with.)

```
git checkout HEAD    -- <file>   (last commit)
git checkout HEAD~   -- <file>   (second to last commit)
git checkout HEAD~2  -- <file>   (third to last commit)
```

What happens if you don't want to override the existing file with an old version, but instead want to save the old version in another file? In this case, you can use the `git show` command mentioned earlier and redirect the output to a new file:

```
git show HEAD:<file>    >  <otherfile>  (last commit)
git show HEAD~:<file>   >  <otherfile>  (second to last commit)
git show HEAD~2:<file>  >  <otherfile>  (third to last commit)
```

3.4.6 Reverting the Last Commits (git revert)

The "most correct" way to revert the last commit is to use the `git revert HEAD` command. This command applies the changes saved in the last commit "backwards," so to speak, to the current changes, thus restoring the previous state, and then executes another commit. When the command is executed, an editor is launched in which you must specify a commit message. (Unlike `git commit`, you cannot pass a commit message with an option.) In `git log`, what happened will be made absolutely clear:

```
git commit -a -m 'stupid commit'
  [main 9d97e6d] stupid commit

git revert HEAD
  [main 521d732] Revert "stupid commit"

git log --oneline -n 3
  521d732  (HEAD -> main) Revert "stupid commit"
  9d97e6d  stupid commit
  98760f1  add function xy
```

`git revert` can't be run if you have made changes to the working directory since the *stupid commit*. You can discard these changes upfront (using `git restore .`) or cache them in the stash area (using `git stash`, described in detail in Section 3.7). A third option consists of saving the changes in a commit and then revoking the last two commits:

```
git revert HEAD
  error: Your local changes to the following files
  would be overwritten by merge: ...
  Aborting

git commit -a -m 'more stupid changes'
  [main f8c18ab] more stupid changes

git revert HEAD HEAD~
```

`git revert` now reverts commits f8c18ab and 9d97e6d in two steps. Accordingly, you must specify two new commit messages.

More generally, `git revert` can revert any commit, not just the last one(s). So, for example, you can use `git revert HEAD~2` to revert only the changes of the third-to-last commit. (The changes made in the last and the penultimate commit will be preserved.)

Finally, you can pass an entire group of commits to `git revert`. The following command undoes the last three commits:

```
git revert HEAD~2^..HEAD
```

In this context, the .. is the syntax for ranges. HEAD~2 denotes the third-to-last commit, and the trailing caret (^) character refers to its predecessor (parent). This notation is necessary because, with the Git range syntax, the starting point is exclusive (i.e., the starting point is not considered). Alternatively, git revert HEAD~3..HEAD would also work.

When you revert a larger commit range, having to specify a commit message for each individual revert operation can be annoying. In this respect, git revert --no-commit or git revert -n can help. These commands combine all revert operations without committing them. As a result, you must then execute the commit command yourself:

```
git revert -n HEAD~2^..HEAD
git commit -m 'revert last three commits at once'
```

3.4.7   Reverting the Last Commits (git reset)

Assuming the commit(s) to be reverted have only been done locally (not yet uploaded to an external repository using git push), a second way is available: You can revert to a previous commit using git reset. Strictly speaking, this command sets the HEAD on an old commit. Everything that happened after that apparently no longer exists. (The commits, including all changes, remain in the Git database for the time being. However, the *garbage collector* or git gc will delete the loose objects sooner or later.)

The git reset procedure is convenient but less transparent than git revert. You're effectively rewriting the history of your commits. Not only does such a *history rewrite* leave a stale taste on a political level but is also considered problematic in Git circles.

The best approach is to look at the log before using git revert:

```
git log --oneline

  bfd78ca (HEAD -> main) stupid 3
  38de270 stupid 2
  1c9048f stupid 1
  4d37367 final tests for feature xy

  ...
```

Then, you must pass the hash code of the desired commit to git reset --hard:

```
git reset --hard 4d37367
  HEAD is now at 4d37367 final tests for feature xy
```

The --hard option means that git reset will also override changes you made after the former last commit (in this example, after bfd78ca). Due to --soft, these changes have remained.

```
git log --oneline
  4d37367 final tests for feature xy
  ...
```

Although the bfd78ca, 38de270, and 1c9048f commits are no longer displayed by git log, they'll continue to exist in the Git repository. Since no references to them exist, they'll be deleted sooner or later. Until then, you can put the HEAD back there with another git reset command. If you don't have the commit numbers at hand, git reflog will help. The reflog logs all recent actions that change the head of the current branch. Besides the commit and revert actions, the reset action is also logged.

3.4.8 Switching Temporarily to an Older Commit (git checkout)

git reset and git revert both have the goal of permanently reverting to a previous commit. git checkout enables you to do that temporarily. Let's assume the initial situation is like before:

```
git log --oneline
  bfd78ca (HEAD -> main) stupid 3
  38de270 stupid 2
  1c9048f stupid 1
  4d37367 final tests for feature xy
  ...
```

git checkout allows you to commit the specified commit to your working directory. Then, you can view the files as they were at the time of this commit. However, the checkout has some side effects, which the command also warns about:

```
git checkout 4d37367
  Note: switching to '4d37367'.

  You are in 'detached HEAD' state. You can look around, make
  experimental changes and commit them, and you can discard
  any commits you make in this state without impacting any
  branches by switching back to a branch.
  If you want to create a new branch to retain commits you
  create, you may do so (now or later) by using -c with the
  switch command. Example:

    git switch -c <new-branch-name>

  Or undo this operation with:
```

```
git switch -
```

```
HEAD is now at 4d37367 final tests for feature xy
```

In plain language, this message means that HEAD points to the desired commit but is no longer connected to the previous branch (hence the word *detached*). You now have two ways to proceed:

- You can make changes and further commits starting from the current state. Thus, a new branch is created at this point that is, for the time being, nameless (anonymous). The checkout command suggests creating and naming this branch permanently with git switch -c <newbranch> if necessary. (The command is only available in Git version 2.23 or later. For older Git versions, you'll need to create the branch via git checkout -b <newbranch>.)
- Alternatively, you can use git switch - or git checkout <oldbranch> to return to the last active branch.

You can only really understand a detached HEAD if you know how Git handles branches (see Section 3.5). Typically, HEAD points to the top of a branch (e.g., to heads/main or to heads/develop). With git checkout <branch>, you can switch between branches, strictly speaking between the heads of branches. git checkout <commitrev>, however, doesn't switch to the head of an existing branch but instead forms a new, nameless branch.

Figure 3.5 shows the revert, reset, and checkout actions we just described. The starting point in all three cases is the commit sequence A, B, C, and D in the main branch. The goal is to return to B.

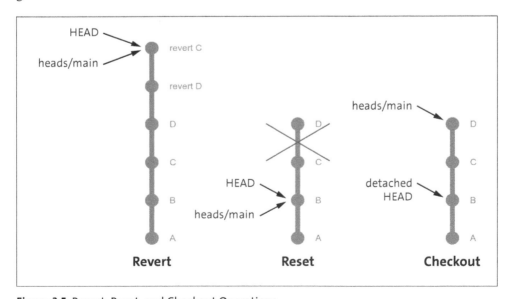

Figure 3.5 Revert, Reset, and Checkout Operations

> **Interpreting Commit Graphs Correctly**
> Figure 3.5 shows the first of many commit graphs in this book. We use such diagrams to visualize Git commits and branches. The most important rule is that the current state is up, not down! While this tendency contradicts common patterns where the sequence runs from left to right and top to bottom, it's consistent with the ubiquitous `git log` command as well as countless visualization tools in the Git environment (e.g., gitk).

3.4.9   Changing the Commit Message

Let's consider what sounds like a trivial problem: You noticed a typo in your commit message and want to correct it:

```
git commit -a -m 'inportant bugfixxes'
```

```
git log --oneline -n 2
  fe696a9  (HEAD -> main) inportant bugfixxes
  98760f1  add feature xy
```

If this message concerns the last commit and the changes haven't been synchronized with other repositories yet, the message can easily be modified via `git commit --amend`. When this command is executed, an editor is started where you can change the commit message. (You cannot specify the new message with -m.)

```
git commit --amend
```

```
git log --oneline -n 2
  0af7157 (HEAD -> main) important bugfixes
  98760f1  add feature xy
```

Behind the scenes, `git commit --amend` causes a reset to the penultimate commit. Then, the changes from the last commit are reapplied but now with a new commit message. This process creates a new commit object with a new hash code, which means you have rewritten history. (True modification of a commit message is impossible because the commit object is secured by a hash code, which is also why a new commit is necessary.)

If you've already committed the erroneous commit to an external repository using `git push`, you should refrain from `git commit --amend`. If you still decide to use this command, you must specify the `--force` option on the next `git push` to upload your modified commit history.

`git push --force` is a decidedly dangerous operation because it overrides commits from other team members that aren't already locally in your repository. Also, the next `git pull` will cause an error for other team members if they've already downloaded your original (incorrect) commit. The other developers will then be forced to run `git fetch` and `git rebase` to restore to their machines the same commit sequence you specified. `git push --force` is a safe way to go if you want to make yourself *really* unpopular with your team. Prior to running this command, you should make sure that you contact someone to help you undo your actions locally.

Long story short: Think for a moment as you formulate your commit messages. Later changes are not provided for in Git and can only be implemented with many undesirable side effects. We'll provide a more detailed description of the possible consequences of a history rewrite in a different context in Chapter 11, Section 11.4. If necessary, you should also check out this excellent article on Stack Overflow:

https://stackoverflow.com/questions/179123

3.5   Branches

Git is designed to manage branches with extremely low overhead. Creating new branches, merging with another branch, switching (checking out) from one branch to another—all this takes just fractions of a second for small repositories, only a few seconds for huge repositories.

Both high speed and straightforward handling of branches were important development goals for Git. Linus Torvalds wanted to create a tool that made the use of branches as convenient and efficient as possible and really invited people to use branches.

You can use branches in many ways: When multiple members of a team work on a project, it's often appropriate for developers to set up their own branches. For example, employee A works in the `new_feature_x` branch, and employee B works in the `other_feature_y` branch. The advantage of this approach is the context of changes made to the code will be much clearer later.

However, this approach not mandatory. Git also allows multiple contributors to work in their own repositories for the same branch. For example, developers A, B, and C can all use the `develop` branch to program new features. The individually performed commits are then merged via `git pull` and `git push`. The merge processes that take place in this context are the same internally in Git, regardless of whether multiple branches have come into play in the meantime or not.

Workflows
We'll cover various techniques for using branches in teams under different conditions in Chapter 8. For now, this section is focused on explaining the underlying mechanisms and commands.

3.5.1   Using Branches

Let's assume you've developed your program to a certain point (commit B). You've committed these changes in the following way:

```
git commit -a -m 'A: basic functions working'
...
git commit -a -m 'B: updated documentation'
```

Your program works, and you've saved the last changes by commit. Now, you want to do two things: First, you want to keep the working code and make tiny corrections if necessary. Second, you want develop a new feature, but you aren't entirely sure if your ideas will really work (experimental code).

For this task, use the following commands to create a new branch and activate it:

```
git branch new_feature
git checkout new_feature
```

Equivalent, but requiring less typing, is git checkout with the -b option, which creates the new branch:

```
git checkout -b new_feature
```

Now, you can work in the new_feature branch for a while, changing files, adding new files, testing the code, and committing occasionally:

```
git commit -a -m 'C: first tests for new feature working'
...
git commit -a -m 'D: fixed some bugs'
```

Suddenly, the (customer) request for a tiny extension in the stable version of your program arises. With a checkout, you switch from the feature back to the main branch:

```
git checkout main
```

You make the change including commit and provide the new (stable) code to your customer:

```
git commit -a -m 'E: minor update'
```

After another checkout, work can continue in the feature branch:

```
git checkout new_feature
..
git commit -a -m 'F: fixed even more bugs for new feature'
```

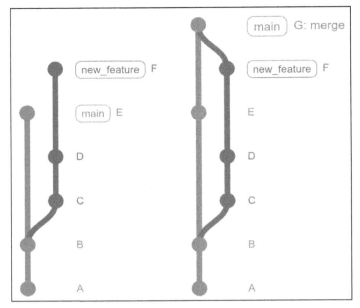

Figure 3.6 Parallel Development of the Main Branch ("main") and of a Feature Branch before and after the Merge Process

---

Setting Up the New Branch before the Commit Is Enough

Sometimes, the complexity of a new feature is not clear from the beginning. Say, for example, you start in the current branch (e.g., main) and make your first changes. After an hour, perhaps you realize that your new feature will keep you busy for hours, maybe days. You should probably do this work in one branch, but you forgot to create it initially.

This omission is no problem for Git! As long as you haven't committed yet, you can set up the new branch (git checkout -b <newbranch>). The changes already made will then automatically apply to the new branch.

"git checkout" versus "git switch"

The git checkout command performs quite different tasks:

- git checkout <branch> changes the active branch.
- git checkout <revision> -- <file> transfers a file from an old commit to the project directory.
- git checkout <revision> transfers all files of a commit to the project directory. HEAD now points to the commit expressed by revision instead of the end of a branch. This option results in the rather confusing (not just for beginners) case of a *detached head*.

To make Git easier to use, the git switch and git restore commands were introduced with Git version 2.23. These commands are user-friendly alternatives to the first and second forms of git checkout we just listed. Thus, with current Git versions, you can also switch the active branch with git switch <branch>. However, we stuck with git checkout <branch> in this book. On one hand, the documentation warns that git switch is still experimental; on the other hand, git checkout <branch> has become second nature to an entire generation of Git users and can be found in countless tutorials online.

3.5.2 Problems Switching between Branches (git checkout)

git checkout <branch> enables you to switch between branches in your project. If you want to know all the branches that exist and which branch is currently active, you must run git branch without any other parameters.

At checkout, all files under Git control are replaced with the versions that were valid at the last commit in the respective branch. Files not under version control won't be touched by git checkout.

Problems occur when Git detects files in the project directory that have been modified since the last commit and that had different contents in the last commits of the two affected branches. In this case, the changes would be overwritten by the checkout and thus lost:

```
git checkout <branch>
  error: Your local changes to the following files would
  be overwritten by checkout: file1
  Please commit your changes or stash them before you switch
  branches. Aborting.
```

You can deal with this situation in various ways:

- **Commit**
  The easiest solution is to commit before checkout, thus saving the last changes made to the current branch.

- **Stashing**
  If the changes are unfinished or if you don't want to commit for other reasons, you can cache the files in the stash area (see Section 3.7). Later, usually after you return to the now valid branch, you can reapply the cached changes.

- **Overriding**
  The most radical solution is to simply override the changes that have been implemented. For this task, you must run git checkout with the --force option. Be careful! This command can't be undone, and the changes will be lost.

3.5.3   Determining "main" as the Default Name for New Repositories

On GitHub and GitLab, main has been the default name for new repositories since 2020. Since Git version 2.28 (July 2020), you can specify the desired default name for the git command in the following way:

```
git config --global init.defaultBranch main
```

3.5.4   Renaming "master" to "main"

For an existing repository, you can easily switch from master to main, provided this repository is a purely local repository that's not connected to an external repository. In the following example, the first command makes master the current branch, and the second one renames the branch:

```
git checkout master
git branch -m main
```

Things get a bit more complex when the local repository is connected to an external repository (e.g., on GitHub or GitLab). More details are provided in Section 3.8, but keeping the master/main topic together in one section seemed to make sense. The key point is that a branch name change must be made both locally and in the external repository:

- **GitHub**
  If your repository is on GitHub, the easiest way is to visit the **Branches** page in the web interface, click the **Edit** button next to the branch master, and give it the new name main. Then, make the name changes locally and connect the local main branch to the GitHub main branch:

  ```
  git checkout master
  git branch -m main
  git fetch origin
  git branch -u origin/main main
  git remote set-head origin -a
  ```

- **GitLab**
  At the time of writing, GitLab's web interface doesn't provide a way to rename a branch. For this reason, you must start locally, give master the new name main, upload the new branch to the GitLab repository, and change the remote configuration in *.git/config* at the same time via push -u:

  ```
  git checkout master
  git branch -m main
  git push -u origin main
  ```

As a result, now both branches are on GitLab (`master` and `main`), which creates confusion. Therefore, you should first go to the **Settings • Repository • Default Branch** and make `main` the default branch. Then, you can delete the `master` branch, which is now no longer needed, under **Repository • Branches**.

Nobody Forces You to Change the Name

The more people use a repository, the more time-consuming changing the name of the default branch will be. Yes, `main` has been the standard for new repositories, but nobody can force you to change repository names that have been established for years.

3.5.5   Internal Details

Behind the scenes, a branch is a tiny file in the *.git/refs/heads* directory. The filename corresponds to the branch name. The text file contains the hash code of the last commit of the branch. In other words, branches in Git are simply *pointers* to a commit.

Now, you'll see why Git's handling of branches is so extraordinarily fast: To set up a branch, you only need to set up a 41-byte text file. (If Git uses a different hashing method in the future, the branch files will may get a few bytes longer.)

A checkout simply copies the last commit of the respective branch into the working directory. (Recall that commits don't save changes in Git. Rather, each commit is a complete snapshot of the project.) Also, the checkout process changes the tiny *.git/HEAD* file, which now contains the name of the currently valid branch, for example, `refs/heads/new_feature` instead of initially `refs/heads/main`.

This extremely simple system also has some disadvantages: In a Git repository, no mapping between commits and branches exists beyond the *.git/refs/heads* file. Although references exist to the respective parent commit(s) for each commit, you can't always tell retrospectively which branch was active when these commits were created.

Branch management in Git also has consequences on delete operations: If you use `git branch -d` to delete a branch that was never connected to a branch that is still active (i.e., this branch turned out to be a dead end during development that's no longer being pursued), then all commits made under that branch are preserved for the time being. But with the next garbage collection (`git gc`), all commits that aren't referenced by other commits or by branch files will then be deleted.

In a nutshell, Git's branch system works wonderfully for active branches. If, on the other hand, you're interested in the historical course, Git often provides little information, simply because that data doesn't exist (anymore). Only the commits remain. Their metadata tells you who committed the file and when, but not in which branch or for which branch.

3.6   Merging

As described in the previous section, working with branches detached from each other is quite a trivial matter. Things get exciting when you want to merge branches again, for example, when you want to apply changes made in branch A to branch B. For this task, you must initiate a merge process via git merge.

3.6.1   Merging Branches (git merge)

We'll use the examples from the previous section to serve as a starting point for the following commands. Thus, we have a main branch with the stable version of the program and a new_feature branch that you'll use to develop a new feature. Your plans for the new feature have worked out; maybe everything works better than expected. Consequently, you now want to transfer the feature to the main branch.

To merge a feature into the main branch, you must go to that branch and then run git merge <otherbranch>:

```
git checkout main        (active branch, will be changed)
git merge new_feature    (new_feature remains unchanged)
```

What happens afterwards depends on the circumstances:

- **"Ordinary" merges**
  With an initial situation, as shown previously in Figure 3.6, Git attempts to merge the commits C and D from the new_feature branch and also to merge commit E from the main branch, which occurred since status B. Provided that code parts other than those changed by C and D have been modified in E, Git can process the changes on its own.

  The changes made are saved as part of a commit, and an editor automatically appears where you can customize a given commit message if necessary, for instance, in the following way:

  ```
  Merge branch 'new_feature'
  # Please enter a commit message to explain why this merge
  # is necessary, especially if it merges an updated upstream
  # into a topic branch.
  #
  # Lines starting with '#' will be ignored, and an empty
  # message aborts the commit.
  ```

  Don't let yourself be confused by the long-winded explanation, nor by the implicit accusation that you want to do a merge process at all. As a rule, it's sufficient to exit the editor immediately and thus confirm the given text. (Only the first line counts; the rest are comments.)

  At this point, you can abort the merge process (including the commit) by deleting the commit message (i.e., saving an empty text in the editor). Conversely, you can avoid the annoying interruption from the editor by passing the desired commit message with the -m option.

By default, Git uses vi, which isn't convenient for beginners. If you don't want to use vi, you can set another default editor (see Chapter 2, Section 2.1).

- **Fast-forward merges**

A special case is a merge process where the base branch (main in our example) has remained unchanged since the split into two branches. In this case, no "real" merge is required. Rather, you can simply set the pointer of the base branch to the last commit. A more detailed explanation of what happens in a fast-forward merge and its advantages/disadvantages is provided in Section 3.6.3.

- **Merge conflicts**

The third option is much more unpleasant: Git fails to independently merge the changes made in the branches. The most common reason for this problem is that certain lines of code were changed differently in the two branches—for example, the original maxvalue=20 has become maxvalue=10 in commit C and maxvalue=30 in commit E. However, Git's automatic mechanisms also fail with binary files. We'll provide several solution strategies in Section 3.9.

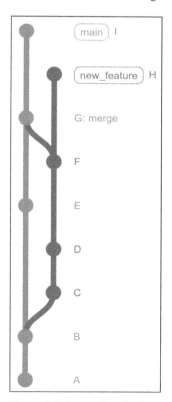

Figure 3.7 Even after the Merge, Both Branches Can Still Be Used

Provided the merge process succeeds, you'll have three Git pointers pointing to the same commit afterwards: at HEAD, at the base branch (main in our example), and at the added branch (new_feature).

The added branch still exists. You can use git checkout <branch> to reactivate the branch and then continue developing the feature (with git commit -a -m 'H', as shown in Figure 3.7). If needed, you can merge these changes back to the main branch later as well (with git merge again).

Git in the Fast Lane

When branches are used concurrently for long periods of time, sometimes we refer to these branches as *lanes* along which the development takes place. So, in this case, we have a main lane and a feature lane. Depending on the Git workflow, more lanes are also conceivable, in which new features pass through various intermediate stages with tests until they finally reach the main lane and thus reach the customer.

Git lacks tools that clearly visualize such lanes. As a result, a separate market in commercial add-on tools has emerged, for example, *https://gfc.io* and *https://www.git-kraken.com/git-client*.

If you lose track of your branches, run git branch. This command lists all branches and highlights the currently active branch. The additional --merged or --no-merged options reduce the output to branches whose last commit has already been merged with the current branch (or hasn't been merged yet).

```
git branch [--merged / --no-merged]
```

If you feel the development of the new feature is complete, you can delete the branch after the merge process has been performed. Commits merged with another branch will be preserved.

```
git merge -d new_feature
```

Rebasing

If you repeatedly merge branches, git log --graph results in a cluttered structure where tiny side branches constantly appear and disappear. You can avoid this complexity by running the git rebase command instead of git merge. We'll provide more detail on rebasing and its advantages/disadvantages in Section 3.10.

Merge for a Single File

git merge takes all the files of a commit into account. If you want to merge only *one* file with the version from another branch, use the git merge-file command after some preparatory work (see Chapter 11, Section 11.3).

3.6.2   Main Merge or Feature Merge?

In the previous example, a new feature was to be integrated into the main branch. As long as you're working on your own, this approach is straightforward.

In practice, however, usually several developers are working in different branches on features of a common project. If all developers change the main branch whenever they have the opportunity, the result will be a horrible mess in no time. Decisions about when and how to integrate a feature into the central main branch is up to the boss of your team.

Conversely, as a team member, you should always stay in sync as much as possible with a central branch when working on your new feature. For this reason, you should always merge the main branch with your feature branch, so you'll perform the merge exactly in the opposite direction:

```
git checkout new_feature    (active branch, will be changed)
git merge main              (main remains unchanged)
```

So, this change to the feature branch is only done so that the merge with the main branch planned for the distant future (whether by a merge command or by a pull request) works as smoothly as possible.

Two Sides of the Same Coin

No matter from which side you start the merge process, the end result in your project directory is the same in both cases. The last commit of new_feature is combined with the last commit of main. Which side you run the merge process from doesn't matter!

- If you merge the feature branch with the main branch (as in the introductory example from the previous section), the main branch is changed. The feature branch will remain as is.

- But if you merge the main branch with the feature branch (as with the two commands before this box), the feature branch will change. In this case, the main branch will remain unchanged.

In any case, you can continue to use both branches afterwards. So, the merge process doesn't "close" any branch. If you no longer need a branch, you must explicitly delete it using git branch -d.

Up to this point, we've always spoken of the main branch for the sake of simplicity. In fact, the central branch into which features are first integrated will probably be called something else. (develop is a popular choice, but other common conventions also exist.)

In this context, we aren't talking about team working techniques; instead, we're focused on how Git handles merge processes from a technical point of view, regardless of on which side the merge is performed. Before using Git in your team, be sure to read Section 3.8 and Chapter 8 and to also familiarize yourself with your team's practices.

3.6.3 Fast-Forward Merges

Let's imagine you created a new branch named new_feature after commit B and performed commits C and D in that new branch. You didn't need to make any changes to the original branch (in this case, main) in the meantime.

If you now switch to the main branch and run git merge new_feature, no real merge process will be required at all. You can simply move the pointer of the main branch to commit D (*fast-forward*). HEAD automatically points to the end of the current branch, in this case also to commit D. As before, new_feature also refers to this commit, as shown in Figure 3.8, in the center.

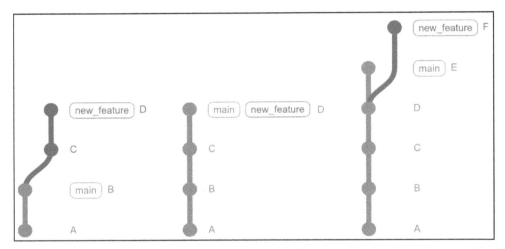

Figure 3.8 Fast-Forward Merge: Before the Merge (Left), after the Merge (Center), and with Subsequent Branches (Right)

Because no change to the Git objects is required when changing the main pointer, no separate commit occurs during the merge process. Accordingly, you don't need to enter a commit message.

The obvious advantage of a fast-forward merge process is its simplicity and speed. Also, the annoying specification of a commit message isn't needed in this case.

However, one drawback is that later you cannot trace that commits C and D originated as part of the new_feature branch. If this lack of transparency is unacceptable, you can run git merge with the --no-ff option.

Of course, even after a fast-forward merge, both branches will be preserved. Development can continue in both branches, for example, with the new commits E in main and F in new_feature, as shown in Figure 3.8, on the right).

3.6.4   Octopus Merges

If you pass not one, but multiple, branches to `git merge`, Git will attempt to merge the current branch with all the branches named as parameters. In the process, the legendary "octopus merge" comes into play, which uses the following syntax:

```
git merge branch1 branch2 branch3
```

We strongly advise against octopus merges: Even an ordinary merge process that merges two branches can cause a lot of problems (see Section 3.9). The more branches involved, the more difficult resolving conflicts or ambiguities becomes.

Our tip is to perform a "simple" merge for each branch. The only advantage of an octopus merge over multiple single merge processes is that (if all goes well) only one merge commit occurs.

However, despite all our warnings, octopus merges do actually occur in practice. In the Linux kernel's Git repository, quite a few octopus merges exist, with one bringing together a considerable 65 branches, as described in the following blog post:

https://www.destroyallsoftware.com/blog/2017/the-biggest-and-weirdest-commits-in-linux-kernel-git-history

Just because Linus Torvalds and other kernel gurus favor the octopus merge doesn't mean you should too!

3.6.5   Merge Process

Internally, Git uses different procedures ("strategies") by which it decides how to integrate changes from one branch into the other. Common methods are `resolve`, `recursive` (applied by default but with various options), `octopus`, and `subtree`. Some methods also consider the commit at which the branches separated (for instance, commit B shown earlier in Figure 3.6).

Typically, Git decides on a suitable procedure on its own. Only in exceedingly rare cases and only with strong knowledge of the intricacies of various merge procedures should you explicitly specify the desired procedure to `git merge` with the `-s <strategyname>` option. Descriptions of merge procedures can be found at the following links:

- *https://git-scm.com/docs/merge-strategies*
- *https://stackoverflow.com/questions/366860*

3.6.6   Cherry-Picking

Cherry-picking in Git refers to applying the changes of a commit *without* immediately merging the entire branch. If this concept seems rather abstract, an example will make everything clear: Let's say you're implementing a great new idea in the `new_feature` branch when a customer reports a serious bug in your software. You drop everything, switch to the main branch, and fix the bug:

```
git checkout main
...
git commit -a -m 'fixed major bug xy'
  [main ad43e20] fixed major bug xy
```

Once you've delivered the software in the new version, you continue working in the new_feature branch. Of course, the error raised by the customer also occurs in that branch. However, you don't want to perform a merge process: The new feature isn't ready yet and can't be transferred to the main branch. Conversely, you also made some other changes in the main branch that you don't want to track in the feature branch (yet).

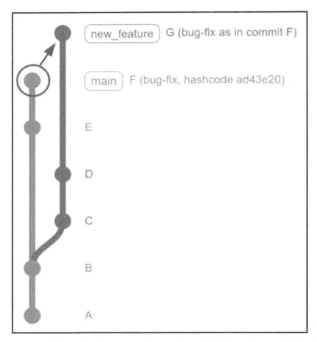

Figure 3.9 Only Changes from Commit F Are Cherry-Picked from the Main Branch to the Feature Branch

The way out of this command is provided by git cherry-pick. This command applies the changes implemented in a commit to the current branch—but only those changes. This feature is remarkable because a commit in Git does *not* store changes but instead takes a complete snapshot of the project. git cherry-pick must therefore compare the commit in question with its *parent*, determine the changes made, and then apply those changes.

```
git checkout new_feature
git cherry-pick ad43e20
```

git cherry-pick can only be applied if no changes in your working directory have occurred since the last commit. The specification of the bugfix commit is indicated by its hash code, which you can identify via git log, if needed. (Before doing so, you should use git checkout to switch to the branch where the bugfix was originally applied—in our example, the main branch.) If the bugfix causes collisions with your code in the feature branch, git cherry-pick may raise conflicts just like git merge. Tips on how to resolve these conflicts are explored in Section 3.9.

3.7   Stashing

With git stash, you can save recent changes to the working directory without committing. "What's the point of that?" you may ask. After all, only a commit saves your changes permanently.

Stashing is handy when you need to interrupt your current work and, for example, temporarily switch to another branch to quickly perform a bug fix there. But you don't want to commit your half-finished new feature to the repository, for example, because you fear that your changes might cause problems for your teammates.

Besides git checkout <branch>, however, various other commands cannot be executed after git stash because Git detects changes in the working directory and doesn't want to override those changes.

3.7.1   Caching and Restoring Changes

git stash restores the state at the last commit and saves all changes in the stash area:

```
git stash
  Saved working directory and index state WIP
  on main: bde1c92 last commit message
```

Later, you can restore the changes with git stash pop. Your working directory must not have changed since the last commit or checkout.

```
git stash pop
  On branch main
  ...
  Dropped refs/stash@{0}
```

If your working directory has changed between git stash and git stash pop, you may experience merge conflicts when applying the cached changes. Tips on how to resolve these conflicts are explored in Section 3.9.

3.7.2   Stashing in Practice

A nice use case for stashing is when you mistakenly work in the wrong branch because you forgot `git checkout <otherbranch>`. If the files you edited have different contents in the two branches (the current branch and the branch you intended to use), Git will warn you that your changes would be overridden by the checkout.

In this case, `git stash` reverts the changes, `git checkout <otherbranch>` switches to the correct branch, and `git stash pop` reapplies the changes in that branch. The whole thing can happen in 10 seconds!

Let's consider another example: You can only run `git pull --rebase` if you haven't made any changes in your project directory since the last commit. (You'll learn what `git pull` can be used for in Section 3.8.) Often, you'll need to know what changes exist in the remote repository without storing the few most recent changes in a separate commit. No problem, if you use the following commands:

```
git stash
git pull --rebase
git stash pop
```

3.7.3   Managing Multiple Changes

You can run `git stash` multiple times to save multiple sets of changes. `git stash pop` processes the changes back in reverse order. (The changes saved last will be applied first—in other words, *first in, last out.*) The larger the stash stack becomes, the more difficult keeping track of it all will be.

If needed, `git stash list` displays a list of all cached stashes, with information about which commit was currently valid when `git stash` was run:

```
git stash list
  stash@{0}: WIP on main: bde1c92  added database connection
                                   logic
  stash@{1}: WIP on main: 78234c9 version bump
```

Using `git stash show -p stash@{<n>}` displays details about the stashes, if needed. `git stash drop` deletes a stash that's no longer needed. `git stash clear` deletes all stashes.

Internally, stashes are stored in the repository as commits (but detached from the current branch). The *.git/refs/stash* file contains references to these commit objects.

3.8   Remote Repositories

Up to this point in this chapter, we've looked at Git as though it were being used purely locally, without access to external (remote) repositories. This scenario is possible but unusual. After all, the whole point of Git is to collaborate with other developers who use their own repositories. That said, we wanted to first explain the basics of Git at a local level before going into further complexity and special cases that can arise in networked operations.

Unlike many other version control programs, Git was designed with decentralized organizations in mind. Developer Anna can communicate via Git directly with developer Ben, and he in turn with programmer Clara. So, the three people can each configure their own machines as a Git server. Then, assuming appropriate access rights or SSH keys, anyone can share commits with anyone else and merge branches, among other things.

As great as the concept is, most developers were overwhelmed with the (albeit small) effort to configure their own Git servers. For teamwork, a centrally administered server that all team members can access is much more convenient.

GitHub was one of the first companies to recognize this dormant market potential and so put together a web interface to offer corresponding services both free of charge and commercially. Microsoft liked this concept so much that it was willing to pay $7.5 billion for GitHub in 2018.

When we speak of a *remote repository* in the following sections, we're referring to any platform of this kind. Which company or service is actually used is not relevant.

3.8.1   Initialization Work

Let's briefly summarize the two most common ways to connect a local repository to a remote repository:

- If the remote repository already exists, you can clone it. git clone takes care of setting up the *.git/config* file so that git pull and git push subsequently work without any additional parameters. The following command applies to GitHub with SSH keys, but analogous commands work with any other Git platform. Of course, you might use HTTPS instead of SSH for authentication. For more details on this topic, see Chapter 2, Section 2.4.

```
git clone git@github.com:<account>/<reponame>.git
cd <reponame>
```

- If the project was started locally first but should be transferred to an initially empty remote repository later, you would use the following required commands:

```
mkdir <reponame>
cd <reponame>
git init
...
git commit -a -m 'commit message'
git remote add origin git@github.com:<account>/<reponame>.git
```

```
git push -u
...
Branch 'main' set up to track remote branch 'main'
from 'origin'.
```

In this case, git remote add origin adds the remote repository origin to the local repository. git push -u makes the repository the default repository.

Depending on which remote repository you're using, git push -u will show you a link to a page on the Git platform where you can initiate a pull request (GitHub) or merge request (GitLab). You don't need to memorize this link; you can also start the request later directly in the web interface of your external repository. More information on this topic is provided in Chapter 5, Section 5.1.

In the following sections, we assume that developer Anna and developer Ben have access to the external repository on their respective machines. Both have freshly downloaded the current repository via git clone or updated via git pull. The remote repository and Anna's and Ben's repositories are all at the same level.

For reasons of simplicity, let's assume that they also refrain from using twigs. So, Anna and Ben are working in the main branch. (We'll describe what will change when they use branches in a moment in Section 3.8.3.)

3.8.2   Push and Pull

After Anna and Ben have cloned the remote repository, they both begin to edit different details in the code. During the course of the day, Anna makes commits A1, and Ben makes commits B1 and B2. For the time being, these commits are only available in their respective local repositories. In the afternoon, Anna decides to end the day and uploads her changes to the remote repository after a second commit:

```
A$ git commit -a -m 'A2'
A$ git push
```

Ben works a little longer, does a final commit, and then tries to upload his changes as well:

```
B$ git commit -a -m 'B3'
B$ git push
 ! [rejected]        main -> main (fetch first)
 error: failed to push some refs to ...
 Updates were rejected because the remote contains work that
 you do not have locally. This is usually caused by another
 repository  pushing to the same ref. You may want to first
 integrate the remote changes (e.g., 'git pull ...') before
 pushing again. See the 'Note about fast-forwards' in
 'git push --help' for details.
```

The process fails. The error message is lengthy but does explain exactly the cause of the problem: git push is only allowed to perform a fast-forward merge in the remote repository. This fast-forward merge in turn is only possible if git push contains only changes that are additive. For this reason, Ben's repository must first be brought up to the state of the remote repository (git pull) before git push can be permitted. (A good practice is to always run git pull before git push.)

git pull downloads the commits available in the remote repository and merges the code with Ben's changes. When running git pull, an editor opens where Ben can change the commit message for the merge process. Typically, he'll simply accept the given text and exit the editor. With luck, the merge process can be performed without any problem. Sometimes, however, a conflict will occur, which then must be resolved by Ben (see Section 3.9)—an unrewarding job when you're already mentally done with work. At least, git push works without problems after all.

```
B$ git pull
  From .../<reponame>
  1268f76..2018bcd  main -> origin/main
  ...
B$ git push
```

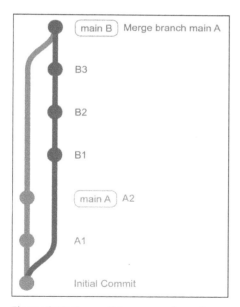

Figure 3.10 Commit Sequence from Ben

Rebasing

When multiple people are working on common branches, git pull merge processes happen all the time. Not only is this annoying, confusing commit sequences result. The solution in this context is git pull --rebase. Before using this option, however, you should refer to Section 3.10, where we provide background, discuss some potential side effects, and show you how to fix the default behavior in the Git configuration.

The next morning, Anna starts the day with git pull, which means bringing her local repository up to date. Unless another developer has made changes, this step only affects yesterday's merge commit from Ben. This commit can be performed as a fast-forward merge:

```
A$ git pull
   From .../<reponame>
   2018bcd..c0d793e  main -> origin/main
   Fast-forward ...
```

Ben also runs git pull first. Since no one has uploaded any changes since its evening use, only the message *Already up to date* appears, as in the following example.

```
B$ git pull
   Already up to date.
```

All three repositories now contain the same commits, and the HEADs of all three repositories also point to this commit.

3.8.3   Remote Branches

Rarely do multiple developers write directly to the main branch. But exceptions exist: For example, we managed the manuscript files for this book in a Git repository. In doing so, we both simply used the main branch. Since we divided up the chapters and sections ahead of time, we almost never had conflicts while working—and thus we had no need for branches.

For software projects, a more appropriate approach is to either use a common develop branch, whose commits are transferred to the main branch only after extensive testing, or to use a separate branch for each new feature.

For example, Anna starts working on the new feature (feature1):

```
A$ git checkout -b feature1
A$ ...
A$ git commit -a -m 'A1'
A$ ...
A$ git commit -a -m 'A2'
A$ ...
A$ git commit -a -m 'A3'
```

A simple git push doesn't work:

```
A$ git push
  fatal: The current branch feature1 has no upstream branch.
  To push the current branch and set the remote as upstream,
  use: ...
```

The git command complains that feature1 isn't known in the remote repository. Therefore, the first time you use the --set-upstream option (shortened to -u), you must
explicitly specify that the remote repository should also be used for feature1:

```
A$ git push --set-upstream origin feature1
```

This step adds three lines to the *.git/config* file:

```
# new in .git/config file
...
[branch "feature1"]
    remote = origin
    merge = refs/heads/feature1
```

From now on, Anna can simply upload further commits to the remote repository again
with git push.

Private Branches

An important consideration to note is that nobody forces you to synchronize your
branches with the remote repository. If you never run git push for a branch, nor merge
these commits with another (public) branch, the commits will remain in your repository. Thus, the branch is private, which is often useful if you want to try something out.

Keep in mind that now the backup feature associated with remote repositories is gone.
Typically, once you run git commit and git push, you have a backup of your work on the
Git server. Then, as soon as other team members run git pull, your code will end up on
their machines too. By analogy, if you leave your laptop on a train, you suffer a financial
loss, but at least your work can be reconstructed. The only difference is that this coverage doesn't apply to private branches.

The next time Ben runs git pull, the command downloads all new commits and indicates that a new branch now exists in the remote repository:

```
B$ git pull
  ...
  [new branch]      feature1   -> origin/feature1
```

Ben, however, isn't interested in this branch for the time being. On the contrary, he sets
up the new feature2 branch for himself:

```
B$ git checkout -b feature2
B$ ...
B$ git commit -a -m 'B1'
B$ ...
B$ git commit -a -m 'B2'
B$ git push --set-upstream origin feature2
```

Now, let's say Anna sends an email to Ben asking him to briefly test her code for feature 1. Ben switches to the feature1 branch. (The commits are already there thanks to git pull, although he has never dealt with feature1.) He finds a small error, which he immediately fixes, saves, and uploads:

```
B$ git pull
B$ git checkout feature1
    Switched to a new branch 'feature1'
    Branch 'feature1' set up to track remote branch 'feature1'
    from 'origin'.
B$ ...
B$ git commit -a -m 'B3, bugfix for feature1'
B$ git push
```

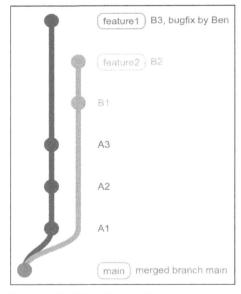

Figure 3.11 Using Feature Branches

Pull for All Branches, Push Only for the Active Branch

git pull basically downloads all new commits but only performs a merge process for the currently active branch. If you later switch to another branch, Git will advise you to run git pull again. With this step, Git looks to see if additional commits exist in the remote repository and then initiates the pending merge process. (Behind the scenes, git pull is actually a combination of two commands executed in sequence: git fetch downloads the new commits, and git merge initiates the merge process for the current commit.)

git push, on the other hand, always takes only the active branch into account. So, if you've committed to main, feature1, and feature7, but currently main is active, then git push will transfer only the commits for main to the remote repository. Thus, you must explicitly run git push for each branch where you've saved changes. Alternatively, git push --all origin leads to the same goal.

3.8.4   Internal Details

Any branch that's pushed to or pulled from the remote repository is subsequently considered a *tracking branch* (sometimes more accurately, a *remote tracking branch*) in Git terminology. So, Git tracks the status of such branches both locally and in the remote repository. The *.git/refs* directory contains pointers to the latest commit (local and external):

```
tree .git/refs/

  .git/refs/
     heads
         feature1
         feature2
       main
     remotes
       origin
            feature1
            feature2
          HEAD
          main
```

git branch -vv (i.e., twice -v or --verbose) lists the local branches, the associated tracking branches (in square brackets), and the last commit message in each case:

```
A$ ...  (more changes to feature1)
A$ git commit -a -m 'A5'
A$ git branch -vv
  * feature1 3f47639 [origin/feature1: ahead 1] A5
    feature2 e25c407 [origin/feature3]          B1
    main     c0d793e [origin/main]              Merge branch ...
```

When you run git status, the command checks whether the commits are in sync and, if so, tells you to run git push or git pull:

```
A$ git status
    On branch feature1
    Your branch is ahead of 'origin/feature1' by 1 commit.
    (use "git push" to publish your local commits)
A$ git push
```

Note that git status only considers local data and doesn't "query" the remote repository. In this respect, the designation *tracking* is a bit misleading. To determine whether changes in the remote repository have occurred since the last git pull command, you must explicitly run git fetch or git remote update before git status. (Functionally, both commands are largely identical.) In the following example, we can run git status on Ben's machine, which thinks the feature1 branch is up to date. But after git fetch is run, the branch is not up to date.

```
B$ git status
    On branch feature1
    Your branch is up to date with 'origin/feature1'.
B$ git fetch
    ...
B$ git status
    Your branch is behind 'origin/feature1' by 1 commit, and can
    be fast-forwarded. (use git pull to update your local branch)
```

Remember that git status only looks at the active local branch. To determine what's going on in the other branches, you must first checkout a different branch.

3.8.5 Multiple Remote Repositories

Until now, we've assumed that there is *one* remote repository, which, following Git conventions, is usually called origin. However, Git can also handle multiple remote repositories.

With git remote add, you can easily add another remote repository to your configuration. In the following example, we assume that the first remote repository (origin) is located on GitHub. However, you may also want to move your project to a GitLab server, either because GitLab has a feature that's missing from GitHub or because you're considering a platform change in general. Make sure that you don't specify origin as the remote name after the add keyword (this name is already taken) but instead specify another name. (In our example, we simply used gitlab.)

git push transfers all branches to the new repository. If you also specify the -u option, the new repository will also become the default repository. (We're assuming in this case that you don't want to make the new repository the default.)

```
git remote add gitlab git@gitlab.com:<accout>/<repo>.git
git push gitlab --all
```

If you subsequently commit and run git push, the previous remote repository will be taken into account (i.e., origin). To explicitly push commits to the secondary repository, you must pass the name of the repository to git push:

```
git push            ('normal' push to origin)
git push gitlab     (explicit push to gitlab)
```

The *.git/config* file records which remote repositories exist and which branch uses which repository by default:

```
# in .git/config
...
[remote "origin"]
    url = git@github.com:<account>/<repo>.git
    fetch = +refs/heads/*:refs/remotes/origin/*
[remote "gitlab"]
    url = git@gitlab.com:<account>/<repo>.git
    fetch = +refs/heads/*:refs/remotes/gitlab/*
[branch "main]
    remote = origin
    merge = refs/heads/main
[branch "feature1"]
    remote = origin
    merge = refs/heads/feature1
[branch "feature2"]
    remote = origin
    merge = refs/heads/feature2
```

Basically, you can use different default repositories for different branches. If required, you can even configure different defaults for push and pull operations, as described in the following link:

https://stackoverflow.com/questions/4523496

> **Repository Mirroring**
>
> To set up a remote repository in GitHub and in GitLab with just a few git commands, and to synchronize them as conveniently as possible at the same time, check out the following tutorial:

https://github.com/isse-augsburg/minibrass/wiki/Setting-up-a-new-git-repo-with-two-remotes

Separate from the Git techniques described in this section, some Git platforms provide features that mirror the contents of repositories between two platforms. Consider, for example, the following GitLab help page:

https://docs.gitlab.com/ee/user/project/repository/mirror/index.html

Note, however, that these platform-specific functions aren't anchored in the `git` command.

3.8.6   Workflows

Let's say we assume multiple team members have the right to perform push actions in a shared repository. This access requires a high level of discipline from everyone involved. Not only can each team member change their own branches; they can also change the main branch. When careless, this access can be pretty disastrous or at least cause a lot of turmoil and aggravation.

Thus, all team members should agree on who can/should use which branches. Alternatively, you can set up Git so only selected developers have write access to the master repository. The rest of the development team must use their own repositories and can only submit new features as pull requests. We'll present these workflow and other working techniques in Chapter 8.

3.8.7   Configuring Your Own Git Server

You don't need witchcraft to set up a Git server on a web and SSH server (i.e., practically on any Linux server with minimal configuration). A good guide for this topic is the following chapter of the official Git documentation:

https://git-scm.com/book/en/v2/Git-on-the-Server-The-Protocols

The result is then, in a sense, "GitHub self-built in ten minutes," but the comparison is a bit misleading: Although you can synchronize repositories as on GitHub or GitLab, all additional features are missing, from the web interface to the bug database (for issues) to two-factor authentication—all reasons why Microsoft spent so much money to acquire GitHub.

We won't describe configuring your own minimal Git server in this book because, in our view, doing so is no longer a modern approach. What we'll describe, however, is how you can configure a "real" Git platform based on GitLab. So, if you need a Git platform for your organization or for your company, but you don't want to hand over all your data, GitLab is *the* ideal solution. The big difference between GitHub and GitLab is not the features or the pricing model, but the fact that the GitLab source code is subject to an open-source license. Therefore, you can set up your own server that looks and functions as much as possible like *https://gitlab.com* (see Chapter 6).

3.9   Resolving Merge Conflicts

The nightmare of every Git user is the error message *merge failed*. In this case, Git has failed to merge two commits independently. As a result, you must analyze and solve the problem by yourself. Of course, this situation always occurs at the worst possible time; for example, you're about to leave your office and want to do a quick pull/push after your last commit to save your work in the remote repository.

As the name suggests, merge conflicts are triggered by a merge process. However, since Git applies the merge code to other commands as well, a merge conflict can occur with various commands, such as `git pull`, `git stash pop`, or `git rebase`, to name the three "most popular" candidates.

In this section, we'll explain why merge conflicts occur and provide tips on how to resolve them. We'll also point to an even bigger problem: Sometimes, Git doesn't see a conflict and performs the merge operation without a hitch. But the next time you test it, the code doesn't work, and all the developers blame each other. Such problems can occur when two separate parts of the code are changed so that they no longer fit together.

Fewer Conflicts Due to Frequent Merge Processes

For Git, whether you perform dozens of commits in either of two branches and only then do a merge, or if you regularly initiate a merge every two or three commits, doesn't matter. In each case, Git compares only the latest commit from both branches and the common base (i.e., the first parent commit from both branches).

However, if conflicts do occur, the fewer files or locations in the code that are affected and the younger the code, the easier problems will be to resolve. You and your fellow developers will then know immediately why the changes were made and can determine which change is correct more quickly.

For this reason, you should run `git merge` or `git pull` regularly (unless other reasons exist not to do so).

3.9.1   Collisions in the Code

The most common cause of merge conflicts are changes to the same code made in different branches or by different developers. Let's assume the following statement exists in a source file (*code.py*):

```
# original code (main)
maxvalue = 20
```

Then, developer Anna changes the line in the following way:

```
# in the branch of Anna (branch1)
maxvalue = 30
```

Simultaneously, Ben finds that a smaller maxvalue is also sufficient and saves memory and so writes the following code:

```
# in the branch of Ben (branch2)
maxvalue = 10
```

The attempt to merge branch1 starting from branch2 fails. Git cannot determine which of the two changes is better or "more correct."

```
git checkout branch2
git merge branch1
  Auto-merging code.py
  CONFLICT (content): Merge conflict in code.py
  Automatic merge failed; fix conflicts and then commit
  the result.
```

First, you'll now need to realize what state your project directory is in. Git has already changed the files where the changes can be made without any problems and marked them for the next commit. The problematic files have also been changed, but they now contain both versions of the code with special markers.

```
git status
  On branch branch2
  You have unmerged paths.
    (fix conflicts and run "git commit")
    (use "git merge --abort" to abort the merge)

  Unmerged paths:
    (use "git add <file>..." to mark resolution)
    both modified:   code.py
```

Git expects you to edit the *code.py* file with an editor, manually resolve the conflicts, mark the file for the next commit, and finally commit the file yourself. In an editor, the code in question now has the following lines:

```
<<<<<<< HEAD
maxvalue = 10
=======
maxvalue = 30
>>>>>>> branch1
```

In this case, the first variant (between <<< and ===) contains the code of the current branch or (in case of a merge conflict on a pull) your own code. Between === and >>> follows the code of the foreign branch or (in case of a pull) the code from the remote repository. Depending on the editor, the two branches are highlighted in a color, and commands may be available to quickly activate one or the other variant.

In any case, you must now remove the conflict markers and decide on a code variant. Usually, an appropriate step is to also leave a comment to document how the code came to be:

```
# maxvalue set as proposed by Anna
# (merge conflict Jan 2022)
maxvalue = 30
```

Now, you need to provide the file for the next commit and perform the commit. This completes the merge process:

```
git add code.py
git commit -m 'merge branch1 into branch2'
```

In practice, larger merge processes often involve multiple files and code passages. Accordingly, resolving all conflicts can be tedious.

3.9.2 Merge Tools

You can resolve merge conflicts in any editor by searching for the text passages in question, deciding on a variant in those places, and deleting the alternative suggestion along with the conflict markers. In difficult cases, however, seeing all three code versions side by side could be helpful. The git mergetool command can provide help in this regard:

```
git mergetool --tool meld
  Merging: f2settings.py

  Normal merge conflict for 'f2settings.py':
    {local}:  modified file
    {remote}: modified file

git commit
```

git mergetool launches an external program (for our example, we used meld) that juxtaposes two or three code versions of the file in conflict (see Figure 3.12):

- On the left, the version that was current when the two branches were split (i.e., the first common parent of both branches)
- In the middle, the local/current version (i.e., the file from the active branch)
- On the right, the version from the branch to be added or (in case of a pull operation) the version from the remote repository

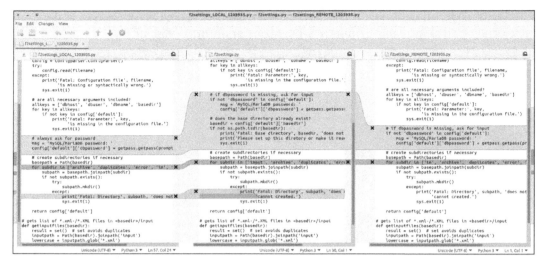

Figure 3.12 "meld" Merge Tool with Three Variants of a PHP File

Some merge tools don't display the parent version. The operation of each tool also varies. The goal is to change the local version of the file so that the correct changes are there. Then, you can save the file and exit the program. Finally, you must use git commit to complete the merge process.

git mergetool requires that a suitable external tool be installed beforehand. When you run git mergetool --tool-help, the command shows which tools are relevant and which are installed. We've had good experiences with meld (see *https://meldmerge.org*). A Windows version is available for download from the project website. The Linux version can be easily installed on many distributions (e.g., on Ubuntu) with apt install meld. macOS isn't officially supported, but the package management systems *brew*, *Fink*, and *MacPorts* contain corresponding packages. On Windows, the tortoisemerge command from *TortoiseGit* is also a good choice.

git mergetool is designed to help resolve merge conflicts as conveniently as possible. However, we want to be upfront that the operation of various merge tools is not trivial and will require practice. In simple cases, you'll typically reach your goal more quickly without an explicit merge tool.

3.9.3   Binary File Conflicts

For text files, Git can determine the changes between two or three versions of the file. This comparison isn't possible with binary files (i.e., images, Word documents, PDF, ZIP files, etc.). If a binary file has different contents in two branches, Git has no clue which is the "better" file. You cannot integrate parts of one binary file into another; a binary file can only be considered in its entirety.

```
git checkout branch1
git merge branch2
    warning: Cannot merge binary files: image.png
    (HEAD vs. branch1)
    CONFLICT (content): Merge conflict in image.png
    Automatic merge failed; fix conflicts and then commit
    the result.
```

In this case, you can use `git checkout` to explicitly use either the version of the current/own branch (`--ours`, namely, `branch1`) or that of the other/foreign branch (`--theirs`, namely, `branch2`). The double hyphens separate the options and references of `git checkout` from the filename that follows.

Using `git commit -a`, you can complete the commit. The `-a` option is required for the file modified with `git checkout` to be included. (Alternatively, of course, you can run `git add <file>` upfront.) We've intentionally not specified the `-m` option. This option launches an editor, as is usual with `git merge`, where you can change the default commit message for the merge process.

```
git checkout --ours -- image.png      (use 'own' version)
git commit -a                         (perform commit)

git checkout --theirs -- image.png    (use 'foreign' version)
git commit -a                         (perform commit)
```

> **Inverse Meaning of "Ours" and "Theirs" in Rebasing**
>
> If a merge conflict occurs during rebasing (see Section 3.10), the `checkout` options `--ours` and `--theirs` have the inverse meaning!
>
> This almost absurd behavior stems from the fact that, during rebasing, foreign commits are used as the basis, and the own ones are adjusted accordingly. The merge process therefore takes place in the reverse direction.

3.9.4 Merge Abort and Undo

A merge process that has been started but that has been interrupted due to a conflict can be canceled quite easily with the following command:

```
git merge --abort
```

Your project will then be in the same state as it was before you started the merge process. If the merge conflict occurred as part of `git pull`, the new commits have already been downloaded, which means `git fetch` is already done. Only the merge process belonging to the pull action is still pending.

Of course, git merge --abort won't solve all your problems, but you can at least enjoy the weekend in peace. You should by all means avoid trying to force a merge process through; you shouldn't simply throw up your hands and say, "It'll work somehow."

If aborting the merge is already too late, you can use git reset to return to the last commit *before* the merge process. For this task, you must pass the hash code of the last commit to the command. As a rule, you can specify HEAD~ instead of the hash code. This notation denotes the predecessor of the current commit (see Section 3.12):

```
git reset --hard <lasthash> resp. HEAD~
```

Whitespace Issues

By default, Git also takes into account *whitespace* (i.e., blank spaces and tab characters) when comparing code files. If two developers disagree on the best way to indent code, significant merge problems may arise.

On one hand, the issue can be resolved by implementing clear rules (i.e., "No one changes the indentation of other people's files!"). On the other hand, you could use the command git merge -X ignore-all-space, which allows Git to ignore whitespace and tab characters when comparing code files. (man git-diff documents some additional whitespace options.)

3.9.5   Content-Related Merge Conflicts

A syntax error in the code is usually easier to fix than a logic error, where the code is syntactically correct but returns incorrect results. The same is true with Git: If Git reports a conflict, you can usually fix it quickly with a little practice or after consulting with the other members.

What's much more annoying is when Git *does not* detect a conflict, but your code doesn't work (correctly) anymore after the merge process. How can this happen?

Imagine that Ben has programmed the function myfunc in file B and also called it in a few places. He finds out that the design of the function isn't ideal and so changes the order of the first two parameters and adds an optional third parameter. Then, he accordingly adjusts the places in the code where he calls myfunc. With a quick grep, he makes sure that nobody else uses his function yet—so nothing can happen. Commit, pull/push, and end of work.

On the same day, Anna also works on the code. After a pull in the morning, she discovers myfunc and uses it to greatly simplify her code in file A. "A godsend," she thinks. (At that point, myfunc is still in its original state.) She also ends the day with commit, a pull, and a push. Git doesn't recognize any problem. Ben only changed file B, Anna only changed A, and the code can be merged effortlessly.

The next day begins with frustration for both team members: Already at the first attempt errors occur when running the program (with what is now for both sides current versions of the files A and B).

In the scenario described, the correction is of course trivial. Much worse is when an error isn't that obvious, only occurs in a rare constellation of circumstances, and is discovered a month later or when the interaction of two apparently unrelated changes in the code triggers a security problem.

How can such problems be avoided? Only through the consistent use of automated (unit) tests. You should always keep in mind that Git applies formal rules to the merge process, but it doesn't "understand" your code at all.

3.9.6 MERGE Files

You're already familiar with the *.git/HEAD* file from Section 3.2. This file contains a reference to the head file of the current branch. In the case of a merge process that failed due to a conflict, the *.git* directory contains a whole bunch of other files with status information:

- MERGE_HEAD contains the hash code of the branch to be merged. In an octopus merge, the file contains the hash codes of all branches accordingly.

- Typically, MERGE_MODE is empty. Only if you run git merge --no-ff will the file contain appropriate information.

- MERGE_MSG contains the intended commit message. (The COMMIT_EDITMSG file also contains the text of the last commit message and isn't relevant for the merge process.)

- ORIG_HEAD contains the hash code of the active branch.

As soon as you complete or cancel the commit, the MERGE files will disappear again. (ORIG_HEAD will be retained.)

3.10 Rebasing

When several people work on the same branch, the commit sequence is constantly disrupted by merge processes. git log --oneline --graph shows a structure where short branches of commits from one developer constantly appear and disappear. The same structure is created when developers create their own development branches for a short period of time and connect them to the main branch on a regular basis. Basically, this constant change isn't a structural problem, but a cosmetic one: Git doesn't mind the short-lived forks, but for us humans, keeping track of such complicated commit sequences and separating important commits from unimportant ones can be quite difficult.

The git rebase command can help in these cases. git rebase can be used instead of git merge or combined with a pull in the form git pull --rebase. In this case, instead of the git merge required by the pull process, git rebase is executed.

> **Caution**
>
> Never use git rebase to modify the history of commits in a public branch (i.e., one that is synchronized with a remote repository) if the commits have already been uploaded. The main branch is completely off-limits in this respect. If you use rebasing carelessly, you'll quickly make yourself unpopular with your team.

3.10.1 Example

Let's consider an example is the following scenario: Our develop branch is shared by multiple developers via a remote repository. You now start working on a new feature and create a private feature branch for this purpose. Then, you perform two commits: F1 and F2. In the meantime, however, changes in the develop branch have occurred with commits D1 and D2, as shown in Figure 3.13, on the left.

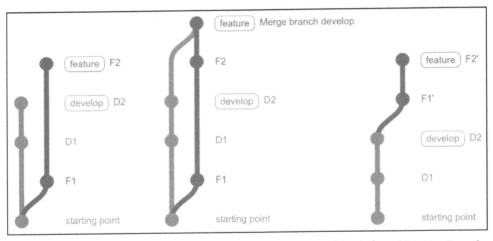

Figure 3.13 Initial Scenario (Left), Feature Branch after a Merge (Center), and Feature Branch after a Rebase (Right)

The new feature is to be incorporated into the develop branch in the distant future. You're not done yet, but to stay as close as possible to the develop branch and thus avoid future merge problems, you should transfer the last changes made in develop to your feature branch. For this task, you have two options:

- You can use the following commands:

```
git checkout feature    (feature will be extended)
git merge develop       (develop remains unchanged)
```

Now, the commits D1 and D2 are merged with your branch, as shown in Figure 3.13, in the center. In the process, a commit merge is added to your feature branch.

- Alternatively, you can use the following commands:

```
git checkout feature    (feature will be rebuilt + extended)
git rebase develop      (develop remains unchanged)
```

In this case, we're pretending that commits D1 and D2 already existed in our feature branch. Git will *rebase* your commits (F1 and F2) to make them look as if the changes were made after D2, as shown in Figure 3.13, on the right. This approach has the following advantage: No separate merge commit is required, so the commit sequence looks "nicer."

Whether you run git merge or git rebase, both branches remain available for further commits.

3.10.2 Concept

As a general rule, every Git commit is immutable. Changing a commit after the fact is not intended and, due to the hash code associated with each commit, is also simply impossible. But no one can stop you from creating new commits (with new hash codes) based on existing commits and then forgetting the old commits, which is exactly what happens with rebasing.

During rebasing, Git takes the D1 and D2 commits and pretends they are part of the feature branch, which is technically not a problem because nothing changes in the commits. In the feature branch, F1 and F2 will now first be reverted. Two new commits (F1' and F2') are then created to repackage the original changes of F1 and F2, but as if the changes had been made based on commit D2.

F1' and F2' are therefore completely new commits. Although the metadata (i.e., the commit message, the time, and the author) is taken from the original commits, the state of the files is different, and so is the hash code, of course! (Since the commit message remains unchanged, in git log, it's not obvious that F1 and F2 have changed. Only checking the hash codes will make changes clear. As shown in Figure 3.13, we've added the ' character after the commit name for clarity.)

The advantage of the rebasing approach is that no merge commit is required. A fast-forward merge without its own commit is sufficient.

3.10.3 Merge Conflicts during Rebasing

If Git notices any conflicts during the rebuilding process, you must resolve them manually (see Section 3.9), save them in a commit, and then continue the rebasing process with git rebase --continue.

During conflict resolution, note that the `--ours` and `--theirs` checkout options have the opposite effect to what happens in an ordinary merge process. In our introductory example, `--ours` would denote the `develop` branch, and `--theirs` would denote our own `feature` branch. This fact defies all human logic but can be justified by the way rebasing works, as we've outlined, where your own commits are rebuilt into new commits to match the existing commits of the "foreign" branch. Internally, a merge process occurs in the opposite direction. More information can be found at the following link:

https://stackoverflow.com/questions/8146289

3.10.4   Side Effects

The result of `commit log --graph` looks much tidier after rebasing, of course. However, we'd like to draw your attention to two side effects:

- Commits `F1'` and `F2'` never existed in this form. `git rebase` created artificial commits that combined data from various commits. Git is quite clever about this scenario, but sometimes things do go wrong. At some point, as a developer of commit `F1'`, you may need to justify why a bug exists in `F1'` that didn't exist in commit `F1` at all.

  Whether you can then still refer to the original commit `F1` is unclear. This commit is preserved for the time being when running `git rebase`. However, since no branch refers to the commit anymore, the original commit will fall victim to a garbage collection sooner or later.

- Along with each commit, *two* timestamps are stored: the *author date* and the *commit date*. Typically, both times are identical. When rebasing, the commit date of the newly created commit is updated with the current date. The author date, on the other hand, remains unchanged.

  `git log` normally takes the commit date into account unless you use the `--author-date-order` option. We'll cover this topic and other subtleties of sorting commits in Chapter 4, Section 4.1.

3.10.5   Pull with Rebasing

Probably the most common use of rebasing is in combination with `git pull`. The additional option `--rebase` makes sure that no merge process will occur, but that your own commits are adapted to the new upstream commits by `git rebase`:

```
git pull --rebase
```

Binary File Conflicts

If a conflict occurs with a binary file during the pull process with rebasing and you want to fix it using `git checkout --ours` or `--theirs`, the inversion of these options

> mentioned earlier will also apply. `--ours` denotes the remote repository's commits, while `--theirs` denotes your own.

Instead of `--rebase`, you can also pass the `--ff-only` option to `git pull`. This pull operation only takes place if the changes can be imported directly (i.e., if a fast-forward merge is possible without an explicit merge commit).

Starting with Git version 2.27 (available since mid-2020), `git pull` displays a warning every time the command is executed without concrete information about the desired pull behavior. You can avoid this warning by specifying one of the `--ff-only` (fast-forward or error), `--no-rebase` (fast-forward or merge commit), or `--rebase` options. Alternatively, you can make the desired behavior permanent in the configuration by using one of the following three commands:

```
git config [--global] pull.ff only        (FF or error)
git config [--global] pull.rebase false   (FF or merge)
git config [--global] pull.rebase true    (always rebasing)
```

Rebasing as a default behavior is especially recommended when multiple developers are working on a common branch and trust each other well. Accordingly, the Visual Studio Code (VS Code) editor also provides a similar option. Under **Settings**, search for "git rebase" and then enable the **Git: Rebase when Sync** option. Now, every time you click the **Sync** button, a pull will be performed with rebasing.

3.10.6 Special Rebasing Cases and Undo

Instead of running `git rebase <other>`, you can run `git rebase -i <other>`. This approach will take you to an editor that summarizes the actions to be performed. You can then modify the commands, for example, to set the commit messages of the new commits (`edit`) or to combine two old commits into a single new commit (`squash`). A good practice is to try out this process in a test project first. You can find more details on this topic at the following links:

- *https://git-scm.com/book/en/v2/Git-Tools-Rewriting-History*
- *https://thoughtbot.com/blog/git-interactive-rebase-squash-amend-rewriting-history*

You can use `git rebase <hash>` to start rebasing at a specific point. The hash code must point to the commit *before* the first commit where the rebasing process should start. (As mentioned before, don't apply `git rebase` to commits that you have already uploaded to a remote repository using `git push`.)

`git rebase --onto <newbase> <other>` transfers the branch `other` to a new location away from the main branch. A good example of how to use this option can be found on Stack Overflow:

https://stackoverflow.com/questions/21148512

If you must undo a rebasing operation, simply run `git reset --hard <hash>` using the hash code of your last original commit. (In our previous example, we would use the hash code of commit F2.) You can determine the hash code via `git reflog`.

3.10.7 Squashing

If your primary concern is a tidy commit history, you might consider `git merge --squash <other>`; `git commit` instead of `git rebase <other>`. In this context, all commits of the other branch will be combined into a new large commit. This commit is considered an "ordinary" commit. The only parent is the previous commit of the active branch. Unlike a merge commit, however, no parent reference to the other branch exists. Ultimately, no rebasing occurs, and thus, the original commits of `<other>` remain as they were.

As shown in Figure 3.14, we have a main branch and a bugfix branch. The two commits B1 and B2 are built into the main branch with the following commands:

```
git checkout main
git merge --squash bugfix
```

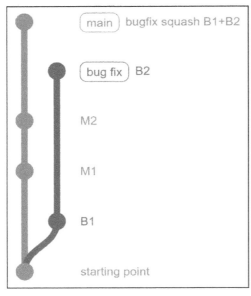

Figure 3.14 Commits B1 and B2 of the Bugfix Branch Transferred into the Main Branch via Squashing

`git merge --squash` is useful, for example, to merge a bugfix consisting of several commits into the develop or main branch with only one commit. The drawback of squashing is that the commit details of the bug fix are lost in the history of the main branch. The commit sequence doesn't indicate that a merge process has taken place at all.

140

3.11   Tags

By default, access to commits and other Git objects occurs through hash codes. For instance, the command `git show 991f2` shows details about an object whose hash code starts with `991f2`. (If the hash codes of several objects start with the same 5 hexadecimal characters, `git` will complain that the code isn't unique. Then, you must simply specify 6 or 7 digits. Unless your repository is the Linux kernel, 5 digits, which results in about a million possibilities, is often enough.)

Despite all the benefits of hash codes, this type of addressing isn't really elegant. Git therefore provides the option of tagging (literally "labeling") particularly important commits. Often, this feature is used to mark the commits at which your product reaches a certain version number.

```
git commit -m 'final work for version 1.0 done'
git tag v1.0
```

Tag names cannot contain spaces. Restrictions also exist for various special characters (see `man git-check-ref-format`).

3.11.1   Listing Tags

With tags, you can use `git tag` or the equivalent `git tag --list` command to list all tags. The following example shows only the last five tags because of `tail`:

```
git tag | tail 5
  v0.8
  v0.9.beta
  v0.9.rc1
  v0.9.rc2
  v1.0
```

Sorting Tags Correctly

`git tag` returns the tags in alphabetical order by default. Because of the character-by-character comparison, `v0.12` *is placed before* `v0.7`. If you want tags with version numbers to appear automatically in the correct order, you'll need to devise an appropriate terminology. For example, you could provide 2 digits for the version number if you expect more than 10 version numbers (`v0.01`, `v0.02`, etc.).

Of course, you can sort tags by all sorts of criteria using `git tag --sort=xxx`, such as by commit date with `--sort=committerdate`, but having to specify this option all the time can be quite tedious.

Often, you need to also display the commit date with the tag list. For this purpose, you have two options: One option is to pass the `--format` option to `git tag -l`. The `%09` corresponds to a tab character. The syntax for `--format` is documented by `git-for-each-ref`:

```
git tag -l --format='%(committerdate) %09 %(refname)' | tail -5
  Wed Mar 10 10:45:46 2021     refs/tags/iprot_v3.7.5
  Tue May 18 21:00:40 2021     refs/tags/iprot_v3.8.0
  Tue May 18 22:25:46 2021     refs/tags/iprot_v3.8.1
  Mon Jun 28 15:03:05 2021     refs/tags/iprot_v3.8.2
  Sun Dec 5  10:16:02 2021     refs/tags/iprot_v3.9.0
```

The other variant is to use `git log` but now eliminating all commits without tags or other additional information via `--simplify-by-decoration`. Formatting is then performed using the `--pretty` option (see `man git-log` for its syntax). The head filters out the five most recent commits:

```
git log --simplify-by-decoration --pretty='format:%ai %d' | \
                                                   head -5

  2022-01-21 07:51:21  (HEAD -> main)
  2022-01-11 10:50:36  (origin/main, origin/develop)
  2021-12-20 08:31:17  (develop)
  2021-12-05 10:16:02  (tag: iprot_v3.9.0)
  2021-06-28 15:03:05  (tag: iprot_v3.8.2)
```

3.11.2   Simple Tags versus Annotated Tags

Git uses two types of tags:

- With `git tag <tagname>`, you can create a simple tag, called a *lightweight tag*, to reference the last commit in the active branch. Internally, such tags are stored as references in the form of tiny text files in the *.git/refs/tag* directory, where the name of each file corresponds to the tag text. The file contains the hash code of the commit.

- `git tag -a <tagname>` creates an *annotated tag*. In addition to the tag text, this tag stores various additional information (e.g., when the tag was created and by whom). In addition, a second, detailed message text can be stored via the `-m` option. (If you use `-m`, you can omit `-a`.)

  Internally in Git, annotated tags are separate objects. `.git/ref/tags/<tagname>` then refers to the tag object rather than the commit. The tag object contains the date, time, the tag message, and of course the reference to the currently valid commit.

But when should you use each kind of tag? This choice depends solely on whether the additional data of annotated tags is important for you or not. Don't let the *lightweight* designation mislead you! Even with annotated tags, the management overhead is minimal. You don't need to bother about losing efficiency when you use annotated tags.

An argument exists in favor of annotated tags: If you use `git push` with the `--follow-tags` option (which we'll describe next), annotated tags will automatically be committed to the remote repository with the commits. For simple tags, on the other hand, a separate command is required for synchronization.

3.11.3 Synchronizing Tags

Git considers tags to be private information. Therefore, `git push` with no options pushes commits to the remote repository but does not push tags. To upload tags to the remote repository, you have three options, which can be quite confusing:

- `git push origin <tagname>` transfers only the specified tag. The command works for both lightweight and annotated tags. You must specify `origin` or another remote identifier because otherwise `git` interprets the tag name as the remote identifier.
- `git push --tags` transfers all tags of the active branch. This command also takes into account both lightweight and annotated tags. Commits, on the other hand, won't be transferred. To push both the commits and the tags, you need two commands: `git push` and `git push --tags`.
- `git push --follow-tags` commits both commits and associated tags to the remote repository. While this approach seems like the ideal way to commit *and* tag at the same time, this option only considers annotated tags, not simple tags!

With `git config --global push.followTags true`, you can make the option the default behavior of `git push` (but even here the restriction to annotated tags remains).

Tags and Releases

Once tags have been committed to a Git platform's repository, they'll show up on the platform as well. Depending on the platform (e.g., GitHub), you can find the tags under the **Releases** label.

Note, however, that some platforms differentiate between tags and releases. A *release* isn't a Git term, but a platform-specific way of marking particularly important versions of your project and making them available for download if necessary.

3.11.4 Setting Tags Subsequently

`git tag` applies to the current commit by default. However, if you forgot to set a tag in the past, that omission isn't a problem. You can use `commit log` to find the relevant commit and pass the first digits of the hash code to `git tag`. In the following listing, the hash codes and commit messages are heavily truncated due to space limitations:

```
git log --oneline
  1409ad45... (HEAD -> main, tag: iprot_v3.6.1 ...) Merge ...
  b916b955... (origin/develop) bump version
```

```
53ab1904... minor bugfix (PDF tuning)
612410cd... Merge branch 'develop' into 'main'
aa1b2195... add release-notes blog link
99ad895c... Merge branch 'develop' into 'main'
cf22c207... bump version
...
```

```
git tag 'iprot_v3.6.0' 612410cd
```

In this example, we forgot to set the tag for version 3.6.0 in the 612410... commit. This problem wouldn't have been noticed until the tag for version 3.6.1 was created after a tiny fix.

3.11.5   Deleting Tags

`git tag --delete <tagname>` deletes the specified tag in the local repository. If the tag has previously been transferred to a remote repository, the tag will remain in that remove repository. To delete it there as well, you must run `git push origin --delete <tagname>`, replacing `origin` with the remote repository's name if necessary.

3.11.6   Modifying or Correcting Tags (Retagging)

To change the name of a local tag, you must create a new tag for that commit and then delete the old one. Pay attention to the correct syntax for annotated tags: By simply specifying the previous tag (old), the new tag would refer to the old one. But you want the new tag to point to the same commit as the old tag!

```
git tag <new> <old>       (for simple tags)
git tag <new> <old>^{}    (for annotated tags)
git tag --delete <old>
```

If the erroneous tag has already been transferred to an external repository as well, you can synchronize these changes in the following way:

```
git push origin <new>
git push origin --delete <old>
```

You're out of luck if other team members have already downloaded the erroneous tag from the remote repository (via `git pull`). Of course, you have no influence on the local repositories of the other developers. However, you can ask your team to run `git pull --prune --tags` (see *https://stackoverflow.com/questions/1028649*).

3.11.7 Signed Tags

A special form of annotated tags, signed tags include information so that other developers can verify that you (and not someone else) created the tag. For this verification, the other developers need the public part of your GNU Privacy Guard (GnuPG) key. In this respect, signed tags are only appropriate if GnuPG keys are used in your company and all relevant developers can handle them.

Before you can create a signed tag, you need a key. The `gpg --list-keys` command lists all keys that are known on your machine:

```
gpg --list-keys
  pub   rsa3072 2021-05-07 [SC] [expires: 2023-05-07]
        351AB58F1E800FA0EFFDBD1464AAA3485BCC01AD
  uid          [ultimate] Michael Kofler
               <MichaelKofler@users.noreply.github.com>
  sub   rsa3072 2021-05-07 [E] [expires: 2023-05-07]
  ...
```

With `gpg --gen-key`, you can create a new key, if necessary.

Usually, `git` searches your GnuPG keyring for the key that matches your Git email address. Alternatively, you can explicitly specify the desired key using `git config`:

```
git config user.signingkey 351AB58F1E800FA0EFFDBD1464AAA3485BCC01AD
```

If you want the setting to apply not only to the current project, but to all Git repositories on your machine, you must pass the `--global` option as well.

To create a signed tag, you must use the `-s` option instead of `-a` with `git tag`. If your key is secured with a password, you'll be asked for it.

```
git tag -s 'v2.0.0' -m 'finally: version 2.0 with feature xy'
```

Signed Commits

You can also sign commits in the same way; simply pass the additional `-S` option to `git commit`.

3.12 References to Commits

For some `git commands`, a parameter references a commit or another object in the Git repository. In this context, the terminology for Git speaks of *revisions*, that is, states or versions of an object in the Git repository.

The simplest way to pass a reference to a particular commit, or more generally to specify a particular revision, is to use the object's hash code. You can quickly determine the hash codes of the latest commits using `git log --oneline`, if needed.

Usually, naming the first characters of the hexadecimal object is sufficient, unless you have 2 objects whose hash codes start with the same characters. In any case, you must specify 4 characters. More usual is the specification of the first 7 digits. (Having 7 hexadecimal digits results in 16^7 or about 270 million possibilities. Even in large Git repositories, the chance that two objects have hash codes starting with the same string is small.)

Computers find it easier to handle hash codes than people. Thus, Git provides numerous other options to point to a specific revision of an object. One approach is tags, which we introduced to you in the previous section.

In the following sections, we'll show you some other ways to reference commits. Before we get lost in the details, let's consider a few examples:

- `HEAD@{4}` denotes the commit that occurred four local actions before the last commit. The `{date}` notation refers to the reflog, and actions include pull, push, and checkout commands in addition to commits.
- `develop@{2 weeks ago}` represents the last state in the `develop` branch that is at least two weeks old. This notation also refers to the reflog.
- `HEAD~2` refers to the predecessor of the current commit. Instead of the reflog, the parent information of the commit objects is evaluated in this case.
- `@^2` denotes the second parent of the current commit. (In a merge process, a commit can have multiple parents.) `@` is a short notation for `HEAD`.

In this section, we'll try to stay as close as possible to the official documentation with regard to terminology. We recommend running `man gitrevisions` too or reading *https://git-scm.com/docs/gitrevisions*. Some more variants and special cases of the revision syntax can be described, but we don't think they are relevant for everyday Git practice.

3.12.1   Reference Names

Reference names are names used in *.git/refs* for the names of local or remote branches, such as `main` or `refs/remote/origin/develop`. Also allowed is `HEAD` to designate the most recent commit of the current branch. Depending on the context (e.g., during a merge process), `FETCH_HEAD`, `MERGE_HEAD`, `ORIG_HEAD`, and `CHERRY_PICK_HEAD` are also valid names. The `@` character by itself is a short notation for `HEAD`.

In the following commands, the first two commands are equivalent—as is the third one if the `main` branch is currently active:

```
git show @
git show HEAD
```

```
git show main
git show refs/heads/feature_xy
git show refs/remotes/origin/develop
```

> **Tip**
>
> To try out the revision syntax, consider passing the `--oneline` and `--no-patch` options to git show. This approach shortens the output of commits to a single line. To make our examples more clear, we refrained from stating these options all the time.

3.12.2   refname@{date} and refname@{n}

With `refname@{date}`, you can add a time to reference names. You can use time to denote the first object *before* the time specification in the relevant branch. Thus, `HEAD@{2 weeks ago}` is the youngest (newest) object that's older than 2 weeks. If no object in the reflog is that old, Git uses the oldest available object and displays a warning. For time specifications relative to `HEAD`, the short notation `@{date}` is allowed.

Remember that you must enclose expressions that contain spaces in quotation marks. In Bash, you can use single and double quotes (i.e., ' and "); in `cmd.exe`, you can only use double apostrophes. Alternatively, you can use periods instead of spaces, as in `HEAD@{2.weeks.ago}`; in this case, you don't need the quotation marks.

```
git show HEAD@{yesterday}
git show '@{1 day ago}'                  (equivalent)
git show 'develop@{2 hours ago}'
git show 'main@{2 months 3 weeks ago}'
```

The notation `refname@{n}` denotes the state of the object n actions earlier. Note that, with this syntax, actions include not only commits but also the git `checkout` or git `reset` commands. `HEAD@{2}` can therefore be the penultimate commit but may not be. (You can get to the penultimate commit safely with `HEAD^^` or `HEAD~2`. Details about this syntax variant are provided in the next section.)

> **Reflogs as a Prerequisite**
>
> The reflog logs Git actions that change the head of a branch of the local repository. (Pull and push commands also get logged for remote repositories.)
>
> Which actions are logged in the reflog can be shown via git `reflog` (for `HEAD`) or git `reflog --all`. Note that occasionally old entries are removed from reflog due to space limitations.
>
> The two notations `refname@{date}` and `refname@{n}` only work for Git objects that are known to the reflog. For a repository that you're just downloading with git `clone`, no

reflog exists initially. Any attempt to access older commits (@{2 days ago} or develop@{1 week ago}) will then result in error messages.

The syntax refname@{date} and refname@{n} isn't suitable for tags (error message *unknown revision or path*).

3.12.3   Accessing Previous Versions

Starting from the rev commit, you can access its predecessor using rev~n or rev^n as well as various syntax variants. You can specify the revision by using the @ abbreviation, the HEAD keyword, or the name of a branch, as described earlier. Unlike reference names, tags may also be used as starting points.

Let's start with the syntax using the tilde character, which is easy to understand:

- rev~ refers to the parent of the specified revision.
- rev~1 is equivalent to rev~.
- rev~2 references the ancestor (grandfather or grandmother, so to speak).
- rev~3, rev~4, etc. references even older predecessors.

With the tilde syntax, you can address only the first parent in each case. The caret syntax (with the ^ character) is relevant when a commit has multiple parents, for example, after a merge process. Let's consider some examples:

- Like rev~, rev^ denotes the first parent (biologically, for example, the mother).
- rev^1 is equivalent to rev^.
- rev^2 denotes the second parent (e.g., the father). In a merge process, rev^ was the active branch at the time, rev^2 was the other branch.
- rev^3, rev^4 etc. denote further predecessors of the same level in the order in which they were specified in the merge command. (Biological comparisons now become difficult.) However, the rarely used octopus merge can be used to merge several branches at once.

The caret character may also be specified more than once. In this context, the following rules apply:

- rev^ = rev~
- rev^^ = rev~2
- rev^^^ = rev~3

> **Trouble in cmd.exe**
>
> The ^ character is a special character in cmd.exe. For this character to be considered correctly, you must either duplicate it or enclose it in quotation marks. We recommend the latter approach because duplicating easily causes confusion. For instance, HEAD^^ in cmd.exe would be equivalent to HEAD^ in Bash.

3.12.4 Examples

The commit history shown in Figure 3.15 serves as a starting point for the following examples. The commands show the use of the tilde and caret syntaxes. We've greatly shortened the result of git show so you can focus on the hash codes. At the time we executed these commands, the main branch was active, so HEAD and main were equivalent.

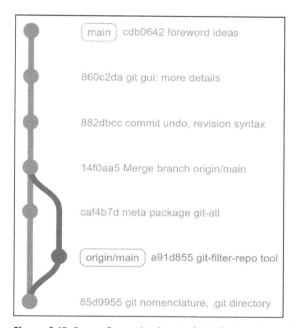

Figure 3.15 Some Commits Created While We Wrote This Book

```
git show HEAD
  cdb0642  foreword ideas

git show HEAD~
  860c2da  git gui: more details

git show @~         (equivalent)
  860c2da  git gui: more details
git show main~     (equivalent)
  860c2da  git gui: more details

git show @^         (equivalent, there is only one predecessor)
  860c2da  git gui: more details

git show @~2
  882dbcc  commit undo, revision syntax
```

```
git show @~3
  14f0aa5  Merge branch ...

git show 14f0aa5^      (first parent, active branch)
  caf4b7d  meta package git-all

git show 14f0aa5^2     (second parent, added branch)
  a91d855  git-filter-repo tool
```

3.12.5   References to Files

If a reference points to a commit or to a tree object, all syntax forms described so far can be extended by :<file>. For example, git show 3cb2907:file1 shows file1 in the state it was in at commit 3cb2907.

3.13   Internal Details of Git

This section continues where we left off in Section 3.2. After that introductory overview of how the Git database works, let's dive into some more details to close the chapter.

3.13.1   Object Packages

With large repositories, thousands of files can end up in the objects directory. This situation is inefficient, especially if repositories are to be transferred over a network connection. Thus, Git provides the option to combine objects into one file. Redundancies also are eliminated in the process. The resulting object packages (*.pack) and the associated index files *(.idx)* end up in the *.git/objects/pack* directory.

The git gc command (for *garbage collection*) is responsible for such cleanup actions. You can call it manually, but git gc also runs automatically from time to time. Background information on the package format is provided by the man pages on the git pack-objects or git gc commands and the following pages from the Git manual:

- *https://git-scm.com/book/en/v2/Git-Internals-Packfiles*
- *https://git-scm.com/book/en/v2/Git-Internals-Maintenance-and-Data-Recovery*

When you clone a project from a Git host like GitHub or GitLab, you always get the repository in packed format. Later commits are then stored again "normally" (i.e., in files of the format .git/object/xx/yyyy, where xxyyy together form the hash code). The entire object database then consists of a package and several individual files.

3.13.2   SHA-1 Hash Codes

In Git, hash codes are everywhere. These numbers are comparable to checksums, even if their calculation is internally different. Hash codes perform two tasks in Git: They provide quick access to objects in the Git database, and they can verify that the object hasn't changed.

To calculate hash codes, Git uses the rather old SHA-1 algorithm (see also *https://stack-overflow.com/questions/7225313*). Among security experts, this algorithm has long been considered outdated. With SHA-2 and SHA-3, already two successors can be used. Their greatest advantage (somewhat simplified) is that specifically manipulating a file in such a way to result in the same hash code (despite having different contents) is almost impossible. SHA-1 can be tricked in this respect and is therefore obsolete for security-relevant tasks.

The choice of SHA-1 as the hashing algorithm has been debated in developer circles from the start. Linus Torvalds originally argued that targeted SHA-1 collisions are relatively difficult to exploit for attacks. However, this vulnerability can't be completely ruled out: One conceivable scenario would be a manipulated firmware file.

In 2018, the Git development community decided to move Git to SHA-2 for the longer term (SHA-256 to be precise). An experimental implementation has been available since October 2020 (Git version 2.29). The following command creates a new Git repository with SHA-256 codes:

```
git init --object-format=sha256
```

However, you cannot switch between SHA-1 and SHA-256 in existing repositories. At the time of writing, no schedule for when SHA-256 will be used by default has been set. You can find more details on this topic at the following links:

- *https://github.blog/2020-10-19-git-2-29-released*
- *https://lwn.net/Articles/823352*

3.13.3   The .git/index File

Git's handling of the staging area is a mystery for many Git beginners. In Section 3.3, we described the concept of the staging area from a user's point of view. Internally, Git memorizes which file from your project directory is in which state in the staging area through the *.git/index* file. The index file is in a binary format, the structure of which is documented at the following links:

- *https://mincong.io/2018/04/28/git-index*
- *https://stackoverflow.com/questions/4084921*
- *https://github.com/git/git/blob/master/Documentation/technical/index-format.txt*

3.13.4   Commands for Managing the Git Database

This book focuses on the `git` commands you need to operate Git (`git add`, `git commit`, etc.). Most Git users will agree that those first few are already more than enough commands. If you want to explore or evaluate the internal details of the Git database beyond that, you'll need to focus on the more low-level commands responsible for the *plumbing* (i.e., they serve as a foundation for all other commands).

We lack the space in this book to go into detail about plumbing commands or even to provide a complete reference. However, the following list may serve as a starting point:

- `git cat-file <hashcode>` displays details about the Git object specified by its hash code. With the option `-p` (for *pretty print*), the command shows the contents of the object; with `-t`, the command shows the object type. A variant to this command with partly similar functions is `git show`.

- `git gc` triggers garbage collection in the Git database. This process removes Git objects to which no further references exist and which are therefore (presumably) no longer needed.

- `git hash-object <file>` calculates the hash code of a file.

- `git ls-files` shows the files under version control, filtered by various criteria, depending on the option.

- `git ls-tree` displays the contents of a Git tree object.

- `git pack-objects` creates a package of Git objects (*.git/objects/pack/**).

- `git rev-list` lists commits similarly to `git log` but returns only their hash codes. This command allows for further processing of this data by other commands or in scripts.

- `git rev-parse` evaluates a reference to a Git object (`HEAD~`, to give a conceivably simple example) and returns the associated hash code.

- `git update-index` adds a file from the project directory to the staging area (the *index*).

Further Reading

To delve further into the internal workings of Git, two more links may be helpful:

- *https://git-scm.com/book/en/v2/Git-Internals-Plumbing-and-Porcelain*
- *https://githowto.com/git_internals_working_directly_with_git_objects*

Chapter 4
Data Analysis in the Git Repository

This chapter is about searching a repository for specific data: Which files are under version control? In which commits was a file last modified? What changes were made in the process? In which commits does a particular term appear in the commit message?

In this chapter, we'll cover the following tasks:

- Searching commits with git log, git reflog, git tag, and git shortlog
- Searching files with git show, git diff, git grep, and git blame
- Searching errors with git bisect
- Generating statistics and visualizations with git shortlog, gitstats, and GitGraph.js

As in the previous chapter, we'll focus on using the git command and only discuss other tools in passing. However, many development environments, editors, Git platform web interfaces, and special (often commercial) programs like GitKraken are more comfortable for browsing the Git repository. We've already mentioned our personal favorite several times: Visual Studio Code (VS Code) with the GitLens extension.

As is often the case, once you understand how Git works internally and what features are available at the command level, using tools will be all the easier. Besides, every tool is limited in comparison to the scope of the git command!

4.1   Searching Commits (git log)

The git log command displays previous commits, starting from the current commit. This view is possible because a reference to the parent commit is stored along with each commit. (Correspondingly, merge commits have at least two parents.)

By default, git log displays all metadata (date, author, branch, etc.) for each commit, as well as the respective commit message. If more commits exist than can fit in the terminal window, you can use the cursor keys to scroll through the commit sequence. Pressing Q ends the display.

Figure 4.1 Commits of the Linux Kernel in a Terminal Window

The Linux Kernel as a Playground

If you're just getting started with Git, you probably don't have a large Git repository of your own to play with. Just use the Linux kernel! With nearly a million commits from countless developers and over 700 tagged releases (as of early 2022), you'll find a wonderful playground—and also see how fast Git works even with huge repositories. The only drawback is that, with more than 5 GB, the space requirement on your hard drive is considerable. You can clone the Linux kernel with the following command:

```
git clone https://github.com/torvalds/linux.git
```

Internally, the output of git log is routed through a *pager*, usually using the less command. Accordingly, the usual keyboard shortcuts for less apply as well. The search function, which you can start via ⌧, is particularly useful.

Shortcut	Function
Cursor keys	Scrolls through the text
G	Jumps to the beginning of the text
Shift + G	Jumps to the end of the text
/ abc Enter	Searches forwards
? abc Enter	Searches backwards
N	Repeats the last search (forward)
Shift + N	Repeats the last search (backward)
Q	Ends less
H	Displays the online help

Table 4.1 Shortcuts for "less"

If Git displays international characters or emojis incorrectly, an incorrect interaction between git and the text display command less has occurred. The --no-pager option provides a temporary workaround, while the following command provides a permanent solution:

```
git config --global core.pager 'less --raw-control-chars'
```

4.1.1   Clear Logging

Often, git log shows more detail than you actually need, while other information may be missing. The following options provide remedies:

- --graph visualizes branches (ASCII style).
- --oneline combines metadata and a commit message into a single line.

Conversely, the logging may be missing the very information you're looking for:

- --all shows also commits of other branches.
- --decorate also displays tags.
- --name-only lists the modified files.
- --name-status lists the type of changes per file (e.g., M for *modified*, D for *deleted*, or A for *added*).
- --pretty=online|short|medium|full|fuller|... feature predefined output formats for the metadata and the commit message.
- --numstat lists the number of changed lines per file.
- --stat shows the scope of changes per file as a bar chart.

A good idea is to simply try out the effect of each option. Some options can be combined with others. Figure 4.2 shows the Linux kernel's commits again, this time with the `--graph` and `--oneline` options. A more detailed description of the `git log` syntax will follow in Chapter 12, Section 12.1.19.

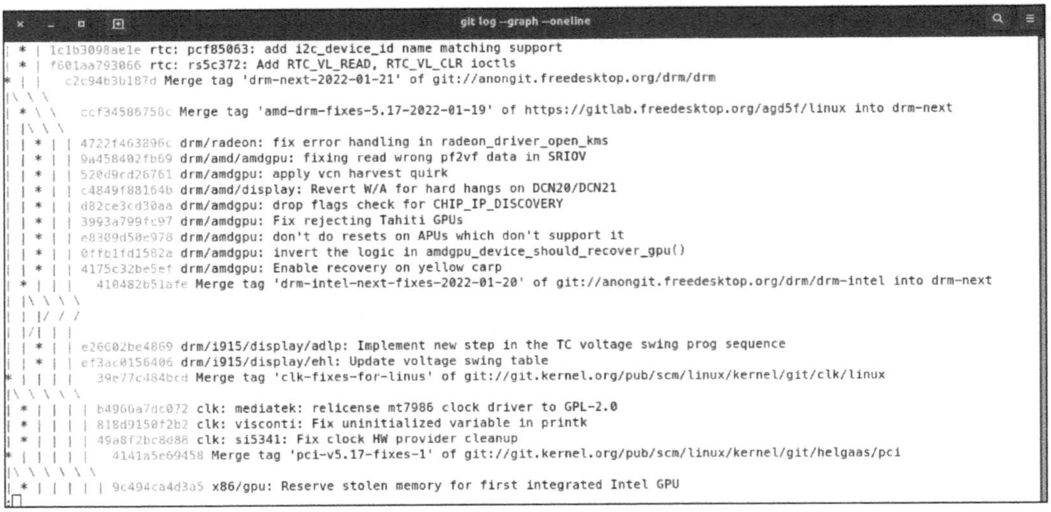

Figure 4.2 Compact Commit Display with Branch Visualization

4.1.2   Custom Formatting (Pretty Syntax)

If you aren't happy about the default formats, you can format the output of the commits yourself by using the `--pretty=format'<fmt>'` option. In this case, `<fmt>` is composed of codes that are similar to `printf`. Countless other codes are documented in man `git-log`. The format for the output of date and time can additionally be influenced by the `--date=iso|local|short|...` option.

In the following example, only the 7-character commit code, the first 20 characters of the developer's name, and the first line of the commit message are supposed to be displayed:

```
git log --pretty=format:'%h %<(20)%an %s'
  35870e2  Michael Kofler      bugfix y
  ebdb53f  Bernd Öggl          added validation
  9ae3fb8  Michael Kofler      feature x
```

To display the author's name in red, the format string must be modified in the following way:

```
git log --pretty=format:'%h %>(20)%Cred%an%Creset %s'
```

The most important codes are listed in Table 4.2.

Code	Meaning
%H	Complete hash code
%h	7-digit hash code
%ad	Author date
%cd	Commit date
%an	Name of the developer (*author*)
%ae	Email address of the developer
%s	First line of the commit message (*subject*)
%b	Remaining part of the commit message (*body*)
%n	New line
%<(20)	Next column 20 characters left aligned
%>(20)	Next column 20 characters right aligned
%Cred	Show output in red from here on
%Cgreen	Show output in green from here on
%C...	Various other colors
%Creset	Reset colors

Table 4.2 Pretty Format Codes

4.1.3   Searching Commit Messages

With the --grep 'pattern' option, git log displays only the commits that have the search term in their message. This search is also case sensitive. If you want to ignore case, you should specify the -i option in addition.

The following command searches *all* commits (not just those on the current branch) for the search term "CVE" irrespective of case:

```
git log --all -i --grep CVE
```

Unfortunately, the search terms found aren't highlighted in color. You can achieve this goal by first running git log without the --grep option, then filtering the resulting text with the grep command, and finally passing it through less. However, this approach isn't particularly efficient and provides fewer options when displaying the commits. (The grep option -5 causes the five lines above and below the found line to be displayed. The read option -R is necessary so that the color codes passed by grep are processed correctly.)

```
git log --all | grep -i -5 --color=always CVE | less -R
```

4.1.4   Searching Commits That Modify Specific Files

Often, you aren't interested in *all* commits, but only in commits in which a particular file or any file from a particular directory is modified. For this scenario, you must pass the file or directory name to git log. If identical names in terms of tags, branches, and so on, you must use the -- prefix.

The following command filters out the Linux kernel commits in which files of the ext4 driver (in the *fs/ext4* directory) have been modified. Thanks to the --stat option, the names of the changed files and the extent of the changes are also displayed at the same time.

```
git log --oneline --stat -- fs/ext4
  959f75845129 ext4: fix fiemap size checks for bitmap files
   fs/ext4/extents.c | 31 +++++++++++++++++++++++++++++++++++
   fs/ext4/ioctl.c   | 33 ++-------------------------------
   2 files changed, 33 insertions(+), 31 deletions(-)
   ...
  54d3adbc29f0 ext4: save all error info in save_error_info()
                   and drop ext4_set_errno()
   fs/ext4/balloc.c         |  7 +++----
   fs/ext4/block_validity.c | 18 +++++++-----------
   fs/ext4/ext4.h           | 54 ++++++++++++++++++++++++++++++++++++
                              ++++++------------------
   fs/ext4/ext4_jbd2.c      | 13 ++++---------
   ...
```

Tracking Renamed Files

git log -- <file> has problems when the name of a file changes. In such cases, you must use the additional --follow option, as in git log --follow -- <file>.

4.1.5   Searching Commits of a Specific Developer

You can use the --author <name> or --author <email> options to filter out the commits of a particular developer. As with --grep, <name> and <email> are interpreted as patterns.

In the following example, we'll continue to use the file system code for the Linux kernel and search for commits made by *Theodore Ts'o*. The apostrophe in the name won't make the search any easier. We'll simply use a period (.) instead. (The period is interpreted as a placeholder for any character according to the syntax of regular expressions.)

```
git log --oneline  --author 'Theodore Ts.o'
```

The second example searches for email addresses that contain *ibm.com*:

```
git log   --author 'ibm\.com'
```

4.1.6 Restricting the Commit Range (Range Syntax)

Typically, git log [<branch>] returns all commits of the current or specified branch back to the beginning of the commit sequence, up to the first commit of the repository. This behavior isn't always useful, however. Often, you're only interested in commits that are specific to a branch or to a few branches, not the entire common ground. In such cases, you can use the range syntax <branch1>..<branch2> or <branch1>...<branch2>. Instead of branch names, you can also use hash codes or other revision information (see Chapter 3, Section 3.12).

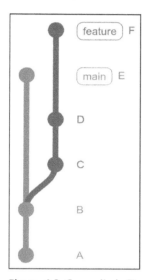

Figure 4.3 Commits in Two Branches

The starting point for the following examples is the commit sequence shown in Figure 4.3, where the commit messages are simply A, B, C, and so on. Currently, the main branch is active. Without the range syntax, all commits back to the initial commit A will be displayed:

```
git checkout main
git log --oneline
   ebdb53f (HEAD -> main) E
   c9bb505 B
   45c6cd4 A

git log --oneline feature
   35870e2 (feature) F
   9ae3fb8 D
```

```
b115d39 C
c9bb505 B
45c6cd4 A
```

git log main..feature shows only the feature branch commits not merged with main.
The common base is dropped (in this case, the commits A and B). Instead of main..fea-
ture, two alternative notations are actually syntactically clearer but rarely occur in
practice:

```
git log --oneline main..feature
git log --oneline feature --not main   (equivalent)
git log --oneline feature ^main        (also equivalent)
  35870e2 (feature) F
  9ae3fb8 D
  b115d39 C
```

git log main...feature with three periods works like the first command, but additionally takes into account the commits made since the branches were separated in main.
(By the way, you'll get the same result if you swap the branch names.)

```
git log --oneline main...feature
git log --oneline feature...main       (equivalent)
  35870e2 (feature) F
  ebdb53f (HEAD -> main) E
  9ae3fb8 D
  b115d39 C
```

4.1.7 Limiting Commits in Time

Instead of the range syntax presented in the previous section, which limits the commit
range based on logical criteria, you can also use options to limit the commits supplied
by git log in time, with the following options:

- --since <date> or --after <date> shows only commits that originated after <date>.
- --until <date> or --before <date> will only show commits done before/until <date>.

For example, to view the commits created in January 2022, you would run the following
command:

```
git log  --after 2022-01-01 --until 2022-01-31
```

4.1.8 Sorting Commits

By default, git log sorts commits by time, showing the most recent commit first. However, this behavior changes once you add the --graph option. git log then bundles
related commits. If you want to order the commits in terms of time despite --graph,

you can use the additional option --date-order. Conversely, you can achieve a grouping of commits, by branch, without --graph by using --topo-order.

The following examples again refer to the diagram shown earlier in Figure 4.3. However, the branches were connected with merge:

```
git checkout main
git merge feature
```

Typically, git log orders the commits strictly chronologically. (The --pretty option allows a one-line display including the commit date. To improve the overview, we reformatted the original editions a bit and removed weekdays and years.)

```
git log --pretty=format:"%h %cd %s" --date=local
```

```
52003e9  Jan 13 07:06:25     Merge branch 'feature'
35870e2  Jan 10 10:32:56     F
ebdb53f  Jan 10 10:32:38     E
9ae3fb8  Jan 10 10:32:04     D
b115d39  Jan 10 10:30:36     C
c9bb505  Jan 10 10:29:24     B
45c6cd4  Jan 10 10:29:16     A
```

The --graph option groups commits C, D, and F:

```
git log --pretty=format:"%h %cd %s" --date=local --graph
```

```
*      52003e9  Jan 13 07:06:25     Merge branch 'feature'
|\
| *  35870e2  Jan 10 10:32:56     F
| *  9ae3fb8  Jan 10 10:32:04     D
| *  b115d39  Jan 10 10:30:36     C
* |  ebdb53f  Jan 10 10:32:38     E
|/
*      c9bb505  Jan 10 10:29:24     B
*      45c6cd4  Jan 10 10:29:16     A
```

The --date-order option restores the original order despite the branch representation:

```
git log --pretty=format:"%h %cd %s" --date=local --graph \
      --date-order
```

```
*      52003e9  Jan 13 07:06:25     Merge branch 'feature'
|\
| *  35870e2  Jan 10 10:32:56     F
* |  ebdb53f  Jan 10 10:32:38     E
| *  9ae3fb8  Jan 10 10:32:04     D
```

```
| *   b115d39  Jan 10 10:30:36    C
|/
*     c9bb505  Jan 10 10:29:24    B
*     45c6cd4  Jan 10 10:29:16    A
```

Author Date versus Commit Date

Along with each commit, *two* timestamps are stored: the *author date* and the *commit date*. Normally, both times agree. However, this rule isn't true for commits that have been modified by rebasing: In this case, the author date indicates the time when the original commit was created. The commit date refers to the time of rebasing.

To consider the author date when sorting commits, you must use the --author-date-order option. The commits are then grouped as with --topo-order, but within the branches (now fewer or none, thanks to rebasing), the author date is used as the sorting criterion.

4.1.9   Tagged Commits (git tag)

git tag returns a list of all tags. git tag <pattern> restricts the result to tags that match the search pattern. Once you've determined the tag you want, you can use git log <tagname> to view the commits that led to that release.

Alternatively, you can use git log --simplify-by-decoration to show only those commits that contain tags or are referenced by a branch. In large repositories, however, this approach is comparatively slow.

Usually, git log doesn't display tags. If you want this additional information, you must pass the --decorate option to git log. If you still want a compact display, you can combine --decorate with --oneline as before.

4.1.10   Reference Log (git reflog)

Whenever we talk about the commit sequence (i.e., the *commit log*), we must also refer to the *reference log (reflog)*. The reflog contains all locally executed commands that changed the global HEAD or the head of a branch. The git reflog command lists these actions along with the hash codes of the commits:

git reflog

```
  ebdb53f (HEAD -> main) HEAD@{0}: checkout: moving from
                                   feature to main
  35870e2 (feature) HEAD@{1}: commit: F
  9ae3fb8 HEAD@{2}: checkout: moving from main to feature
  ebdb53f (HEAD -> main) HEAD@{3}: commit: E
```

```
c9bb505 HEAD@{4}: checkout: moving from feature to main
9ae3fb8 HEAD@{5}: commit: D
```

If you want the detailed output of git log, but at the same time want to see exactly the commits that git reflog returns, you should run git log with the --walk-reflog option, as in the following example:

```
git log --walk-reflogs

commit ebdb53f0db624c6dd4d754940903c3be905a9be (HEAD -> main)
Reflog: HEAD@{0} (Michael Kofler <...>)
Reflog message: checkout: moving from feature to main
Author: Michael Kofler <...>
Date:   Mon Jan 10 10:32:38 2022 +0200

    E

commit 35870e24fb49bb77622e17f5844cfaeb515c0a00 (feature)
Reflog: HEAD@{1} (Michael Kofler <...>)
Reflog message: commit: F
Author: Michael Kofler <...>
Date:   Mon Jan 10 10:32:56 2022 +0200

    F
```

Instead of --walk-reflog, you can also use the --reflog option. In this case, each commit will be displayed only once. (With --walk-reflog, the same commit may show up multiple times, for example, whenever you previously switched branches using git checkout.)

4.2   Searching Files

In Section 4.1, we focused on searching the metadata of a repository. In this section, we're interested in the content: What was the content of a particular file at an earlier time? What has changed since then? And who is responsible for this change? Numerous commands, including git show, git diff, and git blame, can help answer these and other questions.

4.2.1   Viewing Old Versions of a File (git show)

We introduced the git show <revision>:<file> command in Chapter 3, Section 3.4. This command outputs the <file> file in the state it was in when the <revision> commit was current. So, if you've tagged version 2.0 of your program with the v2.0 tag and you want to know what the *index.php* file looked like back then, you would run the following command:

```
git show v2.0:index.php
```

Of course, you can also redirect the output to another file so that you have both versions (the current one and the old one) available in parallel with the following command:

```
git show v2.0:index.php > old_index.php
```

4.2.2   Viewing Differences between Files (git diff)

To determine what has changed between the current version and an old version of a file, you should use git diff. Let's consider how the *index.php* file has changed since version 2.0. The output consists of several blocks, which are introduced with @@ and indicate the position. For orientation, a few lines of code help set the context. This information is followed by the changed lines, preceded by - or + depending on whether the line was deleted or added. (In the terminal, the deleted lines are highlighted in red, and the added lines are in green, which unfortunately can't be displayed in this book.)

```
git diff v2.0 index.php
```

```
diff --git a/index.php b/index.php
index a41783c..d1e3af2 100644
--- a/index.php
+++ b/index.php
@@ -10,9 +10,9 @@ try {
   exit();
 }
-try {
-   $ctl->checkAccess();
-} catch (Exception $e) {
+if ($ctl->checkAccess() === TRUE) {
+   $ctl->showRequestedPage();
+} else {
   if ($ctl->isJSONRequest()) {
     $data = new stdClass();
     $data->error = true;
@@ -29,4 +29,3 @@ try {
     exit();
   }
 }
-$ctl->showRequestedPage();
```

If you're only interested in the scope of the changes, you can additionally pass the `--compact-summary` option:

```
git diff --compact-summary v2.0 index.php
 index.php | 7 +++----
 1 file changed, 3 insertions(+), 4 deletions(-)
```

The `git diff <revision1>..<revision2> <file>` command shows the changes between two old versions:

```
git diff --compact-summary v1.0..v2.0 index.php
```

Of course, to `git diff`, you can pass the hash codes of commits, the names of branches, or other references instead of tags or versions (see Chapter 3, Section 3.12). Note that the rather convenient `HEAD@{2.weeks.ago}` notation for timing only works for locally performed commits (i.e., only for actions stored in the reflog). Apart from this notation, no other options can time a comparison commit. You may need to first use `git log` to find a timed commit and then pass its hash code to `git diff`.

Range Syntax with Three Periods

The `git diff <rev1>...<rev2>` variant is especially useful when the revisions are branches. In this case, `git diff` first determines the last common base of both branches and then shows what has changed in `<rev2>` compared to the last common commit. Unlike `<rev1>..<rev2>`, however, all changes that have happened in `<rev1>` since then are ignored.

4.2.3   Viewing Differences between Commits

If you choose not to specify a file in `git diff`, Git will show you *all* files changed since the specified version or between two versions/commits. Again, the `--compact-summary` option is useful if you just want an overview for the time being.

In case of extensive changes, not enough space is available to output a + or a - for each changed line. Instead, the total number of changed lines is specified after |. The number of plus signs and minus signs is relative to the file with the largest number of changes. The longer the bar of characters, the more extensive the changes.

```
git diff --compact-summary v1.0..v2.0 index.php
```

```
css/autocompleteList.css                  |  225 +-
css/editproject.css (new)                 |   13 +
css/edituser.css                          |   99 +-
css/iprot.css                             |  648 ++++-
css/iprot/jquery-ui-1.8.13.custom.css     |    2 +-
```

```
css/mobile.css (new)                        |    17 +
...
269 files changed, 22819 insertions(+), 12792 deletions(-)
```

In rare cases, you're simply interested in all the changes. Two options can help you to specifically limit the result:

- You can use -G <pattern> to specify a search pattern (a regular expression). git diff will then return only the text files whose changes contain the search expression, with exact case matching.

- --diff-filter=A|C|D|M|R filters out those files that have been *added*, *copied*, *deleted*, *modified*, or *renamed*, respectively.

For example, the following command returns the files that have been modified between version 1.0 and 2.0 and whose code contains the search text PDF:

```
git diff  -G PDF --diff-filter=M --compact-summary v1.0..v2.0
```

Changes since the Last Commit

Before running git commit, a good idea is to retrieve an overview of the changes in all the files flagged for commit, which is exactly what git diff --staged does.

If you haven't run git add yet or plan to use git commit -a, the git diff command will display all recent changes without any additional parameters. (This option doesn't include new files that aren't yet under version control.)

4.2.4   Searching Files (git grep)

In the numerous files of your huge project, at what points is function *X* called or an object of class *Y* created? The answer to such questions is provided by git grep <pattern>. By default, this command considers all files in the project directory and lists the lines where the search expression occurs in exact case. (If you don't want to differentiate between uppercase and lowercase, add the -i option.)

```
git grep SKAction
  ios-pacman/Maze.swift:   let setGlitter = SKAction.setTextur...
  ios-pacman/Maze.swift:   let setStandard  = SKAction.setText...
  ios-pacman/Maze.swift:   let waitShort = SKAction.wait(forDu...
  ...
```

You can get a more compact search result by using --count. In this case, git grep only shows how many times the search expression occurs in each file:

```
git grep --count CGSize
  ios-pacman/CGOperators.swift:6
  ios-pacman/Global.swift:1
  ios-pacman/Maze.swift:4
  ...
```

You can limit the search by specifying files or directories. The following command searches the files in the *css* directory for the keyword margin. Because of the -n option, the line number is also given for each location:

```
git grep -n margin css/
  css/config.json:100:     "@form-group-margin-bottom": "15px",
  css/config.json:144:     "@navbar-margin-bottom": "@line-heig...
  css/editglobal.css:25:   margin-top: 1px;
  css/editglobal.css:29:   margin-top: 0px;
  ...
```

Of course, you can also search old versions of your code by specifying the desired revision before the filenames or directories. If the search expression contains special characters or spaces, you must place it between apostrophes. For instance, the following example looks for UPDATE commands in version 2.0 of the program that modify the person table:

```
git grep 'UPDATE person' v2.0
  v2.0:lib/delete.php:          $sql = "UPDATE person SET sta...
  v2.0:lib/person.php:          $sql = sprintf("UPDATE person...
  v2.0:lib/personengruppe.php: $sql = sprintf("UPDATE person...
  ...
```

What makes git grep difficult to use is when you don't know which commit to look in or when you're dealing with changes that were only made temporarily and later removed from the codebase. In these cases, use git rev-list v1.0..v2.0 to create a list of the hash codes for all the commits during the period in question. You can then process this list using git grep.

For example, you can use git grep to count how many times the SQL keyword UPDATE occurs in various versions of the *lib/chapter.php* file. As with git log, the latest commit is considered first. The -- characters separate the hash code list generated by git rev-list from the filename:

```
git grep -c 'UPDATE'  $(git rev-list v1.0..v2.0) -- user.php
  262d67fed686cda939092e7b0cb337bbc1e2dbe9:user.php:5
  96d0a06d389784ec93f252a097185ee3678a2c1c:user.php:5
  c07c2f0ce5682bea898ba3a65a15bf5230dd23dc:user.php:4
  ...
```

4.2.5   Determining the Authorship of Code (git blame)

When you've found the file you're actually interested in with the commands we've described so far, the next question is of course: Who is responsible for the code contained there? A great tool for this purpose is git blame <file>. Without any further options, this command displays the file in question line by line and indicates, for each line, some key information, including which commit changed the line, by which author, and on what date.

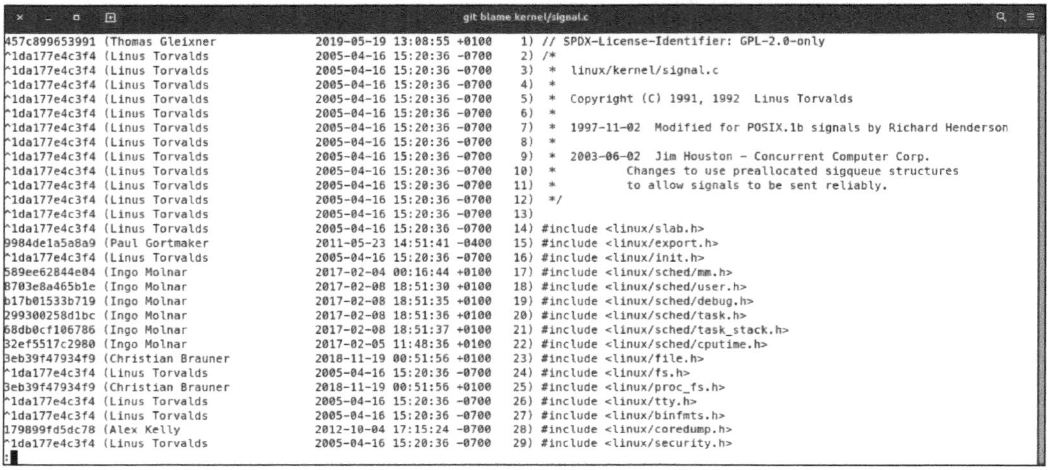

```
457c899653991 (Thomas Gleixner      2019-05-19 13:08:55 +0100    1) // SPDX-License-Identifier: GPL-2.0-only
^1da177e4c3f4 (Linus Torvalds       2005-04-16 15:20:36 -0700    2) /*
^1da177e4c3f4 (Linus Torvalds       2005-04-16 15:20:36 -0700    3)  *  linux/kernel/signal.c
^1da177e4c3f4 (Linus Torvalds       2005-04-16 15:20:36 -0700    4)  *
^1da177e4c3f4 (Linus Torvalds       2005-04-16 15:20:36 -0700    5)  *  Copyright (C) 1991, 1992  Linus Torvalds
^1da177e4c3f4 (Linus Torvalds       2005-04-16 15:20:36 -0700    6)  *
^1da177e4c3f4 (Linus Torvalds       2005-04-16 15:20:36 -0700    7)  *  1997-11-02  Modified for POSIX.1b signals by Richard Henderson
^1da177e4c3f4 (Linus Torvalds       2005-04-16 15:20:36 -0700    8)  *
^1da177e4c3f4 (Linus Torvalds       2005-04-16 15:20:36 -0700    9)  *  2003-06-02  Jim Houston - Concurrent Computer Corp.
^1da177e4c3f4 (Linus Torvalds       2005-04-16 15:20:36 -0700   10)  *      Changes to use preallocated sigqueue structures
^1da177e4c3f4 (Linus Torvalds       2005-04-16 15:20:36 -0700   11)  *      to allow signals to be sent reliably.
^1da177e4c3f4 (Linus Torvalds       2005-04-16 15:20:36 -0700   12)  */
^1da177e4c3f4 (Linus Torvalds       2005-04-16 15:20:36 -0700   13)
^1da177e4c3f4 (Linus Torvalds       2005-04-16 15:20:36 -0700   14) #include <linux/slab.h>
9984de1a5a8a9 (Paul Gortmaker       2011-05-23 14:51:41 -0400   15) #include <linux/export.h>
^1da177e4c3f4 (Linus Torvalds       2005-04-16 15:20:36 -0700   16) #include <linux/init.h>
589ee62844e04 (Ingo Molnar          2017-02-04 00:16:44 +0100   17) #include <linux/sched/mm.h>
8703e8a465b1e (Ingo Molnar          2017-02-08 18:51:30 +0100   18) #include <linux/sched/user.h>
b17b01533b719 (Ingo Molnar          2017-02-08 18:51:35 +0100   19) #include <linux/sched/debug.h>
299300258d1bc (Ingo Molnar          2017-02-08 18:51:36 +0100   20) #include <linux/sched/task.h>
68db0cf106786 (Ingo Molnar          2017-02-08 18:51:37 +0100   21) #include <linux/sched/task_stack.h>
32ef5517c2980 (Ingo Molnar          2017-02-05 11:48:36 +0100   22) #include <linux/sched/cputime.h>
3eb39f47934f9 (Christian Brauner    2018-11-19 00:51:56 +0100   23) #include <linux/file.h>
^1da177e4c3f4 (Linus Torvalds       2005-04-16 15:20:36 -0700   24) #include <linux/fs.h>
3eb39f47934f9 (Christian Brauner    2018-11-19 00:51:56 +0100   25) #include <linux/proc_fs.h>
^1da177e4c3f4 (Linus Torvalds       2005-04-16 15:20:36 -0700   26) #include <linux/tty.h>
^1da177e4c3f4 (Linus Torvalds       2005-04-16 15:20:36 -0700   27) #include <linux/binfmts.h>
179899fd5dc78 (Alex Kelly           2012-10-04 17:15:24 -0700   28) #include <linux/coredump.h>
^1da177e4c3f4 (Linus Torvalds       2005-04-16 15:20:36 -0700   29) #include <linux/security.h>
```

Figure 4.4 Authorship of the Linux Kernel File "signal.c"

The option -L 100, 200 considers only the line numbers 100 to 200. A great help in reading the outputs are the following two options:

- --color-lines displays continuation lines from the same commit in blue color.

- --color-by-age indicates freshly changed code in red (changes in the preceding month) and moderately new code in white (changes in the preceding year).

An even clearer representation of the use of git blame is provided by the websites for GitLab, GitHub, etc. In addition, you can view the relevant commit directly on those platforms with just a few clicks.

Boundary Commits

If not all commits are contained in the local repository, individual hash codes are prefixed with the ^ character (called a *caret*), as in ^1da177e4c3f4. This character points to a *boundary commit*, that is, the last commit available in the repository.

4.3 Searching for Errors (git bisect)

Imagine you notice that an error occurs in a feature of your program, but you fail to find or even isolate its cause. Presumably, this interaction has only arisen as a result of changes in several files.

You're sure that the error didn't occur earlier. With git checkout v1.5, you can temporarily revert to version 1.5 and tested it again. At that point, everything is still alright. But since that version, 357 commits have occurred. The git rev-list command is a simpler variant to git log, which usually just returns the hash codes of the commits in question instead of commit messages. With the --count option, git rev-list counts the commits between two points on a branch:

```
git rev-list v1.5..HEAD --count
  357
```

To determine the cause of the error, you'll need to find the first commit in which the error occurs, which can be like searching for a needle in a haystack.

Fortunately, git bisect supports you in this endeavor. The concept behind git bisect is that you first specify the last known "good" and "bad" commit—in this example, the commit tagged v1.5 and the current commit (i.e., HEAD). git bisect then does a checkout in the middle of the commit area, so it bisects the search area. Now, we have a detached HEAD. In other words, HEAD doesn't reference the end of a branch but instead references some commit in the past.

```
git bisect start
git bisect bad HEAD
git bisect good v1.5
  Bisecting: 178 revisions left to test after this
    (roughly 8 steps)
  [e84fd83319c1280bcef38400299fd55925ea25e6] Merge branch ...
```

Now, you'll test if the error still occurs with this commit. *How* you perform this test depends entirely on the type of code. You may need to compile your program to test it. With a web application, on the other hand, a test in the browser is usually sufficient. Depending on how the test turns out, you must report the result using either git bisect bad or git bisect good:

```
git bisect bad
  Bisecting: 89 revisions left to test after this
    (roughly 7 steps)
  [cea22541893ded6e6e9f6a9d40bf6d0c2ec806d8] bugfix xy ...
```

Depending on your answer, git bisect then knows whether to continue looking in the top half or the bottom half of the commit area. The command performs another checkout in the middle of the remaining search area. The search area was thus reduced to about a quarter.

Again, you must then repeat the test to see if the error still occurs or not and pass this information to Git. Continue in this way until `git bisect` finally reports:

```
git bisect good
  4127d9d06ecbae0d4d9babaaa8aacebc0c8853cb is the first bad
  commit ...
```

This message lets you know at what point in the past the error first occurred. The search for the cause of the error is still pending, but actually `git diff HEAD^` (i.e., the summary of changes compared to the previous commit) should put you on the right track.

Finally, with `git bisect reset`, you can exit `git bisect` and return to the head of the branch you were in at the beginning of the search. Now, you must try to finally fix the error.

```
git bisect reset
  Previous HEAD position was ef81d5c fix: getLink for csv ...
  Switched to branch 'develop'
```

4.4   Statistics and Visualization

With large repositories, you often can't see the forest for the trees (in our case, "for the branches"). In this section, we'll therefore introduce you to `git` commands and other tools to help you get back on track.

4.4.1   Simple Number Games (git shortlog)

A useful command to obtain a first overview is `git shortlog`. In its simplest form, this command provides an alphabetically ordered list of all commit authors, with the number of commits for each author, and the first line of each commit message.

Various options allow you to further shorten the output. The following command provides a list of the Linux kernel developers who've had the most commits since the beginning of 2021, not counting merge commits:

```
git shortlog --summary --numbered --email --no-merges \
          --since 2021-01-01

  967  Christoph Hellwig <hch@lst.de>
  737  Lee Jones <lee.jones@linaro.org>
  672  Andy Shevchenko <andriy.shevchenko@linux.intel.com>
  642  Mauro Carvalho Chehab <mchehab+huawei@kernel.org>
```

```
625   Pavel Begunkov <asml.silence@gmail.com>
606   Vladimir Oltean <vladimir.oltean@nxp.com>
...
```

You can get the total number of commits (across all branches) using `git rev-list` in the following way:

```
git rev-list --all --count
  1071789
```

To find out the number of files in the current branch, you must pass the output of `git ls-files` to `wc` (which stands for *word count*) with the following command:

```
git ls-files | wc -l
  75014
```

In a similar way, you can find out the number of branches and tags, as in the following example:

```
git branch -a | wc -l
  3
```

```
git tag | wc -l
  728
```

You can determine the number of changes between two versions/branches/revisions of your project using `git diff --shortstat`, as in the following example:

```
git diff --shortstat v5.5..v5.6
   11999 files changed
  680199 insertions(+)
  258909 deletions(-)
```

4.4.2   Statistical Tools and Scripts

The internet is teeming with scripts and programs that can extract more details from a Git repository than the commands we've covered so far. A good starting point is the following Stack Overflow article:

https://stackoverflow.com/questions/1828874

Popular and easy to use on Linux is the Python script `gitstats`. After installation, you must pass to the script the path to the repository and provide a directory where the result files should be stored. Starting from the *index.html* file, you can then view various statistical evaluations in a web browser. However, the appearance of the accompanying graphics is rather minimalistic.

```
sudo apt install gnuplot
git clone git://repo.or.cz/gitstats.git
mkdir result
gitstats/gitstats <path/to/repo> results/
google-chrome results/index.html
```

4.4.3   Visualizing Branches

Especially during training or when trying to explain to co-workers how Git works, you may need to "neatly" visualize many commits distributed across multiple branches. However, the results of git log --graph are unsuitable for this purpose.

A better representation is available from the gitk program that's installed on many computers. You can usually start gitk from the terminal to show the commit sequence for the current branch.

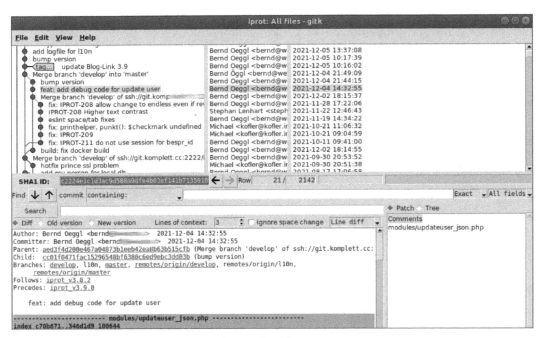

Figure 4.5 Visualization of Branches via "gitk"

For clearer representations of branches, we recommend the following suggestions:

- The commercial program *GitKraken* not only displays commit sequences in an attractive style but also provides numerous other functions to help with the administration of Git repositories. The free version can only be used for public repositories.

- Some Git platforms also include visualization features. For example, GitLab shows a clear representation of the commit history at **Repository • Graph**.

172

- GitHub users, who are less spoiled in this regard, should look at the commercial project *Git Flow Chart (GFC)*. At *https://gfc.io*, you can visualize the commit sequence of repositories on GitHub and Bitbucket. The basic functions are available free of charge for public repositories. If you want to use GFC for private repositories or in combination with the GitHub team features, you must pay a monthly fee.

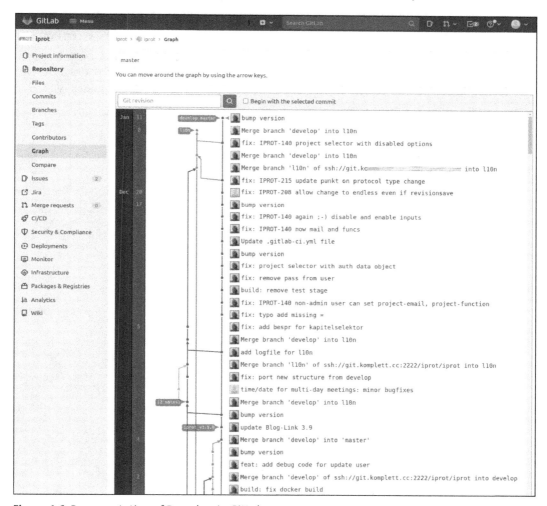

Figure 4.6 Representation of Branches in GitLab

4.4.4   GitGraph.js

You may have noticed the following: All figures in this book that show the commit sequence of multiple branches have a consistent appearance. Of course, this consistency is no coincidence. With the open-source library *GitGraph.js* and a few lines of custom JavaScript code, many visualization needs can be met. The result can then be admired in a web browser. The GitGraph.js project website (*https://www.nicoespeon.com/gitgraph.js*) summarizes some elementary working techniques in a presentation.

Unfortunately, GitGraph.js can't draw real commits from a repository. So, you must assemble the commit structure using appropriate JavaScript statements, which involves some effort (which we haven't shied away from for this book, of course).

Let's go back to the code in the diagram shown earlier in Figure 4.3. graphContainer points to the place in the HTML code where the graph should be displayed. mytemplate contains some options to display commits without authors and hash codes, but with branches with their names. createGitGraph creates the commit sequence, which is empty for now. Commits and branches are then added with branch and commit.

```
<!doctype html>
<html><head>
<script src="https://cdn.jsdelivr.net/npm/@gitgraph/js">
</script>
</head>
<body>
<div id="graph"></div>
<script>
const graphContainer = document.getElementById("graph");
const mytemplate =  GitgraphJS.templateExtend(
   GitgraphJS.TemplateName.Metro, {
       commit: {  message: { displayAuthor: false,
                             displayHash: false    } },
       branch: {  label:    { display: true } }
      });
const gitgraph = GitgraphJS.createGitgraph(
  graphContainer,
  { author: " ", template: mytemplate } );
const main  = gitgraph.branch("main").commit("A").commit("B")
const develop = main.branch("feature").commit("C").commit("D")
main.commit("E")
develop.commit("F")
</script>
</body></html>
```

Chapter 5
GitHub

When GitHub was launched in 2008, the idea of an online web platform for version control was no longer entirely new: SourceForge had already proven itself in many projects since the turn of the millennium. The fact that so many developers switched sides and moved to GitHub in the following years shows that GitHub did something right. Its acquisition by Microsoft in 2018 for an astronomical $7.5 billion reinforces this impression.

GitHub has presented itself then, as now, in a clear interface for the large range of functions, without advertising but with good performance and sufficient resources.

The main components provided by GitHub include the following:

- Git repositories
- Collaborative work with forks and pull requests
- GitHub Actions
- Automatic safety checks
- A ticket system (issue tracker) with milestones
- A discussion forum for teams
- Package management for Docker, Node Package Manager (npm), and other package formats
- Wiki
- GitHub Pages
- Gists
- The GitHub command-line interface (CLI)

You can choose between a free account and among different payment models. To attract as many users as possible to the platform, the functions offered in the free version are constantly being expanded. Recently, restrictions on private repositories were lifted, so you can now create unlimited projects that are visible only to selected users. The advantages of paid accounts are essentially in the amount of storage available, in the ability to include enterprise servers for authentication (*single sign-on*), and in the support provided by GitHub.

If you use GitHub for all your software projects, then you effectively have a cloud solution for your source code. You won't have to search for the data of one of your projects on different computers or in old backups because you know you can find everything on

GitHub. But reducing GitHub to just another cloud storage service falls short, as you'll see in this chapter.

> **Prerequisites**
>
> In this chapter, we assume that you've already created a GitHub account and are familiar with the basic features of the web interface (see Chapter 2, Section 2.2). With this basic knowledge, we can immediately start this chapter with the "special features" that set GitHub apart from a pure Git repository or from other Git platforms.

5.1   Pull Requests

Pull requests are among the most important features of GitHub. Basically, the aim is to formalize the merge process: Developer A writes code for a new feature and then asks developer B to look at the code and put it into the main development branch (e.g., `main` or `develop`).

Basically, of course, this process can work completely without GitHub. For instance, developer A sets up the new branch (`git checkout -b newfeature`), writes the code, performs various commits, commits the branch to a remote repository (`git push`), and emails developer B to ask her to look at the code. Developer B downloads the branch (`git pull`), tests the code, and finally runs `git merge` or asks developer A to make some improvements upfront.

GitHub was probably the first Git platform to elegantly map this process in a web interface, which has several advantages:

- Communication from the start of the pull request to its completion (or denial) is documented transparently for all parties involved.

- The implementation requires only a minimum of Git knowledge. Both sides basically only need to click a few buttons in the web interface.

- Cross-repository pull requests are possible based on forks. This feature makes working on projects in which the helper isn't a team member at all possible.

> **The Term "Pull Request"**
>
> The term *pull request* isn't linguistically perfect. Developer A actually asks for a merge operation. In this respect, one would have to speak of a *merge request*. In fact, GitLab's web interface uses this term for the equivalent function.
>
> The name *pull request* results from a time when Linus Torvalds still managed the code of the Linux kernel with other version management tools. After another developer had programmed a new function, he asked Torvalds to download the code to his computer via pull and look at it.

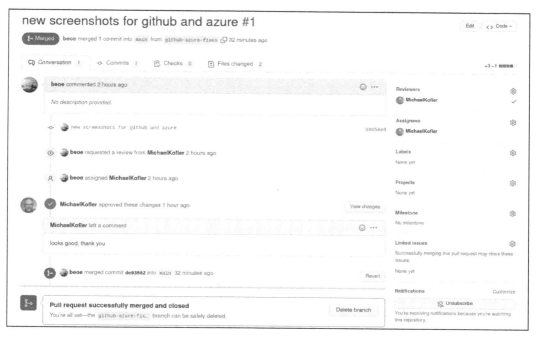

Figure 5.1 While Writing This Book, We Proofread Each Other's Chapters, Saved the Changes in a Designated Branch, and Submitted Changes via Pull Requests to the Other Author for Review

5.1.1   Pull Requests on a Team

When multiple developers have access to a GitHub repository, two scenarios are possible:

- In one case, all developers have the same rights and can modify all branches without restriction. In this scenario, pull requests are optional but are possible, of course, and promote transparency. Each developer can merge their own changes into the main branch (git merge) and upload them to the GitHub repository.

- In the other case, rules for some branches (for example, for main or develop) restrict the actions developers are allowed to perform. Then, for example, everyone is allowed to upload their own branches, but not upload to central branches like main or develop. Such rules can be set in the GitHub interface in the repository's **Settings**, under **Branches**—but only for public projects or if you have a paid GitHub account.

  When such restrictions apply, pull requests are the only way developers can get new code into the central (development) branch of the repository.

In both cases, you perform the development of the new feature in a branch. You should always make sure that you're up to date with the branch into which your code will later go (main in the following example). Finally, after the last commit, you must commit it to the remote repository (i.e., GitHub) using `git push`. You'll need to specify the `--set-upstream` option only on the first push.

```
git checkout -b new_feature
...
git commit -a -m 'working on new feature, xy done'
...
git merge main
...
git commit -a -m 'finished new feature'
git push  [--set-upstream origin pr_in_github]
```

Then, you can initiate the pull request on the GitHub website, either in the **Pull requests** dialog box or in the **All branches** dialog box, which displays all the branches of the project.

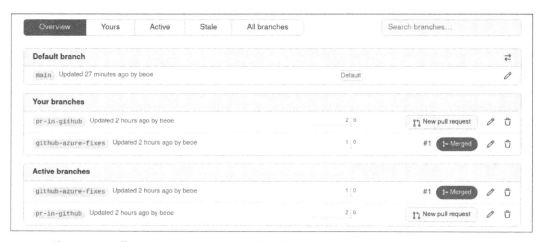

Figure 5.2 Pull Requests Can Be Initiated in the Branches Dialog Box, among Others

Subsequently, you must justify your pull request (as shown in Figure 2.16 in Chapter 2, Section 2.7.2) and specify who on your team is responsible for it. If this teammate approves the pull request, the corresponding merge process will be performed directly in the GitHub repository. Once you subsequently run `git pull` locally, the changes made as part of the pull request will also become visible in your local repository.

Workflows

In Chapter 8, we describe several variations on how a team can collaborate in a shared Git repository without reference to specific platforms such as GitHub or GitLab. In that context, we'll return to the topic of pull requests again; not from a technical point of view as in this chapter, but from a workflow perspective instead.

5.1.2   Pull Requests in Public Projects

Especially in large open-source projects, you cannot give all developers the right to make changes in the repository. The risk would be too great that someone would inadvertently (or even intentionally) wreak havoc. To create an uncomplicated form of collaboration in these cases as well, GitHub has extended pull requests by means of *forks*.

We've already described the basic procedure for forking in Chapter 2, Section 2.7: To contribute code to someone else's project, you must first create a fork of that other person's repository, that is, you make a copy of the repository in your own GitHub account.

Forking projects has a long tradition in software development. In open-source projects, forks sometimes arise because the development team can't agree on what the future holds and thus a group splits off with a copy of the source code and does its own development. The fork and the original project often exist in parallel for a while but continue to evolve independently until one variant prevails.

In a way, forks on GitHub work the same way, but with one big advantage over a copy: A GitHub fork still has a link to the original and can update changes with git fetch. So, GitHub forks were designed for collaboration, not for separate development.

> **Fork Details**
>
> In fact, of course, a repository isn't copied in its entirety in a fork. Doing so would take a long time and require a lot of memory. GitHub can share Git objects across multiple repositories as *shallow copies*. Details about this topic and other internal GitHub optimization measures can be found at the following link:
>
> *https://github.blog/2015-09-22-counting-objects*

As with working on a team, you must ensure that your codebase is at the same level as the original project before initiating the pull request. If the original project has been modified since the fork, this consistency requirement is no longer met. GitHub then displays a notice in the web interface: *This branch is <n> commits behind <origrepo>:main*.

To update the local repository on your machine, you must also add the remote repository of the original project to it. A common practice is to call this remote repository the upstream repository:

```
git remote add upstream \
  https://github.com/<origaccount>/<origrepo>.git
```

Now, you can periodically (specifically, right before you prepare a pull request) add any new additions from the original repository to your own repository via the following call. In the pull process, merge conflicts between your own code and the latest changes made in the external repository may arise. For your pull request to have a chance for success, you'll have to resolve these conflicts.

```
git pull upstream main
```

The `git push` command uploads the updated repository to the GitHub fork of your account:

The GitHub interface then displays the text *This branch is <n> commits ahead of <orgrepo>:main* in the repository description. These *<n> commits* are the changes you've made. The **New pull request** button then takes you to a dialog box where you can initiate your pull request. Normally, a pull request would only be possible within a project. But because GitHub knows that you originally forked the project, it sort of recognizes the relationship between your repository and the original one.

5.2   Actions

In Chapter 9, Section 9.1, we describe the ability to use *hooks* in Git to run programs on the client and server before or after a commit or push. *GitHub Actions* takes this concept a bit further by allowing all GitHub events to be used for hooks (for example, when a new ticket is created).

For execution, GitHub provides *runners*. As of February 2022, you could choose between Windows Server (2022, 2019 or 2016), Ubuntu Linux (20.04 or 18.04), and macOS (10.15 or 11) in this context. The virtual machines (VMs) are equipped with sufficient resources and an SSD. Depending on the operating system, you have different options for building and testing your software.

> **Runner Software**
>
> An overview of the currently available operating systems for GitHub Actions and the software installed in them can be found in the GitHub repository at the following link:
>
> *https://github.com/actions/virtual-environments*

The list of installed software on a runner can be impressively long. Docker and `docker-compose` also run on the VMs, which is especially useful if your software runs in containers.

Now, you may wonder if GitHub really provides unlimited compute time for your actions free of charge, which of course is not the case. For private repositories, 2,000 minutes and 500 MB per month are free of charge (in spring 2022); anything above that usage must be paid for. If your actions don't run on Linux, this time span will be significantly reduced: The Windows runner exists only for half the time; macOS, only a tenth of the time.

An alternative is to use *self-hosted runners*, which are computers you make available to perform certain actions. You would install a special GitHub program on your computer and connect it to GitHub. You can find detailed instructions for this setup by clicking **Add Runner** under **Settings • Actions** in your repository. Since runners also exist for the ARM hardware platform, a Raspberry Pi mini computer, for example, can perform this service. Your Arduino team can thus trigger automatic tests of their own hardware through GitHub Actions.

Regardless of the type of runner you run the action on, you can define the individual steps in a configuration file in the YAML Ain't Markup Language (YAML) format, which we'll cover next.

5.2.1 YAML Syntax

For configuration files in a continuous integration (CI) environment, the YAML file format has become immensely popular, in addition to other uses. Let's briefly summarize the syntax rules for YAML now:

- `---` introduces a new section.
- `#` starts a comment that extends to the end of the line.
- Strings can be expressed as `"abc"` or `'abc'`. However, these quotation marks are only mandatory in exceptional cases, for example, if the string contains special characters or can be interpreted as another YAML expression.
- Several expressions introduced with `-` form a list:

  ```
  - red
  - green
  - blue
  ```

  Alternatively, lists can be enclosed in square brackets:

  ```
  [red, green, blue]
  ```

- Associative lists (key-value pairs) are created in the format, `key: value`:

  ```
  name: Howard Hollow
  age: 37
  ```

  A space-saving variant of this format uses curly brackets:

  ```
  {name: Howard Hollow, age: 37}
  ```

- `|` introduces a text block in which the line breaks are preserved:

  ```
  codeblock: |
    Line 1
    Line 2
  ```

- > introduces a text block in which line breaks are ignored. However, empty lines are kept:

```
textblock: >
  Text that
  belongs together.

  Here begins the
  second paragraph.
```

All these elements can be nested within each other. The structure is created by indentations. Note that spaces must be used in YAML (no tabs!). When accessing the elements, the identifiers (keys) are strung together.

```
# sample.yaml file
data:
  list:
    - item1
    - item2
  key1: >
    This text is assigned to the
    'data.key1' key.
  key2: |
    code line 1
    code line 2
```

Some advanced syntax elements of YAML, which usually don't play a role in GitHub Actions, are documented at Wikipedia:

https://en.wikipedia.org/wiki/YAML

To avoid too much typing work, you can select existing actions from the GitHub Marketplace and use them in your repository, which is exactly what we'll demonstrate in the next section through a simple example.

5.2.2 Notification to Slack

As a first demonstration of GitHub Actions, let's try to send automatic notifications to the popular messenger *Slack*. If you prefer to notify Telegram or the Matrix network instead of Slack, you can simply use the appropriate action from the GitHub Marketplace.

For this purpose, we've created the repository `git-compendium/slack-notification` where we've placed an HTML file to demonstrate how it works.

To enable actions for your project, you should either click the **Actions** tab in your project's web interface or create the *.github/workflows/* folder structure in the root of your

GitHub repository. The editor in the GitHub web interface works particularly well in this case: First, it suggests possible entries, and second, it immediately flags syntax errors.

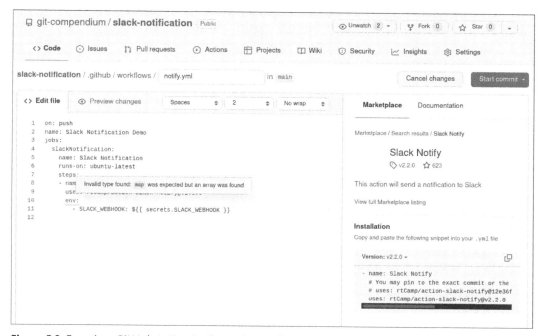

Figure 5.3 Error in a GitHub Action in the Web Interface

Let's now define the action in the *notify.yml* file, containing the following lines:

```
# git-compendium/slack-notification/.github/workflows/notify.yml
on: push
name: Slack Notification Demo
jobs:
  slackNotification:
    name: Slack Notification
    runs-on: ubuntu-latest
    steps:
    - name: Slack Notification
      uses: rtCamp/action-slack-notify@v2.2.0
      env:
        SLACK_WEBHOOK: ${{ secrets.SLACK_WEBHOOK }}
```

The file begins with the `on: push` statement, which enables the execution of the action on each `git push`. The name in the next line is displayed in the GitHub Actions overview in the web interface and should be a good description of the operations in the file. The subsequent `jobs` section may contain one or more entries that are executed in parallel or in a dependency with each other.

Each *job* runs on a runner, which in this case is Ubuntu Linux in the latest available version on GitHub (`runs-on: ubuntu-latest`). One or more `steps` are then executed on this runner. In our example, only one step starts the `action-slack-notify` action from the GitHub Marketplace. You can find these and other actions via the search function to the right of the web editor.

The action is provided with the `SLACK_WEBHOOK` environment variable, which is where you'll find the URL where GitHub must send the message for the message to show up in your *Slack channel*. You can create this URL in your Slack account settings under **Apps • Incoming Webhooks**.

To ensure that only authorized applications post messages to your Slack channel, this URL contains a security token that should remain secret and should never be found in a public repository on GitHub. Nevertheless, the action needs this address to send the messages. GitHub has provided a concept of secret variables, called *secrets*, with the scope for a repository for this purpose. You can create such variables in the **Settings** tab via the **Secrets • Actions • Repository Secrets** menu item. Once such a variable is created, even you can't view its contents any longer.

Once you've created the variable and committed and pushed the *notify.yml* file, you should receive your first notification in the Slack channel of your choice.

Figure 5.4 Notification for a Push to GitHub in Slack

5.2.3   The Continuous Integration Pipeline

While the notification in the previous section can be dismissed as a nice gimmick, we're now getting to the serious scenarios for GitHub Actions. CI is a booming area in software development. In general, CI means that all parts of an application are brought together and tested. Ideally, this approach is fully automatic and frequent (preferably after each push). GitHub Actions are predestined for running CI pipelines.

In a CI pipeline, several stages usually are passed through:

1. *Build:* The application is packed with all its components.
2. *Test:* The application goes through automatic tests.
3. *Release:* If the tests were successful, the application is saved as a new version.
4. *Deploy:* Optionally, the application can be rolled out. Generally, the automatic deploy process is only started for beta and test versions.

For this example, we created a `git-compendium/ci-first` repository with an action in the *start.yml* file. The first step is to check the *index.html* file in this repository for syntax errors. We'll use the program `prettier` for this purpose, which formats HTML files and issues a corresponding message in case of errors.

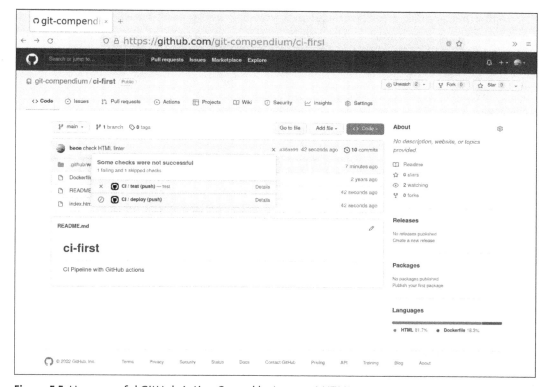

Figure 5.5 Unsuccessful GitHub Action Caused by Incorrect HTML

Since this program is a module from the Node.js environment, you can install it using `npx prettier` and run it immediately. The entire process is logged in the *start.yml* file in the newly created directory.

```
# File: ci-first/.github/workflows/start.yml
name: CI
on:
  push:
    branches: [ main ]
```

```
jobs:
  test:
    runs-on: ubuntu-latest
    steps:
    - uses: actions/checkout@v2
    - name: Check syntax of html files
      run: npx prettier *.html
```

Now, let's verify that `prettier` works by adding a bug to the *index.html* file, committing the changes, and pushing them to GitHub. In our case, we removed the <h1> tag, which thus invalidates the closing </h1>.

But that's not all: After successful tests, you can now upload your website to the server. For this task, you must create another job named `deploy` that will also be run on the Ubuntu Linux system. We want to copy the HTML file via the SSH protocol to the server of your choice using the `rsync` program.

Since the execution of the jobs of an action normally runs in parallel, you must use the `needs: test` statement now to specify that the first job must be successfully completed. The short script is executed in the Linux `bash` interpreter and recorded in multiple lines, which enables the `run: |` statement in YAML syntax. Another important point in this job is the environment variable `SSH_KEY`. This variable contains an SSH private key, the secret key that gives you SSH access to the server where the HTML file is to be copied.

For our deploy workflow, ideally, you would set up a separate user on the server; let's call it `deploy`. On this server, you should store the public part of the SSH key, which allows logon with these credentials. For our example, the user only needs write permissions in the */var/www/test* folder to which the HTML files are copied.

The Bash script starts by checking whether the ~/.ssh folder already exists on the Ubuntu runner and creates the folder if necessary. Then, the secret key is copied to a file in that folder, and the file permissions are restricted so that only the current user can read the file. Finally, the `rsync` command is executed. To make `rsync` pass the correct SSH key without asking for confirmation of the server's authenticity, the parameters -i ~/.ssh/key and -o StrictHostKeyChecking=no are passed when called.

```
# File: ci-first/.github/workflows/start.yml (continued)
  deploy:
    runs-on: ubuntu-latest
    needs: test
    steps:
    - uses: actions/checkout@v2
    - name: Deploy HTML with rsync
      shell: bash
      env:
```

```
    SSH_KEY: ${{ secrets.SSHKEY }}
  run: |
    if [ ! -d ~/.ssh ]; then mkdir ~/.ssh; fi
    echo "$SSH_KEY" > ~/.ssh/key
    chmod 600 ~/.ssh/key
    rsync -rv --exclude=.git \
      -e "ssh -i ~/.ssh/key -o StrictHostKeyChecking=no" \
      $GITHUB_WORKSPACE/ deploy@server.com:/var/www/test/
```

As in the previous section, we'll also use a GitHub secret in this case. The secret SSH key available in the SSH_KEY environment variable in the script that originates from such a GitHub variable. You can create it via **Settings • Secrets** with the name "SSHKEY" and copy the secret part of the SSH key into the text field.

Figure 5.6 GitHub Secrets in the "ci-first" Repository

The workflow we've presented is admittedly a simplified representation of a productive CI/continuous deployment (CD) pipeline. Even for simple web applications, a now common practice to optimize and package the code. Deployment is often not done via SSH but instead delivered in a Docker container. We'll describe this procedure in the following section.

To troubleshoot complex actions, you can trace each step in the web interface and initiate a restart, if necessary. In the **View raw logs** context menu, you can find detailed messages about each step.

Figure 5.7 Troubleshooting an Unsuccessful GitHub Action

Finally, a note about repositories you create with a fork from another repository: In these cases, GitHub disables actions by default. Although the configuration files are provided, in the **Actions** tab, you'll find a note that they won't be executed unless you manually confirm the operation.

5.3   Package Manager (GitHub Packages)

The CI technique presented in the previous section often ends with the creation of software packages. Different programming languages use different formats for this purpose and are often supported by a package manager that takes care of dependencies and updates. In the Node.js environment, for example, this package manager is npm (which Microsoft also acquired in 2020 and thus fits well into the "family"). For C#, *NuGet* is mostly used, and in the Java environment, the preferred tool is currently *Maven*. Container technology extends the concept of packages to include the necessary parts of an operating system, which is packaged with the software in the container images.

To access the packages in the build process of your application, they're stored on central servers from where package managers load them as needed. For Docker, this location is the *Docker Hub* (*https://hub.docker.com*), whereas for npm, it's the *NPM Registry* (*https://www.npmjs.com*). For developers, this scenario means they must manage another, perhaps paid account with the credentials for this server.

GitHub aims to unify all software development functions on one platform as much as possible and has therefore started to integrate a repository for common package formats into every GitHub repository. You can place your Docker, npm, Maven, RubyGems, or NuGet packages directly in the repository where the source code for them resides. With GitHub's large server infrastructure in the background, this inclusion of packages also makes a lot of sense because a reliable internet connection is absolutely important for such central software sites.

We'll use GitHub Actions to package a simple Node.js application into a Docker image, automatically test it, and, if the tests are successful, save it as a new version in the GitHub Docker Package Manager.

5.3.1   Example

The repository we created for this example is called `git-compendium/ci-docker`, and it contains the Node.js and HTML code for a simple online image database. The *test/* folder contains an end-to-end test that fully tests the application's functionality. We use the Node.js library *testcafe* for this purpose:

```
# File: ci-docker/test/e2e.js
import { Selector } from 'testcafe';

fixture `Webpage`
  .page('http://localhost:3001/')

test(`Header 1 on main page`, async t => {
  const h1 = Selector('h1');
  await t
    .expect(h1.exists).ok()
    .expect(h1.textContent).eql('Simple picture db');
})

test(`Upload picture with exif date check`, async t => {
  const pics = Selector('#pics>li')
  const picDate = Selector('#pics>li>span')
  await t
    .setFilesToUpload('input[type="file"]', [
      'demo.jpg'
    ])
    .expect(pics.count).eql(1)
    .expect(picDate.textContent).eql('Sat Feb 12 2022')
})
```

```
test(`Delete picture`, async t => {
  const pics = Selector('#pics>li')
  await t
    .click('#pics>li>button')
    .expect(pics.count).eql(0)
})
```

The first of the three tests is quite simple: We're searching for the heading of the first category (h1), checking if the element exists on the page, and then comparing the text with the *Simple picture db* string. More interesting is the second test, where the *demo.jpg* image is uploaded. The image is also located in the *test* folder and therefore doesn't need a path specification. For this test to be successful, the number of list items after upload must be exactly one, and the date entry on the image must be February 12, 2022. This date is read from the metadata generated by the camera, in the *exchangeable image file format (Exif)*. In the last test, the delete button next to the image is clicked, and the number of list entries must be zero again afterwards.

If you start the web application locally (npm start), you can also run the tests on your computer before asking a runner to do it. You'll see the Firefox browser open and run the tests in order.

```
> npx testcafe firefox test/e2e.js
Running tests in:
- Firefox 97.0 / Linux 0.0

Webpage
✓ Header 1 on main page
✓ Upload picture with exif date check
✓ Delete picture


3 passed (1s)
~/work/git/ci-docker main >
```

Figure 5.8 Output of End-to-End Tests in the Console

Everything so far has been pretty simple, but how can the GitHub action running on some VM in a data center control a browser with these statements, and where is the web service running that is supposed to be tested? testcafe can launch a browser in *headless* mode, so it doesn't need a connected screen to run the tests. In the *package.json* file, we've added the entry for the test:

```
"scripts": {
  "test": "testcafe firefox:headless test/e2e.js"
  ...
},
```

The Firefox browser is already installed on the *runner* we use with Ubuntu. In the following section, we'll show you how to start the web service on the runner at http://localhost:3001.

The GitHub action will perform the following steps:

1. Check out the source code

2. Create a Docker image for production use, tag it as a test image, and upload it to the GitHub Docker registry

3. Launch a Docker image and test it using the end-to-end tests shown

4. In the event of successful tests, tag the Docker image as `latest` and upload it again to the GitHub Docker registry

The advantage of this approach is that the Docker image created for production runs through the tests and can be deployed unchanged upon successful completion. We start with the GitHub action, as you already know from the previous sections:

```
# File: ci-docker/.github/workflows/main.yml
name: CI/CD with docker
on:
  push:
    branches: [ main ]
env:
  API_IMG_TEST: "ghcr.io/git-compendium/ci-docker/api:test"
  API_IMG_STABLE: "ghcr.io/git-compendium/ci-docker/api:latest"
```

The only new element in this case is that we'll create two environment variables named `API_IMG_TEST` and `API_IMG_STABLE` at the top level. They contain the server name of the GitHub Docker registry and the path to our repository in addition to the name of the image (`api`) and the version (`latest` and `test`, respectively) separated by a colon. The action is executed on every push to the main branch. Then, three `jobs` are run, first to create and upload the Docker test image, then to carry out the test, and finally to tag the Docker production image (`latest`). To prevent the jobs from running in parallel, the test and publish jobs each contain the `needs` statement with a reference to the previous job.

```
# File: ci-docker/.github/workflows/main.yml (continued)
jobs:
  build:
    runs-on: ubuntu-latest
    steps:
      - uses: actions/checkout@v2
      - name: Build docker image
        run: docker build -t "${API_IMG_TEST}" .
      - name: Log in to registry
        run: |
          echo "${{ secrets.GITHUB_TOKEN }}" |\
            docker login ghcr.io -u ${{ github.actor }} \
            --password-stdin
```

```
      - name: Push docker image
        run: docker push "${API_IMG_TEST}"
  test:
    needs: build
    runs-on: ubuntu-latest
    services:
      api:
        image: ghcr.io/git-compendium/ci-docker/api:test
        ports:
          - 3001:3001
    steps:
      - uses: actions/checkout@v2
      - name: test running container
        run: |
          npm install
          npm test
  publish:
    runs-on: ubuntu-latest
    needs: test
    steps:
      - name: Log in to registry
        run: |
          echo "${{ secrets.GITHUB_TOKEN }}" |\
            docker login ghcr.io -u ${{ github.actor }} \
            --password-stdin
      - name: Tag docker image
        run: |
          docker pull "${API_IMG_TEST}"
          docker tag "${API_IMG_TEST}" "${API_IMG_STABLE}"
          docker push "${API_IMG_STABLE}"
```

In the build job, the source code is first checked out on a current Ubuntu Linux version, and then the Docker test image is created using docker build. To upload the image to the GitHub Docker registry, we need to log on first (docker login ghcr.io). The variables used for the user name (github.actor) and the secret token (secrets.GITHUB_TOKEN) are automatically available on each runner.

The test job contains the exciting part: Now, we'll start a service that loads our Docker image from the GitHub Docker registry and connects port 3001 on the container to the same port on the runner. Unfortunately, in the current version of GitHub Actions, we couldn't also use the variable name of the test image in the service definition, but GitHub may have resolved this problem by the time you read this.

In parallel with the start of the service, the source code is checked out, and npm install is used to install the necessary modules (including those required for development).

Then, the end-to-end tests are started on the runner using npm test. The port mapping of 3001:3001 makes the web service accessible at *http://localhost:3001*. Note that our Docker image only contains the necessary files for production operation, but not the environment for end-to-end testing.

The final publish job no longer needs the source code. Simply log on to the GitHub Docker registry again, download the successfully tested image, and tag it with the lat-est tag. The final push uploads the tag to the registry, where it replaces the image previously marked as latest. If you've now acquired a taste for using Docker, you should not skip Chapter 6, Section 6.4.

Figure 5.9 Successful GitHub Action in the "ci-docker" Repository

5.4   Automatic Security Scans

The advance of automation in software development makes detecting problems in the source code almost automatic. This automation works quite well, for example, with included libraries that are known to have a security gap. Also, security tokens or passwords that were forgotten in the source code can be found automatically with appropriate tools. GitHub can check the structure of tokens from 20 cloud service providers and will notify you if found.

In this section, we'll create a representational state transfer (REST) application programming interface (API) based on Node.js and use GitHub security features.

5.4.1   Node.js Security

Especially in a Node.js environment, the concept of small, reusable modules is widely used. The dependency of the modules on each other often means that you quickly have more than 100 modules in use, even for applications that aren't particularly large. Those who take security updates seriously will be happy to use a system that sends automated warnings for all modules in use, which is where GitHub's security scanners come into play.

We'll use the small example from the previous section. Our example consists of a REST backend that sends and receives data in JavaScript Object Notation (JSON) format to and from the frontend. You can upload images via an HTML page, which will be checked for metadata (*Exif tags*) and then stored in a SQLite database. To run the example, you only need the Node.js runtime. For this purpose, you must install the associated Node.js modules using the npm install command and start the server via npm start. After that step, the web server should be running on port 3001, and you can reach the simple web page at *http://localhost:3001*.

The backend code where the images are parsed uses several Node.js modules, such as the following:

- better-sqlite3 communicates with the local database.
- debug is the Node.js debugging module.
- exif-parser reads the metadata from the images.
- express simplifies HTTP communication.
- jimp places a preview image in the database.
- multer extracts the files from the HTTP post request.
- uuid generates universally unique identifiers (UUIDs) according to RFC 4122.

For development, we also use the nodemon module, which can automatically restart the backend when changes are made to the source code, and testcafe for end-to-end testing of the software. Since these modules themselves use other modules, after calling npm install, you go from 9 packages installed, to over 700, as the npm command outputs:

```
added 739 packages, and audited 740 packages in 4s
```

A security gap appearing in one of these packages would be no big surprise. Of course, this vulnerability was anticipated by Node.js developers, which is why there has been an *auditing function* included in the npm command for some time. Using npm audit, your Node.js project is scanned for modules with known security issues, and with the npm audit fix extension, these issues can even often be fixed automatically (provided the new version doesn't contain incompatible changes).

Undoubtedly a valuable tool, npm requires you initiate processes yourself. GitHub automatically handles this process for you and sends you alerts via email and in your GitHub Notification Center.

Figure 5.10 Security Warnings in the GitHub Repository

But GitHub can do even more: If a security gap is found and an updated package is available that's marked as compatible, GitHub will generate a pull request. For this purpose, an automated running program (also referred to as a *bot*) creates a branch in your repository, runs the update there, and pushes the branch to GitHub with a pull request.

Let's demonstrate this concept with a concrete example: For the image database, we'll install the widely used lodash module, which provides some convenience functions for objects and arrays in JavaScript. The version we use of the lodash module (4.17.20) has a security gap that can be used to inject code.

After the push, the automatic scanner finds the problem and checks for a possible update. In the current version 4.17.21, the problem has been fixed, and no incompatibilities exist with the old version, according to the developers of the module. The dependabot user (GitHub's automatic package update program) creates the dependabot/npm_and_yarn/lodash-4.17.21 branch and performs the module update there. Then, the pull request is created, and you'll receive two emails: one containing the notice of the security problem and a second one containing the pull request.

When you now run git pull on your local computer, the newly created branch is loaded from GitHub and created locally:

```
git pull
```

```
remote: Enumerating objects: 5, done.
remote: Counting objects: 100% (5/5), done.
remote: Compressing objects: 100% (3/3), done.
remote: Total 3 (delta 2), reused 0 (delta 0), pack-reused 0
Unpacking objects: 100% (3/3), 1000 bytes | 90.00 KiB/s, done.
```

```
From github.com:git-compendium/npm-security
* [new branch]          dependabot/npm_and_yarn/lodash-4.17.21 ->
origin/dependabot/npm_and_yarn/lodash-4.17.21
```

We can now pull in the pull request as usual, either via the web interface or by merging the local branch with the local main branch and then pushing. When merging via the web interface, dependabot cleans up and deletes the branch that's no longer needed.

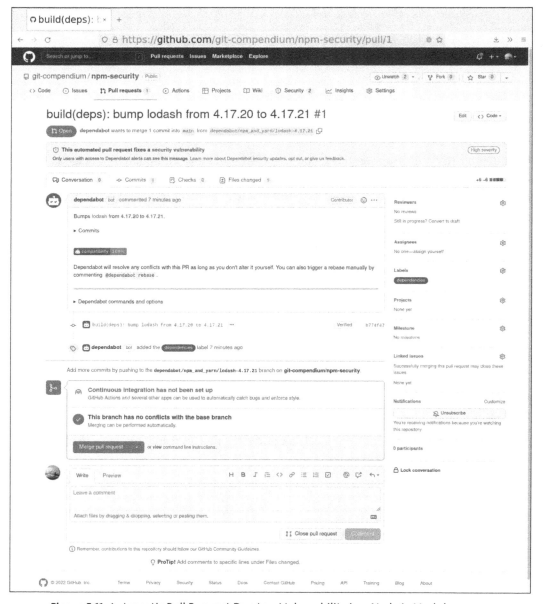

Figure 5.11 Automatic Pull Request Due to a Vulnerability in a Node.js Module

dependabot has even more tricks up its sleeve: Before we noticed the security warning from GitHub, perhaps we had continued working on the project and installed the additional Node.js module moment. After pushing the new version to GitHub, we received the following message in the console about a problem in our repository:

```
git push

  Counting objects: 7, done.
  ...
  remote: Resolving deltas: 100% (3/3), completed with 3 local...
  remote:
  remote: GitHub found 2 vulnerabilities on
  git-compendium/npm-security's default branch (1 high,
  1 moderate). To find out more, visit:
  remote:   https://github.com/git-compendium/npm-security/secu...
  ...
```

But what will happen to the existing pull request? During our installation of the moment module, the *package.json* and *package-lock.json* files, which are responsible for module management, have changed. So, the pull request, which modifies the same files, can't be brought in easily anymore. dependabot also takes care of this problem by performing an automatic rebase of the dependabot/npm_and_yarn/lodash-4.17.21 branch to the new main branch.

5.5   Other GitHub Features

In this section, we'll briefly point out some other GitHub features, without describing their application in great detail.

5.5.1   Collaboration

One of the great merits of the GitHub platform has undoubtedly been its simple process for developers to contribute code to projects. Even without in-depth knowledge of branches and merges, an existing project can be modified and incorporated as a clear pull request. If the project manager approves the change, only a few clicks in the web interface are required for the new function to be adopted. The commit messages of the contributing developer are preserved. You can find more information about forks and pull requests in Chapter 2, Section 2.7.

5.5.2   Issues

In modern software development, with multiple people involved, an issue tracking or bug tracking system is considered an absolute must. Users can use this system to express wishes for further development and to report bugs. Issues in GitHub are labeled and can be assigned to *milestones*.

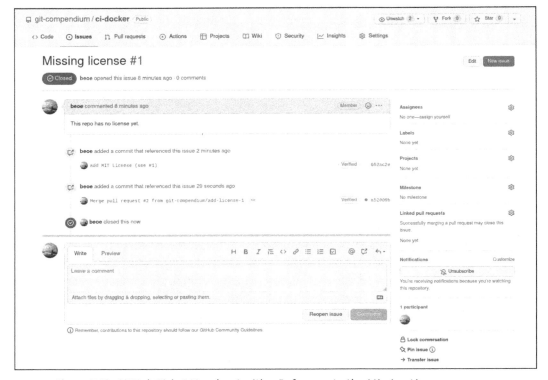

Figure 5.12 GitHub Ticket Number 1 with a Reference to the Missing License

A valuable characteristic of this feature is the ability to reference issues via keywords in the text of the commit message. For example, let's say your message reads:

```
add MIT License (see #1)
```

You'll now see a link in your commit message in the GitHub web interface. Additionally, GitHub creates an entry in the ticket with the number 2, indicating that the ticket was mentioned in a commit. Of course, a link will be created to the ticket as well.

Since 2016, GitHub only supports the English language for menus and all other generated text. You can of course write your commit messages in another language, but the rest of GitHub remains in English. In larger projects and public projects, therefore, common practice is to formulate commit messages in English.

5.5.3   Discussions and Teams

The opportunity to comment on issues is often used so extensively that GitHub's developers felt the platform needed its own area for discussion.

GitHub Discussions is a relatively new component that works at the team level. Teams can be created in GitHub underneath an organization and provide the option of a nested structure. For example, you might have a team of *employees* and below that other teams such as *IT staff* and *sales*, each of which are subgroups of employees. Using teams, you can quickly manage access to individual GitHub repositories. Entire teams can be given read-only access or full access.

During discussions, you can simply mention people or other teams (@ syntax). Issues and pull requests are also linked if you add a # prefix to the corresponding number. Access is restricted to the repositories and teams assigned to the team.

Now, of course, you might rightly ask if there aren't already enough other discussion forums on the internet and whether GitHub really needed to create another one. However, the interlocking with the source code and ease with which you can link issues and pull requests are actually quite helpful during discussions. If the people involved are already registered on GitHub anyway, then the forum is a useful extension.

5.5.4   Wiki

The traditional notebook has also found its counterpart in the digital world with the wiki. For projects where people aren't working in the same area but from remote places, a wiki enables simultaneous access for everyone and can serve as a way to share common knowledge. Important for the success of such electronic documents is that you follow a certain structure, but a wiki can also be handled simply, just like a notebook where you can quickly jot something down.

In this context, wikis allow simple formatting, linking to each other, and incorporating graphics (often screenshots for technical documents). Each GitHub repository can be commented and documented via a wiki integrated into the interface. A big advantage of this interface is that you don't have to search for the documents because one click on the **Wiki** tab helps you to find the information you need. GitHub doesn't place the files in your Git repository; it creates its own Git repository for them, with the same name as the GitHub repository plus the `.wiki` extension.

The easiest way to use this wiki feature is directly in the browser. GitHub provides a toolbar for simple formatting, images, and links. If you prefer to edit the wiki in an editor on your computer, you can check out, modify, commit, and push the corresponding wiki Git repository locally. Note that you run the risk of merge conflicts if both workflows are used at the same time.

As a format for text documents of all kinds, Markdown has become widely accepted. GitHub also suggests writing the wiki pages in this format by default but isn't limited to it. You can also write your wiki in *AsciiDoc*, *reStructuredText*, or another format.

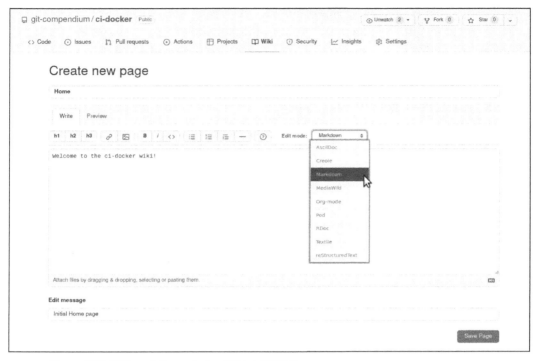

Figure 5.13 Different Formats for GitHub Wiki Pages

Limited Collaboration in the Wiki

Especially in public GitHub projects, a fundamental disadvantage of the wiki function becomes obvious: The documentation contained there is outside the actual repository. This separation makes having external people help with the documentation difficult because the usual procedure (i.e., fork first, pull request later) isn't possible. Stack Overflow describes a possible way out of this dilemma:

https://stackoverflow.com/questions/10642928

Alternatively, you should consider foregoing the wiki and simply creating documentation in Markdown files in a directory of your repository (usually, the *doc* directory).

5.5.5   Gists

What wikis are to notes, *gists* are to program code snippets and configuration files. The syntax highlighting, colored according to the file type, makes reading easier. Logged on users can comment directly below a gist or award a gist a star. Another handy feature includes embedding a gist via a JavaScript snippet that can be copied from the web interface. (Especially in tech blogs, you'll see this form of linking.)

Figure 5.14 Short JavaScript File as a GitHub Gist

5.5.6   GitHub Pages

The wikis mentioned earlier are a great way to quickly take notes. However, the layout and interaction options with the resulting web pages are limited.

GitHub Pages also enables you to publish entire websites to your GitHub account on the web. Activating this module is quite simple: Simply create a GitHub repository with the name `username.github.io` in your account, and soon the files in this repository will be accessible at the web address *https://username.github.io*. Make sure your GitHub user name is spelled exactly the same in the repository name!

Especially for software developers, one great advantage is that the website is managed in a Git repository just like the source code of the software. Although you may not have any databases available now, as is often the case with web hosting packages, a frontend web application based on *Vue.js*, *Angular*, or *React* runs without problem.

If you prefer to create the website for your project using less elaborate means, you can use a *static site generator*. These programs use templates (*themes*) to convert Markdown to HTML files. You can also create navigation elements or loop structured data (for example, CSV or JSON). Well-known representatives of this category are *Hugo*, *Hexo*, or *Jekyll*, the latter being particularly interesting in the context of GitHub. In fact, in your project website settings, you can select a Jekyll theme, which will convert all Markdown files to your website using the Jekyll program.

More details about Jekyll can be found in our sample repository and on the Jekyll website:

- *https://github.com/git-compendium/git-compendium.github.io*
- *https://jekyllrb.com*

Figure 5.15 GitHub Pages Settings with a Theme for Jekyll

GitHub Pages aren't limited to the single repository `username.github.io`. You can enable GitHub Pages in any of your GitHub repositories. You can find the setting under **Settings • Pages**, where you can choose whether the HTML or Markdown files should be located in the *docs* subfolder or in the main repository directory. If you enable a repository other than *username.github.io* for GitHub Pages, the files will be available at the following address: *https://username.github.io/repositoryname*.

> **Custom Domain Names**
>
> GitHub provides the option to have your own domains reference GitHub Pages. For this task, you must adjust the Domain Name System (DNS) settings at your DNS provider accordingly. You can find information on this topic at the following link:
>
> *https://docs.github.com/en/pages/configuring-a-custom-domain-for-your-github-pages-site*

5.6   GitHub Command-Line Interface

Throughout this chapter, we've repeated that GitHub is a web platform for managing your Git repositories—what's a command-line interface (CLI) doing here now? *GitHub CLI* is still a young project that enables you to perform frequently used operations on GitHub from the console. The CLI clearly aimed at power users (i.e., users who work with the GitHub platform a great deal).

Currently, you can use the gh command to process issues, pull requests, and repositories. If you're in a repository checked out from GitHub when you invoke the command, all commands will work for that repository; alternatively, you can select a repository from any directory using the -D <user/repo> option.

"hub" versus "gh"

In addition to the GitHub CLI, a similar project called hub has its roots in the early days of GitHub, provides significantly more functionality, and is correspondingly popular:

https://github.com/github/hub

However, hub takes the approach of integrating the git command into hub. Over time, this approach has turned out to be a misguided decision: Again and again, incompatibilities occurred after git updates, which could only be fixed with great effort. The main developer of both tools described how he saw the future of both projects, now that his focus was completely on the new CLI, at the following blog post:

https://mislav.net/2020/01/github-cli

For this reason, hub isn't expected to have much of a future. Accordingly, we refrain from documenting its functions further.

5.6.1   Installation

The installation of this program, written in the Go programming language, is quite simple: You can simply download the binary for your platform from its GitHub page *https://github.com/cli/cli/releases* and copy it to your operating system's search path. Alternatively, installation packages also exist for the common operating systems.

Figure 5.16 GitHub CLI Authentication in the Web Browser

When using the CLI for the first time, you must log on with the gh auth logon command and grant the program the right to access your GitHub account, which can conveniently be achieved via a web browser. At the command line, you'll be presented with a one-time code that you must enter into the web browser to subsequently authorize the program.

5.6.2   Examples of Use

Once installation and authentication are complete, you can create a new GitHub repository using a tiny command:

```
gh repo create

    ? What would you like to do?
      Create a new repository on GitHub from scratch
    ? Repository name
      git-compendium/gh-cli
    ? Description
      gh command test
    ? Visibility
      Public
    ? Would you like to add a .gitignore?
      No
    ? Would you like to add a license?
      Yes
    ? Choose a license MIT License
      MIT
    ? This will create "git-compendium/gh-cli" as a public
    repository on GitHub. Continue? Yes
    - Created repository git-compendium/gh-cli on GitHub
    ? Clone the new repository locally?
      Yes
    Cloning into 'gh-cli'...
    ...
```

The interactive dialog guides you through the necessary specifications before the command is executed. Alternatively, you can skip this dialog by specifying the repository name directly at the command line and adding the necessary --public switch. Now, let's create your first commit in this repository. We've agreed that a license file should be created in the repository. This choice has an advantage in that, unlike an empty repository, the main branch has already been created.

Now, create an initial issue for the new repository with the following command:

```
gh issue create -t "Create README.md" \
  -b "Add project description in markdown file"

  Creating issue in git-compendium/gh-cli
  https://github.com/git-compendium/gh-cli/issues/1
```

Create the requested *README.md* file in your repository on a new add-readme branch and then commit and push the branch. Next, create a pull request with the CLI on this branch with the following command:

```
gh pr create

  Creating pull request for add-readme into main in git-compen...

  ? Title fix: #1 add README
  ? Body <Received>
  ? What's next? Submit
  https://github.com/git-compendium/gh-cli/pull/2
```

The title is taken from the commit message, in this case with the reference to the issue (#1). If the pull request is good, the branch can be merged into the main branch using the git command.

```
git merge add-readme     # on the main branch

  Updating 2cc0bfd..5aad2c3
  Fast-forward
  README.md | 3 +++
  1 file changed, 3 insertions(+)
  create mode 100644 README.md
```

When you now push the main branch, GitHub detects that the pull request was successful and closes it automatically. In addition, our commit message starts another flow. Since the message starts with fix: #1, the associated issue 1 is also automatically closed.

In the web interface, you'll see that the full documentation for this issue has been logged, including the issue, pull request, and merge link.

If you're not a huge fan of the command line, you may find this manual work a bit excessive and prefer to create issues in the web browser, which you probably have open anyway during your daily work.

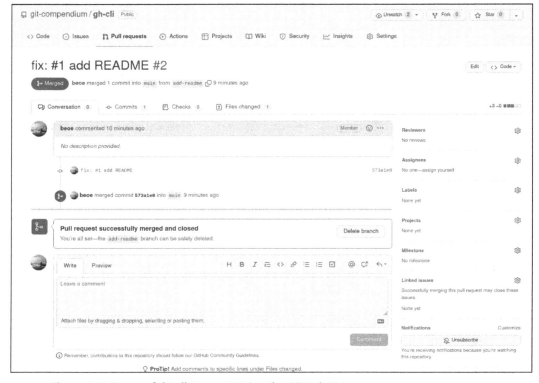

Figure 5.17 Successful Pull Request Using the GitHub CLI

5.7   Codespaces

Finally, we'd like to introduce you to *codespaces* in this chapter. This concept is still fairly new, but its potential shouldn't be underestimated.

Imagine the weekend has arrived, and you're on the slopes in perfect conditions at the ski resort of your choice. Unfortunately, a call from one of your co-workers disturbs you, pointing out that a small change on Friday evening was probably not a great idea after all because the project's website just stopped working. You didn't even bring a laptop with you, and if the bug needs to be fixed quickly, you must cancel your ski trip now. Even if you could find a computer somewhere in the ski resort, installing the development environment with all the necessary tools is unrealistic.

Now is when GitHub Codespaces could come into play: This tool provides you with a complete development environment including editor (VS Code) in the web browser, and you can operate it from your cell phone as well. The screenshot shown in Figure 5.18 has actually been taken from the cell phone of one of the authors. Of course, you can't write large blocks of code this way, but to fix a typo and run simple commands like git add, git commit, and git push, all is well and good.

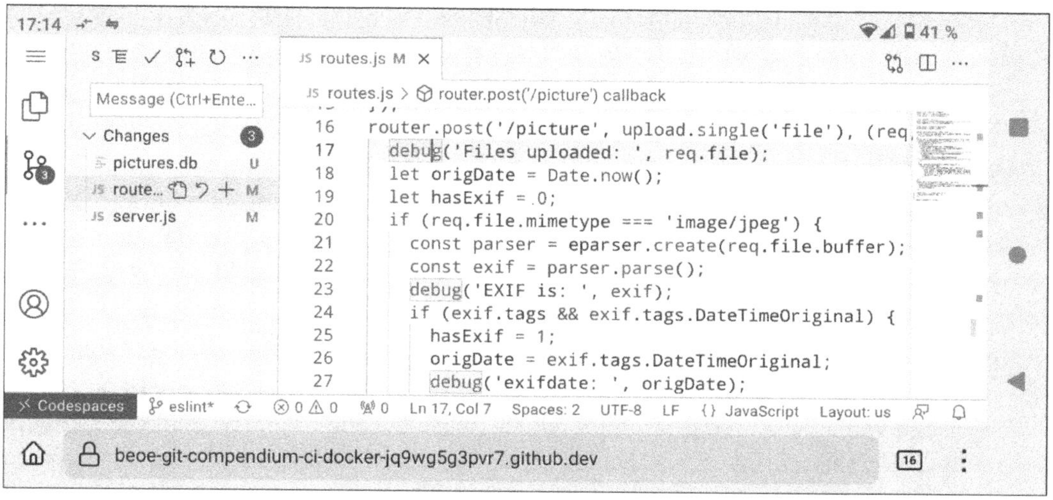

Figure 5.18 GitHub Codespaces on an Android Cell Phone

What at first seems a bit like magic is made possible by virtualization and Docker containers. Starting a codespace on GitHub creates a virtual Linux environment for your project, where you even have access to a real shell (command line).

Figure 5.19 GitHub Codespaces

The botched ski trip scenario we described was probably not the main motive behind this development. Rather, the focus of codespaces is to provide a unified and complete development environment for all team members. Especially for complex projects that use different programming languages or frameworks, this unified experience can save a lot of time.

For our simple Node.js example, the required modules were automatically installed, and the program was started using npm start. Port forwarding (through port 3001) is even implemented in such a way that the website is accessible with valid HTTPS encryption on a subdomain of githubpreview.dev.

GitHub/Microsoft doesn't give you this computing power for free, of course. Billing for your team or enterprise account is based on time and disk space used and can be roughly calculated using an online calculator on the GitHub website. In the spring of 2022, the service was still available for free for individual accounts, but the help pages stated that the service could be used for no charge at all. We can't say how pricing will look in the future.

Dev Containers

A detailed treatment of the configuration of codespaces is beyond the scope of this book. If this use case sounds interesting to you, we recommend reviewing the GitHub help pages for setting up *dev containers*, as GitHub calls its virtual environments:

https://docs.github.com/en/codespaces

Chapter 6
GitLab

GitLab is a direct competitor to GitHub, which we've described in detail in Chapter 5. Both platforms provide a variety of useful tools for software development, with the central element in both cases being a Git repository.

A significant difference between the two rivals is that GitLab maintains the source code of the application publicly on the internet under an open-source license (as a project on its own platform, of course). Unlike GitHub, therefore, you can run a GitLab server in your own data center (*on-premise*), which might be a decisive factor for companies that need to decide on a specific software.

Figure 6.1 First Project in GitLab Based on a Template from Node.js Express

At first glance, GitLab's web interface is quite different from the one you may know from GitHub. On closer inspection, an essential difference stands out: In GitLab, the central menu is placed vertically on the left, whereas it's located horizontally above the main content in GitHub. For us as users, the competition has its advantages: Both platforms are constantly outdoing each other with new features, which are often provided free of charge.

But before we dive into the technical details of the GitLab platform, we'd like to spend a few words about the extraordinary company that is GitLab. Since the first release in 2011, the GitLab program (written in the Ruby on Rails programming language, by the way) was available as an open-source software.

In keeping with the spirit of the times, the founders considered it normal for tools to be available to developers in source code. As the popularity of the software grew, an enterprise version and a community version were developed, which is apparently a veritable business model for the company: GitLab says it had more than 1,500 employees from 65 countries by spring 2022, but no office building. Everyone on the team works remotely, making GitLab the largest company in the world to operate exclusively via remote work.

Another unusual circumstance for a company of this size is the transparency in software development and the rapid development cycles. *Patch-level updates* occur several times a week in some cases, and a new *minor release* occurs every month on the 22nd, which is an impressive feat given the scope of the software.

6.1   On-Premise versus Cloud

As we mentioned earlier, probably the biggest difference between GitLab and GitHub is that you can install the GitLab platform, the server for managing Git projects, by yourself. You can then use the software for the development of your commercial or open-source projects without your data falling into foreign hands.

If you decide to use a self-hosted GitLab instance, we assume that you already have server administration experience. Thus, you're aware of the amount of work required to keep a server running securely. GitLab consists of several components that must run on one or more servers:

- Web application based on Ruby on Rails
- PostgreSQL database server
- SSH server
- Gitaly server (a quasi-upstream Git server)
- Redis database server
- Nginx web server

Further services are necessary for the operation of GitLab. If you're still not deterred, here's the good news: GitLab provides different installation variants that work easily and quickly. All variants have been designed for Linux systems, and operation on Windows isn't intended.

6.2 Installation

In this section, we'll walk you through installing a GitLab server on your own hardware step by step. To avoid difficulties as much as possible, we recommend a dedicated server or an appropriate cloud instance that is reserved exclusively for GitLab. You can rent a virtual server that meets the hardware requirements for a few dollars per month. In this section, we'll describe the recommended installation method using the operating system's package manager; however, you can also run GitLab as a Docker container or compile it from the source code.

The (virtual) hardware for our test server has the following key data:

- 2 (v) CPUs
- 4 GB RAM
- 40 GB SSD

Of course, your server must be accessible via the internet and should have a valid Domain Name System (DNS) record because of transmissions are encrypted. We'll use `gitlab.git-compendium.info` for this purpose. Our operating system is Ubuntu 20.04, which is officially supported with packages from GitLab alongside Debian, CentOS, and openSUSE.

Cloud Installation

GitLab also provides images and installation instructions for self-hosted GitLab instances in the cloud. Whether through Microsoft Azure, Google, or Amazon or in an existing Kubernetes cluster, the instructions on the GitLab website are quite detailed and are available at the following link:

https://about.gitlab.com/install

From many years of experience, we're used to installing complex systems and know the time involved. For this reason, we were astonished when we got GitLab running and fully operational with valid SSL certificates on our server in less than 5 minutes and in only one installation attempt.

First, you must install the necessary add-on packages and configure `postfix` to allow your server to send email. GitLab needs the email functionality for notifications, especially for resetting passwords.

```
sudo apt update
sudo apt install curl openssh-server ca-certificates postfix
```

We'll use `gitlab.git-compendium.info` as the system mail name in the `postfix` configuration, which allows for the sent emails to have `gitlab@gitlab.git-compendium.info` as the sender. Next, you must add the GitLab packages directory to your package manager. GitLab has a small shell script that will do this step for you automatically:

```
curl https://packages.gitlab.com/install/repositories/gitlab/\
  gitlab-ee/script.deb.sh | sudo bash
```

Note that the URL must be written on one line, of course. The APT package manager has been extended with the entry /etc/apt/sources.list.d/gitlab_gitlab-ee.list. In addition, the script updated the local package cache.

Finally, enter the following command:

```
sudo EXTERNAL_URL="https://gitlab.git-compendium.info" apt-get \
  install gitlab-ee
```

At this point, you've started the installation process. All components for the system are packed into one package (of over 800 MB). Now is a good time to grab a cup of coffee because unpacking the files, initializing the databases, and creating the certificates will take a few minutes. In the console window, you can closely follow the progress of the installation, with important information highlighted in color. Among the final output on the console, you'll see the following note that the initial password is in a file on your server:

```
Notes:
Default admin account has been configured with following details:
Username: root
Password: You didn't opt-in to print initial root password to
STDOUT.
Password stored to /etc/gitlab/initial_root_password. This file
will be cleaned up in first reconfigure run after 24 hours.
```

Next, open *https://gitlab.git-compendium.info* in your browser or the address you used during the installation.

On the start page, you must use the password stored in the file for the administrator account with the user name root.

Perhaps you noticed the **Register now** link in the logon window? After the default installation, users can create an account on your new server. If you don't want this feature available, you should log on as the root user and disable the function under **Menu • Admin • Settings • General • Sign-up restrictions**. GitLab also indicates this condition clearly in the user interface (UI).

Now, you can create a first user in your GitLab instance. (We recommend that you don't use the root user for normal work with GitLab.) After logging on with your own user, GitLab alerts you that you haven't stored an SSH key yet. Your GitLab instance is now fully operational.

Figure 6.2 First Logon to the Newly Created GitLab Instance

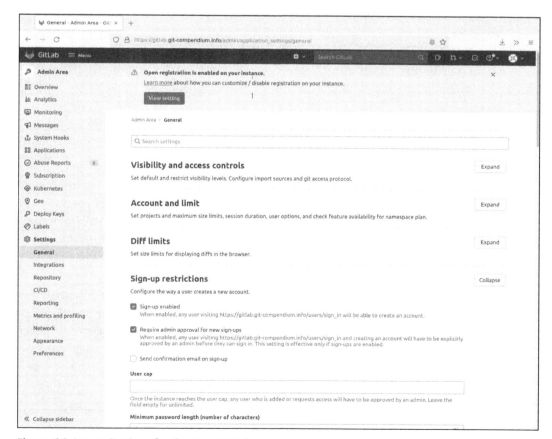

Figure 6.3 Logon Settings for the New GitLab Instance

6.2.1   Installing GitLab Runner

As a final step of the installation, we'll show you how to install and activate *GitLab Runner*. The continuous integration (CI) pipelines are an outstanding feature of GitLab. Basically, pipelines aren't unlike Git hooks. Upon closer inspection, however, you'll quickly see that pipelines are far more flexible and powerful. In a pipeline, different sections (*jobs*) are executed, either simultaneously or sequentially, and jobs can be logically linked to the result of other sections.

Pipelines aren't executed directly on the GitLab instance but instead operate on any computer, the *runner*, which communicates with GitLab over the internet. The system is extremely flexible since the runners can run on different operating systems and serve different *executors* simultaneously. Behind this terminology is the environment in which the jobs are processed. The following three components in particular are worth mentioning:

- **Shell**
  Jobs are executed in the shell of the operating system: on Linux/macOS, in Bash and, on Windows, in PowerShell. The execution is performed as a standalone user on the computer running the runner, and the programs needed to run the pipeline must be installed on the computer.

- **Docker**
  Provides a clean environment at every startup. You can use your own Docker images for pipeline execution with all necessary programs installed. Compared to the shell runner, this environment is much more flexible and scalable.

- **Kubernetes**
  Uses containers in an existing Kubernetes cluster. If you already use Kubernetes anyway, you can run your runners here as well without requiring any more hardware.

Runners can also start a virtual machine (VM) like *VirtualBox* or *Parallels* or access a remote server via SSH and run pipelines there. We won't describe these special cases any further, but we will install a runner on a current Ubuntu Linux system. Quite commonly, a GitLab instance will have multiple runners registered from different computers. For example, a runner can also be installed on your laptop, which is online only when you're working.

To install a runner on a current Ubuntu/Debian system, you should download the Debian package (`gitlab-runner_amd64.deb`) from *https://gitlab-runner-downloads.s3. amazonaws.com/latest/index.html*. Before doing so, make sure that the Git and Docker programs are installed:

```
sudo apt install git docker.io
curl -LJO https://gitlab-runner-downloads.s3.amazonaws.com/\
  latest/deb/gitlab-runner_amd64.deb
sudo dpkg -i gitlab-runner_amd64.deb
```

During the installation of the Debian package, a new `gitlab-runner` user was added. To allow this user to use Docker, you still need to add it to the appropriate group with the following command:

```
sudo usermod -aG docker gitlab-runner
```

This step completes the installation of the runner, and you should see the active status in the output of the following command:

```
systemctl status gitlab-runner
```

```
. gitlab-runner.service - GitLab Runner
    Loaded: loaded (/etc/systemd/system/gitlab-runner.servi...
    Active: active (running) since Sat 2022-02-19 10:39:31 ...
...
```

To register the runner with your GitLab instance, you must navigate to **Admin • Runners** on the web interface. Click the **Register an instance runner** button to find the token you need for the following registration. Now, start the registration process in the command line of your future runner:

```
sudo gitlab-runner register --non-interactive \

    --registration-token xxxxxxxxxxxxxxxxxxx \
    --run-untagged \
    --name cloudRunner1 \
    --url https://gitlab.git-compendium.info/ \
    --executor docker \
    --locked=false \
    --docker-privileged \
    --docker-image ubuntu:latest
    Runtime platform      arch=amd64 os=linux pid=2076146 rev...
    Running in system-mode.

    Registering runner... succeeded              runner=xxxxxxxx
    Runner registered successfully. Feel free to start it, but...
```

This command shown starts the installation in non-interactive mode. You can also call `sudo gitlab-runner register` to be guided through the steps on the command line. Note, however, that the `--docker-privileged` and `--locked=false` settings can only be set directly via a command-line call.

Unfortunately, to enable certain operations in Docker executor, the container must be started in privileged mode. This approach, however, isn't a particularly good idea from a security point of view, but since the runner shouldn't run on an important server anyway, the security aspect isn't a priority in this context. By default, runners are available only for pipelines that use a tag that is also assigned to the runner. You can either set this setting at the command line with `--tag-list` or change it in the web interface under **Admin • Runners • Tags**.

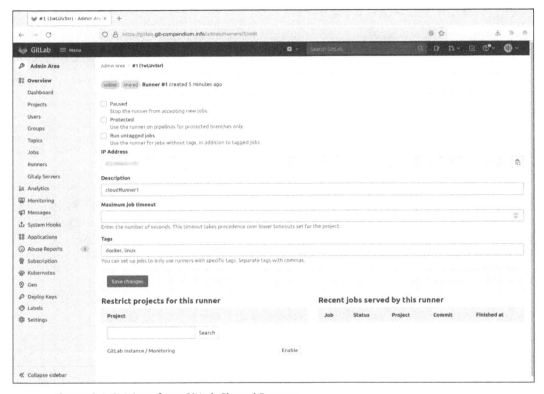

Figure 6.4 Settings for a GitLab Shared Runner

If the runner has been successfully registered, nothing stands in the way of CI/continuous deployment (CD) pipelines on your GitLab instance.

6.2.2 Backup

Before you dive into the GitLab interface after this fairly simple installation and as server administration tasks take a back seat, let's consider how you can set up an automatic backup for your GitLab platform. Even if you only use your GitLab instance for personal purposes and a server failure doesn't have far-reaching consequences, a backup is still essential, especially when it's as easy to do as with GitLab.

> **Not for Runners**
> The configuration of GitLab Runner resides on the particular computer on which the runner is running. However, since a runner can be re-registered with only one command, we don't include special backup instructions for runners here.

The installation of GitLab includes its own backup script that creates a database dump for you and backs up all other files belonging to your GitLab projects. For this process, you must simply call the script gitlab-backup:

root@gitlab:~# gitlab-backup

```
2022-02-19 11:05:10 +0000 -- Dumping database ...
Dumping PostgreSQL database gitlabhq_production ... [DONE]
2022-02-19 11:05:13 +0000 -- done
2022-02-19 11:05:13 +0000 -- Dumping repositories ...
...
Deleting old backups ... skipping
Warning: Your gitlab.rb and gitlab-secrets.json files contain
sensitive data and are not included in this backup. You will
need these files to restore a backup. Please back them up
manually.
Backup task is done.
```

The script creates a TAR file in the */var/opt/gitlab/backups* folder, using the timestamp, the current date, and the extension *-ee_gitlab_backup.tar* as the filename. As this file is a backup of the application data, it doesn't include the configuration files of your GitLab instance, as indicated by the warning message at the end of the backup process. The central configuration file *gitlab.rb* and the JavaScript Object Notation (JSON) file *gitlab-secrets.json* must be backed up separately. GitLab provides a script for this requirement as well, activated by the following command:

gitlab-ctl backup-etc /var/backups/gitlab-etc

This step saves the configuration files in a TAR file in the */var/backups/gitlab-etc* folder. GitLab recommends storing this backup separately from the application data backup. In the GitLab interface, among other things, you can create secret variables that are encrypted by the settings in *gitlab-secrets.json*. If an attacker gets a hold of a backup of the application data but doesn't have the secret keys, the information is still unreadable.

For an automated backup via Cron, we recommend some more parameters when calling the backup script. For instance, CRON=1 suppresses the output of messages when no errors occur, which results in you only receiving email notifications from Cron when something has gone wrong. In addition, not backing up the container registry with every backup may make sense since exceptionally large amounts of data can accumulate in the container registry. You can use SKIP=registry to prevent Docker images from being backed up. With a comma separator, you can exclude other modules too, for example, uploads for attachments in the wiki or lfs for Git large-file support (LFS) objects.

> **Backup Functions**
>
> Other useful features when creating backups of GitLab application data include uploading finished backups to cloud storage or automatically deleting old backups. These and other options for GitLab backups can be found on the relevant help pages at the following link:
>
> *https://docs.gitlab.com/ee/raketasks/backup_restore.html*

6.3   The First Project

In the remaining parts of this chapter, we'll use a hosted variant of GitLab in the free version (*free plan*). If you followed the installation process in the previous section and are already working on your own GitLab instance, you can try the following examples there as well.

We'll start by creating a new project via the web interface. In comparison to GitHub, note that, apart from importing existing projects, you have the option of creating a project from a template (**Create from template**). With this option, you'll find some basic frameworks for projects in common programming languages as well as for Android and iOS apps—a nice bonus, especially if you want to get into a new topic.

When importing projects, GitLab shows its versatility: In addition to its well-known competitors, such as GitHub, Bitbucket, Gitea, or the no longer active platform Google Code, a custom GitLab export format can also be imported. This option is especially interesting if you need to transfer a project between different self-hosted GitLab instances.

With the option to use a project only as a CI/CD pipeline for other platforms (especially GitHub), GitLab underlines its expertise in this area. Pipelines have long been an integral part of the platform. Like some competitors, GitHub had long outsourced this functionality before rolling out GitHub Actions (see Chapter 5, Section 5.2).

We'll create a new project (`pictures`) without templates (**Blank project**), and we won't create a README file now because we'll push an existing Git repository to the new project. Once the project has been created, the web interface displays instructions on how to use the empty repository. Our use case is **Push an existing Git repository**, following the instructions on the website.

In the local *ci-docker* folder is located a small HTML/Node.js project, which we used in Chapter 5, Section 5.3. The functionality of the application isn't important; what matters is that we have a Node.js project in which we've already made some commits.

```
cd ci-docker
git remote rename origin old-origin
git remote add origin git@gitlab.com:git-compendium/pictures.git
```

```
git push -u origin --all

  Enumerating objects: 223, done.
  Counting objects: 100% (223/223), done.
  ...
  Compressing objects: 100% (102/102), done.
  To gitlab.com:git-compendium/pictures.git
   * [new branch]      main -> main
  Branch 'main' set up to track remote branch 'main' from 'ori...
```

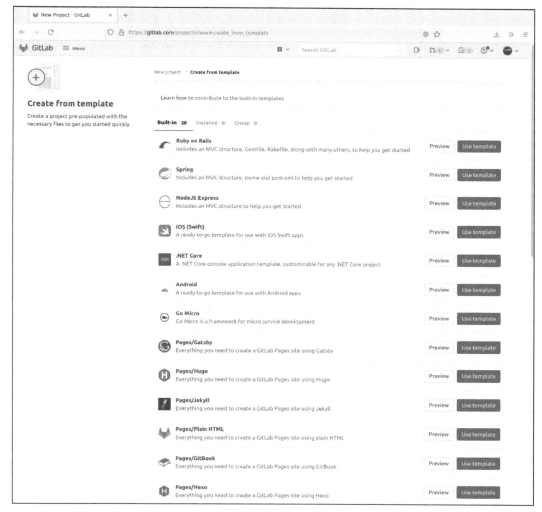

Figure 6.5 Templates for a New Project in GitLab

Now, we're ready to get into the exciting stuff on the GitLab platform, starting with *pipelines.*

6.4   Pipelines

Once you've pushed a Git repository, GitLab alerts you, through its web interface, that you can enable **Auto DevOps**. Let's give automation a chance and activate the setting in the **Settings** section for our project.

Figure 6.6 GitLab Suggests Enabling Auto DevOps for New Projects

6.4.1   Auto DevOps

Unfortunately, selecting one checkbox isn't quite enough: Auto DevOps wants to complete the successful pipeline with the deployment of the application, in other words, set up a full CD workflow. For this step to work, you'll need properly configured Kubernetes cluster, which seems slightly over the top for a sample program. Fortunately, however, you can also restrict the Auto DevOps pipeline to the CI part, as the GitLab interface makes clear.

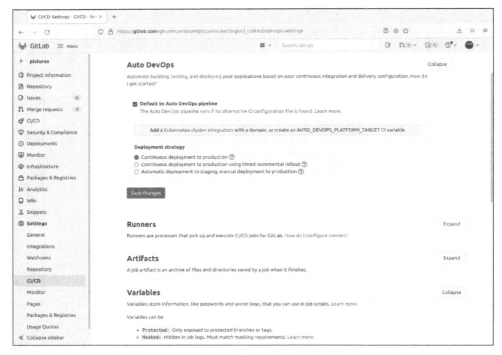

Figure 6.7 To Restrict the Auto DevOps Pipeline to CI, You Must Set the AUTO_DEVOPS_ PLATFORM_TARGET Variable

Following the instructions on the web interface, add the variable named AUTO_DEVOPS_ PLATFORM_TARGET and assign it the value CI.

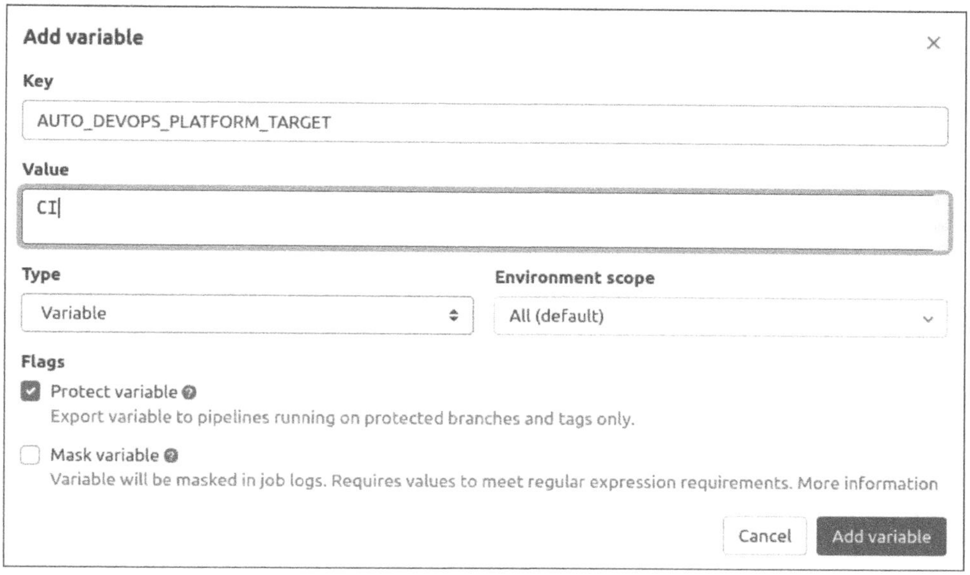

Figure 6.8 New AUTO_DEVOPS_PLATFORM_TARGET Variable

If you try the example on gitlab.com and followed the steps described earlier, everything is now ready, and the pipeline should already be running. For self-hosted instances, you must have a runner installed for this feature (see Section 6.2.1); on a cloud instance, shared runners should be available to run the pipeline.

GitLab is so confident about Auto DevOps that this feature has been enabled by default since version 11 of the platform. What's great about Auto DevOps is that, without writing a line of code, you can use an automated workflow of build, test, and code quality review on every push.

The pipeline that was automatically created for the Node.js project contains two sections:

- **Build**
  Since you have a Dockerfile in the repository, this step creates an image and uploads it to the Docker registry assigned to the project.

- **Test**
  In this section, different analyses are performed with the source code, using the Node Package Manager (npm). First, npm test is called, which starts the test script in the *package.json* file (at the bottom of the list of tests shown in Figure 6.9). Second, this section also loads publicly available Docker test images that, among other things, check code quality or look for forgotten passwords in the source code.

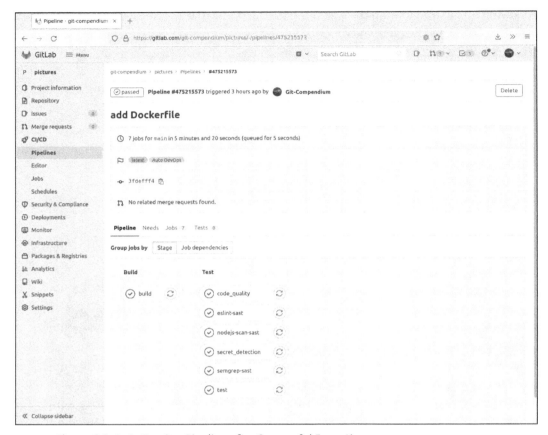

Figure 6.9 Auto DevOps Pipeline after Successful Execution

For the test section, GitLab uses *Heroku buildpacks* in the background. These build-packs are open-source components from the Heroku cloud platform, which specializes in running modern applications in containers. For the pipeline to be set up automatically, different criteria must be met depending on the programming language. In this example, the system recognizes that our Node.js project from its *package.json* file (besides other JavaScript files) and sets up the sections accordingly. For example, for Python, the necessary file would be *requirements.txt*, or in the case of PHP, *composer.json*.

If you use GitLab in a paid variant (*Ultimate* or *Gold*), even more sections will be activated in your Auto DevOps pipeline, which then examines the application for security-related aspects. These features include, for example, static application security testing (SAST) and dynamic application security testing (DAST), container scanning, dependency scanning, and license compliance.

Conclusion

We think the Auto DevOps feature is a successful development for entering the world of CI/CD pipelines, and it's a unique selling point for GitLab compared to other Git hosting platforms. When working on concrete projects, we usually quickly switch to manually created pipelines since the flexibility is incomparably greater and the effort required to create them remains quite manageable. The next section provides more information on this topic.

6.4.2 Manual Pipelines

The great attention GitLab pays to pipeline development has led to an increasing number of complex tasks being handled in pipelines. For example, you can equip different parts of a project with different pipelines and control them in a central file (*parent-child pipeline*) or even define pipelines across multiple projects.

We'll now turn our attention to the *basic pipelines*. This concept involves defining various jobs in a central configuration file (*.gitlab-ci.yml*). A job contains one or more commands that are executed on a runner. Jobs are divided into sections (*stages*), and these sections can be started in parallel or as dependent on each other. We described the syntax rules for the YAML Ain't Markup Language (YAML) file format in detail in Chapter 5, Section 5.2.1.

The typical flow of a CI/CD pipeline is divided into the build, test, and deployment sections, but no rigid rules are at play. Without the deployment section, the flow is just referred to as a *CI pipeline*.

Container Technology (Docker)

While containers aren't a mandatory part of CI pipelines, they are commonly used in this context. The background is that the automatic execution of a pipeline works reliably if the environment in which the execution takes place can be defined exactly, which is exactly the case with (Docker) containers. Each newly launched container has exactly the state defined in the Docker image.

If containers are involved, then for the build section in the pipeline, in many cases, using the docker build command with certain parameters is sufficient. The actual statements for the build process are contained in the Dockerfile.

Let's stick with our simple Node.js example of the image database. The goal for the CI pipeline is to create a production build in the form of a Docker image, then test that image on the fly (*end-to-end testing*), and if the tests are successful tag the image accordingly. We created a new repository (git-compendium/pictures-custom-ci) for this purpose and uploaded the existing code with the Git history there.

> **Docker Tags versus Git Tags**
>
> The names are the same, and their functions are also similar. Both Git tags and Docker tags mark a specific state of the software. Analogous to the main branch in Git, usually a Docker image is tagged latest.
>
> For Docker images, the tags are appended to the end of a name, separated by a colon. Git tags are often used directly as tags for Docker images, which can then result in a Docker image with the name pictures:1.1.0, for example.

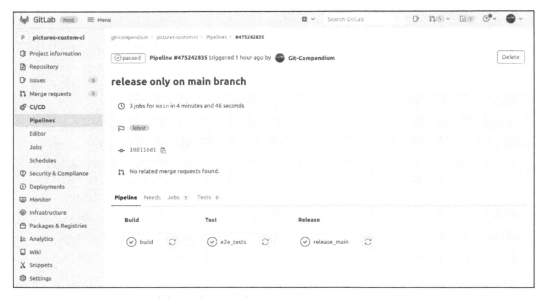

Figure 6.10 Successful GitLab CI Pipeline

As in our earlier discussion on GitHub Actions in Chapter 5, Section 5.2, we'll create a production Docker image, test it, and then put it into use as is. This process eliminates the possibility that tests running in the development environment will miss a potential bug in the production environment.

The configuration file for the pipeline, which must run on a Docker runner with advanced privileges, begins by defining variables, the default image, and the sections that will be traversed. The variables are defined for convenience and to save typing work further down the line.

TEST_IMAGE is composed of CI_REGISTRY_IMAGE and CI_COMMIT_SHA. The first variable consists of the name of the Docker registry for the current project and the path to the current project.

We'll use the GitLab cloud for our example, so the content of the CI_REGISTRY_IMAGE variable is registry.gitlab.com/git-compendium/pictures-custom-ci. Unsurprisingly, the CI_COMMIT_SHA variable contains the Git commit hash for the commit that started the pipeline. The RELEASE_IMAGE variable receives the contents of the CI_COMMIT_REF_NAME variable as a Docker tag, which is either the name of the branch on which the push occurred or the name of the Git tag.

The image statement specifies the *default Docker image* for all sections. Unless otherwise specified, all script commands are executed inside the docker:19 image. We'll use this image to create the Docker image for this project and load it into the registry.

Under stages, entries that are referenced in the further course of the file (build, test, and release) are defined:

```
# File: .gitlab-ci.yml
variables:
  TEST_IMAGE: $CI_REGISTRY_IMAGE:$CI_COMMIT_SHA
  RELEASE_IMAGE: $CI_REGISTRY_IMAGE:$CI_COMMIT_REF_NAME
image: docker:19
stages:
  - build
  - test
  - release
```

The build section is compact, as mentioned earlier, because the configuration for it is stored in the Dockerfile. After the (successful) docker build, the image is uploaded to the registry (docker push), in our case, registry.gitlab.com. Before the push, a logon to the Docker registry must still take place. The gitlab-ci-token user and secret token are present by default in the GitLab instance.

```
# File: .gitlab-ci.yml (continued)
build:
  stage: build
  script:
    - docker build -t $TEST_IMAGE .
    - docker login -u gitlab-ci-token -p $CI_JOB_TOKEN
      $CI_REGISTRY
    - docker push $TEST_IMAGE
```

6.4.3   Test Stage in the Manual Pipeline

To test the image on the fly, we'll use another Docker image called testcafe. Basically, we could also load the server's web pages with curl or wget and analyze the output, but using testcafe, we can simply access the Document Object Model (DOM) elements of the web page and check if the output is as expected. In the background, testcafe does even more: This image actually launches a web browser and loads the web page in the browser engine, which results in the JavaScript contained in the web page being executed and interpreted as well.

In our example, running JavaScript is critical for high-quality testing. The image database is implemented as a *single-page application*, which means that JavaScript handles most of the control. Uploading an image, which is the core of this simple application, works only through the JavaScript support of the browser. You can use testcafe to test this functionality without any user interaction.

```
# File: .gitlab-ci.yml (continued)
e2e_tests:
  services:
    - name: $TEST_IMAGE
      alias: webpage
  stage: test
  image:
    name: testcafe/testcafe
    entrypoint: ["/bin/sh", "-c"]
  script:
    - /opt/testcafe/docker/testcafe-docker.sh firefox:headless
      test/e2e.js
```

The e2e_tests section has another specialty to offer: In the services section, the Docker image created earlier is listed and given an alias. The GitLab Runner starts the image as a service parallel to the actual image testcafe/testcafe. Docker containers run on their own network, and the container being tested can be reached at the address *http://webpage:3001* (port 3001 is defined this way in the application).

Overwriting the entrypoint in the image section is a specific Docker feature, which we won't discuss further.

6.4.4   Release Stage in the Manual Pipeline

The last section is used to tag the successfully tested Docker image with latest and push it to the registry again. Similar to Git tags, the entire Docker image is not transferred from the runner to the Docker registry of the GitLab instance; only the few bytes of the new tag.

What's new is the GIT_STRATEGY variable, which is assigned with none. By default, the repository source code in each section is copied to the working directory using git clone. Since we're only testing with the final Docker image in this section, we don't need a copy of the source code and will turn off this process. What's also new is the only keyword, which we used in this example to include only commits on the main branch:

```
release_main:
  stage: release
  variables:
    GIT_STRATEGY: none
```

```
  script:
    - docker login -u gitlab-ci-token -p $CI_JOB_TOKEN
      $CI_REGISTRY
    - docker pull $TEST_IMAGE
    - docker tag $TEST_IMAGE $CI_REGISTRY_IMAGE:latest
    - docker push $CI_REGISTRY_IMAGE:latest
  only:
    - main
```

We ran the presented pipeline in a dedicated runner on one of our laptops. The runner with the Docker Executor was configured to have the Docker socket available in the container:

```
# in file /etc/gitlab-runner/config.toml
[runners.docker]
  ...
  disable_cache = false
  volumes = ["/var/run/docker.sock:/var/run/docker.sock","/cache"]
```

Using this (somewhat insecure) trick, working with the Docker command line also works inside a container. The commands are executed on the host, that is, by the Docker daemon on the laptop. If you use a shared runner from gitlab.com, you'll need to slightly customize the YAML file. You'll need a global service with the image docker:19.03.12-dind for the build to work, as shown in the following example:

```
services:
  - docker:19.03.12-dind
```

6.4.5 Debugging Pipelines

Especially when developing more complex pipelines, setbacks in the form of typos, YAML syntax errors, and logical errors are common. Since the workflow of *fix file, commit*, *push*, and *wait for feedback* isn't what you want as a developer, there's an option to take a shortcut.

Syntax errors in the YAML file can be rather annoying and are easily prevented. Every GitLab project therefore includes a syntax check for pipeline files with the URL fragment /-/ci/lint. In our example, the full address is *https://gitlab.com/git-compendium/pictures-custom-ci/-/ci/lint*.

To test the pipeline locally, you can install a GitLab Runner on your computer and invoke it with the exec option and a section of the *.gitlab-ci.yml* file. For example, you could use the following command:

```
gitlab-runner exec docker build
```

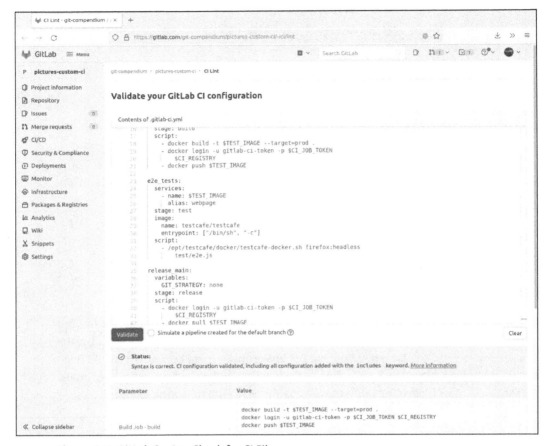

Figure 6.11 GitLab Syntax Check for CI Files

This step starts a runner with the Docker executor and processes the build section locally. Note that git commit must be run upfront in any case, but the cloning is performed from the local repository (i.e., your working directory). This workflow results in massive time savings and also enables you to clean up the Git history before the push. While you must commit locally, you can simply cancel the last commit with the following command:

```
git reset --soft HEAD~1
```

This command deletes the last commit but doesn't change the files. The changes since the second-to-last commit are *staged* and can be changed before another commit. In reality, of course, the commit won't be deleted. Only the HEAD will be set to the previous commit, and the actual commit will remain somewhere in limbo until garbage collection is started.

In our example, we unfortunately had bad luck our attempts to run the pipeline locally. The problem stems from the CI_REGISTRY_IMAGE, CI_JOB_TOKEN, and CI_REGISTRY variables, which aren't set in a local GitLab Runner. This problem is known and also discussed in the GitLab Issue Tracker:

- *https://gitlab.com/groups/gitlab-org/-/epics/1335*
- *https://gitlab.com/gitlab-org/gitlab-runner/-/issues/2797*

A final note on debugging pipelines: You can launch any program present in the active Docker image in the `script` section, and you'll see their output in the browser. For example, for a list of variables present in the `bash` shell, add the `export` call to the section, as in the following example:

```
...
script:
  - export
  - docker build -t $TEST_IMAGE .
...
```

6.5 Merge Requests

If you've already read Chapter 5, the next few lines will sound familiar. What in GitHub is called *pull requests*, GitLab refers to as *merge requests*. Since the concepts work the same way, we won't go into all the details again in this section, but simply perform a merge request via the Gitlab's well designed web interface.

You start with a new issue: The requirement states that the backend code should be stored in its own subdirectory.

In the web interface, you can create a merge request directly on the issue, which will result in a new branch being created with the name of the issue. Back on your PC, you can call `git pull` in the working directory, and the new branch will be created. After switching to the branch, you must move the files and adjust the paths in the Dockerfile.

```
git pull
```

```
From gitlab.com:git-compendium/pictures-custom-ci
 * [new branch]      1-move-backend-code-to-separate-folder ->
origin/1-move-backend-code-to-separate-folder
Already up to date.
```

```
git checkout 1-move-backend-code-to-separate-folder
```

```
Branch '1-move-backend-code-to-separate-folder' set up to track
remote branch '1-move-backend-code-to-separate-folder' from
'origin'.
Switched to a new branch '1-move-backend-code-to-separate-fo...
```

```
# edit files ...

git add .
git commit -a -m 'feat: move backend code to server dir'
git push
```

Once the branch has been set up as a tracking branch, the `git push` command without any other parameters is sufficient to push the changes to the server.

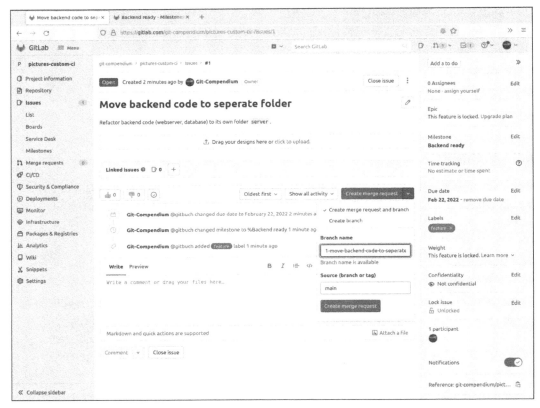

Figure 6.12 New Issue in GitLab That Requires a Reorganization of the Backend Code

Now, let's continue working in the web interface: The merge request has automatically been given the status `Draft`. This status shows clearly that work on this branch isn't yet complete. Also, the CI pipeline we defined earlier in the Section 6.4 automatically ran and executed the end-to-end tests on the Docker image. Note that only two of the three sections in the pipeline are executed in this case since the third section applies only to the main branch.

Once the tests are successful, you can cancel the temporary status by clicking the **Mark as ready** button in the web interface.

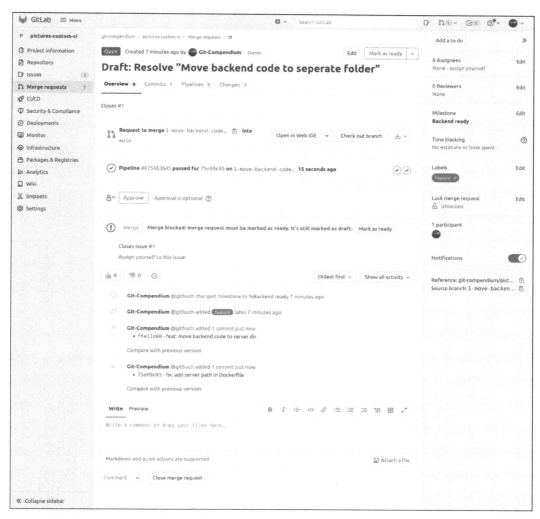

Figure 6.13 Merge Request with the Draft Status

Then, you can confirm the merge request. This step merges the feature branch with the main branch.

Finally, the CI pipeline runs again but this time at the main branch. In the third section of the pipeline, the new Docker image is tagged as `latest` and uploaded to the registry. If you now call `docker pull` with the image name on your server in the cloud, you'll get the latest tested version of the software.

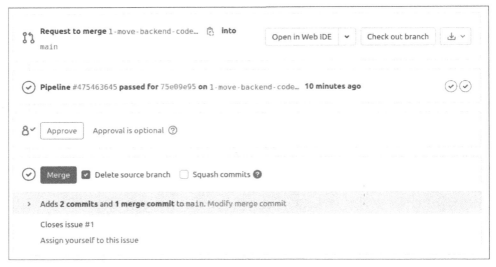

Figure 6.14 Confirmation of the Merge Request Including Deletion of the Feature Branch

6.6   Web IDE

Another feature that sets GitLab apart from its competitors is its editor built into the web interface. This feature isn't just a text editor with syntax highlighting that runs in a browser. Multiple files can be opened in tabs and changes can be committed immediately. For some languages like JavaScript, HTML, or CSS, the editor offers additional features like code completion and error displays.

The editor isn't a proprietary development of GitLab but instead is based on the open-source project *Monaco Editor*, which also powers the desktop editor Visual Studio Code (VS Code). Thus, this component comes from GitLab's biggest competitor, GitHub's owner Microsoft.

Web IDE cannot be a direct replacement for the desktop editor for us. If you're familiar with VS Code, you'll no doubt have already added extensions, such as GitLens, which we introduced in Chapter 2, Section 2.6.5. None of these extensions run in the browser.

But the bigger limitation is that, when we develop, we usually test the application immediately, in the sense of "trying it out." This testing works perfectly on the desktop since you can start the program right away in a shell that's open at the same time, or in the case of a web application, you load it in the browser.

GitLab is currently working on a possible solution to this problem: The *Web Terminal* feature (still in beta as of spring 2022) launches a shell on a designated runner. The environment on this runner can be freely configured; that is, you can install the necessary libraries there to run the software. When the terminal is started, the source code is copied to the runner. However, GitLab shared runners can't be used for this purpose.

But even now, GitLab's Web IDE is perfect for a code review. Clicking the **Web IDE** button on a merge request opens the changed files in a different view.

Figure 6.15 Web IDE in GitLab with JavaScript Programming Support

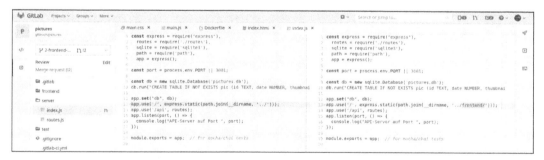

Figure 6.16 Code Review with GitLab Web IDE

6.7   Gitpod

The integration of Gitpod goes even one step further. Gitpod is first and foremost an independent, open-source project (*https://github.com/gitpod-io*), but it's also a cloud platform (*https://gitpod.io*), which provides its services as a paid *software as a service (SaaS)*. In the free version, you can work 50 hours per month in four parallel workspaces in the Gitpod cloud. Based on the open-source project, you can also run your own self-hosted variant of Gitpod. Currently, however, installation instructions are only available for the three major cloud providers (Amazon, Microsoft, and Google).

If you enable this extension for your account (near your avatar icon under **Preferences •
Integrations • GitPod**), you can develop your project in a browser via a virtual environment in the cloud.

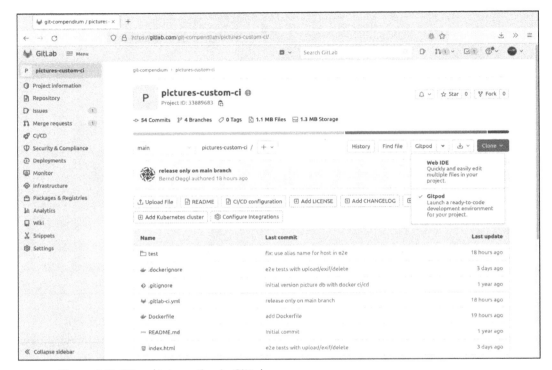

Figure 6.17 Gitpod Integration in GitLab

After agreeing once to authenticate with GitLab, a virtual environment is launched
where you can use a version of the VS Code editor that also supports many extensions
you know from the desktop version. But that's not all—the built-in terminal function
makes *real* Linux terminals available to you in the browser. For our simple JavaScript
application, npm install and npm start were also called automatically. The necessary
port mapping for testing an application also works smoothly, and another browser tab
opens with the application running. You can use these features to develop and test
your web application entirely in the browser.

If you've read Chapter 5 on GitHub to the end, you might just be experiencing déjà vu.
In fact, GitHub Codespaces and Gitpod are remarkably similar and are based on the
same technology. The trend towards having a development environment in a browser
is still quite young but suggests considerable potential. Not only can you develop
regardless of your endpoint device, but no work is involved in the initial project setup.
Depending on the focus of your project, the concept may work better or worse. While
you probably can't completely forgo a desktop environment for hardware-related projects, browser-based development can be a convenient solution for web applications.

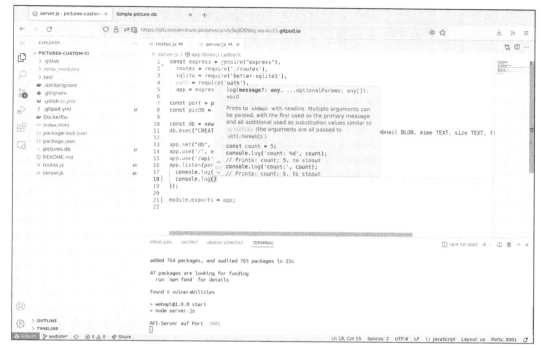

Figure 6.18 Developing in the Browser in Gitpod

Chapter 7
Azure DevOps, Bitbucket, Gitea, and Gitolite

In addition to the top dogs GitHub and GitLab, various alternatives have established themselves over time. In this chapter, we'll briefly introduce four platforms: *Azure DevOps* and *Bitbucket* are large vendors that have been active in the market for a long time but have relied on other version control systems in the past. *Gitea* and *Gitolite*, on the other hand, are comparatively lean programs that help host Git itself.

7.1 Azure DevOps

Azure DevOps is Microsoft's offering for companies to conduct modern software development with *continuous integration/continuous deployment (CI/CD)* and a dash of project management. In terms of web interface, Azure DevOps is more reminiscent of its competitor GitLab than GitHub, probably due to the vertical main menu bar on the left.

Azure DevOps evolved from Microsoft Visual Studio Team Services (VSTS), which in turn was the successor to Visual Studio Online. These two predecessor products were actually only known to die-hard Microsoft users who practiced software development in Microsoft Visual Studio. With Microsoft's move to the cloud and the Microsoft Azure platform, this limited audience is changing somewhat since Microsoft Azure is also interesting for customers who don't rely on Microsoft for an operating system.

Azure Cloud versus Azure DevOps

The naming and pricing policies of Microsoft's cloud offerings aren't always easy to understand. With a free Azure DevOps account, you can currently create an unlimited number of Git repositories and also create and run pipelines. If your project isn't open source, you're limited with regard to automatic test runs. To use other services from the Azure Cloud (for example, Kubernetes or the container registry), you must submit your credit card details. Billing depends on the individual services.

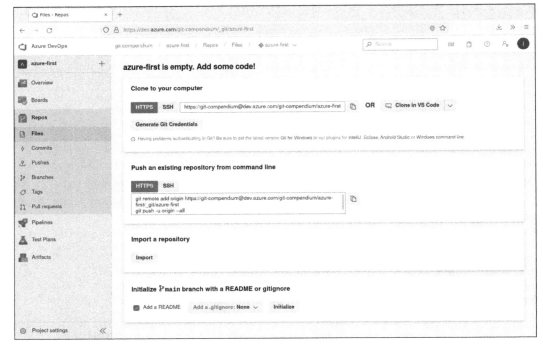

Figure 7.1 First Project in Microsoft Azure DevOps

7.1.1   Trying Out Azure DevOps

Compared to GitHub and GitLab, Azure DevOps wants to score with (even) more team functions, as shown in the prominent placement of agile tools, such as Kanban boards, backlogs, and sprint planning in the web interface. In this section, we'll show you a workflow with Azure DevOps using a simple Node.js project.

Using our Microsoft account, the first step is to create a new project in the web interface at *https://dev.azure.com/*. Then, we'll import the oft-used Node.js example from the ci-docker repository from our GitHub account. For this task, we'll simply specify the GitHub URL when importing, and the code is imported. An interesting difference from GitHub and GitLab becomes apparent upon closer inspection: An Azure DevOps project isn't limited to a Git repository, which is also evident when cloning our repository. Use the following command to clone a repository via SSH:

```
git clone git@ssh.dev.azure.com:v3/git-compendium/simple-picture-
db/simple-picture-db
```

In this case, the first simple-picture-db denotes the project, and the second stands for the Git repository of the same name. Azure DevOps additionally provides a convenient way to clone a Git repository directly in the integrated development environment (IDE) of your choice: Behind the dropdown button with the default setting **Clone in VS Code**,

238

other common IDEs can be accessed, such as *Android Studio, IntelliJ IDEA, WebStorm*, or *PyCharm*. Our tests with VS Code worked fine (even on Linux), whereas the other options may rely on an installed version of Visual Studio.

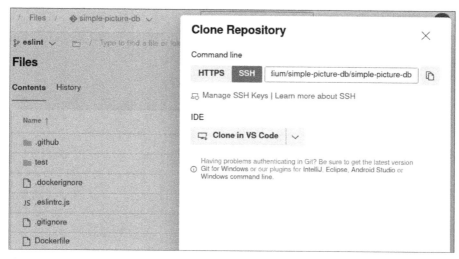

Figure 7.2 Option to Clone with an IDE in Azure DevOps

Pipelines are created and edited directly in the browser. First, you'll select the source code, and in Azure DevOps, this selection isn't limited to your own Git repository. You can also tap into sources from Git hosts.

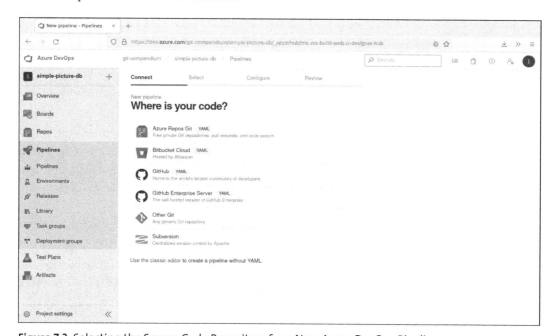

Figure 7.3 Selecting the Source Code Repository for a New Azure DevOps Pipeline

A convenient feature for newcomers to the pipeline business is the selection of pre-
defined actions. You can choose from many tasks for different programming languages. The result is a YAML Ain't Markup Language (YAML) file remarkably similar to
what we've already seen in Chapter 5, Section 5.2.1, and in Chapter 6, Section 6.4. For our
project, we selected the **Docker** option, which generated the full syntax for creating a
Docker image.

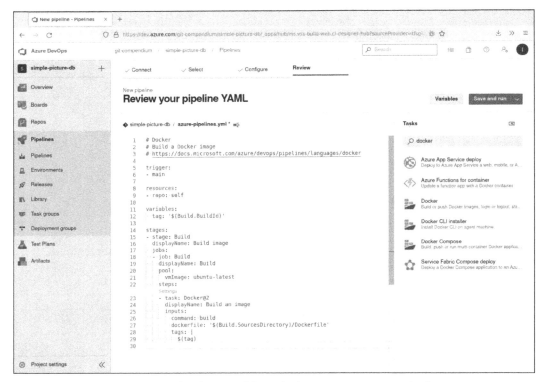

Figure 7.4 YAML File and Other Possible Tasks for an Azure DevOps Pipeline

As a final point in the short Azure DevOps demonstration, we'll walk through the life-
cycle of a work item. First, create an **issue** in the **To-Do** board. The requirement is that
frontend code of our application should be organized into separate HTML, CSS, and
JavaScript files. When creating the **issue** element, you can create a branch for development right away by using frontend-code-splitup. When we now call git pull on our
computer in the cloned directory, a new branch is created following the remote frontend-code-splitup.

You could have accomplished the same thing by first creating the branch locally and
pushing it after making changes to the source code, for example, with the following
commands:

```
git checkout -b frontend-code-splitup
# change code ...
git add .
git commit -m "fix: split up frontend code (see #1)"
git push --set-upstream frontend-code-splitup
```

Once you push the changed branch, you'll see a notice in the web interface indicating that we can now create a pull request from the changes. Unlike in GitLab and GitHub, this notice won't be displayed in the console after the push. Microsoft probably assumes that Azure DevOps users won't have as much contact with the command line but rather use Git integrated in an IDE.

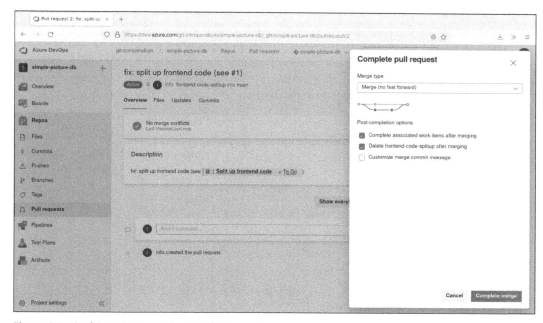

Figure 7.5 Final Step in Accepting a Pull Request

7.1.2 Test Plans

An important aspect of CI/CD pipelines is automated testing. The concept behind this feature is that, if the source code has an extremely high coverage with tests, shipping a new version won't cause any problems and can be done automatically (provided the tests are all green).

Azure DevOps dedicates a separate menu item in the web interface to testing, namely, **Test Plans**. You can't get started with test plans until you either provide your credit card details or activate the free trial month. (You can access these settings via **Organization Settings • Billing • Basic + Test Plans** at the bottom level of Azure DevOps, *https://dev.azure.com/*). Test runs can be performed on different hardware and for web applications also with different browsers. Microsoft needs to be paid for the computing power to be applied.

The configuration Microsoft provides for test plans is rather complex, to say the least. You'll need to create *test plans*, which in turn are assigned to individual issues and can be performed by members of your team and then assessed positively or negatively. Describing all these tasks would take us too far away from Git, but we recommend the following tutorial at Azure DevOps Labs if you're interested:

https://azuredevopslabs.com/labs/azuredevops/testmanagement

7.1.3   Conclusion

If you already use Azure Cloud Services anyway, Azure DevOps is certainly a good place for your Git repositories. Integrated project management with agile techniques can be the all-round, carefree package for many companies. Presumably, your corporate credit card is already on file with Microsoft, and the additional cost won't create any additional work for your accounting department.

On the other hand, if you choose a Git host without a Microsoft background, Azure DevOps probably won't be your first choice. Both GitLab and GitHub offer solutions that don't require tight integration with a Microsoft account and provide the full package with CI pipelines and actions, respectively. For a leaner system (without integrated CI/CD), a particularly good choice is Gitea (see Section 7.3).

7.2   Bitbucket

Bitbucket is another major player in the cloud-based Git hosting solutions market. Back in 2008, Atlassian, the company behind Bitbucket, presented the software on the internet. With the rapid rise of GitHub, Bitbucket lost importance but remains a good alternative for customers who already use other Atlassian products. *Jira*, a popular issue-tracking software, and *Confluence*, a wiki-based documentation software, may play a role in this choice in particular.

Of course, you can also create a free account with Bitbucket. Both private and public repositories are possible. If you've read Chapter 5 and Chapter 6 on GitHub or GitLab, respectively, the menu items in the web interface will seem familiar. With Bitbucket, too, you can access your Git repository, pull requests, and pipelines, among other things, although the latter are limited to 50 minutes of runtime per month in the free version. Pipeline definitions are also written in YAML syntax, and execution takes place in Docker containers.

What's missing compared to GitHub or GitLab is a wiki and an issue system. But you've probably guessed it already: Atlassian offers other software products in their portfolio with particularly good integration with Bitbucket. You can try both for 7 days, but then

Atlassian charges you for these services. Prices start at $10 per month (for less than 10 users) if you store your data on Atlassian servers. In return, you'll enjoy robust integration between issue tracking and Git hosting functionalities.

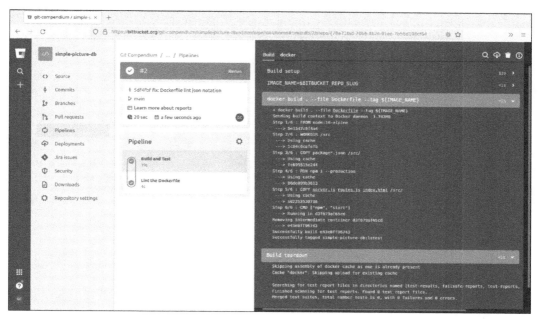

Figure 7.6 Bitbucket Pipeline during the Creation of a Docker Image

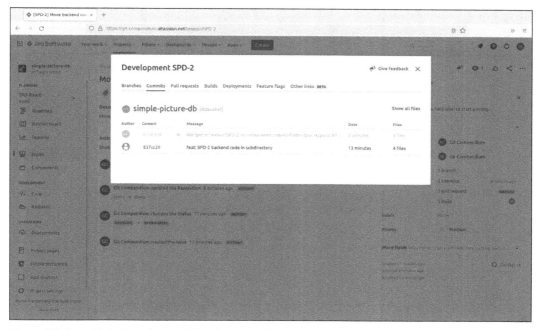

Figure 7.7 Smooth Integration of Bitbucket with Jira

7.3   Gitea

The Git hosting solutions we've presented so far are all heavyweights with complex web interfaces, caches, and databases that consume a lot of resources. Gitea takes a different approach: This relatively young project (first released in 2016) was developed in the Go programming language and is characterized by high performance and a rather tidy web interface.

Figure 7.8 Gitea Web Interface with a Sample Project: The Similarities with GitHub Are Undeniable

7.3.1   Trying Out Gitea

A trial installation can be set up easily: Simply download the binary file for your platform from GitHub or via Gitea (*https://dl.gitea.io*) and run it on your computer. Then, you can open the *http://localhost:3000* address in the browser and access your Gitea instance. In the initial configuration, which can be done completely via the web interface, you'll be asked for the access data to a database server. For a test run, select the file-based SQLite3 format and complete the setup without making any further changes.

Don't underestimate Gitea because of its simple setup! You've just installed a web application with a ticket system, a wiki, and the option of pull requests. Two-factor authentication with one-time passwords or hardware keys works without any further configuration effort. The operation of the web interface is strongly reminiscent of GitHub, which makes a possible switch extremely easy.

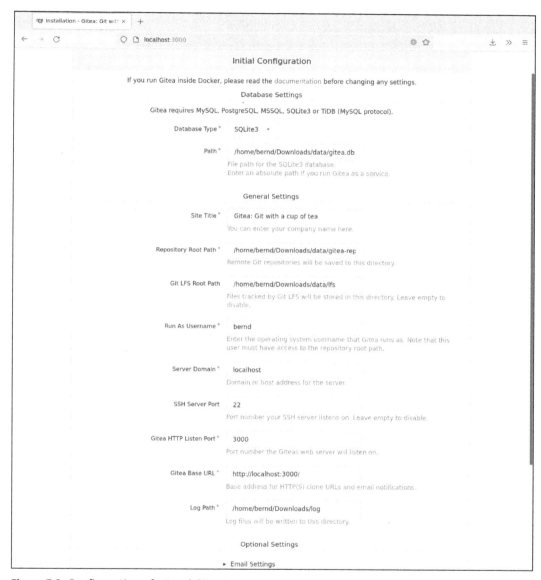

Figure 7.9 Configuration of a Local Gitea Instance

7.3.2   Server Installation with Docker

In this section, we assume that you've worked with Docker before. The following setup also uses `docker-compose`, a component you should certainly be familiar with as a Docker user.

Gitea developers support installation with Docker by providing up-to-date images on Docker Hub and the option to configure the application server via environment variables. For us, we'll use a *docker-compose.yml* file to configure a ready-made system that can be run in production using one command.

```yaml
# File: gitea/docker/docker-compose.yml
version: "3"
services:
  server:
    image: gitea/gitea:1.16.1
    environment:
      - USER_UID=1000
      - USER_GID=1000
      - DB_TYPE=mysql
      - DB_HOST=db:3306
      - DB_NAME=gitea
      - DB_USER=gitea
      - DB_PASSWD=quaequo5eN6b
      - DISABLE_REGISTRATION=true
      - SSH_PORT=2221
      - SSH_DOMAIN=gitea.git-compendium.info
    restart: always
    volumes:
      - gitea:/data
    ports:
      - "2221:2221"
      - "3000:3000"
    depends_on:
      - db
  db:
    image: mariadb:10
    restart: always
    environment:
      - MYSQL_ROOT_PASSWORD=aGh3beex0eit
      - MYSQL_USER=gitea
      - MYSQL_PASSWORD=quaequo5eN6b
      - MYSQL_DATABASE=gitea
    volumes:
      - mariavol:/var/lib/mysql
volumes:
  gitea:
  mariavol:
```

In our example, we'll use version 1.16.1 of Gitea for the first service (server), as shown in the line image: gitea/gitea:1.16.1. For a test run, you can also set gitea/gitea:latest, which will test the latest developer version. However, not all modules functioned smoothly during our tests.

The environment variables first define under which user and group the application server runs in the container. The variables marked with DB_* define the connection to the database (in this case, MariaDB). DISABLE_REGISTRATION disables the registration for all users, and SSH_PORT sets a different port for the internal SSH server since such a service is probably already running on the server system. The SSH_DOMAIN entry is needed so that the links to clone via SSH show the correct address.

Essential to this setup is that you assign the /data folder in the container to a volume, which is the only way to ensure that you don't lose your data during an upgrade. We'll use a *named volume* in this case, which of course must be mounted in an automatic backup. The named volume is where the Git repositories, SSH keys, and application configuration reside.

The second service (db) launches an instance of MariaDB version 10. The database data is also stored in a named volume.

With this configuration, your web server runs on port 3000, while the SSH server runs on port 2221. In the Docker environment, a reverse proxy is often used for encrypted HTTP connections. This proxy refers to an upstream web server that manages the necessary certificates and terminates the encrypted traffic. For this configuration to work, you must add the ROOT_URL=your.hostname.com entry in the environment section of the server service to the setup with your host name.

7.3.3   Server Installation on Ubuntu 20.04

Unfortunately, no ready-made packages for Gitea are available for Linux distributions like Ubuntu or Debian. Therefore, if you don't want to use Docker, you must make some manual adjustments to run Gitea. In this section, we'll show you the procedure for Ubuntu 20.04.

Your server must have Git installed, and if you want to use a database other than SQLite, you'll need the credentials for that database. For security reasons, we recommend that you don't run the application server as the root user. The best approach is to create a separate user that otherwise has no rights on the system, for example, the gitea user, as in the following example:

```
sudo adduser --system --shell /bin/bash --group \
  --disabled-password --home /home/gitea gitea
```

As a storage location for all files managed by Gitea, the */var/lib/gitea* folder is suitable on Ubuntu. In that folder, create the subfolders *custom*, *data*, and *log* and give the gitea user and group permissions to these folders, with the following commands:

```
sudo mkdir -p /var/lib/gitea/custom /var/lib/gitea/log \
  /var/lib/gitea/data
sudo chown -R gitea:gitea /var/lib/gitea/
sudo chmod -R o-rwx /var/lib/gitea/
```

Finally, the central Gitea configuration file should be stored in the */etc/gitea* folder. Create this folder and set the permissions so that the gitea group has write access to it, with the following commands:

```
sudo mkdir /etc/gitea
sudo chown root:gitea /etc/gitea
sudo chmod o-rwx,ug+rwx /etc/gitea
```

Now, only two things are missing: the Gitea server itself and a startup script so that the server is started automatically on every restart. You should load the server into the */usr/local/bin* folder and mark this file as executable, with the following commands:

```
sudo wget -O /usr/local/bin/gitea \
  https://dl.gitea.io/gitea/1.16.1/gitea-1.16.1-linux-amd64
sudo chmod 755 /usr/local/bin/gitea
```

On Ubuntu, systemd takes care of starting and stopping services. A minimal configuration file (gitea.service) for the Gitea service is shown in the following:

```
[Unit]
Description=Gitea
After=syslog.target
After=network.target
[Service]
RestartSec=2s
Type=simple
User=gitea
Group=gitea
WorkingDirectory=/var/lib/gitea/
ExecStart=/usr/local/bin/gitea web --config /etc/gitea/app.ini
Restart=always
Environment=USER=gitea HOME=/home/gitea GITEA_WORK_DIR=/var/lib/gitea
[Install]
WantedBy=multi-user.target
```

Copy the file to the */etc/systemd/system/* folder on your Linux system and enable the service using the following command:

```
sudo systemctl enable gitea --now
```

Your Gitea server is now running on port 3000. Once you click **Login** or **Register**, you'll be taken to the installation page. If you don't have any other web services enabled on this server, you can also run Gitea on the default port for secure HTTP, and Gitea can even generate certificates for you by itself via *Let's Encrypt*.

For HTTPS to work on the designated default port 443 with the certificates, you still need to make two small changes in the files. In the service file for systemd, you can grant the gitea user permissions to use ports 80 and 443. For this task, you must insert the following two lines in the [Service] section:

```
CapabilityBoundingSet=CAP_NET_BIND_SERVICE
AmbientCapabilities=CAP_NET_BIND_SERVICE
```

Next, you must restart the systemd process via the systemctl daemon-reload command. In the configuration of the application server, the entries for HTTPS and Let's Encrypt are now missing. Add the following lines to the beginning of the */etc/gitea/app.ini* file:

```
[server]
PROTOCOL=https
DOMAIN=tea.git-compendium.info
HTTP_PORT = 443
ENABLE_LETSENCRYPT=true
LETSENCRYPT_ACCEPTTOS=true
LETSENCRYPT_DIRECTORY=https
LETSENCRYPT_EMAIL=root@git-compendium.info
```

For DOMAIN and LETSENCRYPT_EMAIL, you must adjust to the real domain name of your server, of course. When you now restart the Gitea process (systemctl restart gitea.service), Gitea will take care of the certificates; after a while, you can access your server via HTTPS.

To use Gitea in production, we recommend a database system other than SQLite. To use MariaDB with this installation on Ubuntu 20.04, the following commands are sufficient:

```
apt install mariadb-server
mysqladmin create gitea
mysql gitea -e "GRANT ALL PRIVILEGES ON gitea.* TO \
  gitea@localhost IDENTIFIED BY 'einohD8ith3I'"
```

You can now leave the default selection for MySQL in the database setting in the web interface and enterohD8ith3I or use the string you have chosen as the password.

7.3.4   A First Example with Gitea

To demonstrate a few of Gitea's features, let's now import an existing project into Gitea. Unlike GitHub or GitLab, Gitea doesn't provide importers for repositories hosted by its competitors. However, you can import an existing Git repository in any case.

First, create a new project named `pictures` via the web interface on the Gitea server. This project will contain the Node.js application we used in Chapter 5, Section 5.4. We'll then clone the existing GitHub repository to the local computer using the `--mirror` flag:

```
git clone --mirror git@gitlab.com:git-compendium/pictures.git

  Cloning into bare repository 'pictures.git'...
  ...
```

Figure 7.10 New Gitea Repository for the Image Database Example

We now have created a `bare` repository in the *pictures.git* folder that contains all references such as tags and remote tracking branches. Now, copy this repository to the new project created on Gitea by going to the new folder and calling `git push` with the mirror option, as in the following example:

```
git push --mirror gitea@tea.git-compendium.info:git-compendium/pi
ctures.git
  Enumerating objects: 229, done.
  ...
  To tea.git-compendium.info:git-compendium/pictures.git
   * [new branch]      main -> main
```

Now, let's get started with Gitea and create a first entry (*issue*) in the ticket system. The suggestion for improvement (*feature request*) is that the Dockerfile in the project be rebuilt to support multistage builds for development and production use.

Notice that Gitea supports multiple languages in the web interface. If your operating system is set to another language than English, you'll also see the menus in Gitea in that language—a luxury that neither GitHub nor GitLab provide so far.

To avoid losing your overview in the ticket system, you can assign one or more *labels* and a milestone to an entry. Labels must either be created manually for new projects, or you can import a preset label set consisting of seven useful labels such as *bug, duplicate*, or *wontfix*.

For our example, we'll locally develop the desired changes on the Git branch `multistage-dev`:

```
git clone clone gitea@tea.git-compendium.info:git-compendium/pict
ures.git
  Cloning into 'pictures'...
  ...
  Resolving deltas: 100% (102/102), done.

cd pictures

git checkout -b multistage-dev
  Switched to a new branch 'multistage-dev'
```

After making the changes in the Dockerfile file, commit and push the feature branch. Note the reference in the commit message to the issue in the ticket system (see #1):

```
git commit -am "feat: multistage build for Docker image (see #1)"
  [multistage-dev 757a103] feat: multistage build for Docker i...
   Date: Tue Feb 22 11:03:31 2022 +0100
   1 file changed, 13 insertions(+), 3 deletions(-)

git push --set-upstream origin multistage-dev
  Enumerating objects: 5, done.
  Counting objects: 100% (5/5), done.
```

```
Delta compression using up to 8 threads
Compressing objects: 100% (3/3), done.
Writing objects: 100% (3/3), 478 bytes | 478.00 KiB/s, done.
Total 3 (delta 1), reused 1 (delta 0)
remote:
remote: Create a new pull request for 'multistage-dev':
remote:    https://tea.git-compendium.info/git-compendium/pic...
remote:
remote: . Processing 1 references
remote: Processed 1 references in total
To tea.git-compendium.info:git-compendium/pictures.git
 * [new branch]      multistage-dev -> multistage-dev
Branch 'multistage-dev' set up to track remote branch 'multi...
```

Now, open the link to create a new pull request that was issued in the console after the push command. In the web interface, you'll see the changes. Clicking the green button will actually create the pull request.

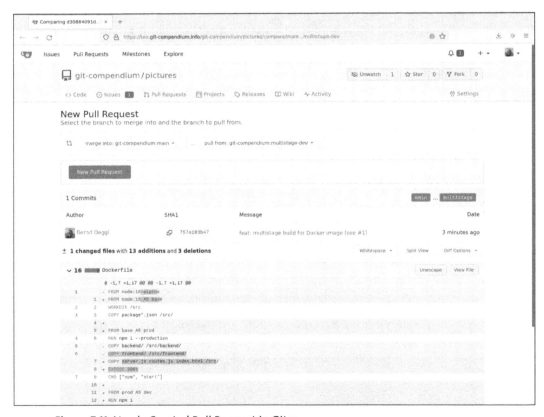

Figure 7.11 Newly Created Pull Request in Gitea

The task of reviewing and accepting/rejecting a pull request is usually the responsibility of different individuals on a team. In our example, however, we'll accept the pull request ourselves right away. In this case, we'll accept the pull request with the default setting **Merge Pull Request**. This option will create a new commit indicating the merge of the feature branch. If we had selected the **Rebase and Merge** option from the dropdown list, this entry wouldn't appear in the commit history. After merging, delete the multistage-dev branch directly via the red button.

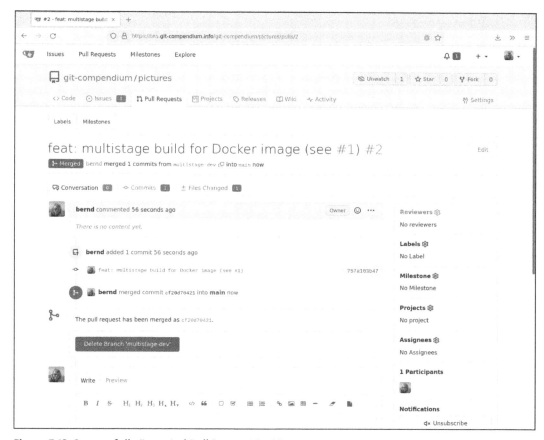

Figure 7.12 Successfully Executed Pull Request in Gitea

The issue in the ticket system contains references to all operations that were related to the pull request because the commit message contains a reference to the issue.

To conclude this short example, let's create a release of our software. Click on **Releases • New Release**. We'll use v1.0.0 as the tag name and Docker multistage as the title. Gitea generates the desired tag and two compressed files: one in the *.zip* format, which is more common on Windows, and one in the *.tag.gz* format, which is more common on Linux and macOS.

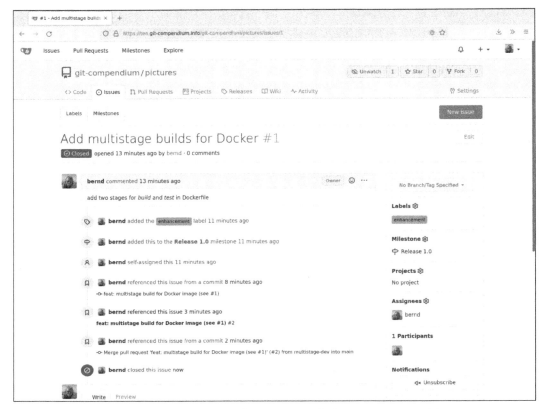

Figure 7.13 Closed Issue #1 in the Ticket System with the Entire Merge History

Figure 7.14 Release Tagged "v1.0.0" in Gitea

Now, when you run a git pull on your local computer, the new tag is downloaded:

git pull

```
remote: Enumerating objects: 1, done.
...
  * [new tag]          v1.0.0      -> v1.0.0
```

7.4   Gitolite

Gitolite is the program that's currently the most streamlined of all for managing your own Git hosting. In this program, everything happens on the command line—no web interface and of course no ticket system, wiki, or similar features. For Gitolite, the software requirements are minimal:

- OpenSSH server
- Git
- Perl (with the JavaScript Object Notation [JSON] module, if you want this output)

Since the system doesn't use a database or application server, the hardware requirements are also quite low: As long as the SSH server is running and access to permanent storage is snappy, you won't have any performance issues for your private repositories. For this reason, you can also use mini servers (like a Raspberry Pi) as Gitolite servers.

7.4.1   Installation

Unlike the Git hosting programs presented so far, Gitolite handles remote access to Git repositories exclusively via SSH. All SSH access occurs via a user account on the Linux system, and this account manages the rights for the projects. The other hosts we've described do the same. You can recognize this by the address of the remote Git repository: Using the address git@gitolite.git-compendium.info:gitolite-first, you can connect as user git to the server gitolite.git-compendium.info and use the repository gitolite-first.

For the most straightforward installation, re-create this user on your server and let Gitolite initialize the SSH settings. If you're familiar with Docker, we recommend looking at the repository at *https://github.com/git-compendium/gitolite-docker*, where you'll find a Docker setup that starts the Gitolite server with a command. For example, on an Ubuntu or Debian server, you can perform the manual setup with the following commands:

```
sudo useradd -m git
sudo su - git
git clone https://github.com/sitaramc/gitolite
mkdir /home/git/bin
/home/git/gitolite/install -ln
```

With this step, you're almost done with the installation. What's still missing is the administrator user for your Git repositories. Now, you must generate a SSH key on your workstation/laptop (or use an existing SSH key).

```
ssh-keygen -f ~/.ssh/gitoliteroot -N ''
scp ~/.ssh/gitoliteroot.pub gitolite.git-compendium.info:/tmp
```

Then, copy the public part of the key to the server and complete the installation (still as user git), as shown in the following example:

```
/home/git/bin/gitolite setup -pk /tmp/gitoliteroot.pub

  Initialized empty Git repository in
    /home/git/repositories/gitolite-admin.git/
  Initialized empty Git repository in
    /home/git/repositories/testing.git/
  WARNING: /home/git/.ssh missing; creating a new one
      (this is normal on a brand new install)
  WARNING: /home/git/.ssh/authorized_keys missing; creating a ...
      (this is normal on a brand new install)
```

7.4.2   Application

The Gitolite server is now ready. As shown in the output earlier, two Git repositories have been created: gitolite-admin and testing. Creating users or new Git repositories can be performed by modifying the gitolite-admin repository. You must clone the repository on your laptop or workstation where you previously generated the SSH keys:

```
git clone git@gitolite.git-compendium.info:gitolite-admin

  Cloning into 'gitolite-admin'...
  ...
```

The new directory contains the *conf* and *keydir* folders. The latter contains the SSH public key for gitoliteroot, which you imported during setup.

```
tree --charset=ascii

  .
  |-- conf
```

```
|    `-- gitolite.conf
`-- keydir
    `-- gitoliteroot.pub
```

To create new users, you must simply copy their public SSH keys to the *keydir* folder. Note that the name of the file corresponds to the user name. To create new Git repositories, edit the *conf/gitolite.conf* file and add a new `repo` entry:

```
repo gitolite-first
    RW+    = gitoliteroot
```

This step creates the `gitolite-first` repository, and the user `gitoliteroot` now has read and write permissions. Still, you must commit and push these changes:

```
git commit -a -m "add gitolite-first repo"

  [master 0fcc024] add gitolite-first repo
   1 file changed, 3 insertions(+)


git push

  Enumerating objects: 7, done.
  Counting objects: 100% (7/7), done.
  Delta compression using up to 8 threads
  Compressing objects: 100% (3/3), done.
  Writing objects: 100% (4/4), 393 bytes | 393.00 KiB/s, done.
  Total 4 (delta 0), reused 0 (delta 0)
  remote: Initialized empty Git repository in
    /home/git/repositories/gitolite-first.git/
  To gitolite:gitolite-admin
     7b33ac2..bb8b85f  master -> master
```

In the output of `git push`, notice that Gitolite has created a new Git repository for you. In the current version of Gitolite, a branch named `master` must be used. This name is referenced in many places in the Perl source code of the program.

Conclusion

Although both authors are quite fond of the command line, we still found Gitolite to be *very ascetic*. The web interfaces of GitHub, GitLab, or Gitea provide much more comfortable interfaces.

Chapter 8
Workflows

In this chapter, we'll show you how to work successfully and productively with Git, both on your own and, especially, on a team. Requirements in software development are truly diverse. Modern (web) applications are often developed and published continuously, which requires different workflows than a *fat client program*, for which a new release occurs only once every few years.

The good news is that Git is the right tool to master a wide variety of workflows. Which process is right for you and your team depends not only on the product, but also on personal taste.

8.1 Instructions for the Team

You should regard the workflows we present in this chapter as proven suggestions for how teamwork can function with Git. However, for *your* team to function well, you shouldn't follow these instructions without question. Maybe your project is a prototype where the focus isn't on a flawless implementation but instead on a fast implementation. You can then probably plan some steps differently than you would for software for a product, for instance, an Internet of Things (IoT) gadget that is produced in large numbers and is difficult or impossible to update later.

In any case, establishing certain rules for collaboration on the source code makes sense prior to a project's start. Ideally, the list of instructions is written on a sheet of paper physically displayed at workstations or digitally displayed on desktops for quick access. That some developers on your team will be completely without Git experience is quite unlikely these days. However, a short list of git commands related to the workflow you're using, as shown in Figure 8.1, won't do any harm.

Depending on the team's size, designating a Git tutor to serve as a point of contact in case problems arise may make sense. This person can certainly save valuable time when an inexperienced developer becomes despondent during a merge conflict or even accepts the wrong changes.

Git is an immensely powerful tool, but it can't stop team members from permanently deleting valuable information from a repository. Inexperienced developers, in particular, should be advised that --force with git push on important branches is most definitely a bad decision and therefore forbidden.

259

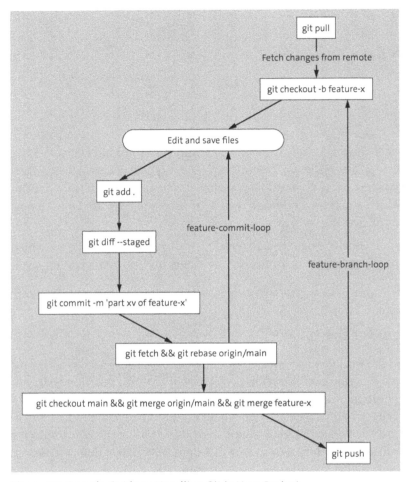

Figure 8.1 Sample Guide to Handling Git in Your Project

8.2   Solo Development

To get started, we'll describe the simplest scenario imaginable, namely, that you're developing a software project on your own. As soon as your program leaves the "Hello World!" status, using version management makes sense in any case. Software that fulfills this purpose is free, and the extra effort in your workflows is tiny. Yet, the gain from additional documentation is certainly worth the extra effort. Moreover, your private pet project may develop into something bigger, and other people might participate in its development at a later stage.

As long as you develop on your own and don't make your source code publicly available, you can of course do without the techniques we've presented, such as merge/pull requests, feature branches, or code reviews. Your development takes place only in the main branch, and you commit from time to time and push to a remote repository that serves as a backup for your source code.

If, in the course of development, a new idea comes to mind that you would like to try out, you may start this development on a new branch. Why? After some time, you may realize that the idea wasn't so good after all, and you can simply switch back to the main branch. To return to the stable version, you don't need to search the Git history for the point in time you want to jump back to. If you don't delete the feature branch, the development won't be lost. You can look at this idea again at a later time and perhaps use it in a different way.

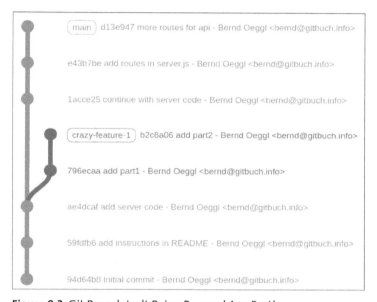

Figure 8.2 Git Branch Isn't Being Pursued Any Further

If the new idea is what you want, you can simply merge the branch into the main branch. Since you haven't made any commits to the main branch in the meantime, a fast-forward merge is generated, and the feature branch can simply be deleted, which then no longer appears in the Git history.

8.2.1 Conclusion

To summarize, the benefits of using Git (or more generally a version control system) include the following:

- The work is documented.
- You can go back to previous versions.
- Testing ideas using different branches is easy.
- A backup exists when using remote repositories.

Some drawbacks of using Git include the following:

- Workload is increased due to commits/pushes.

8.3   Feature Branches for Teams

The optional branching model just presented can also be applied to teams. The concept of *feature branches* introduced in this section will also appear in other workflows in this chapter. At this point, however, we want to focus on how you can reduce annoying merge conflicts despite feature branches.

8.3.1   New Function, New Branch

An inevitable problem for teams working together on a project occurs when different people modify the same files (or possibly modify the same passages in those files) at the same time. We discussed this topic in Chapter 3, Section 3.9.

With feature branches, the potential for conflict can be reduced by dividing work packages among individuals and having each development package take place in its own branch (the feature branch). Write access to the main branch is thus less frequent, resulting in fewer merges and uncomplicated development on the feature branch. In the extreme case, only one person is allowed to write to the branch. Everyone else on the team develops in their own feature branches, and once they're done, they send a merge/pull request to the authorized person.

8.3.2   Example

An example scenario is shown in Figure 8.3. Only Jane Doe has write access to the main branch, while the other team members each develop on their own feature branches. feature-1 was a *quick win*: Two commits from Manuel, a merge to the main branch, and the new feature is available to all.

The workflow on Manuel's computer would involve the following commands:

```
git pull

  Already up to date.

git checkout -b feature-1

  Switched to a new branch 'feature-1'
```

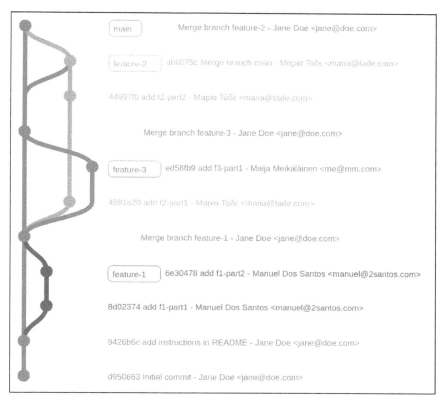

Figure 8.3 Possible Feature Branch Scenario: Development Team Working on Three Features

Now, Manuel creates the new file *feat1.py*, references it in the existing file *main.py*, and makes the first commit. After making further changes to *feat1.py*, he commits the file again and pushes its branch to the remote repository, as shown in the following example:

```
git add feat1.py
git commit -a -m "add f1-part1"

  [feature-1 8d02374] add f1-part1
   2 files changed, 3 insertions(+)
   create mode 100644 feat1.py
# other changes in feat1.py
git commit -m "add f1-part2" feat1.py

  [feature-1 6e30478] add f1-part2
   1 file changed, 2 insertions(+)

git push --set-upstream origin feature-1
```

```
Enumerating objects: 9, done.
...
 * [new branch]      feature-1 -> feature-1
Branch 'feature-1' set up to track remote branch 'feature-1'...
```

For Jane to merge the feature branch, she first performs a pull on her working copy of the repository, with the following commands:

```
git pull
```

```
...
 * [new branch]      feature-1  -> origin/feature-1
Already up to date
```

In the pull, the new branch origin/feature-1 was created in Jane's repository. She can now take another look at the changes (git diff) and then merge the branch into the main branch, in the following way:

```
git diff main..origin/feature-1
git merge origin/feature-1
```

```
Updating 9426b6c..6e30478
Fast-forward
main.py  | 2 ++
feat1.py | 3 +++
2 files changed, 5 insertions(+)
create mode 100644 feat1.py
```

The other branches are a bit more complicated: feature-2 and feature-3 are developed in parallel, whereas the latter branch is finished more quickly by Maija and is merged into the main branch. To make sure that the feature-2 branch of our Greek co-worker Maria doesn't cause problems with main, Maria merges the changed main branch (commit ab6075c) after finishing her new feature and tests the changes thoroughly again. Maria places the following commands on the feature-2 branch:

```
git checkout feature-2
git -a -m "add f2-part2"
  [feature-2 44997f0] add f2-part2
  1 file changed, 2 insertions(+)
```

```
git pull
  From ...
    6e30478..ed58fb9  main     -> origin/main
  Already up to date.
```

Note that Maria starts a pull, from the remote repository, from the feature branch. In this process, the changes of the changed `main` branch are fetched from the server but not merged with the local `main` branch. So, as a result, Maria needs to merge the `origin/main` with her feature branch, with the following commands:

```
git merge origin/main
```

```
  Merge made by the 'recursive' strategy.
    feat3.py | 3 +++
    1 file changed, 3 insertions(+)
    create mode 100644 feat3.py
```

```
git push --set-upstream origin feature-2
```

As no merge conflict exists and the new feature still works, Maria pushes the `feature-2` branch to the remote repository, and Jane can merge that branch into the `main` branch as well. The new features will be available for the next release.

All of this works with the out-of-the-box tools of Git. You can use `git branch` to create branches and use `git merge` to merge the `main` branch into a feature branch and finally merge a feature branch into `main`. If you use a Git platform like GitLab or GitHub, alternatively, these steps occur via the web interface. If you're already familiar with the Git command-line interface (CLI), you'll reach your goal more quickly than with the web interface.

Figure 8.4 Settings for Write-Protection of Branches in GitLab

Git itself doesn't contain any functions for limiting writes to the main branch (or any other branch). If you don't want to rely on team discipline to limit write access, you can enable this functionality on your Git platform. All the programs we described in previous chapters provide an option to protect branches from unauthorized write access. With GitHub, however, you'll need a paid subscription (e.g., GitHub Pro) for private projects.

So far, we haven't explicitly talked about merge or pull requests in this section because we've always equated these terms with the corresponding functions of Git hosting platforms in this book. Theoretically, of course, a merge request can be a simple email to the person with write permissions on the main branch requesting a merge.

8.3.3   Code Review

A responsible developer (like Jane in our example) will, of course, review these changes before merging the branch. Even better, perhaps the whole team, or at least a designated group, carries out this reviewing process.

Code reviews are often an integral part of agile software development processes. With feature branches, reviewing changes is quite easy. Going back to the previous example, you could conduct a code review before the merge from the feature-2 branch by starting a diff from the main branch with the feature branch:

```
git diff main..origin/feature-2
```

The syntax used in the git diff command shows the changes made to the main branch during a merge. To check if any changes on the main branch aren't in the feature-2 branch prior to reviewing, you can use the following command:

```
git diff origin/feature-2...main
```

Note the three periods between the branches. In our example, the output remains empty because Maria committed ab6075c to the current state of main. She did this commit via a merge commit, but she could also have rebased main to her branch, which we'll describe in the next section. If problems still occur in the code review of feature-2, Maria can fix these problems with further commits before the merge is performed.

8.3.4   Merge

You may have noticed that the merges shown in Figure 8.3 are depicted with a circle, but that no hash code appears in their relevant descriptions. We chose this display to show you how the branches evolve over time. The Git history after the commits and merge processes is shown in Figure 8.5.

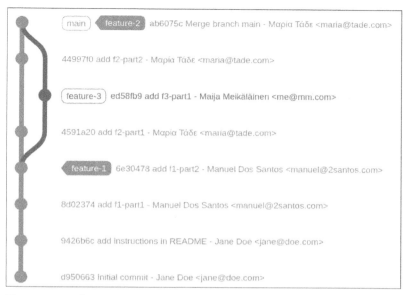

Figure 8.5 Real Git History after Commits and Merges

Since merges on the main branch are always fast-forward merges, the actual merge no longer appears in the Git history. To avoid losing the merges, you must call git merge with the --no-ff option to force an explicit commit. Whether this information will be important to you later, however, you must decide for yourself. Without merge commits, the Git history will definitely be tidier.

8.3.5   Rebasing

However, we still do have such a merge commit in the history. Maria created commit ab6075c by merging main into her feature branch. This inclusion can be useful for documentation purposes since it shows that the ed58fb9 commit was included in her branch before her feature was merged into main. A fast-forward merge isn't possible in this case because different commits have occurred on main and on feature-2.

If Maria does a rebase from main on her feature branch, then this merge commit will also get dropped, and the Git history will look quite straightforward.

```
git rebase origin/main
```

```
First, rewinding head to replay your work on top of it...
Applying: add f2-part1
Applying: add f2-part2
```

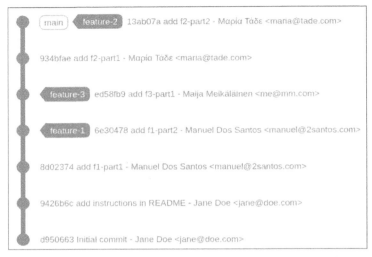

Figure 8.6 Git History with Rebasing from the Main to the Feature Branch

The basic rule is that rebasing must never be applied to a public branch that has already been uploaded. For this reason, you should only use rebasing if the feature branch hasn't been uploaded yet to a remote repository via git push. The commits on the feature branch are rewritten by main during rebasing (compare the difference in the hash codes for commits f2-part1 and f2-part2, as shown in Figure 8.5 and Figure 8.6). We describe the problems that can arise when making changes to the Git history in Chapter 11, Section 11.4, among others.

8.3.6   Conclusion

With the mini feature branches described in this section, the workflow is quite straightforward in theory. In real software projects, however, often feature branches involve several developers working for days or even weeks.

During that time, developers can always merge or rebase their feature branch with the main branch so that the final merge into the main branch doesn't become too complicated. At the same time, however, other team members can't see the code of the feature branch team. If functions are developed in the course of the project that are also needed by other developers, parallel developments may occur. This problem can be prevented with good communication, but the problem should still be considered in the workflow.

Some advantages of using feature branches include the following:

- Undisturbed development of new functions
- Code reviews before feature branch merges
- Clear Git history
- The main branch remains stable

Some drawbacks of using feature branches include the following:

- Possible code duplication in shared libraries
- Overly complicated merges because of long development periods

8.4   Merge/Pull Requests

Based on the feature branch model, the major Git platforms have extended the work-flow to include merge/pull requests as integral parts. At this point, we'll deviate from pure Git functionality and use workflows in a web interface on a platform.

The major enhancement (compared to the feature branch workflow described in Chapter 7, Section 7.3.4) is the mandatory review process. Picking up from our earlier scenario, let's have Manuel develop a new function. He does so by creating the `feature-1` branch and adding two commits (a8503d6 and 70996c6). When pushing to the remote repository, Manuel receives the following response:

```
git push --set-upstream origin feature-1

  Enumerating objects: 7, done.
  ...
  remote:
  remote: To create a merge request for feature-1, visit:
  remote:    https://gitlab.com/git-compendium/workflows-github...
  remote:
  To gitlab.com:git-compendium/workflows-github.git
   * [new branch]      feature-1 -> feature-1
  Branch 'feature-1' set up to track remote branch 'feature-1'...
```

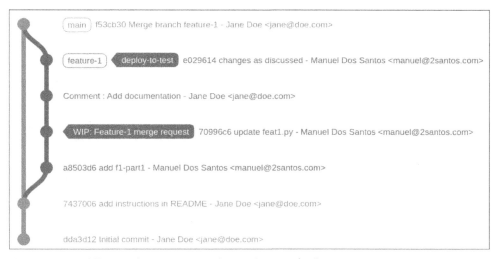

Figure 8.7 Workflow with Feature Branches and Merge/Pull Requests

The lines beginning with `remote` indicate the response by the Git server. In modern terminals on Linux and macOS, you can click the link directly (possibly together by holding down `Ctrl`). Alternatively, you can create the merge request via the web interface.

Figure 8.8 Merge Request in GitLab Created via the Web Interface

Manuel creates the merge request via the web interface and enters the name "Feature-1 merge request." Note that this merge request isn't a feature of Git itself, and you won't find a reference to this request anywhere via `git log`. The metadata about the merge request, such as who created the request and when, is stored in the Git hosting provider's database. If you switch providers at some point, this information is likely to be lost. A commendable exception is GitLab, which can import both the pull requests from GitHub and those from Gitea, including comments, as we verified during our tests.

Manuel enters Jane as the person responsible for the merge request. Jane reviews the new feature and asks for additional documentation for the new feature. Manuel adds the comment and commits the changes (commit e029614). Then, the version from the feature branch is installed on a test system. When the quality assurance (QA) team raises no objections to the new feature, Jane merges the changes into the `main` branch.

The workflow we've described is certainly widely used, not least because of the popularity of GitHub and GitLab. The processes aren't complicated, and code review can eliminate errors before they reach the main branch. The workflow inherits the problem of branches running in parallel for too long when features are too large from the feature branch model. An additional problem with this workflow can arise if the time span between the pull/merge request and the merge itself is too long. Reasons for this delay

can be that the code review doesn't take place quickly enough or that too many problems are found during the pull request. Both extend the parallel runtime of the
branches.

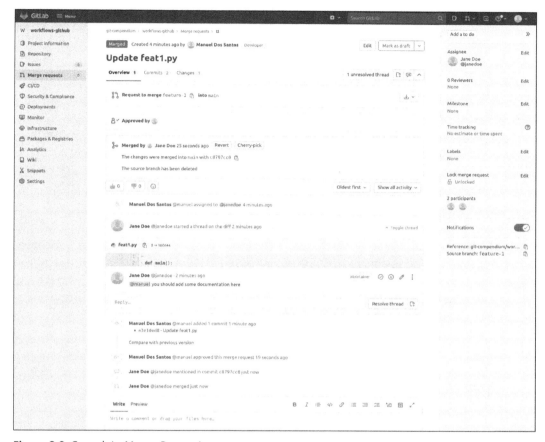

Figure 8.9 Complete Merge Request

In contrast to the previous section, you may notice a few changes in the workflow. We
wanted to highlight the difference between the purely Git-based workflow and the
workflow presented in this section, which can only be implemented with appropriate
Git servers.

8.4.1   Forks

We've described the technique of *forking* foreign repositories in Chapter 2, Section 2.7.1,
and in even more detail in Chapter 5, Section 5.1.2. In combination with merge/pull
requests, you can also establish a workflow where all developers manage their own
repositories to which only they have write access.

This approach is close to Linus Torvalds' original idea. The inventor of Git, who had developed the software primarily to manage the Linux kernel, received a number of suggestions for improvements in the form of patch files as email attachments to the kernel mailing list. To save himself the work of incorporating and testing the patches, Torvalds suggested that patch developers maintain their own Git repositories where they can incorporate and test their own patches. Since GitHub didn't exist back then, developers had to run their own Git servers, from which Torvalds could then pull, which is exactly what Git's built-in server `git daemon` is for.

Origin of Git

In a tech talk worth watching, Git's creator Linus Torvalds presented his motivation for creating Git in 2007, when it was just two years old. In his rather opinionated way, he condemned every other version control system, first and foremost Apache Subversion (SVN), which was the most widely used system at the time:

https://www.youtube.com/watch?v=4XpnKHJAok8

Forks with pull/merge requests are an extremely useful workflow for occasional contributions by different people on other people's projects. For the workflows we describe in this chapter, we assume a manageable number of members on your team who are registered with the team in some way and who have permissions to access a central repository. You won't need any forks for your project in this case.

8.4.2   Conclusion

Some advantages of using merge/pull requests include the following:

- Code review before merging on the main branch
- Good documentation of the work processes
- Stable main branch

Some drawbacks of using merge/pull requests include the following:

- Parallel branches when code reviews are too slow

8.5   Long-Running Branches: Gitflow

For a long time, what was called the *Gitflow workflow* was the standard for developing larger projects with Git. The fundamental difference compared to the working methods we've described so far is that, with the Gitflow workflow, two branches run in parallel and are available for the entire duration of the project.

In addition to the `main` branch, at least one other branch, often called `develop` or `next`, is where the actual development takes place. The code on this branch should be stable according to the model and used for nightly builds. On the main branch, only finished versions are merged; *normal* commits don't happen on this branch.

> **The Theory behind Gitflow**
>
> An oft-cited blog post was written by Vincent Driessen in 2010 where he describes clearly and with good graphics his view of this way of working, which he calls *Gitflow*:
>
> *https://nvie.com/posts/a-successful-git-branching-model*
>
> Interestingly, the author added a note to the posting in March 2020, in which he reports from personal experience that many projects can probably be handled just as well with a simpler workflow.

8.5.1   Main, Develop, Feature

The feature branches presented in the previous section can and should be used in the same way with this model, so that the develop branch retains its stability.

The increased complexity of this workflow is shown in Figure 8.10. This time, our team will develop only two new features. You can see the main branch on the far left, followed by the develop branch on the right.

Let's say Manuel develops the first feature in the feature-1 branch, which branches off from the develop branch. Maria merges the two commits back to the develop branch (commit hash 759483c). She uses the --no-ff (*no fast-forward*) option on all her commits so that these commits remain visible in the Git history later. Using the --no-edit option on merge, you can accept the default commit message that says which branch will be merged.

The flow of commands thus looks quite similar to the commands we described in Section 8.3:

```
manuel$ git checkout develop
manuel$ git checkout -b feature-1
manuel$ git commit -m "add f1-part2" feat1.py
manuel$ git push --set-upstream origin feature-1

maria$  git checkout develop
maria$  git pull
maria$  git merge --no-ff --no-edit origin/feature-1
  Merge made by the 'recursive' strategy.
   main.py   | 2 ++
   feat1.py  | 3 +++
   2 files changed, 5 insertions(+)
   create mode 100644 feat1.py
```

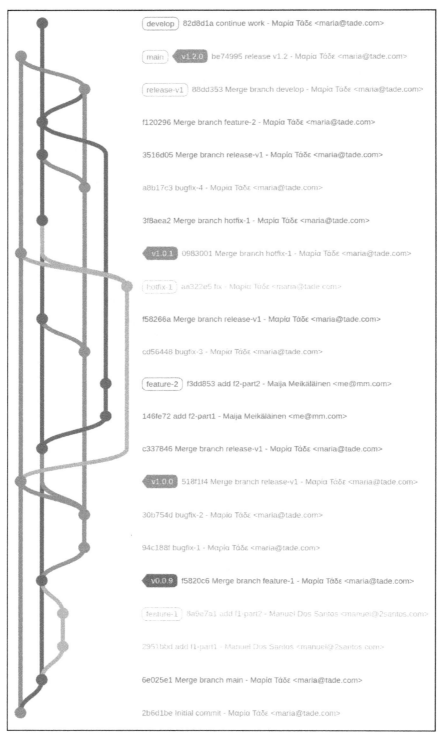

Figure 8.10 Branches, Commits, and Merges in the Gitflow Workflow

After the new feature has been implemented successfully, Maria is now preparing the first release of the software. She marks the current state with the tag v0.0.9. In addition, she creates a new *release branch* (release-v1). During the intensive tests on this branch, two small bugs still appear. Maria fixes these bugs with commits Bugfix-1 and Bugfix-2. To perform these steps, she types the following commands:

```
maria$  git checkout develop
maria$  git tag "v0.0.9"
maria$  git checkout -b release-v1

# Change files for Bugfix 1
maria$  git commit -a -m "bugfix-1"
  [release-v1 94c188f] bugfix-1
   1 file changed, 2 insertions(+)

# more changes for Bugfix 2
maria$  git commit -a -m "bugfix-2"
```

She then merges the release branch to the main branch and tags it v1.0.0. Now is the first time a version of the software can be found on the main branch. Maria merges the release branch to the develop branch to have the two bugfixes available there as well. In the following example, we've omitted the output of the commands:

```
maria$  git checkout main
maria$  git merge --no-ff --no-edit release-v1
maria$  git tag v1.0.0
maria$  git push
maria$  git push --tags

maria$  git checkout develop
maria$  git merge --no-ff --no-edit release-v1
maria$  git push
```

8.5.2   Hot Bugfixes

A serious problem now appears in the operation of the software, which must be fixed immediately. Maria creates the hotfix-1 branch directly from the main branch. She saves the fix with commit aa322e5 and merges the branch back to main. Then, she increases the software version by one patch level to v1.0.1 and tags the repository accordingly.

The hotfix-1 branch must also be merged to the develop branch to eliminate the bug there as well. This section in an enlarged graphic is again shown in Figure 8.11.

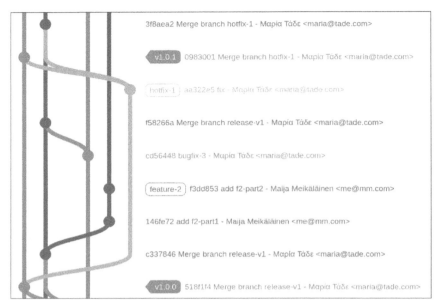

Figure 8.11 Troubleshooting on the "hotfix-1" Branch

8.5.3   Bugfixes in the develop Branch

On the release branch, two more small bugs have been fixed in the meantime (bugfix-3 and bugfix-4). Since these bugs aren't critical, no new software version will be released, but the changes will be included in the next version. However, the bug fixes are immediately merged into the develop branch.

Like the develop branch, the release branch runs parallel to the main branch, but only as long as the version is actively supported. With the completion of a new major version, a new release branch is created (for example, release-v2, not shown in the earlier figure). Whether and how long the old version should still be supported then depends on customer requirements.

8.5.4   Another New Function

Maija has now implemented a new function on the develop branch. She created the feature-2 branch for this purpose and made her two commits in that branch. Maria merges this branch back to develop. Since the interim changes to the develop branch don't overlap with the new feature, the merge goes through without any conflict (commit hash f120296).

To make the new feature available to customers, Maria merges the develop branch to the release branch again (commit 88dd353). As no errors were found, she merges release-v1 back to main and tags the version with v1.2.0.

Figure 8.12 Second Release v1.2.0 on the main Branch

By now, you might be dizzy from the many merges. This workflow places top priority on the stability of the `main` branch and accepts the increased complexity of many branches as a trade-off for this stability. In addition, this workflow enables you to manage multiple versions in parallel. If your software doesn't have these requirements, for example, because you're running a web portal or web service, you can definitely choose a simpler workflow.

If you prefer to work in an *agile* way and aren't scared of continuous integration (CI) pipelines, then the workflow in the next section will certainly appeal to you more.

8.5.5   Conclusion

Some advantages of using Gitflow include the following:

- A stable main branch
- Easily comprehensible versions
- Several versions in production at the same time

Some drawbacks of using Gitflow include the following:

- A large number of merges
- High complexity in the repository
- Branches that can drift apart
- Slow rollout of new software versions
- Strict requirements that make a lot of extra work

8.6   Trunk-Based Development

Trunk-based development refers to a working technique in which all changes are checked in as quickly as possible to the main branch of the development. In Git terminology, you simply replace *trunk* with *main*. Some basic rules of using this technique include the following:

- No long-term branches should exist other than the main branch
- When feature branches are used:
  - One developer per feature branch
  - Maximum duration of 1 to 2 days (even better, a few hours only)

The feature branches used in this context differ primarily in scope from the workflow described in Section 8.3. In trunk-based development, the tasks must be small since only one developer is allowed to work on the problem and only has 1 or 2 days to do so. Also, feature branches are optional in trunk-based development because, in the best case, all team members push directly to the main branch.

At first glance, this scenario sounds a little scary: *All* team members are allowed to push on the main branch? Read on to understand how this workflow can work.

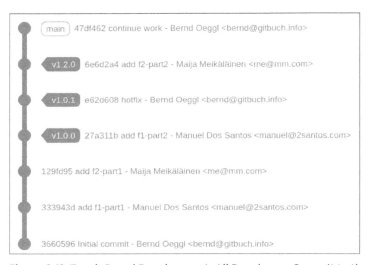

Figure 8.13 Trunk-Based Development: All Developers Commit to the main Branch

8.6.1   Continuous Integration

A prerequisite for this technique to be successful is a functioning CI pipeline that ensures the functionality of the software with sufficient tests. If problems arise in the code, the pipeline sounds an alarm, and the developer who triggered the error is encouraged to fix the error as soon as possible. As long as the pipeline is defective, no commit by a team member will make it into the finished software.

Commonly, teams establish a certain culture where no one likes to destroy the pipeline. As a result, commits are well tested before being pushed to the server, which contributes to the quality of the overall source code. Ideally, a developer can test the CI pipeline, or at least key parts of it, locally before making the push to the server. This approach greatly reduces the risk of a broken pipeline.

8.6.2   Release-Ready

One of the advantages of trunk-based development is that the latest state of development is always (or should be) *release-ready*. Let's say management decides that feature XY, which has existed in the main branch for a few days and was just tested by the QA team, needs to be rolled out today. In the best case, the project manager checks with the development team that everything is going according to plan and brings the last build, which may only be a few minutes old, to the production environment.

This confidence in stable builds derives from a reliable CI pipeline. The pipeline constantly evolves during the project and becomes more and more reliable with every bug weeded out and with every new test.

8.6.3   Continuous Deployment

Once you've gained confidence in your CI pipeline and want to satisfy customer requests as quickly as possible, you can also automate the process of rolling out the finished software. With continuous deployment (CD), you're in the top league of software automation. A developer entering the git push command immediately pushes a new version to the productive environment if the pipeline is successful! Thus, the trunk-based development presented in this section is the ideal basis for CD.

8.6.4   Feature Flags

But how can complex functions be developed that can't be finished and put into production in a day or two? One way to deal with this problem is to use *feature flags* or *feature toggles*. Queries are built into the code that decide whether certain functions are available or not. The conditions for this availability can be specified from a configuration file or from a database during the runtime of the software.

In the simplest case, think of a feature flag as an if query in the software, where the condition isn't version dependent: You could also unlock certain features for certain user groups. For example, functions can be tested by the QA team in productive operations without other users having access to this function. To make the function visible to all users after it has been released, you don't need to install a new version; you can just modify its database entry.

One thing to keep in mind despite all the euphoria surrounding software automation: Demands on developers are higher than in the feature branch workflow, where a newcomer to the team may get valuable tips during a pull request before a bug gets into the main branch. In trunk-based development, an inexperienced developer may disrupt the usual workflow for the entire team because the pipeline stalls after a bug.

To help inexperienced developers get started, *pair programming* works well. If possible, an experienced programmer should sit at a computer with a novice and take turns operating the keyboard.

8.6.5   Conclusion

Some advantages of using trunk-based development include the following:

- Source code that is always *release-ready*
- No complicated merges
- No *code freeze* prior to releases

Some drawbacks of using trunk-based development include the following:

- Difficult start for inexperienced developers, which can be compensated by pair programming

8.7   Which Workflow Is the Right One?

As mentioned at the beginning of this chapter, we can't give you simple answers about what workflows are right for you and your team. On one hand, requirements in software development depend on many different factors, and on the other hand, the choice depends very much on your team.

When working on your own, a best practice is to commit your work to the main branch and create feature branches when you're working on an immature idea or just want to try something out. If you're part of a team, the strategy used will be explained to you anyway, and you'll comply.

When deciding which workflow to use, you should consider the following factors:

- **Experience of team members**
  If all your team members already have in-depth experience with Git, you can choose from any of the suggested workflows. If you have inexperienced developers on your team and pair programming isn't an option, the graphical user interface (GUI) of platforms such as GitHub or GitLab helps tremendously with onboarding. Also, the additional documentation for the merge/pull request workflow can be helpful.

- **Size of the team**
  We think trunk-based development works especially well with smaller teams. The other workflows should scale well even with large teams. However, the fact that team size isn't necessarily a limitation of one workflow over another is impressively demonstrated by Google, where tens of thousands of developers reportedly apply trunk-based development. However, this scenario will no longer have too much in common with the workflow we've described in this chapter because the tools used in such large organizations are rarely useful for organizations of a "normal" size.

- **Type of software**

  If your project requires running multiple stable versions of the software in production, a workflow with parallel branches may be a good choice for you. Despite the increased complexity of Gitflow, you can quickly jump to a version and apply bug fixes there. If you only have one version in production at a time, as is the case with an online platform, for example, an agile workflow like trunk-based development can be more rewarding and lead to higher productivity.

- **Availability of infrastructure**

  While some workflows can do without any additional software other than Git, others require the use of additional programs. Trunk-based development can't function properly in the way we've described without a CI pipeline. The pipelines must be configured and run on a computer infrastructure. In the pull/merge request workflow, you'll need a Git platform, which incurs costs.

The bottom line is that we highly recommend the pull/merge request workflow if you can and want to use a Git platform. This workflow is also well suited for beginners since the processes are clearly documented and are easily retrievable via the web interface.

If you're a bit experimental and rapid development cycles are important to you, you should consider trunk-based development. The effort to create the pipelines must be taken into account at the beginning, but the added value during operations will surely convince you of its efficiency.

Chapter 9
Working Techniques

In this chapter, we'll introduce you to some advanced working techniques, such as the following:

- Hooks can enable you to automatically run a script for certain actions.

- Concise commit messages are essential for the long-term documentation and maintenance of a large project. We'll provide some tips on how to avoid messy commit histories.

- Organizing large projects is a challenge even with Git: Submodules and subtrees provide two ways to separate subprojects in their own directories.

- If you frequently run the git command in terminal windows, you can make your life easier with aliases, bash autocompletion, and ultimately the *Oh My Zsh* extension.

- Finally, enabling two-factor authentication provides for a higher degree of security when accessing Git platforms. In this context, we'll tell you what you need to keep in mind.

9.1   Hooks

A *hook* in Git refers to a script that is executed when a certain event has occurred in your Git repository.

Hooks aren't an invention of Git; other version control systems had and still have a similar concept before Git. Since hooks can also be run before an action occurs (for example, before a commit is accepted), they're popularly used to enforce certain policies or a specific style.

> **Hooks versus Pipelines**
>
> If you've read the previous chapters on Git hosting platforms (see Chapter 5, Section 5.2, and Chapter 6, Section 6.4), you may now be reminded of continuous integration/continuous deployment (CI/CD) pipelines. Hooks are also launched after certain events and work with your Git repository. However, the options *real* pipelines open up for you aren't comparable to the somewhat limited functionality of Git hooks.

9.1.1   Hooks in Real Life

The easiest way to learn about the hook functionality is through an example. We assume that you either work on Linux or macOS or use the Git Bash on Windows. First, you'll need to create a new Git repository on the local computer:

```
mkdir hooks-demo
cd hooks-demo
git init
  Initialized empty Git repository in /src/hooks-demo/.git/
```

Git creates a subfolder with sample hooks:

```
ls .git/hooks
```

```
  applypatch-msg.sample        pre-merge-commit.sample
  commit-msg.sample            prepare-commit-msg.sample
  fsmonitor-watchman.sample    pre-push.sample
  post-update.sample           pre-rebase.sample
  pre-applypatch.sample        pre-receive.sample
  pre-commit.sample            update.sample
```

The files all end in *.sample* to indicate that these are only suggestive. Based on these filenames, you can easily deduce when one of these scripts is used. A common event to execute a hook is pre-commit, which is the time before the changes stored in the staging area are finally committed to the local repository.

Now, let's create the *.git/hooks/pre-commit* file with the following content:

```
#!/bin/sh
untracked=$(git ls-files --others --exclude-standard | wc -l)
if [ $untracked -gt 0 ]
then
  echo "Untracked files, please add or ignore"
  exit 1
fi
```

On Linux and macOS, you still need to make the file executable (chmod +x .git/hooks/pre-commit), which doesn't work on Windows because the NTFS file system doesn't store this information. Git Bash checks the contents of the file and recognizes the file as executable (since the first 2 characters are #!).

Our first hook script should prevent us from committing if files in the working directory aren't intended to be committed. Unfortunately, this case sometimes occurs when major changes are implemented: You might change a few files and then add a new file.

Then, you execute the commit with `git commit -a`. This step causes all modified files to be included in the commit; however, the newly created file falls through the cracks.

Let's check the functionality of our script with two changes. First, we'll add a *README.md* file and then stage and commit it:

```
echo "# Hooks Demo" > README.md
git add README.md
git commit -m "add README"
```

```
[main (root-commit) 1a74605] add README
 1 file changed, 1 insertion(+)
 create mode 100644 README.md
```

No sign of our hook yet, but that's correct because we didn't forget anything with this commit. The second change now affects the *README.md* file again, and we also create a new file called *hello.txt*. Then, we commit everything with the -a switch:

```
echo "A Git pre-commit hook" >> README.md
echo "Hello commit" > hello.txt
git commit -a -m "update README"
```

```
  Untracked files, please add or ignore
```

Now, our pre-commit hook has prevented the commit! The changes weren't included in the repository. As long as files exist in the repository that are neither specified in the *.gitignore* file nor committed to the staging area via `git add`, you can't commit in that repository.

If you're considering scenarios where you use `pre-commit` scripts to demand strict specifications for filenames or require commit messages from all employees, we're sorry to disappoint you. The whole thing is based on voluntariness in a way because, with the `commit` option -n, you can bypass a `pre-commit` hook easily.

To finish our example, we'll check the hook to see if entries in the *.gitignore* file are really ignored:

```
echo "hello.txt" > .gitignore
git add .gitignore
git commit -a -m "update README, add gitignore"
```

```
  [main 69511e6] update README, add gitignore
   2 files changed, 2 insertions(+)
   create mode 100644 .gitignore
```

The commit worked, and the changes were saved in the local repository.

9.1.2   Explanation of the Sample Script

If you look at the code of the hook script presented earlier, even the first line might seem strange to you without prior Linux knowledge. The start of the file, called a *shebang* (#!), determines the interpreter for the statements in the file. In this case, the interpreter is /bin/sh, the default shell on most Unix-based operating systems.

The first statement in our script creates the variable untracked and assigns it the output of the command git ls-files --others --exclude-standard | wc -l. Now, git ls-files outputs a list of files that aren't yet included in the repository, and wc -l counts the lines in the output. For example, if we had two files in the working directory that were neither *staged* nor contained in a *.gitignore* file, the content of the $untracked variable would be the value 2.

The if query checks this value and terminates the script's execution with an error (exit 1) if the value is greater than 0. For shell scripts, a return value of 0 traditionally represents error-free execution, whereas all other values are interpreted as errors.

9.1.3   More Hooks

What we described in the previous section was an example of a local (i.e., client-side) hook. Such scripts are good for pointing out omissions or for suggesting areas of improvement.

The Git hooks help page contains over 20 events for which a hook can be executed. Among them are events related to applying patches from emails or running the garbage collector, which we won't detail any further. Instead, we'll focus on a small selection of local hooks we consider useful, such as the following:

- pre-commit
  This hook, as we've already described, can abort a commit.

- commit-msg
  This hook can check a commit message and abort the commit if necessary. The text of the message can also be changed by your script.

- pre-push
  This hook can prevent a push. At this point, tests could be run to ensure that only *valid* code is uploaded to the remote repository.

- post-commit
  This hook is mainly used to trigger notifications. You can no longer prevent the commit with this script.

- post-checkout
  This hook is called after you've switched to another branch or even after a git clone.

Other hooks can be useful, especially on a server, such as the following:

- **pre-receive**

  This hook starts before a `git push` is accepted on the server. The output of the executed script (both the output of errors and the normal output) is forwarded to the console of the calling program. A user therefore sees the result in response to a `git push`. The `pre-receive` hook is called once per push and can prevent the whole push.

- **update**

  This hook works similar to `pre-receive`, except that it's called once for each pushed branch or tag. This hook allows you to fine-tune and target the pushed objects and allow only parts of a push.

  At this point, you could implement extended user permissions independent of the permissions for the underlying file system. Since the major Git hosting platforms provide such functions conveniently, we're no longer forced to practice complicated shell scripting.

- **post-receive**

  This hook is activated after the push operation has been successfully completed. Previously, these scripts were used for deployment mechanisms to roll out a new software version on a server. As with `pre-receive`, the output is also redirected. Since the proliferation of CI/CD pipelines, these tasks have largely shifted to pipelines.

9.1.4   Hooks versus Actions/Pipelines

At this point, you may wonder how your scripts are executed on a computer running Windows. Interestingly, the script in the previous section also works if you perform your commit in PowerShell on Windows. Responsible for this integration is the *Cygwin* environment, which is included with the Windows Git installation. However, a fundamental problem remains: You don't know in which environment Git hooks are running (unless you know the computer setups of all your team members).

Things are even more difficult when you want to run more complex scripts. Let's say you want to start the automatic tests of your software project before a user can make a push. For testing, you need special libraries that aren't installed in the developer's local environment (and perhaps can't be installed). The developer would thus have no way to push successfully and would always have to bypass the hook using `--no-verify`.

You can already see what the problem boils down to: To guarantee the safe execution of tests or similarly important processes, you want operations to take place in a defined environment. This defined environment is exactly what's provided by pipelines, actions, or CI systems offered by Git platforms such as GitHub or GitLab. However, you must pay for these advantages with certain disadvantages (costs, vendor lock-in, etc.), as listed in Table 9.1.

	Git Hooks	Pipelines/Actions
Complexity	(Shell) scripts	Simple YAML Ain't Markup Language (YAML) syntax
Security	Easy to bypass	Permissions for pipeline stages
Resources	Minimum, no bots/virtual machines (VMs)	Runners as VMs or containers
Lock-In	No vendor lock-in	YAML syntax platform-dependent
Passwords	Difficult to manage safely	Variables in the web interface

Table 9.1 Git Hooks versus Pipelines/Actions

9.2   Concise Commit Messages

If you search the web for "git commit message," depending on your Google profile, you'll be inundated with *best practices* for writing commit messages. In our case, our search found 12.8 million results!

In this section, we want to highlight how important meaningful commit messages are. Of course, commit messages don't determine the success or failure of your project. Nevertheless, we're convinced that a few simple rules can make life easier for you and your team members. Don't worry: Our rules won't require more time writing a commit message than the time required to fix a bug in the code.

Basically, we mostly adhere to three simple rules:

- The first line should be short (preferably less than 50 characters) and describe the changes.
- The second line remains empty if further information exists.
- From the third line on, more information about the commit can follow (but may not).

These rules have become established in many projects and ensure that the essential information is easy to read, especially in the single-line output of the Git history.

9.2.1   Multiline Commit Messages in the Console

If you run git commit without the -m option, you can write the commit message in an editor. But git commit -m also allows multiline commit messages. Just start with git commit -m 'bla ..., and press [Enter].

You can continue the commit message in the next line. According to the rules we discussed, the second line always remains empty, so you want to press [Enter] again. Now, the rest of the message follows until you end the message with the second single

quotation mark. The shell recognizes that the string is now closed, and the command
has thus been entered completely:

```
git commit -m 'first line

more details
still more details'
```

9.2.2   Commit Title and Text

The first line is referred to as the *title* of the commit message. The title is particularly
important because it appears in virtually all log outputs. Any time you or someone else
on your team looks for a change in the Git log, this line is the most important place.

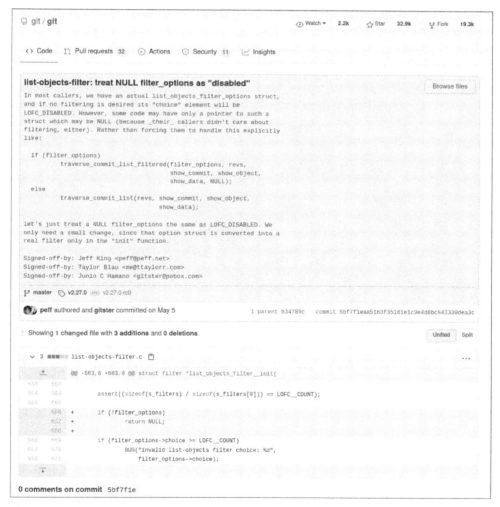

Figure 9.1 Longer Explanations in the Commit Message for a Three-Line Code Change in the
Git Source Repository

Whether you provide information for the text part of the message and how much depends very much on your personal preferences and, of course, on the project's specifications. Even large, successful projects handle this issue in completely different ways. In the repository for the Git software, long explanations with code examples are sometimes included for a code change of three lines. The length of this message is due to the way the Git project works, which involves sending patches to a mailing list, with the email body also being a commit message.

At the other extreme, commit messages may consist of only a few characters. Figure 9.2 shows a commit in the *Atom* editor repository. In this case, an *emoji* is used to describe the commit. This example is not a joke: This particular commit comes from one of the core developers of Atom.

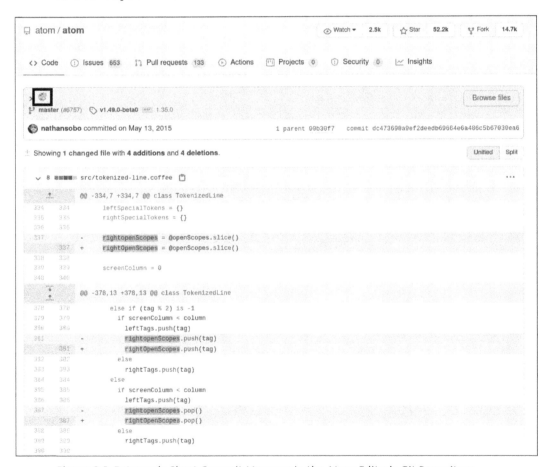

Figure 9.2 Extremely Short Commit Message in the Atom Editor's Git Repository

The Gitmoji project hosted on GitHub (*https://github.com/carloscuesta/gitmoji*) tries to define a standard for which emojis should be used for certain kinds of commits. The emoji used in our earlier example, a color palette, is meant to indicate that the structure or nature of the source code has been improved. (In the actual example, the name of a variable has changed.) That a commit message consisting only of an emoji would be met with acceptance among Git's developers is doubtful.

Git doesn't impose strict rules on commit messages. By default, no commits can be saved without a message, but even this requirement can be worked around with the `--allow-empty-message` option. However, as the `git commit` help page reveals, this option was only included to allow other version control systems to access Git via scripts. You shouldn't use this option at all.

9.2.3   Character Set and Language

Thus, in the end, how you formulate commit messages is up to you. Git supports different character sets in the commit messages, but by default, Git uses UTF-8. As a rule, you're well advised not to change this setting. This character set also supports emojis, which you can copy and paste into a message.

UTF-8 enables you to also write the commit messages in language other than English, including special characters. However, you should keep in mind that you may receive contributions from developers later in the project who don't speak that language. Especially if you host your project publicly on GitHub and your code is of some interest, this problem can happen quickly. For open-source projects, English has therefore become the accepted language for all commit messages.

9.2.4   Links to Issues or Pull Requests

In our opinion, a practical extension for commit messages is to serve as references to issues and pull requests or merge requests (as in GitLab). The Git platforms provide help in this context: You don't need to copy the URL for an issue; you can simply enter the issue/pull request number preceded by the # character (the numbers are assigned consecutively per project).

In GitLab, the situation is slightly different since, in this case, issues and merge requests have two separate counters. Thus, in a GitLab project, an issue might be assigned the number 1, and a merge request might be assigned with the number 1. To map this numbering in the commit messages, you'll need to put a ! character in front of the number in GitLab for merge requests so that GitLab automatically creates a link from it.

Also, you can change the status of issues by placing certain keywords before the issue number. For example, to close issue number 22 on one of the major Git hosting platforms, you can use a commit message like the following:

```
fix: add missing semicolon in server.js (fixes #22)
```

The `fixes` keyword causes the commit to be mentioned in the issue on one hand and to be closed immediately on the other, which avoids a detour into the web browser.

Of course, this feature works with the integrated issue tracking systems. But external systems, such as the widely used *Jira*, can also be integrated via plugins, as in the following example:

```
fix: IPROT-153 overdue settings on project level
```

If the Jira plugin in GitLab is enabled and configured correctly, the commit message in the web interface is automatically linked to the Jira issue tracker.

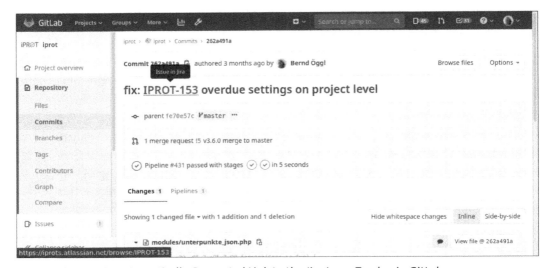

Figure 9.3 Automatically Generated Link to the Jira Issue Tracker in GitLab

The following help pages for the various platforms provide more information:

- *https://docs.gitlab.com/ee/user/project/issues/crosslinking_issues.html*
- *https://docs.github.com/en/github/writing-on-github/autolinked-references-and-urls*
- *https://docs.gitea.io/en-us/automatically-linked-references*

Note that the commit message in Git isn't modified, of course. The insertion of the link occurs only when the message is displayed in the web interface. For this reason, a commit message like the following makes little sense:

```
fix: #44
```

If a member of your team views the Git history in the terminal using `git log`, this message won't be helpful. You should regard the references more as additional information, not as the only information in the commit message.

9.2.5   Commit Messages of the Angular Project

As examples of rules for commit messages, we want to present the guidelines of an Angular project. Angular is a JavaScript/TypeScript framework for building frontend web applications. The project is being further developed by Google and has a wide distribution on the internet. With over 1,500 contributors and approximately 24,000 commits, the project has an extensive and active Git history.

If you want to contribute to the Angular project, your code must follow certain formal guidelines, and the Angular tests must run without errors. Relatively strict rules are also in place for formulating commit messages, which we'll explore next.

Commit messages in Angular are divided into three parts, with an optional footer in addition to the title and body system described earlier. This footer is reserved for references to issues or pull requests and is intended to mark incompatible changes with the string BREAKING CHANGE.

What's interesting are the rules for the title of the message, which in Angular is referred to as the *message header*. The title must begin with a label to indicate the type of commit. The Angular team has specified nine label types, namely, the following:

- `build`
  All changes that have any impact on the build system used (in Angular, these are Node.js modules, among others).

- `ci`
  Changes in the flow of the CI/CD pipeline.

- `docs`
  Changes to the documentation.

- `feat`
  A new function.

- `fix`
  A bugfix.

- `perf`
  Changes that affect the execution speed.

- `refactor`
  Neither a bugfix nor a new function, often a renaming of variables.

- `style`
  No changes to the program logic, often correction of spaces and indentations.

- `test`
  Changes to the automated tests.

After the type, an area for which the commit was made can optionally be specified in parentheses. The ranges are project specific and include, for example, *forms*, *animations*, or *http* in the Angular web application.

293

The last part of the title is the description of the changes, called the *subject* in Angular. Angular is generous with the line lengths and simply says that no line in the entire commit message can be longer than 100 characters.

Figure 9.4 shows a randomly chosen commit from the Angular Git repository. A small typo in the inline documentation for a function of the forms was fixed. You can see the type (docs), the subject, and the reference to a pull request inserted in parentheses. In the footer, you again see the reference to the pull request with the keyword Close, which closes the pull request.

Figure 9.4 Commit Message from the Angular Git Repository

Conventional Commits

The Conventional Commits project has similar specifications. The website, which is also being developed further on GitHub, contains a short specification and examples of appropriate commit messages:

https://conventionalcommits.org/

9.2.6   Conclusion

As mentioned earlier, we don't believe that commit messages will determine the success or failure of a project. No doubt, simple rules are useful—especially for large teams—and can onboarding new members easier.

One advantage of typing commits as we've described is that you can use scripts to automatically extract information from the Git log. In this way, you can reduce the tedious work of manually creating a *changelog* and release notes after the release of a new software version.

With consistent adherence to `feat`, `fix`, and `BREAKING CHANGE`, you can automate this work. Tools for this automation are available at GitHub, among others, at the following link:

https://github.com/conventional-changelog

9.3   Submodules and Subtrees

Both *submodules* and *subtrees* help you to integrate other people's Git projects into your own project. In general, you can incorporate foreign code into your own project in several ways:

- **Copying**
  The easiest way is to copy the source code—or the parts of the source code you need—into a subdirectory and manage it in your own repository from that point on. The big drawback is that bugfixes carried out in the external project won't be noticed in your own repository. Also, you yourself can't contribute to the foreign project.

- **External package manager**
  Many modern programming languages use their own package manager to manage libraries in the correct version for the project. Well-known representatives include, for example, Node Package Manager (npm) for Node.js, `cargo` for Rust, `gem` for Ruby, `pip` for Python, or `NuGet` for `C#`.

  Using such a system and not changing anything in the source code of the foreign project is certainly the easiest way. You can install updates and don't need to customize anything in your Git repository.

- **Submodules or subtrees**
  These two techniques enable you to connect the source code of the foreign repository to your repository in different ways. The following sections show you the advantages and disadvantages of these procedures.

We'll demonstrate these different techniques using our example image database, used many times already in this book. This simple website accesses a Node.js backend, which in turn stores data in a SQLite database. We modified the Node.js backend in such a way that we swapped the image upload process out as a standalone module. Within the module, the metadata about the images is extracted, and small thumbnails are generated.

Check It Out

We've deposited this manageable application on our GitLab account. The source code also includes a Dockerfile and a *docker-compose.yml* file. However, the application also runs without Docker using only the Node.js runtime. For more information, see the *README.md* file in the repository:

- Application: *https://gitlab.com/git-compendium/simple-picture-db*
- Module: *https://gitlab.com/git-compendium/simple-upload-exif*

9.3.1   Copying

The source code for the image upload function changes slightly depending on the technology used. In the first case (*copying*), we'll create the subfolder *server/simple-upload-exif*, copy the *index.js* file from the module to the directory, and extend the *server/routes.js* file with the following line:

```
const uploadExif = require('./simple-upload-exif');
```

In the code, we can then use the loaded module as *middleware* for the express server:

```
router.post("/picture",
  exifUpload.uploadWithExifAndThumbnail('file'), (req, res) => {
  ...
```

Note that we still need to take care of the dependencies of this module ourselves. In this specific case, our `simple-upload-exif` module uses three other Node.js modules, which we must install manually using the package manager:

```
npm install jimp multer exif-parser
```

This step is still possible with this tiny module, but with more complex modules, the manual approach is no longer practical.

9.3.2   Using the Package Manager

Typically, you install Node.js modules using npm package manager from the public npm server `npmjs.com`, which was acquired by Microsoft in April 2020. npm isn't limited to *npmjs.com*, however, and can install modules from a variety of different sources, including GitLab.

Since we've already stored the module in a public GitLab repository, we can include the module in a project using npm. Thus, one advantage of this approach is that, when installing the module, npm takes care of the modules used by our `simple-upload-exif` `module`.

```
npm i gitlab:git-compendium/simple-upload-exif

  + simple-upload-exif@1.0.0
  added 36 packages from 5 contributors and audited 501 packages
```

```
   in 7.396s
 25 packages are looking for funding
   run `npm fund` for details
found 0 vulnerabilities
```

When loading the module, the relative path specification before the module is then omitted:

```
const uploadExif = require('simple-upload-exif');
```

You can find the code for this module at *https://gitlab.com/git-compendium/picture-db-npm*. Now, to implement a small modification to the code of the module, the workflow would use the following sequence:

1. Clone module to another folder with `git clone git@gitlab.com:git-compendium/simple-upload-exif.git`.
2. Edit and save files.
3. Commit with `git add . && git commit -am "fix: ...."`.
4. Push with `git push`.
5. Update the module in the project with `npm update gitlab:git-compendium/simple-upload-exif`.
6. Reload the browser and try it out.

Doesn't sound like the kind of workflow you want all day long, does it? For Node.js modules, one option is to use `npm link` to install local folders in the `node_modules` directory, but using multiple *soft links* feels more like a workaround than the perfect solution. Read on to see how Git submodules can improve the situation.

9.3.3   Submodules

Starting from the same project, let's now add the `simple-upload-exif` module as a Git submodule. The call for this step involves the following command:

```
git submodule add \
  https://gitlab.com/git-compendium/simple-upload-exif.git \
  server/simple-upload-exif

  Cloning into '/src/picture-db-submodule/server/simple-upload...
  remote: Enumerating objects: 18, done.
  ...
  remote: Total 18 (delta 2), reused 0 (delta 0), pack-reused 0
  Unpacking objects: 100% (18/18), 10.18 KiB | 2.54 MiB/s, done.
```

As the output suggests, Git clones the full repository into the *server/simple-upload-exif* subfolder, which we appended as the second parameter to the `git submodule add` command. When you now look at the status of your project repository, you'll see that two changes are ready to commit (i.e., they're in the staging area):

```
git status
```

```
On branch main
Your branch is up to date with 'origin/main'.
Changes to be committed:
  (use "git restore --staged <file>..." to unstage)
  new file:   .gitmodules
  new file:   server/simple-upload-exif
```

These changes are the .gitmodules file and the server/simple-upload-exif folder, which is somewhat misleadingly shown in this case as a new file. The .gitmodules file contains an entry for each module with the relative path and URL to the module's repository; in our case, the entry looks like the following:

```
[submodule "server/simple-upload-exif"]
    path = server/simple-upload-exif
    url = https://gitlab.com/git-compendium/simple-upload-exif.git
```

For our example to be functional again, we still must install the dependencies required by the module. This step is another manual step, but in this case, we can use the configuration file included in the module for the package manager and install the modules there:

```
cd server/simple-upload-exif
npm install
```

The example is now functional, and you can edit the source code of the module without many workarounds by making changes directly to the server/simple-upload-exif/index.js file. The current state of the submodule is without local changes (the output of the hash code is slightly shortened):

```
git submodule status
```

```
  2be3a483a89613ed0b6a... server/simple-upload-exif (heads/main)
```

When we now make changes in the server/simple-upload-exif/index.js file, they'll immediately be visible in the application. The status of the submodule apparently remains unchanged, but changes are displayed in the main project:

```
git status
```

```
On branch main
...
```

```
  modified:   simple-upload-exif (modified content)
no changes added to commit ...
```

But you can't commit in the project; we've to go to the *server/simple-upload-exif* subfolder to commit the changes there. After the commit in the submodule, changes in the actual project can also be committed:

```
git status
```

```
On branch main
...
  modified:   simple-upload-exif (new commits)
no changes added to commit ...
```

Now, the status of the submodule has also changed. It starts with a + sign and shows the modified hash code:

```
git submodule status
```

```
+0bf504bc99c18fac9bd9... server/simple-upload-exif (heads/main)
```

In the main project, the new hash code will be visible when git diff is called:

```
git --no-pager diff
```

```
diff --git a/server/simple-upload-exif b/server/simple-uploa...
index 2be3a48..0bf504b 160000
--- a/server/simple-upload-exif
+++ b/server/simple-upload-exif
@@ -1 +1 @@
-Subproject commit 2be3a483a89613ed0b6a857a4ea6331d2fd162af
+Subproject commit 0bf504bc99c18fac9bd9a71e3445d2178f0683ac
```

If we commit the main project now, the reference to the new commit will be updated in the submodule.

We've described these steps in such detail because things can get awfully confusing when you've made changes in both repositories. You'll see the main project still has uncommitted changes, but git add and git commit -a won't let you commit any files. You must not forget to commit the changes in the submodule separately and also push them at the appropriate time.

If you use submodules in different projects, which is the purpose of modules, you must work even more carefully than with an ordinary repository. In our project, the reference to each commit is stored in the submodule repository. Prior to making changes to this submodule in another project, you should first update the submodule to the latest state (git pull in the submodule's directory); otherwise, you won't be able to push the changes without a merge.

If someone clones our Git repository with submodules, the person must use the `--recurse-submodules` option when doing so; otherwise, only the empty folder for the module will be created.

To load the modules subsequently, you must use the somewhat long command:

```
git submodule update --init --recursive
```

The same applies when you import updates to the main project using git pull. (Note the conflicting naming of the options: While git clone requires the `--recurse-submodules` option, git submodule update requires you to use the `--recursive` option.)

Notice how submodules add a decent amount of complexity to Git. We've not yet talked about submodules that contain other submodules. The administrative overhead with submodules has probably also caused Git developers to program another variant to manage modules in a Git repository. We'll explore the slightly more straightforward method of subtrees in the next section.

9.3.4   Subtrees

If the previous section on submodules scared you off a bit, let's turn to a slightly easier way to use source code from another repository in your own Git repository.

---

contrib

The git subtree command doesn't belong to the Git core commands but is classified in the contrib section. In most installation variants, the command is installed automatically, and no further steps are required. For special Linux distributions, such as *Alpine Linux*, you'll need to install an extra package with apk add git-subtree.

With submodules, while only the reference to the commit in the module is managed by the main project, with subtrees, the entire source code of the module is included. In the standard variant, the entire Git history is also imported, which isn't necessary in most cases. The subtree command provides the `--squash` option for this purpose, which packages the Git history into a single commit.

Let's return to our example with the simple-upload-exif module: Let's add the subtree in the same place as we did before for the submodule, in the *server/simple-upload-exif* subfolder. The git subtree command requires the parameter `--prefix=<prefix>`, passing the path where the foreign code is located, on every call.

To add the module from our public GitLab repository, use git subtree add and specify the URL to the repository in addition to the `--prefix`. In addition, the call requires a revision (see Chapter 12, Section 12.2), where we refer to the current state on the main branch. Finally, use the `--squash` option, mentioned earlier, to compress the Git history into a single commit.

```
git subtree add --prefix=server/simple-upload-exif \
  https://gitlab.com/git-compendium/simple-upload-exif.git \
    main --squash

  git fetch https://gitlab.com/git-compendium/simple-upload-ex...
  warning: no common commits
  ...
  From https://gitlab.com/git-compendium/simple-upload-exif
   * branch            main      -> FETCH_HEAD
  Added dir 'server/simple-upload-exif'
```

The *server/simple-upload-exif* directory now contains all files from the repository except the *.git* directory. Let's look at the Git log after `subtree add`. You'll see two new commits (slightly shortened here):

```
git log --shortstat

  commit 1a6266a32cfaef985c672e882d4d13db7dd18aac
  Merge: 5c212c6 9d0ca75
      Merge commit '9d0ca75415c9b94d0...' as 'server/simple-up...

  commit 9d0ca75415c9b94d07f7d4389187b56092a40ccd
      Squashed 'server/simple-upload-exif/' content from commi...
      git-subtree-dir: server/simple-upload-exif
      git-subtree-split: 2be3a483a89613ed0b6a857a4ea6331d2fd162af
   5 files changed, 816 insertions(+)

  commit 5c212c696e65ee5b5b564752d3722b8a4d43886d
      test: fix number of pics after upload
   2 files changed, 1 insertion(+), 8 deletions(-)
```

Let's examine at the output, from the bottom up, next:

- Commit `5c212c6` was the last commit before we ran `git subtree add`.
- That commit is followed by commit `9d0ca75`, which summarizes the entire Git history of our module (because of the `--squash` option).
- The latest commit considered is `2be3a48`, which is the current state of the main branch in the `git-compendium/simple-upload-exif` module. The automatic commit message contains the two entries `git-subtree-dir` and `git-subtree-split`, which is important information as we'll see in a moment.
- The merge commit `1a6266a` merges the old Git history (commit `5c212c6`) with the new squash commit.

The module's files are now versioned directly via our main project. Other developers who clone our project won't even notice the subtree structure. You can use the repository without bothering with subtrees or submodules.

We might seem to be repeating the beginning of our section, when we simply copied the module's files into the source code. It's indeed quite similar, but with one crucial difference: The time and the hash code of the module repository have been documented during the copying process. In this way, you can push changes to the files back to the module repository or push updates from the module to the main project.

Try this out by downloading the module again via git pull:

```
git subtree pull --prefix=server/simple-upload-exif \
    https://gitlab.com/git-compendium/simple-upload-exif.git \
    main --squash

  From https://gitlab.com/git-compendium/simple-upload-exif
   * branch              main       -> FETCH_HEAD
  Subtree is already at commit 2be3a483a89613ed0b6a857a4ea6331...
```

If changes in the remote repository of the module occurred in the meantime, these changes would have been downloaded, entered into the current Git history, and incorporated into the project with a merge commit.

9.3.5 Internal Details

But how does Git know the status of our subtrees? Unlike submodules, subtrees don't use separate metadata in the *.git* folder but rely on the git-subtree-split and git-subtree-dir strings in the commit messages.

This scenario sounds a bit unusual, but looking at the actual implementation of git subtree brings more clarity and also (at least for us) a surprise. The git-subtree shell script, which runs when we call git subtree, draws on other git commands to determine the commits to merge or push. For example, to find said strings in the commit messages, the script uses git log:

```
git log --grep="^git-subtree-dir:...
```

If we call git subtree pull again later in the work and changes have occurred in our module repository, only the new commits, again with a squash commit, will be integrated into our project. You can see this behavior at work in the first line of the following example, where the area between the commit 2be3a48 and dce31ac is squashed:

```
  Squashed 'server/simple-upload-exif/' changes from  2be3a48....
  dce31ac docs: more precise docs on upload
```

```
git-subtree-dir: server/simple-upload-exif
git-subtree-split: dce31ac16aeab561e573f56fb323d25ad95574e5
```

The opposite direction works just as well. Local changes to the module can be transferred to the remote repository of our module using git subtree push. Note that a commit ideally only affects either the module or the main project. Git can correctly split a commit and push only the changes affecting the subtree to the repository. However, when the module is pulled again, the commit appears once with all changes and once only with the changes to the module. While this behavior doesn't cause any problems in the source code, the entries in the Git history become more complicated to understand.

9.3.6 Subtree Split

So far, this section has described how you can include external modules in your source code. To round out our discussion, we'll introduce you to a convenient method for extracting a module from your source code. We'll go into this topic in more detail later on; in this section, we'll describe the variant with git subtree.

Once again, we'll use the image database repository at *https://gitlab.com/git-compendium/simple-picture-db*. Now, we want to swap out the code affecting the frontend into a separate Git repository. Currently, the code is located in the *client* folder, and no dependencies between this code and the backend code exist.

First, let's call the git subtree command via the split subcommand and pass the name of the new branch to be created with the -b option:

```
git subtree split --prefix=client -b frontend
```

```
Created branch 'frontend'
906cd63b44d61ed9c8cf177134f5a20041e781ee
```

When you now switch to the branch, you'll only see the files from the *client* subfolder, without the folder itself.

```
git switch frontend
ls -a
```

```
.  ..  css  .git  index.html  js
```

Also, the Git history is fully preserved for all changes affecting files in this subfolder. To create a new Git repository with these contents, create a new folder in parallel with the split repository and initialize the new repository. Then, fetch the branch frontend from the parallel folder using git fetch.

```
cd ..
mkdir picture-db-frontend
git init
git fetch ../picture-db frontend
```

```
remote: Enumerating objects: 11, done.
remote: Counting objects: 100% (11/11), done.
remote: Compressing objects: 100% (7/7), done.
remote: Total 11 (delta 0), reused 6 (delta 0)
Unpacking objects: 100% (11/11), 1.53 KiB | 313.00 KiB/s, done.
From ../picture-db
 * branch            frontend    -> FETCH_HEAD
```

The repository now has a peculiar status: We've saved the history of the frontend branch, but it's located in the *Detached FETCH_HEAD*. To change this location and move it to the (still empty) main branch, you must use the following command:

```
git checkout -b main  FETCH_HEAD
```

Now, your new repository is ready to be set up. If you're using a Git hosting platform, you can now create a new project on that platform, add it as a remote repository, and push it.

Submodules versus Subtrees

Finally, we want to highlight what we think is a great comparison of submodules, and subtrees on GitHub, available at the following link:

https://links.git-compendium.info/submodule-subtree

9.3.7   Monorepos

In connection with submodules and subtrees, we want to highlight *monorepos*, which are in use in exceptionally large tech companies. *Mono* refers to using a single repository to manage many different projects within it.

Large companies see advantages in monorepos when different projects collaborate with each other:

- If each developer has access to the source code of all projects via their working copy, preventing duplicate developments is easier.
- The dependencies projects have with each other or with third-party software can be better managed if all projects are located in a single repository.
- Workflows such as *refactoring* can be accomplished across multiple projects with a single commit, providing a tidy history.

The Git repository of the Linux kernel, which we also used as a playground in Chapter 4, currently occupies about 5 GB with the working copy checked out. By our standards, the kernel is definitely a large project, but Git still works superfast with a current-generation laptop. For example, for any given file, `git blame` returns the result in less than a second and has sifted through commits from the last 15 years.

When we talk about monorepos, however, we're referring to repositories that may exceed the size of the Linux kernel by several orders of magnitude! Current figures on the monorepos of big tech companies are hard to find, and their monorepos are of course not open source. A published figure from 2015 puts Google's monorepo at 86 TBs and over 35 million commits (see *https://links.git-compendium.info/google-repo-stats*).

Such amounts of data can no longer be managed with Git without further adjustments. Google and Facebook therefore use self-developed extensions to manage these repositories. For example, Microsoft is working on its *Virtual File System (VFS) for Git* project, intended to manage huge monorepos; however, the software only runs on Windows and requires a customized Git version. But monorepos can only provide a real advantage when tools are able to analyze all the dependencies between projects and then start the necessary tests, builds, and releases.

9.4   Bash and Zsh

This section is intended for Git users who work primarily in the console. In this case, you can make your life easier by using adopting several techniques, such as the following:

- Git aliases allow you to define shortcuts for Git subcommands with frequently needed options.
- Bash users should make sure that `git` command autocompletion works.
- For Zsh users, the *Oh My Zsh* package includes various Git-specific extensions.

9.4.1   Git Aliases

Let's suppose you run the `git log --oneline --stat` command frequently. Entering this command with all its options all the time can become tedious. You can save yourself a lot of typing if you instead define the Git alias `lo` and save this alias in your global Git configuration file using `git config`:

```
git config --global alias.lo 'log --oneline --stat'
```

From now on, you can simply run `git lo`:

```
git lo
```

To list all aliases defined in your environment, use `git config` with the `--get-regexp` option:

```
git config --get-regexp  alias
  aa   = add --all
  br   = branch
  ci   = commit
  co   = checkout
  st   = status
  last = log -1 HEAD
  lo   = log --oneline --stat'
  ...
```

9.4.2 Autocompletion in Bash

Bash is considered the default shell on Linux and is thus responsible for executing commands in terminal windows. After a Git installation on Windows, this command interpreter comes into play in the *Git Bash* window as well.

An important feature of Bash is the completion of command and filenames via the `Tab` key. This feature also is context based. When you type "git com" and then press `Tab`, Bash turns the text into `git commit`. If the initial letters aren't unique (e.g., "git co"), you must press `Tab` twice. Bash then shows the two possible completions (`config` and `commit`) and also includes Git aliases if necessary. Completion also works for the parameters of a git command. When you type "git add" and then press `Tab`, Bash will present you with only the files that have changed.

The completion should work on Windows and Linux without any further configuration. If not the case, you should ensure that the `bash-completion` package is installed on Linux or macOS (using Homebrew or MacPorts).

9.4.3 Oh My Zsh!

In current macOS versions, Zsh is considered the default shell, and this alternative to Bash is also gaining more and more fans among Linux professionals. The autocompletion of `git` commands works the same way as in Bash. You can make Git even more convenient by installing the *Oh My Zsh* extension. The installation instructions can be found at the following link:

https://github.com/ohmyzsh/ohmyzsh

The Git features in *Oh My Zsh* that are of interest in the context of this book are automatically enabled during installation. The first visible consequence is that the currently active branch of a Git repository is now displayed directly in the prompt. Colored symbols indicate whether the last command was executed without errors and whether unsaved changes exist in the current directory.

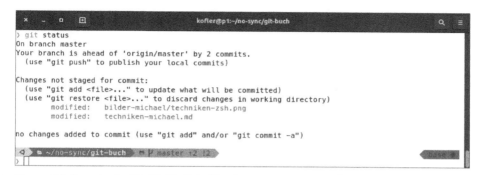

```
> git status
On branch master
Your branch is ahead of 'origin/master' by 2 commits.
  (use "git push" to publish your local commits)

Changes not staged for commit:
  (use "git add <file>..." to update what will be committed)
  (use "git restore <file>..." to discard changes in working directory)
        modified:   bilder-michael/techniken-zsh.png
        modified:   techniken-michael.md

no changes added to commit (use "git add" and/or "git commit -a")
```

Figure 9.5 Terminal with Oh My Zsh: The Current Directory Is "git-book" and the Current Branch Is "master"

As part of the configuration of *Oh My Zsh*, countless aliases are defined. But you must exercise caution: These aliases aren't the same as the Git aliases described earlier, which are processed by the git command; these aliases operate at the shell level. Instead of git add, you can now just run ga; instead of git log --oneline --decorate --graph, it's glog. The almost overwhelming list of all aliases can be found at the following link:

https://github.com/ohmyzsh/ohmyzsh/blob/master/plugins/git/git.plugin.zsh

Alternatively, you can run alias | grep git to list all aliases that contain the search term git.

9.5 Two-Factor Authentication

Usually, your logon to GitHub, GitLab, or any other Git platform is secured by only one factor—your password. If someone manages to guess or steal your password, the thief will have access to all your repositories.

By enabling two-factor authentication, you can significantly improve the security of your account. The second factor can be, for example, an additional code that is sent to your smartphone via text message when you log on or that you generate yourself using a program such as Google Authenticator or Authy.

A logon can then only be performed by someone who knows your password *and* has access to your smartphone or to your code generator. As a rule, an app installed on the smartphone serves as a generator of codes, each of which is valid for only half a minute. Thus, if you lose your smartphone, you may have lost the second factor as well. Various safeguards can ensure that you don't lose access to your Git platform even in this case.

In this section, we'll focus on GitHub's two-factor authentication implementation. Most other Git platforms also support two-factor authentication, though the details may vary. You can find more information about two-factor authentication in GitHub and GitLab at the following links:

- *https://docs.github.com/en/authentication/securing-your-account-with-two-factor-authentication-2fa*
- *https://docs.gitlab.com/ee/user/profile/account/two_factor_authentication.html*

9.5.1   Enabling Two-Factor Authentication on GitHub

To enable two-factor authentication on your GitHub account, log on to the website, open the **Settings • Account Security** page, and click the **Enable two-factor authentication** button. In the next step, you initially have the choice between two variants: an app (i.e., a code generator) or a text message.

Once you've chosen one of the variants, the website displays a set of 16 recovery codes. With each of these codes, you can perform a *one-time* logon if you've lost your second factor or temporarily have no access. GitHub recommends that you don't simply store the codes in a local text file, but instead archive them in a secure manner.

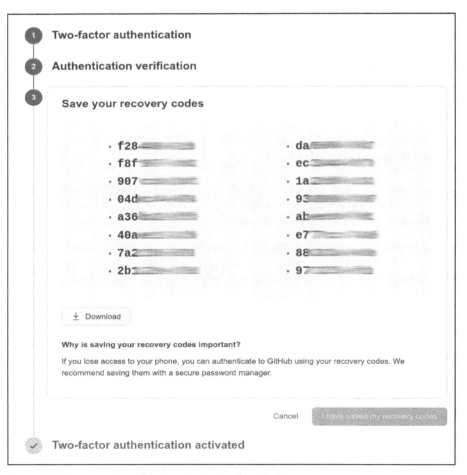

Figure 9.6 Recovery Keys for Two-Factor Authentication

In the app variant, GitHub displays a QR code in the second step, which you photograph with the two-factor authentication app of your smartphone. The most common app in this context is *Google Authenticator*, which is available for free in both the Google Play store and Apple App Store.

However, we recommend the *Authy* app (*https://authy.com*, also available for free in the Google Play store or Apple App Store). Their code generator is compatible with Google Authenticator but has a great advantage: The logons set up in Authy can be synchronized across multiple devices. Not only is this multiple-device feature your plan B if your smartphone becomes defective or is lost; it also provides a useful way to migrate the logons stored in the code generator to a new smartphone. *Authy* can also be installed as a desktop app.

Once the QR scan is successful, the two-factor authentication app starts displaying 6-digit numbers, each of which is valid for 30 seconds. You'll need to enter the current number on the GitHub website to complete the two-factor authentication configuration.

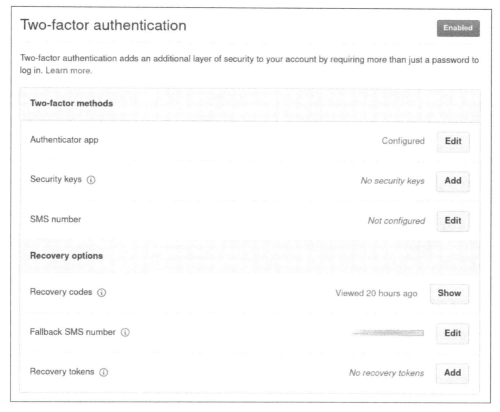

Figure 9.7 Overview of All Enabled Two-Factor Authentication Methods and Recovery Variants

---

Is Authy Really Safe?

Authy has been on the market for several years and has a good reputation. However, we can't guarantee that the mechanism implemented by Authy for encrypted uploads and downloads of your logons to and from the cloud doesn't itself have security vulnerabilities.

If you subsequently visit the **Settings • Security** page on the GitHub website again, you can enable a different two-factor authentication method as well as add various recovery options. For example, you can store another phone number to which a recovery code can be sent as a text message in case of an emergency.

9.5.2   Hardware Security Keys

In addition to the described methods (with an app and via text message), GitHub provides another option for a second factor: hardware security keys, such as those produced by Yubico. These USB dongles support the *WebAuthn* standard, which is now available in all major web browsers. The big advantage over app-based and text message-based authentication is that the mere presence of the device plugged in via USB is enough to be valid as a second factor. The USB key can easily be compared to a *real* key: If you lose it, a malicious person may find it and can use it as well, but only as a second factor. They also must guess your password before using it successfully.

Comfortable and Safe!

If you're serious about two-factor authentication, you should consider purchasing a USB token. These devices, which are considered extremely secure, are available for as little as $45, and they're much more convenient to use than apps and text messages. Typically, they also provide additional features such as secure storage of SSH and GNU Privacy Guard (GnuPG) keys. Not only GitHub, but also other Git hosting software like GitLab and Gitea support such devices.

The biggest obstacle to two-factor authentication is fear of losing the second factor. This loss would lock you out of all accounts or make you rely on recovery keys or other backup strategies. A simple way out is to use *two* USB tokens at the same time and register both tokens with each new account. Then, you always take one token with you, while you keep the other one in a safe place.

9.5.3   Applying Two-Factor Authentication

After enabling two-factor authentication, logging on to the GitHub website becomes a bit more cumbersome: In addition to your user name and password, which is usually stored in the web browser and filled in automatically, you'll then need to enter a 6-digit code generated by the app on your smartphone. Each code is valid for only 30 seconds, after which the next code is generated. If you've registered a hardware security key, no code needs to be entered, and you only need to touch the capacitive area of your security token. As before, a new logon to the website is only required if you explicitly log out or if the current session expires.

Quite little is seen of two-factor authentication in the authentication of Git operations. In detail, the now valid procedure depends on the selected communication mechanism:

- **SSH**
  If you use SSH, authentication is still done with SSH private keys, the public part of which you've deposited with GitHub.

- **HTTPS**
  When accessing repositories via HTTPS, you should use Windows Credential Manager or set up some personal access tokens for authentication (see Chapter 2, Section 2.2).

- **Tools with their own token management**
  The *GitHub Desktop* program and some integrated development environments (IDEs) that request and manage tokens themselves via OAuth (e.g., IntelliJ IDEA) can also handle two-factor authentication.

Two-Factor Authentication Only for the GitHub Website, Not for Git

The additional security provided by two-factor authentication only applies to accessing the GitHub web interface, but not to running Git! Operations such as clone, pull, or push are still only secured by *one* authentication factor, either an SSH key or a token. The crucial aspect in this context is that you don't need to provide your GitHub password for manual HTTPS authentication, only the token.

The limited scope of two-factor authentication stems from the fact that the git command isn't even aware of the concept of two-factor authentication.

Chapter 10
Git in Real Life

In this chapter, we'll present some examples from our Git practice that, for a change, do *not* have to do with managing large codebases. (This "normal case" of the Git application is always in the foreground in the other chapters of this book.)

Specifically, we'll address the following topics:

- *Etckeeper* enables you to manage the configuration files in the */etc* directory of a Linux system via Git.

- In Section 10.2, we'll revisit configuration management, but this time for personal settings. The names of such files or directories usually start with a period (.) on Linux or macOS. The challenge is to manage *only* these files without Git turning the entire home directory into a giant repository.

- With the Git extension `git-svn`, you can access an Apache Subversion (SVN) repository via `git` commands. This feature is useful if you need to collaborate on a project that isn't going to be moved to Git without giving up all the Git benefits.

- This switch from SVN to Git is the topic of the next section. `git-svn` also helps with this task, but a little extra work is required to ensure that all metadata (authors, tags, etc.) is preserved.

- Finally, we'll show you how to use Git in combination with the Hugo blog system to run a simple website or blog. The section is intended for technically savvy authors who prefer a few `git` commands and Markdown syntax to the cluttered web interface of a content management system (CMS).

Along the way, we'll also explain how you can use the *large-file support (LFS)* extension to make Git handle large files more efficiently.

10.1 Etckeeper

In Linux and in other Unix-like systems, (almost) all files for system-wide configuration are stored as text files in the */etc* directory. The *etckeeper* script collection takes care of regularly backing up the contents of */etc* to a Git repository. In this context, "regularly" means once a day, provided that some configuration file has changed. Also, every action of the package management system results in a commit (i.e., every time packages are installed, updated, or deleted).

You may be asking yourself why you should back up or version the */etc* directory separately if you run a daily backup of this directory anyway. (Of course, you do a daily backup, don't you?) The answer is that, with the help of etckeeper or Git, you have much better search and analysis options when problems arise.

10.1.1 Usage Example

Before we describe the installation of etckeeper, let's consider an example from our personal experience where etckeeper saved us a lot of time. In our case, Apache web server log files were kept on Ubuntu servers for a year before being deleted. Archiving was taken care of by the *Logrotate* program, which is started by a cron job and renames, compresses, and deletes log files overnight. Of course, Logrotate also has configuration files that are located in the */etc* directory and managed by etckeeper.

One day, while looking over the previous year's Apache log files, we were shocked to find that only the preceding two weeks were available. A quick look at the list of changes for the affected Logrotate script quickly revealed the culprit, as shown in the following (slightly shortened) listing:

```
etckeeper vcs log -p logrotate.d/apache2
```

```
commit 3452d6d14de58c41dcdf2750e954e697dec81a37
Date:    Sun May 6 14:15:55 2018 +0200
      committing changes in /etc after apt run
diff --git a/logrotate.d/apache2 b/logrotate.d/apache2
index f3d8837..c0cc58a 100644
--- a/logrotate.d/apache2
+++ b/logrotate.d/apache2
@@ -1,7 +1,7 @@
 /var/log/apache2/*.log {
-    weekly
+    daily
     missingok
-    rotate 52
+    rotate 14
     compress
     delaycompress
     notifempty
```

In the output, notice that, in the configuration file, weekly was replaced by daily and rotate was changed from 52 to 14. The commit message shows that the changes were made automatically after a package update (apt run). The mystery is solved, and now you also know exactly until which day you could still count on your log files in the external backup.

10.1.2 Installation and Configuration

The installation of etckeeper is pretty simple. All major Linux distributions provide ready-made packages for etckeeper. To install it, you must run the following command:

```
apt/dnf/yum install etckeeper
```

The install scripts will then take care of the rest. In the current version, Git is the default version control system. etckeeper can also use Mercurial, Bazaar, or Darcs if needed. After installation, a Git repository is set up in */etc*, and the configuration files are stored in */etc/etckeeper/*.

All you need to do now is set up a remote repository where the commits will be uploaded automatically. The developer of etckeeper has already provided for that option, and so two small steps are enough to enable automatic synchronization.

For this example, we created a repository on our private GitLab instance and also set up a custom user there with permissions only for that repository. On the server, we'll create an SSH key (without a password) that's used for the automatic commits. Make sure to execute this command as root! If you use sudo, you must specify the additional -H option to use /root and not your own home directory:

```
sudo -H bash
ssh-keygen -f ~/.ssh/id_rsa -q -N ""
```

We'll store the public key part in GitLab for the newly created user. Now, we just need to set the remote repository on the server. Since etckeeper has created a simple Git repository in the */etc* directory, you can specify the remote repository as the root user:

```
cd /etc
git remote add origin \
    ssh://git@gitlab.git-compendium.info/server/iprot.etc.git
```

As a test, let's call git push to ensure that the SSH key works. In the file */etc/etckeeper/ etckeeper.conf*, activate the line PUSH_REMOTE="origin", which causes a push to be executed after each commit of etckeeper.

From now on, etckeeper runs without any further interaction on your part. On Debian and Ubuntu systems, a Cron script is placed in the */etc/cron.daily* folder during package installation, which causes etckeeper to check for modified files in the */etc* folder every night. If changes occur, a commit is executed and pushed to your server.

Etckeeper is a tool that provides helpful information with little effort and resource utilization. Of course, you could also track the changes using a backup, but accessing a backup is usually more complicated than opening the Git hosting provider's website.

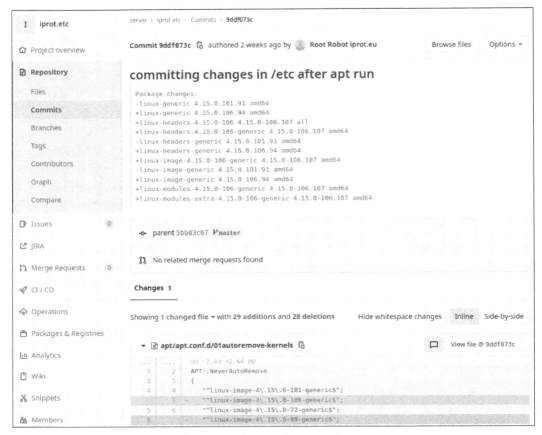

Figure 10.1 One of Our Git Repositories Populated by Etckeeper

10.2   Managing Dotfiles with Git

Dotfiles, that is, files whose names begin with a period, are used to store settings on all Unix-like operating systems. This section shows you how to manage such files on Linux using Git. Of course, you can also adapt these instructions for macOS, Free BSD, and more with little effort.

10.2.1   Dotfiles

Unix has been a multiuser operating system from the beginning. Consequently, configuration files have always been created so that they could be saved for individual users. The concept of a home directory has thus existed from the start. What could be more obvious than to store your configuration files there?

Unwanted Concept

According to Rob Pike, one of the driving forces behind Unix in the 1970s and 1980s, dotfiles actually came about because of a programming error and sloppiness. Previously, no defaults for saving program settings existed at that time. The original post is unfortunately no longer available (since it was written on the discontinued Google Plus network), but a copy is available on Reddit that we have linked for you:

https://links.git-compendium.info/rob-pike-on-dotfiles

Nevertheless, the concept spread quickly, and filenames became established with a convention composed of the program name and an appended suffix (rc, for "resource configuration"). Most Linux users have probably edited their *.bashrc* file at some point to adjust Bash.

In contrast to the binary Windows registry, configuration files on Linux are always in text format. Since you don't need any special software to view and edit the files, such files can also be managed perfectly in Git.

On Windows, the concept of *dotfiles* doesn't actually exist. However, more and more such files are present on Windows as well, for instance, when you use programs that have been ported from the Unix/Linux world for Windows. Nevertheless, we'll explicitly refer to Linux in the following sections.

10.2.2   Dotfiles under Git Control

The longer you work on Linux, the larger the number of dotfiles with beloved shell aliases, editor settings, and more you'll have, as experience shows. The obvious approach is to manage these files in a Git repository; then, a remote repository can serve as a backup and at the same time help quickly transfer files to a new Linux installation.

No sooner said than done! However, we'll quickly run into a problem in a concrete implementation: Do we really want to create a Git repository in the home directory where 200 GB of data might also reside? Not really. We need some Git tricks to separate the dotfiles from the rest of the home directory.

An easy way would be to simply store the dotfiles in a subdirectory *$HOME/dotfiles*. Symbolic links then point from the home directory to the corresponding files in *dotfiles/*. Unfortunately, this approach doesn't work well at all: If new dotfiles are added, they'll need to be moved and linked manually to *dotfiles/*.

10.2.3   git-dir and work-tree

Fortunately, Git provides a much more elegant way: the --git-dir and --work-tree options:

- `--git-dir` specifies the folder where Git manages all internal information (i.e., the Git database), usually the *.git* folder. However, in the following sections, we'll use a different name, namely, *.cfg*.

  Using a different name from *.git* has an advantage in that git then won't assume, for each command, that the command refers to a repository for the entire home directory. Otherwise, you would run the risk that a git command accidentally executed in the wrong directory would automatically refer to the dotfiles repository.

- `--work-tree` specifies the location of the files to be managed. Without this option, Git searches from the current folder up the file system hierarchy for a *.git* directory to determine the worktree.

The two options can be passed to all git commands. As a result, the command in question uses the default Git and worktree directories, regardless of which directory is currently active.

We'll start the configuration process by creating the *.cfg* folder:

```
git init --bare $HOME/.cfg
```

```
Initialized empty Git repository in /home/ubuntu/.cfg/
```

We've now created a *bare repository*, which is a Git directory without the option to check out files. By specifying the two parameters, we can look at the status of our home directory:

```
git --git-dir=$HOME/.cfg/ --work-tree=$HOME status
```

```
On branch main
No commits yet
Untracked files:
(use "git add <file>..." to include in what will be committed)
  .bashrc
  .cfg/
  .profile
  Documents/
  ...
nothing added to commit but untracked files present
(use "git add" to track)
```

Notice that Git has marked all files and folders in the home directory as *untracked files*, including the Git directory *.cfg*. For our first experiments, let's now add the two dotfiles (*.bashrc* and *.profile*) to the Git index and modify a local setting so that unversioned files are no longer shown in the status output:

```
git --git-dir=$HOME/.cfg/ --work-tree=$HOME add .bashrc .profile
git --git-dir=$HOME/.cfg/ --work-tree=$HOME config \
    --local status.showUntrackedFiles no
git --git-dir=$HOME/.cfg/ --work-tree=$HOME status
```

```
On branch main
No commits yet
Changes to be committed:
  (use "git rm --cached <file>..." to unstage)
  new file:   .bashrc
  new file:   .profile
Untracked files not listed
(use -u option to show untracked files)
```

Since typing out these parameters is somewhat tedious and error-prone, we'll add an alias entry to the shell configuration with the following line:

```
alias config='git --git-dir=$HOME/.cfg/ --work-tree=$HOME'
```

Now, you can use the new `config` command like the `git` command, with the difference that `config` always applies to the repository of dotfiles.

Since including the *.cfg* folder itself in the repository never makes sense, create a *.gitignore* file and add that folder with the following command:

```
echo ".cfg" >> ~/.gitignore
```

Even if you were to mistakenly run `config add .` in the home directory, the *~/.cfg* folder wouldn't be included in the staging area.

After the first commits, set up a remote repository (e.g., in GitLab) and store the changes there, with the following commands:

```
config remote add origin \
  https://gitlab.com/git-compendium/dotfiles.git
config push
```

Beware of Git Error Messages

After a short while, the new `config` command feels natural, and we use it to add configuration files to our dotfile repository, commit there, and push-sync them to the remote repository. If an error occurs in the process, for example a merge conflict, Git will help as always with practical tips like the following:

```
use "git merge --abort" to abort the merge.
```

However, remember that you must not copy this command as usual. Rather, you must replace `git` with `config`. (We've had some painful experiences here!)

10.2.4   Setting Up Dotfiles on a New Computer

A dotfile repository is particularly useful for quickly applying personal settings to a newly installed computer. In addition to the editor settings mentioned earlier, this approach also applies to SSH configuration with settings for various server access. Settings for your email program or other software products can also be helpful.

In our experience, a useful step is to additionally include a *README.md* file in the repository. In this file, you can store the necessary installation steps and other comments. Now, when you start up a new Linux system, you can visit the web page of your Git repository, copy the relevant commands from there to clone the repository, and run the commands. After a few minutes, the Linux system is configured in the way you've specified.

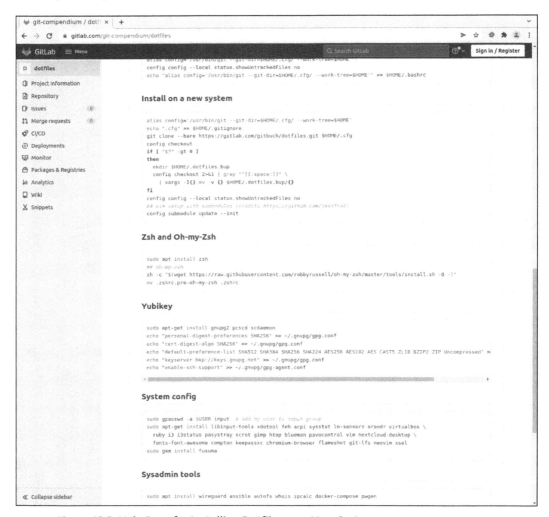

Figure 10.2 Help Page for Installing Dotfiles on a New System

For initialization, only the following commands, presented earlier, are required:

- alias config ... sets up the config command with the --git-dir and --work-tree options.

- echo provides a minimal *.gitignore* configuration.

- git clone downloads the repository. The --bare option ensures that the *$HOME/.cfg* directory will be used.

- config checkout copies the files from the bare repository to the home directory.

However, the config checkout command will fail dotfiles with the same names already exist in the home directory. You can try to solve this problem with a trick, but the solution isn't very elegant:

```
config checkout
if [ "$?" -gt 0 ]
then
    mkdir $HOME/.dotfiles.bup
    config checkout 2>&1 | grep "^[[:space:]]\+" \
    | xargs -I{} mv -v {} $HOME/.dotfiles.bup/{}
fi
```

The command evaluates the output of config checkout and responds to a possible error. Only in case of an error should $? (the return value of the last command) be greater than 0 in shell scripts. If so, the backup directory *$HOME/.dotfiles.bup* will be created, and the output of config checkout will be rewritten into a command.

10.2.5   Shell Commands

Now, let's look at how the following command works:

```
config checkout 2>&1 | grep "^[[:space:]]\+" \
    | xargs -I{} mv -v {} $HOME/.dotfiles.bup/{}
```

(If you aren't interested in shell scripting, you can safely skip this section.)

If config checkout can't be executed successfully (for example, because existing dotfiles are present), the following output occurs:

```
config checkout

  error: The following untracked working tree files would be o...
        .bashrc
  Please move or remove them before you switch branches.
  Aborting
```

We intentionally didn't wrap the second line in the output; instead, we truncated it because the correct output of the characters will become important later. The first problem with the `config checkout` output on an error is that the error output doesn't occur on the same *channel* as the normal output. Errors are output in the shell on the second channel, and we redirect the error to the first channel with the addition 2>&1. This step is necessary to feed the following grep command in the pipeline with the correct data. (Grep searches for *regular expressions* in a string.)

In our example, however, we only want to search for the tab character at the beginning of the line. This search can be defined by using the string `^[[:space:]]`, which in plain language means: Search for the beginning of the line (`^`) followed by a character of the *whitespace* class (which includes the tab). The output of grep is passed to the next command in the Unix pipeline (not to be confused with continuous integration [CI] pipelines). xargs takes the output of the previous program in a pipeline and executes new commands with it. In our case, the output is `.bashrc`, and in the replacement of xargs, you would use the following command:

```
mv -v .bashrc $HOME/.dotfiles.bup/.bashrc
```

This step will move existing dotfiles that are also in the repository into the backup folder. Then, `config checkout` is called again to copy the moved files from the repository, but now without errors.

10.2.6   Vim Configuration

With our dotfiles, one more step involves Git: For the editor *Vim*, possibly the best editor on the planet, you'll need to install some extensions. The original setup originates from Jess Frazelle's impressive GitHub repository, with the dotfiles repository in particular worth looking at:

- *https://github.com/jessfraz/.vim*
- *https://github.com/jessfraz/dotfiles*

The Vim extensions mentioned earlier are loaded as Git submodules (see Chapter 9, Section 9.3) into the *.vim/bundle* subdirectory. To load the submodules after the checkout, you'll need to call the submodule command:

```
config submodule update --init
```

This step will clone all repositories listed in the *.gitmodules* file and store them in the correct subdirectory. To update the plugins, a shell script in the *.vim* folder can be used that starts the git pull call for each submodule with a one-liner:

```
git --git-dir=$HOME/.cfg/ --work-tree=$HOME submodule \
    foreach git pull --recurse-submodules origin main
```

Note the `foreach` statement in the `git submodule` command. To be on the safe side, if the plugins themselves still use Git submodules, call `git pull` with the `--recurse-submodules` option.

10.2.7   Miscellaneous

The other instructions in the *README.md* file refer to installing packages or other configuration settings that don't have anything to do with Git.

We hope that this fairly simple setup whets your appetite for setting up your own dotfiles repository. If you search the internet for "dotfiles repositories," you'll come across many more cool tricks.

10.3   Accessing Apache Subversion (git-svn)

In this section, we want to show you how to participate with Git in a project whose source code is managed in SVN. On Linux, you can install the `git-svn` package to extend Git with the new `git svn` subcommand to create a kind of compatibility mode with SVN:

```
apt/dnf/yum install git-svn
```

You may wonder why you should call `git svn` instead of the SVN client `svn`. But once you've come to know the benefits of Git and its local repositories, you'll never go back to the slow, server-based SVN workflow. So, if you can't convince a project owner to switch from SVN to Git (see Section 10.4), then `git svn` is the next best compromise.

Apache Subversion versus Git

SVN is a version control system that was widely used in the pre-Git era. Especially in the first decade of the 21st century, many projects still used SVN. Git and SVN are fundamentally different in many areas. One of the most important differences is that SVN always has a central repository, and the local working copy doesn't contain a complete history of the project. Learn more about SVN at the following link:

https://subversion.apache.org/

10.3.1   Application

The starting point for the examples in this section is a SVN repository that we used years ago to create a book about HTML5. We've put it in a Docker container and started the SVN server there so that we had a *real* SVN server. So, don't be surprised about the strange server name `svn.server`.

If you're familiar with SVN, you'll know that creating the first working copy is done via `svn checkout <server>`. In contrast, when we work with `git svn`, this step is performed according to Git style via `clone`. We'll pass two more parameters besides the server:

- Since SVN manages tags and branches in a completely different way from Git, `--std-layout` specifies that branches are found in the SVN repository under `/branches` and tags under `/tags`. This scenario isn't always the case in an SVN repository, but this setting is the default setting, which we'll also use in our repository.

- We also set a prefix so that the branches created in Git can be found under `remotes/html5/*`. You should pay attention to the trailing slash, which is crucial for the correct notation of the branch names.

```
git svn clone svn://svn.server/html5 --stdlayout --prefix html5/

  Initialized empty Git repository in /src/git-svn/html5/.git/
  r1 = bb5670d030a0cd84eedfa0f167bc... (refs/remotes/html5/trunk)
    A    tests/form1.html
    A    .svnignore
    A    concept_html5.odt
    A    conversation/[book] missing chapters and more.eml
  r2 = 2005d9359b49e9fd9aec8379777c... (refs/remotes/html5/trunk)
    M    .svnignore
    ...
  r1365 = b6c4265d5dba108b1736ef3a1... (refs/remotes/html5/trunk)
    M   code/chap_intro/timeline.html
  r1366 = a1ef641b8297db7b1ff9b6dc8... (refs/remotes/html5/trunk)
  Auto packing the repository in background for optimum perfor...
  See "git help gc" for manual housekeeping.
  Updating files: 100% (1091/1091), done.
  Checked out HEAD:
    svn://svn.server/html5/trunk r1366
```

The process is surprisingly slow. Unlike cloning a Git repository, in this case, each of the 1,366 commits is loaded *individually* from the SVN server and stored in the local working copy. In the output, you can see how each SVN revision is assigned a Git hash code.

However, the initial time investment is worth it: We now have a real Git repository with the full history from SVN locally on our computer and can accordingly run quick searches in it and compare files. Operations like `git log` and `git diff` run as fast as lightning (as usual), without the detour to a server:

```
git log

  commit a1ef641b8297db7b1ff9b6dc86205b4694448445
  Author: klaus <klaus@c2e5c764-1585-4362-8e61-39aa89b630b5>
  Date:   Tue Nov 27 16:24:17 2012 +0000
```

```
    update timeline
    git-svn-id: svn://svn.server/html5/trunk@1366 c2e5c764-1...
 1 file changed, 11 insertions(+)
commit b6c4265d5dba108b1736ef3a154d4d172bc66b6a
Author: klaus <klaus@c2e5c764-1585-4362-8e61-39aa89b630b5>
Date:   Mon Jul 2 13:52:52 2012 +0000
    fix label position
    git-svn-id: svn://svn.server/html5/trunk@1365 c2e5c764-1...
 1 file changed, 2 insertions(+), 2 deletions(-)
```

In the log output (shortened here by the blank lines), two things stand out:

- First, the authors are saved with weird email addresses. But that shouldn't put you off. You'll learn more about the different handling of authors in SVN and Git in the following section.

- Second, some lines that start with git-svn-id. In these lines, git svn stores metadata about the original SVN commit on import. The first string contains the server URL, the repository, and (after the @ character) the SVN revision. The second string (also truncated here) is the universally unique identifier (UUID) of the SVN repository. You'll also see the same UUID as the domain part of the author email address. SVN assigns such a unique identifier for each new repository. Git uses this value here to assign the commits to the repository.

We'll use the local working copy as we would with a *normal* Git repository. We can create local branches via git branch, work on them locally, and then merge them back into our main branch. As long as we don't upload anything to the SVN server, we have the full freedom to work. No Git remote repository is involved (we'll show you to contribute to the SVN repository shortly), and the local branches are marked with the html5 prefix, as mentioned earlier.

```
git remote -v    # remains without output
git branch -a

  * main
    remotes/html5/first_edition
    remotes/html5/tags/1.0
    remotes/html5/tags/2.0
    remotes/html5/trunk
    remotes/html5/v2
```

10.3.2   Subversion Commits

In SVN projects, commits occur less frequently than in Git projects, if only because each commit requires a round trip to the server and takes what feels like forever. This behavior is one of the big differences between using Git and SVN.

After saving our changes locally in many individual commits, we'll need to synchronize with the SVN server again. For this step, we'll first fetch the changes from the SVN server, still without merging anything, with the following command:

```
git svn fetch
```

If no changes have been made to the SVN server (git svn fetch shows no output), we can push our commits. Since SVN, as the central software, stores every commit immediately on the server, no push command is required, which is why the new command dcommit has been added to git svn, as shown in the following example:

```
git svn dcommit
```

```
Committing to svn://svn.server/html5/trunk ...
Authentication realm: <svn://svn.server:3690> c2e5c764-1585-...
Password for 'bernd':
  M   code/index_en.html
Committed r1367
  M   code/index_en.html
r1367 = a4cd7638710167ecdf1a1c7cb4e36d2c96d84176 (refs/remot...
No changes between ca2a4abfb97565750c872064e9c2b4f54e8dcac6
  and refs/remotes/html5/trunk
Resetting to the latest refs/remotes/html5/trunk
```

With dcommit, our local commits on the SVN server are inserted one by one and receive the revision numbers known from SVN (in this case, r1367). Note that the local commit messages are supplemented with the git-svn-id entry mentioned earlier.

If changes occur on the server, these changes must be imported after git svn fetch via git svn rebase, as shown in the following example:

```
git svn fetch
```

```
  M   code/index.html
r1368 = e652bed7a43d896c42b990ef606113945fbda935 (refs/remot..
```

```
git svn rebase
```

```
First, rewinding head to replay your work on top of it...
Fast-forwarded main to refs/remotes/html5/trunk.
```

Depending on the requirements of the SVN project, the few commands we've presented so far may be sufficient and allow you to stay in your familiar Git world, even though the project is versioned with SVN. You'll then rarely have to deal with the sluggish SVN commands. Your teammates won't even notice that you're working behind the scenes with git instead of svn (except for the typically much higher commit count).

10.4   Migrating from Apache Subversion to Git

In the previous section, we worked as a single developer on an SVN project. In this section, we'll walk you through the main steps for converting an existing SVN repository into a Git repository. Of course, the goal is for the history, authors, branches, and tags to all be transferred correctly from SVN to Git.

For the migration, we'll use the `git svn` command from the `git-svn` package, as described in the previous section. But that's not the end of it—to use the repository cloned from SVN in Git with all its subtleties, we must adjust a few things.

10.4.1   Authors

To contribute to an SVN project, you usually need an account with a user name and password on the SVN server. The user name is also displayed in the log entries, as shown in a slightly shortened example:

```
svn log -l 4

  r1366 | klaus | 2012-11-27 17:24:17 +0100 (...) | 2 lines
    update timeline
  r1365 | klaus | 2012-07-02 15:52:52 +0200 (...) | 2 lines
    fix label position
  r1364 | klaus | 2012-07-02 15:49:26 +0200 (...) | 2 lines
    update timeline, add new browser releases, fix wikipedia links
  r1363 | bernd | 2012-04-17 17:02:15 +0200 (...) | 2 lines
    bugfix for new websocket-server version
```

Git, on the other hand, always uses a name and email address for the author of a commit. For a distributed system like Git, local user names would be worthless since many duplicate users may exist, and when merging different repositories, the true authors would be lost.

For us to store the correct authors in the Git history when switching from SVN to Git, an intermediate manual step is required: For this purpose, we'll generate a list of all authors from the SVN log and equate the authors to Git authors in a text file. The `git svn clone` command has an extra parameter for this, `--authors-file`, which does exactly this translation for us.

First, we'll generate the list of authors from the existing SVN repository. For this step, we'll use the SVN client and check out a working copy from the server:

```
svn checkout svn://svn.server/html5/trunk html5

  A    html5/code
  ...
```

```
A    html5/.svnignore
U    html5
Checked out revision 1366.
```

Then, we'll use svn log to get a list of all authors from the log entries. Unfortunately, SVN doesn't have the log output capabilities we know from Git, so we must use some shell tricks to filter the user names from the list. We use the list output in XML format so we can access the user name more easily. Since we're only interested in the authors, we'll also use the --quiet option, which suppresses the commit messages:

```
svn log -l2 --xml --quiet
```

```
<?xml version="1.0" encoding="UTF-8"?>
<log>
<logentry
    revision="1366">
<author>klaus</author>
<date>2012-11-27T16:24:17.305583Z</date>
</logentry>
<logentry
    revision="1365">
<author>klaus</author>
<date>2012-07-02T13:52:52.268256Z</date>
</logentry>
</log>
```

Using the Linux grep command, we can easily filter this list for lines starting with the <author> tag. To prevent repetitions, the shell command sort -u is used, which sorts the list alphabetically and then displays each entry only once. (The -u option stands for *unique*.) Since the shell pipeline works so well, we continue using it with one more step, putting the output into the format the --authors-file option expects:

```
svn log --xml --quiet | grep '^<author>' | sort -u \
   | sed -e 's/^<author>\(.*\)<\/author>/\1 = \1/'
```

```
bernd = bernd
klaus = klaus
root = root
```

The sed command searches for the string inside the author tag, stores it in the \1 variable, and replaces the entire line with the output of the found user name, the = character, and once again the user name. As we're happy with the result so far, we'll redirect the output to the *authors.txt* file and edit it so that the result looks as follows:

```
bernd = bernd <bernd@git-compendium.info>
klaus = klaus <klaus@openweb.cc>
root  = bernd <bernd@git-compendium.info>
```

Entries mistakenly assigned to the root user in SVN can be assigned to the correct user in this way.

10.4.2 Import

Now, let's start the import with the following command:

```
git svn clone svn://svn.server/html5 --stdlayout --no-metadata \
    --authors-file='authors.txt' --prefix ""
```

The --no-metadata option prevents the log entries for git-svn-id, as we described in the previous section. For a pure Git project, these entries aren't necessary, and they may unnecessarily fill a Git history. Of course, you can also keep the entries in the log.

After the import, the Git history looks the way we want it to:

```
git log --shortstat

  commit 0ea3e24ac7424a4fde0832ce094f8... (HEAD -> main, trunk)
  Author: klaus <klaus@openweb.cc>
  Date:   Tue Nov 27 16:24:17 2012 +0000
    update timeline
   1 file changed, 11 insertions(+)
  commit 6cd390d9f0adbcdaebabe51071103e670a1298d1
  Author: klaus <klaus@openweb.cc>
  Date:   Mon Jul 2 13:52:52 2012 +0000
    fix label position
   1 file changed, 2 insertions(+), 2 deletions(-)
```

10.4.3 Tags and Branches

However, we aren't yet completely happy with our Git repository. After all, git svn imported both tags and branches as remote references rather than what they are supposed to be in our Git repository, namely, actual Git tags and Git branches. To solve this problem, we must go to the shell two more times and deal with low-level git commands. Specifically, we'll use git for-each-ref to run a loop over the tags and another loop over the branches to create the desired Git objects.

After the import, the references look as follows (we've shortened the hash codes):

```
git tag    # no output
git show-ref
```

```
0ea3e24ac... refs/heads/main
be5d53b26... refs/remotes/first_edition
1adc8bd76... refs/remotes/tags/1.0
8b65dd16b... refs/remotes/tags/2.0
0ea3e24ac... refs/remotes/trunk
bce848373... refs/remotes/v2
```

You'll see a reference under refs/remotes/tags/1.0, which was a tag in SVN, which we'll now convert to a tag in Git. Using the git for-each-ref command, you can retrieve a list of all references and filter them.

```
git for-each-ref --format='%(refname:short)' refs/remotes/tags
```

```
tags/1.0
tags/2.0
```

Using this list, we can now start a for loop of the shell and generate the Git tags:

```
for tag in \
$(git for-each-ref --format='%(refname:short)' refs/remotes/tags)
do
  echo "Create $tag"
  git tag ${tag/tags\//} $tag && git branch --delete -r $tag
done
```

```
Create tags/1.0
Deleted remote-tracking branch tags/1.0 (was 1adc8bd).
```

The substitution of variables when setting the tag ${tag/tags\//} causes the tags/ string to be truncated at the beginning. Therefore, the call reads, for example, git tag 1.0 tags/1.0. The remote reference can be deleted afterwards. Now that the tags are done, we still need to convert the remaining branches to local Git branches. The process remains the same, but now, we'll change the filter in refs/remotes. All remaining remote references are to become Git branches:

```
for branch in \
$(git for-each-ref --format='%(refname:short)' refs/remotes)
do
  echo "Create $branch"
  git branch $branch remotes/$branch && \
  git branch --delete -r $branch
done
```

```
Create first_edition
Deleted remote-tracking branch first_edition (was be5d53b).
```

With this step, our local repository is almost finished. We'll only delete the now redundant `trunk` branch of SVN. This branch is an exact copy of `main`:

```
git branch -a -v

   first_edition be5d53b create branch for first edition
 * main          0ea3e24 update timeline
   trunk         0ea3e24 update timeline
   v2            bce8483 use meter elemets for display

git branch --delete trunk

  Deleted branch trunk (was 0ea3e24).
```

Finally, we'll create a new project in our private GitLab instance and add it as a remote repository:

```
git remote add origin \
  ssh://git@git.git-compendium.info/html5/html5.git
git push origin --all
git push origin --tags
```

With these few steps, we transferred the entire history (including the correct authors) from an SVN repository to Git. Although the two systems are quite different in concept (centralized versus decentralized), the effort was manageable.

10.5 Blog with Git and Hugo

Going from Git to a blogging system means we're stretching out the scope of this book. Don't worry, however: We're about to show you that Git can be used quite profitably in combination with certain blog systems and can dramatically simplify the blog workflow. This efficiency is especially true if you're familiar with Markdown, prefer a more technical approach to writing, and have no need for cluttered web interfaces common in CMS administration. Also, this section gives us the opportunity to introduce an interesting Git extension: *Git LFS*.

10.5.1 From WordPress to Hugo

When we talk about software for blogs and CMS, *WordPress* quickly comes to mind: This PHP/MySQL software is a real triumph and is currently the most widely used CMS.

But web technology has evolved, and server-side web page creation (as WordPress does with PHP and MySQL) is no longer state of the art in all areas. *Single-page applications* are becoming increasingly popular. These applications take some of the workload off the server and shift the processing power to the client using JavaScript. Representational state transfer (REST) application programming interfaces (APIs) deliver data to the frontend in JavaScript Object Notation (JSON) format.

In this section, we'll leave PHP and JavaScript aside and introduce you to another web technology that has received a lot of attention in recent years: With a *static site generator*, text in Markdown format can be converted into a complete website with the help of HTML templates. Navigation elements, RSS feeds, links to categories, and tags are all created when the program is called and stored in static files.

What sounds a bit old-fashioned at first brings great advantages: Content can be delivered quickly without burdening your server with database queries. Probably the biggest advantage, however, is the enormous gain in safety: The server itself no longer runs a programming language that attackers often use as a gateway.

A prominent representative of this software is Jekyll, which was developed by Tom Preston-Werner, one of GitHub's founders, back in 2008. The open-source software is still in use today at GitHub and can be used through GitHub Pages. Other prominent representatives of this category include Next.js, Nuxt.js, or Hugo. While Next.js or Nuxt.js are actually JavaScript frameworks for single-page applications, you can use Hugo without any JavaScript knowledge at all. Hugo converts Markdown files to HTML at the blink of an eye and can be easily controlled with templates and themes.

10.5.2 Hugo

We chose Hugo because we've had positive experiences with it in another project; it installs quickly and is quite efficient in operation. Simply download the binary file for the platform from the GitHub project website at the following link:

https://github.com/gohugoio/hugo/releases

The command-line program has an option that's used to set up a new blog, which is where we'll start our little project:

```
hugo new site simple-blog

  Congratulations! Your new Hugo site is created in
  /src/simple-blog.
  ...
```

Hugo has created a directory structure that contains only two files. The *simple-blog* folder has the following structure:

```
|-- archetypes
|    `-- default.md
|-- config.toml
|-- content
```

```
|-- data
|-- layouts
|-- static
`-- themes
```

We'll initialize a new Git repository in it because we want to document all the steps of our blog with the following commands:

```
git init
git add .
git status
```

```
On branch main
No commits yet
Changes to be committed:
  (use "git rm --cached <file>..." to unstage)
    new file:   archetypes/default.md
    new file:   config.toml
```

In doing so, we immediately come across a peculiarity of Git: Although we used `git add .` to add all entries in the current directory to the index, only the two files *default.md* and *config.toml* are provided for the commit. This problem arises because Git only tracks the contents of files; empty directories aren't included.

In our case, this omission isn't a problem. We'll continue to work in the local working copy, and as the directories fill with content, they will automatically be added to the repository. Sometimes, you want to explicitly include an empty directory in the repository. For example, a program might write data to it while it's running without creating the directory first. The only solution to this problem is to create files in the empty directories. You can use *.gitignore* files for this step, as recommended by Git's FAQs (*https://links.git-compendium.info/empty-dir*), but any other file will do as well (see Chapter 11, Section 11.2).

10.5.3 Hugo Themes as Git Submodules

The way in which Hugo converts content to HTML and CSS is controlled by the theme you use. We chose the *Beautiful Hugo* theme, which works well and is responsive on both desktop and mobile devices. This theme can be found on GitHub under the free MIT license at the following link:

https://themes.gohugo.io/beautifulhugo/

To use the theme, add its repository as a submodule (see Chapter 9, Section 9.3) to the *themes* subfolder:

```
git submodule add \
    https://github.com/halogenica/beautifulhugo.git \
    themes/beautifulhugo

  Cloning into '/src/simple-blog/themes/beautifulhugo'...
  ...
```

If the author continues to improve the theme, the submodule technique gives us the opportunity to easily try the update. Using the submodule add call, the theme was cloned, and the changes were added to the index right away. Finally, we'll set the theme in the configuration file and try it out with Hugo's built-in web server:

```
echo 'theme = "beautifulhugo"' >> config.toml
hugo serve

  ...
  Web Server is available at http://localhost:1313/ ...
  Press Ctrl+C to stop
```

Open the given URL *http://localhost:1313* and see the result, which can definitely be improved. At this point, let's make our first commit since the framework for our blog is complete.

Figure 10.3 Hugo Theme "Beautiful Hugo" without Customizations

As shown by the sample page provided with the theme, you can still make some changes in the *config.toml* configuration file. Among other things, let's add a subtitle, the date format, and information about the author. We'll also set the main menu in the `[[menu.main]]` sections.

```
# config.toml file
...
theme = "beautifulhugo"

[Params]
  subtitle = "Travelnotes"
  dateFormat = "January 2, 2006"
  ...
[Author]
  name = "bernd"
  github = "git-compendium"
  gitlab = "git-compendium"
  ...
[[menu.main]]
  name = "Blog"
  url = ""
  weight = 1
[[menu.main]]
  name = "About"
  url = "pages/about/"
  weight = 2
  ...
```

Now would be a good time for another commit. You use this commit to save the settings in the modified *config.toml* file and the submodule settings for the theme.

10.5.4   Filling a Blog with Content

Now, we need to take care of the content. For example, our first entry documents a trip to Switzerland in February 2022. We'll use Hugo to create the structure for the new entry. The entry should be in the *posts/2022-02-10* folder below the *content* folder.

```
hugo new posts/2022-02-10/index.md
```

```
/src/simple-blog/content/posts/2022-02-10/index.md created
```

Although the web browser that's still open reloads the web page every time we change files and has just done so, we don't see anything of our new entry. The culprit is the `draft: true` meta statement in the header of the newly created *index.md* file. As soon as we delete that line or change the value from `true` to `false`, the entry will appear on the blog's home page.

We copy a photo from the trip into the folder and add a few anecdotes from that trip to the Markdown file. Before we commit these changes, we turn to the Git LFS module mentioned earlier.

10.5.5   Git LFS

The *Git LFS* extension was developed to address the issue that Git doesn't handle binary files terribly well. Especially when dealing with large binary files that may be poorly compressible and that change frequently, the size of a repository can grow significantly.

Of course, one could argue that large binary files have no place in a Git repository. But let's return to our example with photos and blog posts: If you were to manage text and images separately, and perhaps back them up separately, the risk of losing data at some point would increase. (Unfortunately, we're speaking from personal experience here.)

Git LFS solves the problem of repositories getting too large by storing files managed by LFS in a different location rather than in the repository itself. The file itself contains only a reference to the file's hash code (called a *pointer* in LFS terminology). LFS uses the hash algorithm SHA-256, which is much more secure than the SHA-1 method currently used by Git (see Chapter 3, Section 3.13).

As users of git lfs, we never get to see the LFS pointers themselves because the sophisticated filter mechanism that replaces the text files with the original binary content. For the filters to take effect, you must first install and enable Git LFS. On Debian or Ubuntu, simply call sudo apt install git-lfs. Installation packages for all major platforms can be found at *https://github.com/git-lfs/git-lfs/releases*. To enable Git LFS for your repository, use the following command:

```
git lfs install
```

```
    Updated git hooks.
    Git LFS initialized.
```

Several steps are performed in this process. When the command is run for the first time on a computer, LFS adds a new section to your personal Git configuration file:

```
[filter "lfs"]
    clean = git-lfs clean -- %f
    smudge = git-lfs smudge -- %f
    process = git-lfs filter-process
    required = true
```

The clean filter stores the binary contents of the file in a subfolder of *.git/lfs* and replaces the original file with the LFS pointer described earlier. This process occurs with git add, which is when the file is added to the Git index. Conversely, the smudge filter retrieves the binary content from the *.git/lfs* folder and replaces the pointer with the correct content.

In addition to the filters, Git hooks are installed which, among other things, take care of uploading and downloading binaries from the LFS storage. But that's enough theory: Let's now add a photo to the LFS memory. For this process to work, we'll need to tell Git which file types are supposed to be managed with LFS:

```
git lfs track '*.jpg'
git add .
git status
```

```
  On branch main
  Changes to be committed:
    (use "git restore --staged <file>..." to unstage)
        new file:   .gitattributes
        new file:   .hugo_build.lock
        new file:   content/posts/2022-02-10/index.md
        new file:   content/posts/2022-02-10/swiss1.jpg
```

So, we want LFS to manage files ending in *.jpg*. We see no change in the subsequent add and status. This scenario illustrates a particularly pleasant aspect of Git LFS: Once LFS has been set up, you don't need to bother about anything, and you won't even notice it's active.

Actually, we don't want to save the *.hugo_build.lock* file to Git. This file only indicates that the hugo serve process is currently still being active. To remove it from the staging area and ignore it afterwards, you can use the following commands:

```
echo ".hugo_build.lock" > .gitignore
git restore --staged .hugo_build.lock
git add .gitignore
git commit -m "first post"
```

For our local repository, LFS doesn't yet provide a decisive advantage: All changes—including to LFS-managed images—remain in the local *.git/lfs* folder. You can now create your remote repository with GitHub and transfer the current state there with the following commands:

```
git remote add origin \
  git@github.com:git-compendium/simple-blog.git
git push -u origin main
```

```
  Uploading LFS objects: 100% (1/1), 193 KB | 0 B/s, done.
  Enumerating objects: 10, done.
  ...
```

```
  * [new branch]      main -> main
Branch 'main' set up to track remote branch 'main' from
'origin'.
```

You'll see a new entry in the otherwise already known output of git push: Via *Uploading LFS objects*, Git tells us that the objects managed by LFS will be uploaded separately from the rest of the repository. As mentioned earlier, the process remains completely transparent, and you don't even notice that the images are being managed differently in any way. Only the note in the GitHub interface *Stored with Git LFS* indicates that the image is now managed by LFS.

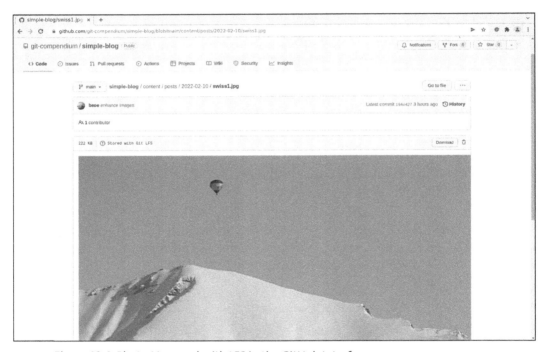

Figure 10.4 Photo Managed with LFS in the GitHub Interface

In the meantime, we've added a second blog entry, and we notice that the quality of the pictures is not so great. For this reason, we edit both images and then commit and push these changes. Before the changes, both images together were 560 KB; afterwards, 660 KB. Our local *.git/lfs* folder now contains two versions of each image, and they occupy a total of 1.3 MB of space (the du program calculates the *disk usage* of a folder).

```
du -h .git/lfs

  372K  .git/lfs/objects/94/ad
  ...
  1.3M  .git/lfs
```

Things get exciting when we create a new clone of our remote repository and examine the size of the *.git/lfs* folder in it. In the final step of `git clone`, the filters mentioned earlier become active: Git now only fetches the exact versions of the images from the LFS space that are needed for the current `HEAD`. The output of `du -h` then results in only 692 KB, which is the total of the two modified images.

```
git clone https://github.com/git-compendium/simple-blog.git

  Cloning into 'simple-blog'...
  ...
  Unpacking objects: 100% (36/36), 4.12 KiB | 469.00 KiB/s, done.

du -h simple-blog/.git/lfs

  ...
  692K  simple-blog/.git/lfs
```

With the exception of Gitolite, all Git hosting providers featured in this book support Git LFS. However, you can't use SSH with Azure Repos if you have LFS enabled in your repository. With Gitea, Git LFS must be explicitly enabled in the configuration file.

To conclude this example, of course, we want to publish our blog. For this purpose, we'll show you two different options right away. The first variant can be activated by a few mouse clicks in your web browser and uses the service of *Netlify*, while the second variant uses GitHub Actions and GitHub Pages.

10.5.6   Deploying with Netlify

Netlify specializes in exactly this use case. The service connects to GitHub (or even GitLab or Bitbucket) and automatically converts your source code using a static site generator of your choice and delivers the finished website to their *content delivery network (CDN)*. To get started, Netlify provides a free account that can host up to 500 projects.

To get our project online on Netlify, start on Netlify's website at *https://www.netlify.com*. Under **Sign Up**, allow access to your GitHub account. The wizard guides you through three steps in which the build command must be specified in addition to the GitHub repository. Since Netlify recognizes that our repository is a Hugo site, the field is already filled in correctly.

Netlify automatically provides you with a domain name (in our case, `elastic-brahma-gupta-a8397d.netlify.app`), and you can optionally specify a custom Domain Name System (DNS) name for the site (we used `simple-blog.git-compendium.info`). In our own DNS management, you must create a `CNAME` entry for the randomly generated Netlify host name and for your own domain name for this purpose. During the first deployment, Netlify automatically creates SSL certificates for both names, and your blog can be online with HTTPS within minutes. That was easy! As soon as we upload a change to GitHub, Netlify starts a new build and deploy process, and the updates are online.

Figure 10.5 Importing Our GitHub Project into Netlify

10.5.7   Deploying with a GitHub Action and GitHub Pages

Of course, if you don't want to use this workflow with Netlify, you can run automatic builds on GitHub. You don't even need to write the GitHub action for these automatic builds by yourself because, unsurprisingly, someone has already done it.

However, in the context of Git LFS and submodules, we want to direct your attention to a few more details. The GitHub action checkout, already known from Chapter 5, Section 5.2, is extended by two parameters so that submodules are cloned correctly and the filters for LFS are activated:

```
on:
  push:
    branches: [ main ]
  pull_request:
    branches: [ main ]
jobs:
  build:
    runs-on: ubuntu-latest
    steps:
      - uses: actions/checkout@v2
        with:
          lfs: true
          submodules: true
```

Within three steps, you can turn your source code into HTML and upload the result to a branch in your repository using push. In our example, we used two actions from GitHub user peaceiris, which are available for download in the GitHub marketplace:

1. The first step, which we called Hugo setup, installs the Hugo program in our environment using the peaceiris/actions-hugo action. The extended: true addition loads the extended Hugo version, which can also convert Sass style sheets.

2. In the Build step, we start Hugo without any other parameters, which saves the finished web page in the *public* folder.

3. In the third and final step, the contents of the *public* folder are uploaded to the gh-pages branch using the peaceiris/actions-gh-pages action (commit and push). The secret GITHUB_TOKEN needed for the push action is automatically available as a variable in all GitHub Actions.

```
- name: Hugo setup
  uses: peaceiris/actions-hugo@v2.4.13
  with:
    extended: true
- name: Build
  run: hugo
- name: Deploy
  uses: peaceiris/actions-gh-pages@v3
  with:
    github_token: ${{ secrets.GITHUB_TOKEN }}
    publish_dir: ./public
```

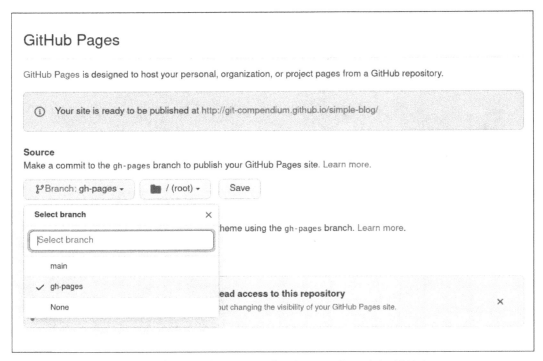

Figure 10.6 Settings for GitHub Pages on the gh-pages Branch in GitHub

Note that the gh-pages branch contains only the finished web page and not the source code from the main branch. The folder structure between main and gh-pages is completely different, which is rather unusual for our previous use of branches. To achieve this behavior, the GitHub web interface provides the option to make the gh-pages branch publicly available. As soon as we enable this setting (under **Settings • Options • GitHub Pages**) and our GitHub Action runs without errors, the blog is online in GitHub.

We've adjusted the layout of the home page (actually the component that generates lists in Hugo) a bit more, so that the images don't take up so much space. The source code for the entire example can be found on our GitHub account at the following link:

https://github.com/git-compendium/simple-blog

Chapter 11
Git Problems and Their Solutions

When working with Git, you may repeatedly come across hurdles or error messages that leave you scratching your head in confusion, asking yourself: What now? Typically, the problems change over time: Git newbies may plague themselves with authentication errors or merge conflicts. Advanced users may look for ways to delete a file that was mistakenly added to the repository or may puzzle over whether or how to move a commit to another branch. Or they're looking for strategies to deal efficiently with really large repositories.

In this chapter, we'll try to provide answers to such questions. We'll start with a section that explains the causes of common Git error messages and outlines ways out and solutions or refers to the relevant chapters of this book. (After all, we don't want to start writing the book from the beginning again!)

11

> **Reading Tip**
>
> The funny page, "Oh Shit, Git!?!" describes other common Git mishaps and provides brief suggestions for solutions:
>
> *https://ohshitgit.com/*
>
> This website is an ideal complement to the first section of this chapter.

The remaining sections then cover the following topics in more detail:

- Handling empty directories
- Merging for single files (git merge-file)
- Permanently deleting files from a repository
- Splitting large projects
- Moving commits to another branch

11.1 Git Error Messages (Root Cause and Solution)

This section consists of many small sections where the heading indicates the essence of a Git error message. The rest of the text then describes the context in which such an error can occur and explains possible root causes and solutions.

11.1.1 Repository Not Found

This error is probably the most trivial Git error: You've tried to execute a `git` command while in a directory that doesn't contain the repository at all. Most often, this problem occurs immediately after `git clone`. Solution: Simply change to the project directory via `cd`.

Conceivably, perhaps no repository (recognizable by the *.git* subdirectory) is available yet for the project in question. In this case, you should use `git init` to set up a new repository.

11.1.2 Please Tell Me Who You Are (git commit)

Along with each commit, your name and email address are stored. Therefore, this data must be preset locally for the current repository or globally for all repositories:

```
git config [--global] user.name  "Howard Hollow"
git config [--global] user.email "hollow@my-company.com"
```

11.1.3 Authentication Failed (git pull, git push)

All commands that access external repositories must be authenticated there. These commands include in particular `git pull` and `git push` and, for private repositories, also `git clone`.

Git supports two basic authentication methods: HTTPS (with a logon name plus password) and SSH (with a key). If a `credential.helper` is set in the Git configuration, the operating system can help with authentication (Windows Credential Manager, macOS Keychain, or Credential Cache).

For troubleshooting, use `git config --list --show-origin` to verify that the URL of the repository is correct (HTTPS/SSH) and that `credential.helper` has been set correctly. If the repository URL contains the @ character, go to the web interface of your Git platform and make sure that you've stored your SSH key there. If you use HTTPS authentication on macOS or Windows, in the respective utility, check if the correct data is stored.

Many more details on the various Git logon mechanisms, including concrete instructions for Windows, macOS, and Linux, are provided in Chapter 2, Section 2.4.

11.1.4 Invalid User Name or Password (git clone, git pull, git push)

This error message also indicates an authentication problem (as in the previous message). Obviously, you're using HTTPS authentication, but either the user name or password is incorrect. If you've enabled two-factor authentication in your Git platform, remember that you must provide the token instead of the password for HTTPS authentication. Be sure to also read Chapter 9, Section 9.5!

11.1.5   Permission Denied, Public Key (git clone, git pull, git push)

Again, an authentication problem has arisen, with a *public key* pointing to SSH authentication, which limits the possible causes somewhat. Most likely, your SSH key isn't stored on the Git platform. If you want to use `git clone` to download a public Git project, you must use an HTTPS URL instead of the SSH URL.

11.1.6   Permission Denied, Unable to Access <repo> (git push)

Once again, we have an access problem. Although in this case the authentication itself worked, you don't have write permissions for the project in question.

If the project is managed by someone else in your company or organization, you should ask them to grant you write permissions. On the other hand, if you want to collaborate on a public project, it's usually best to create a fork (a copy) of the project, make the changes in your fork, and then make a pull request (or in GitLab, a merge request) to the owner of the original project. We described this procedure in detail in Chapter 5, Section 5.1.

11

11.1.7   Changes Not Staged for Commit (git commit)

In this case, you want to save the latest changes you made with `git commit`, but Git finds that there's nothing to save. The cause of this problem is that, in Git, you always must stage the files you want to save before committing with `git add <file>`. For files that are already versioned, it's sufficient to run `git commit` with the `-a` option.

11.1.8   Your Local Changes Would Be Overwritten (git checkout, git switch)

Basically, you are allowed to change the active branch even if you've already modified files in the working directory. If you commit later, the changes will be saved in the current branch. However, changing the branch isn't permitted if the last saved state of the changed file is different in the current and future branches. Switching branches would overwrite the file with its contents in the future branch, and your changes would be lost. And thus, Git refuses to execute the command.

Several ways out, however, exist:

- You can save the changes in a commit before switching branches.
- You can save the changes in the stash area (see Chapter 3, Section 3.7), perform the branch change, and then reapply the changes in the new branch with the following commands:

  `git stash; git checkout <branch>; git stash pop`

- You can force the change using the `--force` option. But you should always act with caution because the last changes you made will be lost.

11.1.9   Your Branch Is Ahead of a Remote/Branch by n Commits (git pull, git status)

This notice from git status (usually after you've previously performed git pull) isn't an error message. Consider the following example:

```
git checkout main
git pull
git status
  Your branch is ahead of origin/main by 3 commits
  ...
```

This message rather documents an entirely normal condition: You've made changes locally and saved them in commits. However, these commits haven't yet been trans-ferred to the appropriate branch of the remote repository (e.g., origin/main). The sim-plest solution in this case is to just upload the commits with the command:

```
git push
```

If you're unsure what the commits are or what changes are being made with them, you may want to investigate instead of running git push and analyze the situation more closely. In this process, you must replace origin and main with the names of the remote repository and the remote branch and use the following commands:

```
git log  origin/main..HEAD
git diff origin/main..HEAD
```

In rare cases, you may realize that you don't want to upload your local commits after all and now want to discard them instead. If that happens, you can use git reset to point the HEAD to the top of the remote branch:

```
git reset --hard origin/main
```

11.1.10   You're in a Detached HEAD State (git checkout)

A detached HEAD isn't an error, so this message isn't an error message. Rather, Git usu-ally indicates, after the git checkout <hashcode> command, that HEAD isn't currently pointing to the end of a branch. This condition is unusual but not incorrect. You can then switch back to a branch via git checkout <branch>, start a new branch at the current location using git checkout -b <newbranch>, or use git reflog to get the hash code of another commit you want to return to.

11.1.11   Pathspec Did Not Match Any Files Known to Git (git checkout)

Your co-developers may have emailed you that they want you to look at a new branch in the remote repository. So, you run the following command:

```
git checkout new_feature_branch
```

However, git returns the error message because git checkout works locally. The new branch doesn't exist yet on your computer; it exists only in the remote repository. The following command can solve this dilemma:

```
git checkout -b new_feature_branch remote/new_feature_branch
```

This command sets up the new branch locally and downloads it from the remote repository.

11.1.12 Please Enter a Commit Message to Explain Why This Merge Is Necessary (git pull)

For once, this message isn't an error message, simply text displayed in an editor. git pull starts the editor unprompted to allow you to enter a commit message.

But why is a commit required at all? Usually, you and other developers have made changes to a branch at the same time. Therefore, git pull can't incorporate the commits coming from the remote repository as a fast-forward merge. Instead, a "real" merge process is required, which is now associated with a commit and a commit message.

Don't let yourself be confused by the insistent tone (*Why this merge is necessary*)! You don't need to justify anything. Simply accept the commit message given in the editor (*Merge branch <name> of <remote repo>*).

11.1.13 Pulling without Specifying How to Reconcile Divergent Branches Is Discouraged (git pull)

git pull returns this warning if you don't specify the desired pull behavior. In the simplest case, git pull can simply incorporate the commits from the remote repository into the local repository using a fast-forward merge. If that approach isn't possible, either a merge process including its own commit (the default behavior) or a rebasing operation is required (see Chapter 3, Section 3.10).

The warning disappears if you pass the --ff-only, --no-rebase, or --rebase options to git pull or if you make the behavior permanent in the configuration, as in the following examples:

```
git config [--global] pull.ff only          (FF or error)
git config [--global] pull.rebase false     (FF or merge)
git config [--global] pull.rebase true      (always rebasing)
```

11.1.14 Cannot Pull with Rebase: You Have Unstaged/Uncommitted Changes (git pull)

This error message occurs when you run git pull --rebase (or git pull without this option, but with the common setting pull.rebasing = true) but open changes exist in the project directory that haven't yet been saved in a commit.

In this case, you have the following two options:

- Saving the open changes in a commit. Then, `git pull` will work.
- If you've changed only minor things since the last commit that don't warrant a separate commit, you can save the changes in the stash area. After `git pull`, you must reactivate the cached changes in the following way:

```
git stash
git pull
git stash pop
```

11.1.15   There Is No Tracking Information for the Current Branch (git pull)

This error message indicates that `git pull` doesn't know from where to download the commits for the current branch. In `.git/config`, a mapping between the current branch and the remote repository is missing. Solution: Establish the mapping with `git branch --set-upstream-to`, for instance, in the following way:

```
git branch --set-upstream-to=origin/<remotebranch> <localbranch>
```

Most times, `<remotebranch>` and `<localbranch>` match, but this rule isn't always true. If you have multiple remote repositories, you should replace `origin` with the name of the repository.

11.1.16   Your Local Changes Would Be Overwritten (git merge, git pull)

This error occurs when `git merge` detects (often as part of a pull process) that you've made changes to the files in the project directory that haven't been saved yet. The `git merge` command can't account for these changes and would overwrite them, and thus, the process is aborted.

You have the option of saving the changes in a commit or temporarily dumping them to the stash area (i.e., `git stash`; `git merge/pull`; `git stash pop`).

11.1.17   Failed to Push Some Refs to <somerepo.git> (git push)

This error message occurs when you try to use `git push` to commit your own commits to a remote repository that itself has commits that aren't yet available to you. This scenario isn't permitted because only fast-forward merge processes are provided at remote repositories. However, such a simple merge process can only be guaranteed if your own repository is up to date and thus your own commits have no conflict with the remote repository.

The solution is simple: First, you must run `git pull` and then `git push`.

11.1.18   The Current Branch <name> Has No Upstream Branch (git push)

This error indicates that you want to commit a local branch to an external repository, but the mapping to a remote repository is missing in .git/config.

Solution: You must specify the repository to which you want to upload the branch in the git push command—for example, git push origin <branchname>. Another often useful action is to also pass the --set-upstream option: Then, git stores the repository mapping in .git/config. Next time, the simple command git push will be sufficient.

11.1.19   Merge Failed, Merge Conflict in <file> (git merge, etc.)

Merge conflicts can occur with all commands that internally trigger a merge process. Besides git merge, other commands include git cherrypick, git pull, git rebase, and git stash pop. When a merge conflict occurs, Git cannot execute two different changes in the same file. Then, you must intervene manually:

- For text files, the solution is to open the file in an editor and choose one of the two variants highlighted with conflict markers. Delete the other code variant and its conflict markers. Finally, you must add the file to the staging area via git add and finish the merge process using git commit.

- For binary files, you must choose one of the two variants. In an ordinary merge process, you would run git checkout --ours if you want to give preference to your file or run git checkout --theirs if you want to use the file from the other branch (or from the remote repository in the case of git pull). git commit completes the merge process. Consider the following examples:

```
git checkout --ours -- <file>      ('own' version)
git checkout --theirs -- <file>    ('others'' Version)
git commit -a                      (perform commit)
```

Caution: With git rebase or git pull --rebase, absurdly, the effect of --ours and --theirs is reversed! Now, --theirs designates your own variant.

- If you feel currently unable to resolve the conflict (e.g., because you simply can't decide which variant is better or more correct), you should abort the merge process, for example, in the following way:

```
git merge --abort
git rebase --abort
```

If you've triggered the conflict via git stash pop, the changes cached in the stash area will be automatically preserved. To restore to the state prior to git stash pop, you must use git restore:

```
git restore <file>
```

For a much more detailed guide on dealing with merge conflicts, see Chapter 3, Section 3.9.

11.2 Saving Empty Directories

Git only processes files, not directories. Of course, Git remembers the location of a file and creates all necessary directories when unpacking, but you cannot process an empty directory as a git object. Although git add emptydir is executed without any problems, the command has no effect.

The easiest way to include a directory without content in a Git repository is to set up an empty, invisible file in the directory. On Linux and macOS, any file that starts with a period is considered invisible. Windows doesn't understand this concept, but a dotfile won't interfere. In the following step, you'll add this file to the repository:

```
mkdir emptydir
touch emptydir/.hiddenfile
git add emptydir/.hiddenfile
```

But if you need to set up an invisible file anyway, you might as well name the file .gitignore and store the following two lines in it:

```
*
!.gitignore
```

This approach prevents files created in the directory from being inadvertently included in the Git repository as well (rule *). The only exception to this rule is the *.gitignore* file. The two rules are useful if the directory is temporary.

11.3 Merge for a Single File

An ordinary merge process always affects all files of the concerned commits. From time to time, however, a requirement may arise to merge only a single file. This scenario isn't actually provided for in Git. But Git wouldn't be Git if a way to do it anyway didn't exist.

11.3.1 git merge-file

The "correct" procedure is unfortunately quite cumbersome: You must first copy the version of the file in question from the other branch to the project directory (preferably to a temporary directory). You also need the version of the file at the last merge process between the two branches. You can determine the hash code of the commit of the last common base using git merge-base.

In the following example, we assume that the main branch is active. You want to merge the changes of file1 from the feature branch. The git merge-base command determines the last common commit between the current branch and feature. The two git show commands create copies of the base version and the feature version of file1.

Finally, git merge-file merges the changes. In this process, file1 is changed. Look at this file before saving the changes with git commit -a. As with git merge, conflicts can occur with git file-merge. In a pinch, you can use git restore file1 to restore file1 to its original state.

```
git checkout main
mkdir tmp
git merge-base HEAD feature
   8ed6b95e1999679b315723fcf98311b2701922cc

git show 8ed6b95:file1 > tmp/file1-base

git show feature:file1 > tmp/file1-feature

git merge-file file1 tmp/file1-base tmp/file1-feature

rm -rf tmp
```

11.3.2   git checkout

An alternative and much simpler approach is provided by the git checkout --patch <branch> <file> command. This command simply overwrites the existing version of the file with that of the specified branch.

However, you should be cautious when using this command: git checkout doesn't perform a true merge operation. The changes made in the current branch since the branches were separated will be lost!

After all, thanks to the --patch option, you can decide interactively for each code block whether you want to apply the changes or not:

```
git checkout main
git checkout --patch feature file1
  diff --git b/file1 a/file1
  ..
  (1/1) Apply this hunk to index and worktree [y,n,q,a,d,e,?]? y
```

11.4   Deleting Files Permanently from Git

At first glance, writing a separate section about how to delete something might seem a bit strange. But that's exactly what Git is particularly good at—preventing you from deleting something (unintentionally).

Once committed, changes are stored in the Git history where they can be traced back to the beginning of the project. Thus, a file that has been checked into a Git repository at some point can always be restored. However, in some situations, this behavior is undesirable, for example, if you accidentally commit a file with secret credentials. Or you mistakenly committed a large file in your repository. Even if you delete this file, in the subsequent commit, all collaborators who have cloned your repository will have to perform this large download once.

To permanently delete the changes, you must modify the Git history. Now, we all know from science fiction that changing history through time travel is tricky and often comes with unexpected side effects. To avoid mishaps with your Git repository, we'll explain several different approaches in detail next.

11.4.1 Local Changes Only, without Push (git rm)

First, let's consider a simple case: You've committed the problematic changes to your Git repository locally but haven't pushed them yet. If it's the last commit, the problem is quickly solved. Let's suppose that you mistakenly added a secret token to a file during a commit:

```
git log --name-status --pretty=short

  commit 390825bea2a26b682ce46b1fb13873fd0d80fd97 (HEAD -> main)
  Author: Bernd Oeggl <bernd@git-compendium.info>
      Add server code
  A       secure_token.txt
  A       server.js

  commit 5c47310ba9f7b90d2322ae6785e40dbd0e24c270
  Author: Bernd Oeggl <bernd@git-compendium.info>
      add README
  A       README.md
```

If you want to completely delete the token, you can just remove it from the repository and make the next commit using --amend:

```
rm secure_token.txt
git add secure_token.txt
git commit --amend --no-edit

  [main 4f7012c] Add server code
   Date: Tue Feb 15 11:59:55 2022 +0000
   1 file changed, 3 insertions(+)
   create mode 100644 server.js
```

The file thus disappears from the Git history. If you want to keep the file, but not manage it in the Git repository, you should delete it only from the Git index:

```
git rm --cached secure_token.txt
```

```
  rm 'secure_token.txt'
```

```
git status
```

```
  On branch main
  Changes to be committed:
  (use "git restore --staged <file>..." to unstage)
      deleted:    secure_token.txt

  Untracked files:
  (use "git add <file>..." to include in what will be committed)
      secure_token.txt
```

After committing with --amend, you must still include the file in the *.gitignore* file so that your Git repository won't continue to show it as an *untracked file.*

If you've only added the one file in the commit that you want to delete later, you'll be warned that the commit with --amend won't create any changes to the previous version and won't be executed unless you use the additional --allow-empty option:

```
git commit --amend
```

```
  On branch main
  Untracked files:
    (use "git add <file>..." to include in what will be commit...
    secure_token.txt
  No changes
  You asked to amend the most recent commit, but doing so would
  make it empty. You can repeat your command with --allow-empty,
  or you can remove the commit entirely with "git reset HEAD^".
```

As the warning in the console also says, now would probably make sense to simply delete the last commit using git reset HEAD^.

11.4.2   Previously Uploaded Changes, with Push (git filter-branch)

If you've already uploaded the commit with the file to be deleted to a remote repository using push, things become much more complicated: Now, you want to delete a file from your Git history that has already been pushed to a server. First, you must realize that all users who have already cloned your repository have this file on their local computer. You can't undo this fact from their computer.

Nevertheless, fixing the problem for the future makes sense. We'll describe three ways to achieve this goal in the this section. Only the first of these options can be run with the git command alone; for the other two solutions, you'll need additional software.

To demonstrate the procedures, we created a Git repository called history-rewrite, which you can find on our GitHub account at *https://github.com/git-compendium/history-rewrite*. The second commit in the Git history inadvertently adds a file named *secure_token.txt* to the repository. Later, the v1.0.0 tag is created and, later, two branches are created (feature-1 and feature-2). In the last commit, the feature-1 branch is merged with the main branch.

Our first option to solve the problem is to use the git command's onboard means, namely, the filter-branch subcommand. The help page for the git filter-branch command starts with an impressive warning: The command has a ton of hidden traps that can put your repository into an unusable state. If possible, you should use an alternative, for example, git filter-repo (which we'll discuss in the next section).

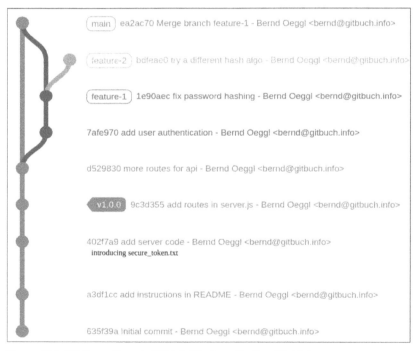

Figure 11.1 Git Repository in Which We Rewrite the Git History

In our test repository, we still want to take a chance and issue the following, somewhat cryptic command:

```
git filter-branch --force --index-filter \
  "git rm --cached --ignore-unmatch secure_token.txt" \
  --prune-empty --tag-name-filter cat -- --all
```

```
WARNING: git-filter-branch has a glut of gotchas generating
  mangled history rewrites.  Hit Ctrl-C before proceeding to
  abort, then use an alternative filtering tool such as
  'git filter-repo'
  (https://github.com/newren/git-filter-repo/) instead.  See
  the filter-branch manual page for more details;
  to squelch this warning, set FILTER_BRANCH_SQUELCH_WARNING=1.
Proceeding with filter-branch...

Rewrite e35bbe0104adf145be37ffdd13bd493651dcf915 (3/33) (0 s...
Rewrite 7495ede732a460687228f4c2d4572f8b0ed9f47e (4/33) (0 s...
Rewrite 75df742dabc122b34c848202cc3c60fbde7a1845 (5/33) (0 s...
...
```

Again, a similar warning as in the help page appears before the command is actually executed. You have the option to cancel the process for a few seconds if you press `Ctrl`+`C` as described in the help text. Otherwise, the execution will start, and all commits in each branch will be analyzed. Since our change starts at the third commit in the history, all subsequent commits must be changed. For our small repository, the time required is manageable, but for repositories with a long history, minutes and hours can quickly pass.

You've now freed your local repository from the security token file. However, the remote repository still needs to be updated. One option is to use the command, `git push origin --force --all`. As with the `filter-branch` command, you must use `--force` in this case to prevent you from carelessly overwriting files or causing other damage. To update tags, they also need to be pushed:

```
git push origin --force --all
git push origin --force --tags
```

If a developer from your team performs a pull from the modified repository into their own local repository, a problem will arise:

```
git pull

  remote: Enumerating objects: 69, done.
  remote: Counting objects: 100% (69/69), done.
  remote: Compressing objects: 100% (52/52), done.
  remote: Total 69 (delta 19), reused 25 (delta 0)
  Unpacking objects: 100% (69/69), 6.46 KiB | 2.15 MiB/s, done.
  From /home/bernd/work/git/tmp/history-rewrite
   + 0d27922...4c15132 main        -> origin/main  (forced update)
  fatal: refusing to merge unrelated histories
```

`fatal` sounds extremely problematic: What happened? `git status` tells you the current status of your local repository:

`git status`

```
On branch main
Your branch and 'origin/main' have diverged,
and have 23 and 23 different commits each, respectively.
  (use "git pull" to merge the remote branch into yours)

nothing to commit, working tree clean
```

The Git history of the local repository and that of `origin/main` are now completely different. Only the first two commits are still the same; then, each commit was changed. You should now tell your collaborators to remove the defective repositories and run `git clone` again. To push in the changes with `--rebase` is dangerous because the now deleted file still exists in the local repository and can go back to the server on a new push.

> **Using git filter-repo**
>
> We'd like to point out that `git filter-branch` shouldn't be used (anymore). Even the official documentation for Git refers to the external tool `git filter-repo`, which we'll describe in the following section.

11.4.3   Previously Uploaded Changes, after Push (git filter-repo)

Fortunately, another tool can handle the problem we just described rather efficiently, through the simple command-line interface (CLI) for users. To remove the file from the Git history with `git filter-repo`, the following call is sufficient:

`git filter-repo --path secure_token.txt --invert-paths`

But first things first: `git filter-repo` is a tool written in the Python programming language that can do much more than just delete files from the Git history. You can find the program, of course, on GitHub:

https://github.com/newren/git-filter-repo

To install this program, all you need to do is download the Python file, make it executable, and save it to your search path. Some help texts and sample applications are included in the Python code.

To install the entire help locally as a Unix man page, then you should download the current release (under the **Releases** tab in GitHub) as a tar archive file (not as the source code from the same folder). In the `Documentation/man1` folder, you'll find the git-filter-repo.1 file. Copy this file to the man search path, for example to /usr/local/man/man1/. Then, you can open the help page as for any other Git module via git filter-repo --help.

For current Linux distributions (for Ubuntu, for example, from version 22.04), ready-made packages can be installed with the respective package manager. An overview can be found in the GitHub repository mentioned earlier.

Let's go back to our task of permanently deleting the *secure_token.txt* file from the Git history. The command git filter-repo returns the following output:

```
git filter-repo --path secure_token.txt --invert-paths

  Parsed 33 commits
  New history written in 0.04 seconds; now repacking/cleaning...
  Repacking your repo and cleaning out old unneeded objects
  HEAD is now at 4c15132 random words in file riverbed.txt
  ...
  Completely finished after 0.08 seconds.
```

So, all 33—admittedly not terribly exciting—commits were processed and rewritten in less than a tenth of a second. The call only works if you use a freshly cloned repository. Once a change has been made to the local repository, git filter-repo refuses to run, stating that you must use the --force parameter if you want to work with the changed copy.

Afterwards, you'll be surprised to see that the remote repository is no longer linked. So, you can't submit a git push in the modified repository. Good reasons exist for this limitation, which we addressed in the previous section. Even if renaming the repository is difficult for you, it's the most consistent way to avoid problems with your collaborators' repositories. Renaming ensures that no one merges the corrected repository with an existing, local repository and possibly reuploads the removed files during a later push.

11.4.4   Previously Uploaded Changes, after Push (BFG Repo Cleaner)

For the sake of completeness, we should also mention the *BFG Repo Cleaner*. Before the availability of git filter-repo, this program was the tool of choice for making changes to the Git history without getting into the dangers of git filter-branch. You can still find this program being recommended on many websites to permanently delete files from Git. The software requires a current Java runtime (we tested it with OpenJDK version 17) and can be downloaded as a JAR file from the Maven repository:

```
wget -O bfg.jar https://repo1.maven.org/maven2/com/madgag/bfg/\
  1.14.0/bfg-1.14.0.jar

  Saving to: 'bfg.jar'
```

```
bfg.jar                           100%[=========>]  13,81M  24...
2022-02-15 14:40:39 (24,6 MB/s) - 'bfg.jar' saved [14483456/...

java -jar bfg.jar

  bfg 1.14.0
  Usage: bfg [options] [<repo>]
  ...
```

Note that the line break in the URL is due to typesetting for this book and must not be entered in this way in the shell. For `bfg` to replace all references, you must clone the repository to be changed with the `--mirror` option, which creates a *bare* repository (i.e., a Git repository without a worktree). You should not then call the program directly in the repository, but instead one level below since `bfg` creates its own folder with statistics for renaming next to the project folder.

```
git clone --mirror git@github.com:git-compendium/history-rewrite.git
java -jar bfg.jar -D secure_token.txt history-rewrite

  Using repo : /home/bernd/work/git/tmp/history-rewrite.git

  Found 24 objects to protect
  Found 5 commit-pointing refs : HEAD, refs/heads/feature-1, r...
  ...
  BFG run is complete! When ready, run: git reflog expire
          --expire=now --all && git gc --prune=now --aggressive
```

The successful execution of the software ends with a hint to clean up the reference log (reflog) and starts the Git garbage collector.

At this point, you may want to go to the changed directory and clean up any references that point to commits that no longer exist:

```
cd history-rewrite

git reflog expire --expire=now --all && \
  git gc --prune=now --aggressive

  Enumerating objects: 100, done.
  Counting objects: 100% (100/100), done.
  ...
  Total 100 (delta 29), reused 38 (delta 0), pack-reused 0
```

Again, what we already said for `git filter-repo` and `git filter-branch` applies in this context as well: Don't load your local repository into the existing remote repository with `git push --force`; the best approach is to create a new repository and push the changed project there.

11.5   Splitting a Project

When you develop a larger project, you may reach a point at which you want to swap out part of the project as a separate module. Maybe other developers can make use of this specific functionality in their own projects as well. To accomplish this spinoff, you could create a new Git repository, copy the appropriate files to it, and commit. However, by doing so, you'd lose the Git history of these files, which—depending on how many commits are involved—can be a great pity.

Using the external command `git filter-repo`, introduced in Section 11.4, you can take all commits involving these files with you. We've already shown you an alternative technique with `git subtree split`, described at the end of Chapter 9, Section 9.3.

Let's say that, in your Node.js project, one component deals with the metadata of photos, that is, data in the *exchangeable image file format (Exif)*. While you initially coded the calls in the file that took care of uploading the photos, the code got bigger and bigger, and you swapped it out into a separate file. This additional file, located in the *server/exif* folder, extracts the Exif data directly when uploading the images and returns an object containing both the image and the broken down Exif data.

Because you can use this functionality in other projects, you should store the file as a separate Node.js module in its own Git repository and not lose the Git history in the process. The `git filter-repo` command makes this step a simple one-liner:

```
git filter-repo --path server/exif

  Parsed 31 commits
  New history written in 0.10 seconds; now repacking/cleaning...
  ...
  Completely finished after 0.13 seconds.
```

After the run, you'll have a Git repository with only one file and no remote repository anymore. You can now create a new Node.js module by calling the Node Package Manager (npm) with `npm init` and registering the necessary components in the *package.json* file. Then, you can create a new project on the Git hosting platform of your choice and add the remote repository to your local repository.

11.6   Moving Commits to a Different Branch

The problem we describe in this section has also caught us unawares several times: We're working on a small project where all our commits occur on the main branch.

After a day's work and various commits, however, it becomes clear that a new feature that seemed so manageable at first won't be ready today after all and that it would actually have been better to develop it on a feature branch.

All commits to date on the main branch haven't yet been uploaded to a remote repository. Isn't there a simple solution to move the existing commits to a branch? Of course, there is—as usual in Git, you have several variants to choose from. We'll explain two procedures in this section: the first using git reset and the second using git cherry-ick. In most cases, the first option is easier.

11.6.1 git reset

Our repository already has seven commits, of which the last five should actually be moved to the feature branch. We're currently on the main branch, and we are at the last commit, which is the HEAD. The last five commits haven't yet been pushed to the remote repository.

We'll create the feature branch big-feature. Both HEAD and big-feature now point to commit 94a920d, as shown in Figure 11.2, in the center.

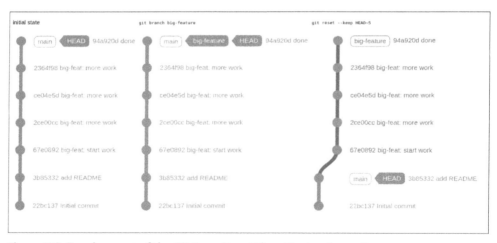

Figure 11.2 Development of the Git Repository When Moving Commits

Now, let's reset HEAD by five commits using reset --keep HEAD~5. (Alternatively, we could specify the hash code 3b85332 directly.) That's it. Finally, to return to the new feature branch, call git switch, as shown in the following example:

```
git branch big-feature
git reset --keep HEAD~5
git switch big-feature  # optionally switch to feature branch
```

11.6.2   git cherrypick

Another option is to first reset the main branch and then `cherry-pick` the five commits from the local reflog (see Chapter 3, Section 3.12).

```
git reset --keep HEAD~5
git branch big-feature
git switch big-feature
git cherry-pick HEAD..HEAD@{2}
```

Two things should be kept in mind regarding this technique: First, the five commits are deleted after the `git reset`; they only exist in the local reflog and would be removed during a garbage collection, as shown in Figure 11.3, in the center. However, since we'll restore these commits right away, that possibility won't be a problem.

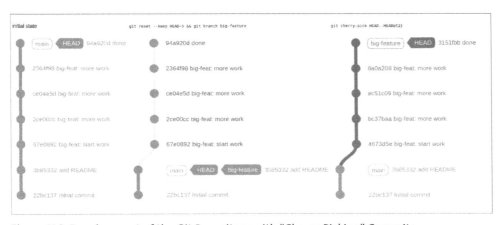

Figure 11.3 Development of the Git Repository with "Cherry-Picking" Commits

Second, the syntax of `cherry-pick` is interesting. You can select a range between the current HEAD and the state to which the reflog pointed before the last two actions (action 1 was the `reset` command; action 2 was the `switch` command). This state corresponds exactly to the last of the five commits by which we first reset the HEAD. Consider the output of the reflog before the `cherry-pick` command:

```
git reflog
```

```
3b85332 (HEAD -> big-feature, main) HEAD@{0}: checkout:
        moving from main to big-feature
3b85332 (HEAD -> big-feature, main) HEAD@{1}: reset:
        moving to HEAD~5
94a920d HEAD@{2}: commit: done
2364f98 HEAD@{3}: commit: big-feat: more work
ce04e5d HEAD@{4}: commit: big-feat: more work
```

```
2ce00cc HEAD@{5}: commit: big-feat: more work
67e0892 HEAD@{6}: commit: big-feat: start work
3b85332 (HEAD -> big-feature, main) HEAD@{7}: commit: add ...
```

The main difference with this technique is the time at which the feature branch from the main branch is inserted correctly in the local reflog. This behavior can be an advantage in a (rather unusual) situation: If the history on the main branch has changed since the feature branch was forked (a push --force must have been used), commits may be lost on with a git pull --rebase main on the big-feature branch.

In terms of background, when rebasing, Git doesn't find the branch point in the local reflog on the modified main and goes back to a common base for rebasing. This behavior isn't a bug in Git, but when rewriting the Git history on previously published branches, strange things can happen. Details about this problem can also be found in the following Stack Overflow article:

https://stackoverflow.com/a/36463546

In case your team doesn't make any changes to already uploaded branches, we recommend the first variant. You'll first create the branch and then perform the reset. However, if you want to be absolutely sure and can't exclude the possibility of a changed history on the main branch, the second variant is more reliable.

Chapter 12
Command Reference

The focus of this chapter is to describe the most important `git` subcommands along with their most commonly used options. Organized alphabetically, we range from `git add` to `git tag` in this chapter.

Our goal in this chapter is *not* to provide a complete description of the `git` command. Instead, we've tried to concentrate, in a manageable way, the information that you'll need in practice. For more exotic subcommands and options, however, refer to the man pages (e.g., `man git-clone`) or to the online documentation available at the following link:

https://git-scm.com/docs

12

> **Cheat Sheet for Printout**
>
> To supplement this chapter, we recommend the following cheat sheet, a 2-page PDF document:
>
> *https://education.github.com/git-cheat-sheet-education.pdf*

In addition to the `git` command, this chapter also summarizes Git's revision syntax, the options Git provides to reference a particular commit or object. The final section explains the functionality and syntax of the main Git configuration files.

12.1   The git Command

The `git` command is executed in the format, `git <subcommand> <options> <parameter>`. The subcommand specifies which action you want to perform (e.g., add, commit, or push). Table 12.1 provides an overview of all the subcommands that we'll describe in more detail on the following pages.

Note that the descriptions in Table 12.1 are considerably shortened. Many `git` subcommands perform *multiple* tasks, provided you pass the appropriate options. On one hand, this overloading is what makes Git so versatile, but on the other hand, subcommands can also be highly confusing: Often, you can do the same task with several commands.

Options are specified in the form --<optionsname>. You may abbreviate options as long as git can understand which option you mean. For this reason, git config --list --show-origin and git config --li --sh are equivalent. (The subcommand itself, however, must always be specified in its entirety.)

You can also formulate particularly important options with 1-letter abbreviations and with only one preceding hyphen. Thus, for git config, you can specify the --list option as -l.

Command	Function
git add	Mark files/directories for the next commit
git bisect	Search commits for a bug or feature
git blame	Show who has changed which line of a file using which commit
git branch	Create, list, and delete branches
git checkout	Switch between branches or restore files from other commits
git cherry-pick	Incorporate changes from another commit into the current branch
git clean	Remove unversioned files
git clone	Create a local copy of an external repository
git commit	Perform a commit
git config	Read or change local/global configuration
git diff	Show changes between two versions of a file or between two commits
git grep	Search versioned files for a text pattern
git fetch	Download commits from external repositories
git gc	Tidy up and shrink repository database
git gui	Launch the Git graphical user interface (GUI)
git init	Set up a new local repository
git log	Show commits
git ls-files	Show all versioned files
git merge	Merge two or more branches
git merge base	Determine the last common commit
git merge file	Merge a file
git mergetool	Fix merge conflicts with external tool

Table 12.1 Git Commands Presented in This Chapter

Command	Function
git mv	Move or rename file in the project directory
git pull	Download and merge remote repository commits
git push	Upload commits of the local branch to a remote repository
git rebase	Rebuilds existing commits to match another branch
git reflog	Show or manipulate reference log (reflog) entries
git remote	Manage remote repositories and tracking branches
git reset	Reset HEAD and head to an older commit
git restore	Restore an old version of a file
git rev-list	List hash codes of commits
git revert	Undo a commit with a new undo commit
git rm	Remove versioned file from project directory
git shortlog	Determine statistical information about commits
git show	Show object of the Git repository
git stage	Mark file for commit (like git add)
git status	Display status information about the working directory
git submodules	Manage submodules (nested repositories)
git subtree	Integrate external repository into subdirectory
git switch	Switch between branches
git tag	Designate commits or list named commits

Table 12.1 Git Commands Presented in This Chapter (Cont.)

12.1.1 Porcelain versus Plumbing

This section focuses on commands and options you'll need in the daily operation of Git. The corresponding commands are sometimes referred to as *porcelain*, meaning the nice, user-friendly side of Git.

In addition to these commands, many other commands are internally responsible for the Git database (i.e., for the files in the *.git* directory). These low-level commands are required for *plumbing*, that is, for installations and pipelines, but in the context of Git, these commands are used more for control functions, for calculating hash codes, for space-saving in the packaging of objects, etc.

We haven't described the majority of those commands at all in this book, although some exceptions were covered in Chapter 3, Section 3.2 and Section 3.13. But even in those cases, we were focused on helping you to understand the way Git works.

12.1.2   General Options

Some options work with any git command, for instance, whether you're running git diff or git log. These options are documented in man git. We've summarized the most important two options here:

- `--git-dir <dir1>` and `--work-dir <dir2>` specify which directories should be used for the Git database and as working directory. Typically, these options are redundant: Git looks for the *.git* directory in the current folder or in the parent folders. The *.git* directory is the default location for the Git database. The directory where *.git* is located is considered the workspace.

  A setting that deviates from the specifications is only possible in special cases. Chapter 10, Section 10.2, describes how both options can be applied.

- `-P` or `--no-pager` disables the redirection of multi-page git output to what's called a *pager* (i.e., a program that allows convenient scrolling through the output).

- `--version` outputs the Git version number.

12.1.3   git add

git add `<files>` marks files to be included in the subsequent commit. Or, more precisely, git add stores the current state of the specified file as an object in the *.git* directory and includes a reference to it in the index (in the staging area).

Although the name suggests otherwise, git add must be run once for files that are to be newly added to the repository but also for all files that have changed and whose changes are to be saved. In the second case, you can omit git add as long as you pass the -a option to commit. Instead of git add, you can also run the equivalent git stage command.

Note that git add applies to the current state of the file. If you make further changes after git add but before git commit, they won't be taken into account! Then, you'll need to run git add again or call git commit with the -a option.

The git add `<dir>` command takes into account all changed or new files in the specified directory and in all subdirectories unless they are excluded from version control by rules in *.gitignore*. Several variants are possible:

- git add `<dir>` takes into account new and changed files, but not deleted files.

- git add `-A <dir>` or git add `--all <dir>` takes into account *all* changes, including deleted files.

- `git add -u <dir>` or `git add --update <dir>` only includes changed files that are already under version control.
- With the additional `-f` or `--force` option, the command takes files into account even if they would normally be ignored according to *.gitignore*.

To exclude an already marked file from the commit after all, you must run `git reset <file>`. The command `git status` provides an overview of all new files or changed files and shows which of these files are marked for commit and which ones aren't.

12.1.4   git bisect

`git bisect` helps you find, from hundreds of commits, the one commit in which the bug *xy* occurred for the first time. The newest and oldest commits to be considered must be specified first. `git bisect` then performs a binary search, halving the number of commits that still need to be searched with each step.

For a detailed example of using `git bisect`, see Chapter 4, Section 4.3. In short, the application of the command works in the following way:

- `git bisect start` activates the bisecting mode.
- `git bisect good <goodrev>` returns the latest known code version in which the bug did not occur.
- `git bisect bad <badrev>` specifies the code version in which the error occurs.

Once the start and end points of the search range are known with `<goodrev>` and `<badrev>`, Git performs a checkout in the middle of this range. You then must test if the error also occurs in this version of your program and tell Git what to do next:

- `git bisect good` or `git bisect bad` continues the search. This process (i.e., testing the version just selected by `git bisect` and returning good or bad) repeats until `git bisect` succeeds in finding the faulty commit. A maximum of 10 steps are required for a search range of 1,000 commits.
- `git bisect reset` terminates the bisecting mode. This command will return you to the branch that was active at startup, and you can then get to work fixing the error.

12.1.5   git blame

`git blame <file>` displays a file. Several columns before each line indicate in which commit (hash code) the file was changed, when, and by whom.

The variant `git blame <revision> -- <file>` of `git blame` only considers commits up to the specified revision (see Section 12.2).

Various options control the output of this command:

- `--color-by-age` marks recently changed lines in red or white. (This option and the next option aren't documented in `man git-blame`, but details more on this topic can be found at *https://stackoverflow.com/questions/3958977*.)

- `--color-lines` marks lines from the same commit in blue.

- `-L <n1>,<n2>` displays only lines with numbers from n1 to n2 (e.g., `git blame -L 100,110 index.php`).

  Alternatively, the syntax `<start>,+<offset>` is also permitted. `-L 100,+11` also displays the lines 100 to 110.

- `--show-stats` adds statistics at the end of the output regarding how many BLOB objects have different versions of the file stored in them, how many commits have changed the file in total, and more.

Incorrect Display of Special Characters

If `git blame` displays international characters and emojis incorrectly, this problem is due to the faulty interaction between `git` and the text display command `less`. The `--no-pager` option provides a temporary workaround, while the following command is a permanent solution:

`git config --global core.pager 'less --raw-control-chars'`

12.1.6 git branch

Without any further parameters or options, `git branch` lists all local branches and marks the currently active branch with the * character.

`git branch <newbranch>` creates a new branch but doesn't activate it. For this purpose, you must also run `git checkout <newbranch>` or `git switch <newbranch>`. Alternatively, you can use `checkout -b <newbranch>` to create and activate a branch at the same time.

Other options for this command include the following:

- `-a` or `--all` displays external repositories in addition to local branches.

- `-d <oldbranch>` deletes the specified branch. The associated commits will be preserved. However, commits of deleted branches that have never been merged and to which no references from other branches exist will be deleted during the next garbage collection process (`git gc`).

- `--merged` or `--no-merged` shows only branches that have already been merged with the current branch or that haven't been merged yet.

  By default, `git branch --merged` tests if the heads of the branches match HEAD. You can optionally specify a commit to use as a comparison point instead of HEAD, for example, `git branch --merged 34ed5a3`. In a similar way, of course, this rule also applies to `git branch --no-merged`.

Remember: `HEAD` is the most recent commit in the active branch. Detached from this commit, each branch has its own head, that is, its last commit in each case (see Chapter 3, Section 3.1).

- `-m [<old>] <new>` or `--move [<old>] <new>` renames a branch. If you don't specify `<old>`, the currently active branch will be renamed.

- `-M [<old>] <new>` also renames the branch but with the `--force` option. If the `<new>` branch already exists, that existing branch will be overwritten.

- `-r` or `--remotes` displays only branches from external repositories instead of local ones.

- `-u` or `--set-upstream-to` sets the upstream repository for the current branch permanently in *.git/config*. The command must be executed as `git branch -u <repo>/<branchname>`, for instance, `git branch -u origin/feature_xy`. (Alternatively, the upstream repository can be set on the first push with `git push -u origin feature_xy`.)

- `--unset-upstream` disconnects the local branch from the *remote tracking* branch assigned in *.git/config*.

12.1.7   git checkout

`git checkout` performs a bewildering number of tasks, although the common denominator can be expressed as follows: The command overwrites files in the project directory with the versions of a different commit. Depending on how the command is called, the pointer may also be changed to the active branch and to the active commit.

Several main variants for calling this command include the following:

- `git checkout <branch>` switches to the specified branch. All files under revision control that had different contents in the last commits of the current branch and the new branch will be overwritten. However, modified files that had the same state in each of the last commits will be preserved.

  If a risk exists that changes will be overwritten, this command will abort the operation. `-f` or `--force` forces the checkout even then. Caution: Overwritten changes cannot be restored afterwards.

- `git checkout -b <newbranch>` creates a new local branch and activates it.

- `git checkout -t <repo>/<branch>` or `git checkout --track <repo>/<branch>` establishes a connection between the local and remote `<branch>` branches and stores the mapping in *.git/config*. With this command, `<branch>` becomes the active branch at the same time.

- `git checkout <revision> -- <file>` overwrites the `<file>` file with the version from the `<revision>` commit. Notations for formulating the revision are summarized in Section 12.2. Note that the two hyphens that must be placed between the revision and file specification to avoid ambiguity. The specification of the revision is optional. If this information is omitted, git checkout will simply be applied to the last commit. This command will undo the changes made to the file since the commit.

The additional --patch option runs git checkout interactively. You can decide for each changed code block whether it should be applied or not. Thus, you have the option of not applying all the changes, instead selectively applying only the changes you're interested in.

- git checkout <revision> works similarly to git checkout <branch> and restores the project directory to its state prior to the <revision> commit. The main difference is that an active branch no longer exists after the command has been executed (called a *detached* HEAD). As a result, only HEAD points to the specified commit, not the head of a branch, and future commits won't be assigned to any branch.

  This checkout variant is useful if you need to look at the state of the project at the time of a past commit or if you want to start a new branch based on this commit. In the first case, you would then return to an existing branch using git checkout <otherbranch>; in the second case, you would start a new branch with git checkout -b <newbranch>.

- In case of a merge conflict, git checkout --ours <file> or git checkout --theirs <file> overwrites the specified file with the version of its own path or with the version of the other path.

  Caution: When a merge conflict occurs during a rebasing operation, the meaning of --ours and --theirs is reversed! --theirs denotes our "own" commits; --ours, the commits of others. This difference is due to Git's internal approach to rebasing, which adds new variants of its own commits to those of others. This behavior reverses the direction of the merge.

The behavior of git checkout can be influenced by additional options.

Alternative Commands

As of 2019, with Git version 2.23, alternative commands are available for certain uses of git checkout:

- Like git checkout <branch>, git switch <branch> switches the active branch.
- git restore -s <revision> <file> restores the specified file from the commit expressed by <revision>. So, this command corresponds to git checkout <revision> -- <file>.

12.1.8   git cherry-pick

git cherry-pick <revision> applies the changes made in the specified commit to the current branch (see Section 12.2). The project directory must not contain any files that have changed since the last commit. You may need to a commit or to use git stash beforehand.

If a conflict occurs in relation to `git cherry-pick`, you must resolve it and commit the change via `git commit` (see Chapter 3, Section 3.9).

12.1.9   git clean

`git clean` deletes all files in the current directory that are neither under version control nor protected by *.gitignore*. This cleanup is an extremely dangerous operation because these files (unlike versioned files) can't be recovered. You should run the command first with the `--dry-run` option!

- `-d` also deletes recursively through all subdirectories. (For security reasons, `git clean` ignores subdirectories by default.)
- `-f` or `--force` forces the deletion. (This option *must be* specified unless the `git config clean.requireForce false` setting applies.)
- `-n` or `--dry-run` outputs the files to be deleted but doesn't touch the files.
- `-x` also deletes files that are excluded (protected) from editing by `git` commands via patterns in *.gitignore*.

12.1.10   git clone

`git clone` creates a copy (a "clone") of another repository. Typically, you pass to `git clone` the address of a repository that can be accessed on the network. You can choose between HTTPS and SSH protocols. If required, authentication is performed accordingly, by the account name and a password/access token or by an SSH key. The general appearance of the URLs is as follows:

```
git clone https://<host name>/<account>/<reponame>.git
git clone <user>@<host name>:<account>/<reponame>.git
```

If the external repository is on GitHub, the URLs look like this:

```
git clone https://github.com/git-compendium/hello-world.git
git clone git@github.com:git-compendium/hello-world.git
```

`git clone` can also copy a repository of the local machine. In this case, authentication isn't required:

```
git clone path/to/repo
```

`git clone` creates a new subdirectory in the current directory with the same name as the repository. Before you can execute further commands, you must switch to this directory using `cd`. If you want the name of the new subdirectory to be different from the repo name, you can specify it explicitly in the following way:

```
git clone git@github.com:git-compendium/hello-world.git my-repo-dir
```

12

git clone sets up the *.git/config* file in the repository directory. Among other things, this file contains the source address of the repository, that is, the location from which the repository was downloaded or copied (keyword url in the [remote "origin"] section). Commands like git pull and git push subsequently work without specifying any further parameters.

The behavior of git clone can be influenced by countless options, the most important of which are listed here:

- --bare sets up the copy in the local directory, so it doesn't create a subdirectory. Only the actual repository is copied in the local director (i.e., the files that are otherwise located in the *.git* subdirectory). No checkout of HEAD occurs.

- --mirror works similar to --bare but also takes external branches and references into account. The goal is to create a complete copy of the external repository. A particularly good explanation of the differences between --bare and --mirror can be found at the following link:

  https://stackoverflow.com/questions/3959924

- --single-branch copies only the commits required to reconstruct HEAD or the branch specified with the --branch=<somebranch> option.

- --recurse-submodules also takes submodules into account.

12.1.11   git commit

git commit performs a commit. In other words, this command creates a snapshot of all files under version control in the local repository. Along with the state of the files, the date and time of the snapshot are stored, as well as your name and email address and a message, the *commit* message.

Typically, git commit considers only files that have been explicitly marked for commit using git add or git stage. (But note the -a option!)

- -a or --all automatically takes into account all changes to files that were already under version control, that is, files for which git add was run at some point in the past. The option has no effect on new files that aren't versioned so far.

- --amend merges the last commit with the changes made since then to form a new commit that replaces the previous commit. The commit message remains unchanged.

  git commit --amend thus allows previously forgotten changes or subsequent corrections to be integrated into the last commit. Since the command changes the history, you should only use --amend if you haven't yet uploaded (pushed) the last commit to a remote repository.

- -C <commit> or --reuse-message=<commit> uses the metadata of an older commit, such as the author, the time, and the commit message.

- `--dry-run` simulates the commit but doesn't actually perform it.

- `-e` or `--edit` opens an editor where the specified commit message can be modified.

- `-m '<text>'` or `--message '<text>'` specifies the commit message. This option is usually mandatory. The only exceptions are commands where the commit message results from another option.

- `-n` or `--no-verify` prevents the *pre-commit* and *commit-msg* hooks from being called.

Commits are only valid locally! To make the commit visible in an external repository, you must run `git push` afterwards.

To revert the last commit, you must run `git revert HEAD`. This process will create a new commit. If you haven't yet committed the current branch to other repositories using `git push`, you can use `git reset --hard HEAD~` to return to the previous commit. We've summarized other ways to revoke one or more commits in Chapter 3, Section 3.4.

12.1.12   git config

`git config` reads the Git configuration or modifies the *.git/config* files in the local repository, *.gitconfig* in the home directory, or */etc/gitconfig* (or on Windows *C:\Program Files\Git\etc\gitconfig*). A detailed description of the configuration concept follows in Section 12.3. For now, let's just focus on the syntax of `git config`:

- `-e` or `--edit` opens the configuration file in an editor.

- `--get <keyname>` reads only this one setting (not all).

- `--get-regexp <pattern>` lists all settings that match the search pattern.

- `--global` reads/modifies the personal configuration (`~/.git/config`).

- `-l` or `--list` lists all valid settings. These settings are composed of system-wide, global, and local settings, with local settings taking precedence. With the additional option `--show-origin`, the command shows which configuration file contains which setting.

- `--local` reads/modifies the configuration of the local repository (`.git/config`). When you change settings, this option applies by default.

- `--system` reads/modifies the system-wide configuration (`/etc/gitconfig`).

The two main uses of the command are to list all settings or to change a single setting:

```
git config --list --show-origin

  file:/home/kofler/.gitconfig    user.name=Michael Kofler
  file:/home/kofler/.gitconfig    user.email=MichaelKofler@...
  ...
  file:.git/config    core.repositoryformatversion=0
```

```
file:.git/config    remote.origin.url=git@github.com:...
...
```

```
git config user.email newmail@samplehost.com
```

12.1.13 git diff

`git diff` shows the differences between two versions of a file or all the changes that make two commits different from each other, depending on how it's used. The main uses of this command include the following:

- `git diff` without further parameters shows all modified lines in all files that have been modified since the last commit. The changes are displayed in a special patch syntax, where added or changed lines are marked with a preceding + and deleted lines with -. Also, at the beginning of each changed block, the position within the file is displayed.

  By default, `git diff` compares the project directory with the last commit. If you want to compare the staging area with the last commit instead, you must additionally specify the `--cached` or `--stage` option.

  Using various other options (that we'll discuss next), you can persuade `git diff` to display only a short version instead of the often sprawling patches.

- `git diff <file>` shows only the change of the specified file (not of all files).

- `git diff <revision> [<file>]` displays all changes between the specified commit and the current state in the project directory (see Section 12.2).

- `git diff <revision1>..<revision2> [file]` shows the changes between two commits.

- `git diff <revision1> <revision2> [file]` is an equivalent syntax variant to the previous item.

- `git diff <rev1>...<rev2> [file]` with three periods between revisions shows the changes in revision 2 compared to the last common basis. For example, `git diff main...develop` returns the changes in develop since the last merge with main. Unlike `main..develop`, however, the changes made in main since then will be ignored.

- `git diff --no-index <file1> <file2>` compares the two files. Using this notation, the command also works outside of a Git repository.

The output of `git diff` can be controlled by various options, but as usual, we only want to mention the most important ones:

- `--compact-summary` displays only a summary instead of the patches, where the number of + and - characters corresponds to the number of lines added and deleted, respectively. The output `<file> ++++--` means that four lines were added and two were deleted.

- `--diff-filter=A|C|D|M|R` processes only files that have been added, copied, deleted, modified, or renamed.

- `-G <pattern>` only considers text files in whose changes (i.e., in whose patch text) the specified search expression occurs. `<pattern>` is a regular pattern; the use of upper-case and lowercase characters must match exactly.

- `--ignore-all-space` ignores spaces and tab characters in the code during the comparison.

- `--name-only` doesn't show the changes made, but only the filename.

- `--numstat` shows only the number of lines added or deleted for each file instead of the patches.

- `--shortstat` only shows how many files have been changed and how many lines have been added or removed in total (summed over all changed files) instead of the patches.

Numerous usage examples for `git diff` can be found in Chapter 4, Section 4.2.

12.1.14   git fetch

`git fetch` downloads commits from external repositories. Without further parameters, all branches of the `origin` repository will be included. If a branch is currently active that has another repository set as the data source in *.git/config*, then `git fetch` will download commits from that repository.

`git fetch <repo>` downloads the commits of all branches of the specified repository. If you only need the commits of a particular branch, you can call the command in the form `git fetch <repo> <branch>`.

`git fetch --all` takes into account all repositories contained in *.git/config* and has the following options:

- `--no-tags` prevents tags from being downloaded along with the commits.

- `--set-upstream` makes the repository the default repository for the current branch. The option is only useful if you execute the command as `git fetch <repo> <url>`, for instance, `git fetch --set-upstream <branch> origin/<branch>`.

`git fetch` is rather rarely executed as a single command. A more common practice is to use `git pull` to combine the fetch operation and the merge operation, which is due afterwards.

12.1.15   git gc

`git gc` cleans up the object database of the local repository (i.e., the *.git/object* directory). The abbreviation gc stands for *garbage collection*. In particular, `git gc` combines many small individual files into packages (`.git/objects/pack/*.pack`) to eliminate redundancies. The space required for the object database can thus be reduced considerably.

12

12.1.16   git gui

git gui starts the *Git GUI* program if already installed, which on Windows is often the case. On some Linux distributions, you can post-install the program using apt install git-gui or a similar command if needed. As described in Chapter 2, Section 2.6, however, Git GUI isn't worth installing: Despite its close interaction with the git command, Git GUI provides some rather unconvincing features.

You can start Git GUI in several different ways:

- Without any additional parameters, git gui opens the local repository.
- git gui blame <file> shows the blame view for a given file (see also the git blame command in Section 12.1.5).
- git gui browser <branch> displays all files of a branch.
- git gui citool shows a dialog box for performing a commit. Git GUI exits immediately after the commit.

12.1.17   git grep

git grep <pattern> searches all versioned text files in the project directory for the search term. git grep thus provides a rather convenient way to search the entire repository for a particular text. <pattern> is a regular expression and is used in the same way as with the Linux command grep.

git grep <pattern> <file1> <file2> restricts the search to the specified files.

git grep <pattern> <revision> searches all files of an old commit referenced by <revision> (see Section 12.2). git grep <pattern> <revision> <filepattern> searches selected files of an old commit. For example, git grep -i 'error' v1.0 '*.c' searches for the text "error" in all version 1.0 C files in your repository. (This example assumes that the commit of version 1.0 was tagged v1.0.)

Other options for this command include the following:

- -a or --text also searches binary files as if they were text files.
- -c or --count shows how often the search term was found in the file (but not the corresponding text passages).
- -E or --extended-regexp accepts extended regular expressions (like the Linux command egrep) in <pattern>.
- -i or --ignore-case ignores case in <pattern>.
- -l or --name-only displays only the files in which the search expression occurs, but not the text passage.
- -n or --line-number specifies the line number for all finds.
- --recurse-submodules also takes submodules into account.
- --untracked also includes files from the project directory that aren't under version control.

12.1.18   git init

git init turns a directory into a Git repository. For this purpose, it sets up the *.git* sub-directory, where project-specific configuration files and the Git database are stored.

If you run git init in an existing repository, the command adds missing files or directories (although these additions may result from the features of a new Git version, for example). Existing data won't be overwritten, however, so there's no danger that you'll wreak havoc.

If you execute the command as git init <directory>, the repository will be created in the specified directory (not the current directory). If the specified repository directory doesn't exist yet, it will be created.

This command has two options:

- --shared=group sets the access rights of the files and directories in *.git* so that all group members are allowed to write in those locations. The option is intended for the rather rare case that a repository is used by several persons (accounts) working on the same computer.

- --shared=world works similarly but makes the files and directories readable by everyone, including people who aren't members of the development group.

12.1.19   git log

Without any other parameters, git log lists the commits of the current branch, with the newest commits first. Along with each commit, the most important metadata is displayed (i.e., hash code, author, date, and commit message).

git log <branch> displays the commits of a different branch. git log <revision> starts the output at the specified commit.

git log <rev1>..<rev2> displays all commits between the two revisions, provided the commits are on the same branch. Things are a bit more complicated when multiple branches are in play: git log <branch1>..<branch2> only shows the commits of <branch2> since the last merge operation with <branch1>. Commits that serve as common ground for both branches aren't included.

git log <branch1>...<branch2> (now with three periods) has yet another meaning: This command displays all commits of <branch1> and of <branch2> since the last merge operation (i.e., the commits of *both* branches). For examples of both variants of this range syntax, see Chapter 4, Section 4.1.

Finally, git log <file> or git log <dir> displays only those commits that result in changes to the files in question. If the filenames are identical to revision names, you should prefix the path names once with -- to prevent misinterpretation. (For example, git log main -- feature returns commits for the branch main that modify the file feature.)

Various options control *how* the commits are displayed:

- `--date=iso|local|short|...` specifies how time information should be formatted.
- `--decorate` additionally shows the tags assigned to the commits.
- `--graph` tries to represent the branches in ASCII style. However, the result can only be moderately inspiring visually.

  On Windows, the graphical commit and branch browser `gitk` can be started as an alternative to `git log --graph`. Usually installed together with Git GUI, `gitk` is also available for Linux, provided you install its package. In addition, countless (often commercial) Git clients can help visualize commit histories.
- `--name-only` lists the files that have changed with each commit (without further details).
- `--name-status` lists all modified files, as with `--name-only`. The letters A, M, and D indicate whether the file was added, modified, or deleted, respectively.
- `--pretty=oneline|short|medium|full|fuller|...` selects between different predefined output formats. By default, the `medium` format is active. `--oneline` is a shorthand for `--pretty=oneline`.
- `--pretty=format:'<fmt>'` allows you to format the output of the metadata as well as the commit message itself, including colors, column widths, etc. Some introductory examples of the `printf-like` syntax are shown in Chapter 4, Section 4.1; a complete reference is provided by man `git-log`.
- `--numstat` lists all modified files, as does `--name-only`. In this case, however, the number of added or deleted lines is additionally indicated in two columns.
- `--oneline` displays the commits line by line to save space (hash code on the left, first line of commit message on the right).
- `--stat` displays the modified files for each commit. For text files, bars consisting of the characters + or - indicate how many lines were changed in the process (as with `git pull`).

Another group of options controls *which* commits are to be displayed or filtered out of the sequence:

- `--after <date>` or `--since <date>` shows only commits that originated after <date>. The parameter <date> is specified in ISO format (e.g., 2020-12-31).
- `--all` displays all commits (including those of other branches).
- `--author <pattern>` displays commits where the developer's name or email address matches the specified pattern.
- `--before <date>` or `--until <date>` will only show commits done before/until <date>.
- `--grep='pattern'` displays commits that contain the search term in their messages. This option can be used multiple times. Git will then return commits that contain at least one of the search terms (an OR link).

The `--all-match` option combines the `grep` search pattern with logical AND. In other words, all search terms must appear in the commit message at the same time.

Typically, uppercase and lowercase must exactly match the search pattern. If you're indifferent to case, you must specify the additional option `-i` or `--regexp-ignore-case`.

With the additional option `--invert-grep`, you can search for commits whose message doesn't contain the search term.

- `-g` or `--walk-reflogs` will only show commits from the reflog, that is, commits that were last created as a result of locally executed `git` commands (see also `git reflog` in Section 12.1.29).
- `--no-merges` ignores merge commits.
- `--reflog`, like `-g`, displays only commits of the reflog but eliminates any duplicates.
- `--simplify-by-decoration` only displays commits that are referenced by a branch or tag.

Finally, you can influence the order in which the commits are displayed with the following options:

- `--author-date-order` groups commits by branch (like `--topo-order`), but within branches, the order considers the author date, not the commit date. (The two timings differ when rebasing is in play. In this case, *author date* specifies the original commit time, while *commit date* specifies the time when the commit was recreated for rebasing.)
- `--date-order` sorts the commits by the commit time (the newest commit first). This setting applies by default.
- `--reverse` reverses the sort direction. The oldest commit is displayed first.
- `--topo-order` groups the commits by branches. This setting applies automatically if you use the `--graph` option.

> **More Details**
>
> The website *https://git-scm.com/docs/git-log* or the command `man git-log` directs you to the official description of the `git log` command. This text would fill about 30 to 40 pages if formatted into this book! Countless other options affect which commits are displayed and how, as illustrated in many use cases for `git log` described in Chapter 4.

12.1.20   git ls-files

Without additional parameters, `git ls-files` displays all files of the repository that are under version control in the current branch and directory (including its subdirectories). This command is thus the easiest way to create a list of all versioned files.

This command has two options:

- -o or --others displays the files that are *not* under version control.
- --stage additionally displays the hash code of the commit of the last change as well as stage-internal information for each file.

12.1.21   git merge

git merge <otherbranch> merges another branch with the current branch. Strictly speaking, this command combines the latest commits of both branches, with the changes usually being saved as a new commit in the current branch. An exception is fast-forward merge operations that don't require a commit, for instance, when no changes have been made in the current branch. For more background details on fast-forward merges, see Chapter 3, Section 3.5 and Section 3.6.

After the merge process, both branches can be reused. The most important merge rule is that only the current branch (mybranch) is changed, but never the other branch (otherbranch):

```
git checkout <mybranch>      (will get changed)
git merge <otherbranch>      (remains unchanged)
```

The details of the merge process can be influenced by numerous options:

- --abort reverses a merge operation that was interrupted due to a conflict. The project directory is then in the same state as it was when the last commit was made.
- --continue resumes an interrupted merge operation. The option is useful after you've manually resolved a merge conflict (see Chapter 3, Section 3.9).
- -m <commitmessage> specifies the message to be stored along with the merge commit. This option avoids starting an editor when running git merge, in which you must type the commit message manually.
- --no-commit performs the merge process but not the subsequent commit. You can view the resulting files in the project directory and, if you're satisfied, run git commit yourself afterwards. Otherwise, you can undo the merge process with git restore.
- --no-ff prevents a fast-forward merge. This option ends the merge process with a commit of its own in any case, even if an explicit commit wouldn't be necessary at all and a resetting of the branch head as well as the HEAD would suffice (see Chapter 3, Section 3.5).
- --squash merges the changes of all commits of the other branch into a new commit in the current branch. This option results in a tidier commit sequence in the current branch. However, the details of the original commits are lost in the process. We described squashing in detail in Chapter 3, Section 3.10.

- `-s <strategy>` or `--strategy <strategy>` determines the merge procedure. Valid keywords for `<strategy>` include `recursive`, `resolve`, `octopus`, and `subtree`. Git generally decides on the most appropriate method on its own (usually `recursive`).
- `-X <stratopt>` or `--strategy-option <stratopt>` specifies an option for the selected or default merge method `recursive`:
  - `-X ignore-all-space` ignores all space and tab characters during the merge process. Other whitespace options are described in detail in `man git-diff`.
  - `-X ours` prefers its own branch in case of conflicts (and only then). Thus, when `git merge` notices a conflict in a passage of code, it uses its own code for that passage instead of triggering a merge conflict and requesting that it be resolved manually.
  - `-X theirs` works similarly to `-X ours` but prefers the other branch in case of conflicts.

12.1.22   git merge-base

`git merge-base <branch1> <branch2>` determines the hash code of the last common commit (the common base) of both branches. Instead of the current branch, you can of course simply specify `HEAD`.

12.1.23   git merge-file

`git merge-file <file> <base> <other>` runs a merge process for the file `<file>` and modifies this file. `<base>` is the version of the file between the current branch and a second branch. `<other>` is the version of the file in another branch. The command is cumbersome and only recommended if you want to merge only a single file (and not all files of two commits). For an application example, see Chapter 11, Section 11.3.

12.1.24   git mergetool

`git mergetool` starts an external program to help resolve the current merge conflict (see Chapter 3, Section 3.9).

- `--tool <cmd>` determines which program should be started. Appropriate programs are `meld` (Linux) or `tortoisemerge` (Windows). Note that usually you need to install the desired merge tool first.
- `--toolhelp` lists the installed merge tools.

12.1.25   git mv

`git mv <oldfile> <newfile>` renames a versioned file or moves it to another subdirectory within the project directory.

12.1.26   git pull

git pull transfers all commits from an external repository (like git fetch) and integrates them into the local repository (like git merge or git rebase). During the merge or rebasing process, the command considers only the current branch. If you switch branches later, Git will prompt you to repeat git pull.

Without any additional parameters, git pull assumes that the remote repository is configured for the current branch in *.git/config*. If not true, you must explicitly specify the desired repository with git pull <reponame>. If the remote repository has never been used before (not even for another branch), you must also specify its address with git pull <reponame> <url>.

The behavior of git pull can be influenced by numerous options. Some of the most important include the following:

■ --ff-only performs a fast-forward merge after the pull process. If this isn't possible, the command will abort with an error.

■ --no-commit performs the merge or rebasing operation, but not the commit. You can view the changes and then cancel the process using git restore . or finish with git commit -a -m '<message>'.

Note that the option has no effect if no "real" merge process is required at all because the fast-forward change of the HEAD is sufficient. As a result, --no-commit is often used in combination with --no-ff.

■ --no-ff forces a commit even if a fast-forward change of the HEAD is sufficient instead of a proper merge operation, for instance, when no changes have occurred in the local branch. (We described fast-forward merges in detail in Chapter 3, Section 3.6.)

■ -r or --rebase doesn't perform an ordinary merge process, but a rebasing (see Chapter 3, Section 3.10). In this process, the commits of others are downloaded first and then the own commits are rebuilt into new commits so that they fit the changed starting point in the branch. The advantage of this option is that the commit sequence isn't constantly broken by merge commits. However, one disadvantage is creating commits that never existed in this form.

When conflicts occur in rebasing, the meaning of --theirs and --ours is inverted! For example, git checkout --theirs <file> falls back to its own version of a file.

The desired default behavior of git pull can be defined in the configuration (parameters pull.ff and pull.rebase).

You can use the -s <strategy> and X <option> options to influence the details of the merge process. These options are described in the context of git merge in Section 12.1.21.

12.1.27 git push

git push transfers the commits of the current branch to the remote repository. The command is only permitted if no new commits exist in the remote repository that aren't yet available locally. To fulfill this requirement, you should always run git pull upfront.

git push works without any other parameters only if *.git/config* can map a branch in a remote repository to the local branch. After git clone, this is only the case for the default branch (i.e., usually for main).

If another branch is to be uploaded, you must use git push <repo> <remotebranch> to specify which remote repository to use (often origin) and which branch to use there. Typically, you'll specify the name of the active local branch in the <remotebranch> parameter; however, local and remote branch names can be different. The --set-upstream option can be used to permanently save the mapping.

The git push documentation describes countless other syntax variants for specifying the branch in the remote repository, but we won't explore them in this book. In practice, however, the following options are more frequently of importance:

- --all commits all commits to the remote repository, not just those of the current branch.

- -d or --delete deletes all external references specified in the additional arguments. The command is usually used to delete tags in the remote repository (i.e., git push origin -d <tagname>).

- --follow-tags transfers the associated annotated tags to the remote repository along with the commits. git config --global push.followTags true makes this behavior the default behavior.

  Simple tags (*lightweight tags*) are ignored by --follow-tags. To push them, you need to run git push origin <tagname> or git push --tags.

- -f or --force forces the upload of commits even if they conflict with existing remote commits and thus cause a change in the commit sequence in the remote repository. You should avoid this option at all costs because, as a result, git pull will cause problems for other team members.

- --tags transfers all simple and annotated tags of the active branch to the remote repository. Note that git push --tags *only* transfers the tags, not the commits.

- -u or --set-upstream <repo> <remotebranch> causes the mapping between the current local branch and the <remotebranch> in the specified remote repository to be permanently stored in *.git/config*. This option has an advantage in that git push can subsequently be called without any further parameters. The external branch is then sometimes called the *remote tracking branch*.

12

12.1.28   git rebase

git rebase <otherbranch> is a variant of git merge <otherbranch>. The goal of both commands is to merge another branch with the current branch. With git merge, this merging is performed through a merge commit that merges the other branch's changes. With git rebase, on the other hand, the merge takes the other branch's commits unchanged and then creates new commits for its own branch, remodeling them as if they had been created from the beginning based on the other branch's commits. The original commits are no longer used and may be deleted later.

git rebase has an advantage over git merge in that the commit sequence is "nicer" and isn't broken by merge commits. git rebase has one disadvantage, however: The local commits are re-created in a form that doesn't correspond to the actual state of the project directory. You must not use git rebase if the local commits of the current branch have already been uploaded to a remote repository using git push. Background and further details on this topic can be found in Chapter 3, Section 3.10.

With the git rebase <revision> variant, the rebasing process starts at a specific location. <revision> refers to the commit *before* the first commit to be processed (see Section 12.2).

- --abort and --continue revoke an interrupted rebasing operation and resume it after a manual conflict resolution, respectively.
- -i or --interactive runs the command interactively. Git will launch an editor in which you can specify how to process the individual commits of the local branch.
- --onto <newbase> transfers <otherbranch> to a new location away from the main branch (just <newbase>).

12.1.29   git reflog

The reference log, or *reflog* for short, logs Git actions that are performed locally. The reflog is located internally in the *.git/logs/refs* directory.

git reflog displays all available actions relative to HEAD (HEAD, HEAD@{1}, HEAD@{2}, etc.). With the --all option, the command also considers other references. git reflog <branch> only displays actions for the named branch.

You can use git reflog delete to delete individual entries from the reflog and use git reflog expire to remove all entries that exceed a certain age.

The reflog isn't synchronized with other repositories and is therefore purely local data. In a freshly cloned repository, the reflog is empty.

12.1.30   git remote

git remote helps you manage remote repositories. Without any additional parameters, the command lists all known remote repositories (i.e., those stored in *.git/config*). In this case, the command with the -v or --verbose option provides more detailed information, including the addresses of the repositories and their associated actions (e.g., fetch or push).

The command can also be executed with a subcommand, for example, in the form git remote add or git remote remove. The following list describes the most important subcommands:

- git remote add <reponame> <url> adds a remote repository.
- git remote get-url <reponame> returns the address of the repository.
- git remote remove <reponame> deletes the remote repository and all associated tracking branches from *.git/config*.
- git remote set-url <reponame> <newurl> changes the address of the repository. This command is convenient, for example, if you want to switch from HTTPS to SSH communication.
- git remote show <reponame> provides detailed information about a remote repository, including which branches are provided by the repository and which are associated as tracking branches with local branches.

git remote is *not* suitable for establishing a mapping between local and remote branches (i.e., for setting up remote tracking branches). For this task, you must use the following commands, depending on the context:

- If you have a remote branch but no local counterpart, you should call git checkout --track <repo>/<branch> (for example, git checkout --track origin/feature_x).
- Conversely, if you've created a local branch and want to upload it to the remote repository for the first time while also setting up a persistent configuration, you must run git push -u <repo> <branch> (e.g., git push --set-upstream origin feature_y).
- If the local and remote branches already exist, but you've always passed the remote repository and branch as parameters in git pull or git push so far, and it isn't yet a tracking branch, you can create the connection retroactively in the following way:

```
git checkout feature_z
git branch --set-upstream-to <repo>
```

Conversely, to clear the connection to the remote tracking branch, you must call git branch with the --unset-upstream option, as in the following example:

```
git checkout feature_z
git branch --unset-upstream
```

12.1.31   git reset

Like many other commands, git reset performs completely different tasks depending on which parameters and options you pass:

- `git reset <revision>` sets the HEAD as well as the head of the current branch to the specified commit (see Section 12.2). This option is equivalent to resetting the branch to a previous state. The commits made subsequently are preserved but no longer used.

  `git reset` can thus undo commits. However, the command changes the commit history in the process. If you've already uploaded the commits to an external repository using `git push`, you should avoid using `git reset` and use `git revert` instead (see Chapter 3, Section 3.4).

  `git reset` results in an error message if any files in the project directory have changed since the last commit. With the `--hard` option, `git reset` overwrites these changes as well as the staging area. This operation can't be undone.

- `git reset <file>` removes the file from the staging area. So, the command undoes `git add <file>`. The file in the project directory is left untouched.

Reset versus Restore versus Revert

Since confusion is common between `git reset`, `git restore`, and `git revert`, let's briefly summarize the basic purpose of the three commands:

- `git reset` changes the pointer to the current commit (both HEAD and the head of the current branch).
- `git restore` (new since Git version 2.23) restores a file in the project directory to an old version.
- `git revert` creates a new commit that reverts the changes made in the previous commit.

Just like most other commands, `git reset`, `git restore`, and `git revert` typically perform tasks beyond their basic functions, provided you pass appropriate options.

12.1.32   git restore

Since Git version 2.23 (August 2019), you can use `git restore` to restore an older version of a file in the project directory. `git restore` was created to swap out one of the many uses of `git checkout` into a simpler command. So that things don't become *too* simple, `git restore` also supports various variants, the most important ones of which are listed next:

- `git restore <file>` restores the state of the file from the last commit. Changes made since then will be overwritten without confirmation and thus lost.

- `git restore .` (with a period) restores all files located in the current directory as far as they are under version control. Of course, you can also specify a different directory instead.

- `git restore -s <revision> <file>` or `git restore --source <revision> <file>` overwrites the file in the project directory with an older version. In this context, `<revision>` references the desired commit (see Section 12.2).

- git restore --ours <file> or git restore --theirs <file> overwrites the file with the last valid version from its own branch or from the other branch (in case of a pull operation, the one from the remote repository) during a merge conflict.

By default, git restore overwrites the specified file only in the project directory. The --staged option makes sure that the file in the project directory remains unchanged, while the state of the file stored in the stage area is overwritten. With --staged --worktree, both variants of the file will be overwritten. (This behavior applies to git checkout by default.)

12.1.33 git rev-list

git rev-list <rev> lists all commits starting from the specified starting point. In this regard, the command is a variant of git log. The main difference is that, by default, git rev-list doesn't provide any details about the commits, only returns their hash codes. git rev-list is therefore well suited for script programming and for tasks where a second command processes the commits whose hash codes are provided by git rev-list.

git rev-list <rev1>..<rev2> takes into account the specified range within a branch. If <rev1> and <rev2> are located in different branches, only the changes in <rev2> that occurred since the last merge operation will be included. In general, git ref-list works quite similar to git log. In addition, parameters like --all, --after, --before, --grep, --no-merge, --since, and --until are evaluated as in git log (see Section 12.1.19).

If you simply want to know how many commits exist between two points in the commit sequence, you can pass the additional --count option. The git rev-list --count --all command determines the number of all commits in the repository.

12.1.34 git revert

git revert HEAD creates a new, inverse commit after the last commit and reverts the last changes made. git revert thus provides a transparent commit-undo function that doesn't subsequently change the commit sequence. However, an unsightly commit sequence results from it. If you haven't yet committed the last commit to the remote repository using git push, you might consider using git reset instead of git revert.

In its variant git revert <revision1> <rev2> <rev3> ..., the command reverts any commits picked out of the commit sequence. This approach adds a corresponding number of inverse commits to the commit sequence.

You can use git revert <revstart>..<revend> to undo an entire commit range. In this context, you should keep in mind that the start commit <revstart> itself will *not* be taken into account, only the subsequent commits.

The following options are also available:

■ `-n` or `--no-commit` only performs the required changes in the project directory, not the subsequent commit. You must initiate this commit yourself via `commit -a -m '<message>'`.

■ `--no-edit` uses automatically generated commit messages and thus avoids the repeated call of the editor to enter/modify the commit message.

12.1.35   git rm

`git rm <file>` deletes the specified file. If the file has been modified since the last commit, you must force the deletion using `--force`. Note that `git rm` can only be used for files that are under version control.

Using `git rm --cached <file>`, you can remove a file from the staging area, thus undoing `git add <file>`. This variant won't touch the file in the project directory. `git rm --cached <file>` is equivalent to `git reset <file>`.

12.1.36   git shortlog

`git shortlog` isn't a variant of `git log` but a simple statistics tool. This command retrieves a list of all commit authors and displays the first line of each of their associated commit messages. You can further shorten the output by using other options, such as the following:

■ `-<n>` only considers the most recent `<n>` commits. Thus, `git shortlog -100` shows who was responsible for the last 100 commits.

■ `--after <date>` or `--since <date>` shows only commits that originated after `<date>`. The value of `<date>` is specified in ISO format (e.g., `2020-12-31`).

■ `--before <date>` or `--until <date>` will only show commits done before/until `<date>`.

■ `-e` or `--email` also displays the email address. Consequently, commits from a developer with multiple email accounts are counted separately.

■ `-n` or `--numbered` sorts the author list by the number of commits (instead of alphabetically by default).

■ `--no-merges` ignores merge commits.

■ `-s` or `--summary` only shows the number of commits, not their commit messages.

12.1.37   git show

`git show <obj>` displays the object in question from the Git repository. The desired object can be specified by its hash code or by references (see Section 12.2).

The following options are available:

■ `--oneline` shortens the object specification to one line.

■ `--no-patch` shows only the metadata for commits, not the changes made.

Often, `git show` is used to display different versions of a file. The following examples show some syntax variants:

- `git show <file>` shows the file from the project directory in the current state.
- `git show :<file>` shows the file as it was saved in the staging area.
- `git show <revision>:<file>` shows the file in the state it was in when the commit expressed by `<revision>` took place. `git show HEAD-:db.py` shows the `db.py` file two commits ago.

A low-level alternative to `git show` is the `git cat-file <obj>` command. For commits, `git cat-file -p` reveals the hash codes of the parent commit and the associated tree. You can also determine what kind of object it is (with the `-t` option) and how its size (with the `-s` option).

12.1.38   git stage

`git stage` is equivalent to `git add`, so it saves the current state of files for the next commit.

12.1.39   git status

Without additional parameters, `git status` summarizes the status of the working directory. In particular, the command lists all files that have changed since the last commit and indicates whether or not they've been marked for the next commit. `git status` compares the working directory, the staging area, and the last commit of the active branch.

In addition, `git status` shows a list of all files that aren't under version control but have also not been explicitly excluded in *.gitignore*. (Conversely, if `git status` outputs many unversioned files you don't want to include in your repository anyway, you should take the trouble to adapt *.gitignore* accordingly.)

The following options are available:

- `-s` or `--short` displays the information in a clear shorthand notation. Tip: You can permanently enable the short notation via `git config --global status.short true`. Then, if you still want the full status output as an exception, you can run `git status --long`.
- `-u` or `--untracked-files` lists only files that aren't versioned.

12.1.40   git submodule

In Git terminology, we use the term *submodules* when a repository itself contains other repositories (see Chapter 9, Section 9.3). In this case, `git submodule` takes care of their administration. Without any additional parameters, the command lists all known submodules stored in the *.gitmodules* file.

With `git submodule <cmd> <options>`, you can then perform various actions. We'll only briefly summarize the most important three:

- `add <url>` adds the submodule specified by its address to the current repository and stores a reference in the *.gitmodules* file.

- `status` lists all submodules together with the currently active commits. Submodules that haven't been initialized yet are marked with -, while submodules that have been changed compared to the remote repository are marked with +. If the submodules themselves contain other submodules, you also need the `--recursive` option.

- `update` updates the content of the submodules. The `--init` option must be specified for the first execution. The submodules will then be downloaded from the remote repository for the first time. (For an ordinary repository, this option would correspond to `git clone`.)

12.1.41 git subtree

`git subtree` provides a second option (in addition to `git submodule`) to include the files of an external repository in a subdirectory of the local repository (see Chapter 9, Section 9.3). Many users prefer subtrees because they're easier to handle.

Consider the following examples:

- `git subtree add --prefix <subdir> <url> <rev>` inserts the project directory of an external repository in a specific revision (e.g., `v2.0` or simply `HEAD`) into the `<subdir>` subdirectory. `<subdir>` thus becomes part of the current repository. Neither does this command result in repository nesting, nor does it create another Git database in `<subdir>/.git`.

- `git subtree merge --prefix <subdir> <rev>` merges the files in the subdirectory with the specified `<rev>` commit.

- `git subtree pull --prefix <subdir> <url> <rev>` updates `<subdir>` with a different version of the external repository.

- `git subtree push --prefix <subdir> <url> <rev>` uploads changes made in the subdirectory into the specified repository. Before the push, `git subtree split` is run internally to create a commit that includes only files inside `<subdir>`.

For the `git subtree add`, `merge`, and `pull` commands, specifying the `--squash` option is often useful: This option combines all changes into a single commit.

12.1.42 git switch

Since Git version 2.23 (August 2019), you can use `git switch <branch>` instead of `git checkout <branch>` to switch the active branch, with the following option:

- `-c <newbranch>` or `--create <newbranch>` creates the new branch and activates it.

`git switch -` switches to the last valid branch. If you execute the command twice, you'll be back in the initially active branch.

12.1.43   git tag

git tag manages *tags* (markers, i.e., named commits). Without additional parameters, git tag lists all known tags.

git tag <tagname> provides the current commit (i.e., HEAD) with a lightweight tag. Alternatively, you can create annotated tags (-a option) and annotated signed tags (-s or -u option). Tag names must not contain spaces. Restrictions also exist for other special characters (see man git-check-ref-format).

To tag another commit or object, you must call the command in its variant, git tag <tagname> <commitid> or git tag <tagname> <objid>.

The following options are available:

- -a or --annotate creates a new annotated tag. The name of the tag must be specified in the command (e.g., git tag -a 'v1.0'). Optionally, you can save a message together with the tag using -m or --message.

- -d or --delete deletes the specified tag in the local repository. (To delete a tag in a remote repository, you should run git push origin --delete <tagname>.)

- -f or --force allows overwriting an already existing tag.

- -l or --list lists all tags in alphabetical order. A different sort order can be enforced by the Git configuration versionsort.suffix or the --sort option. If you're only interested in the first or last tags, you should append head or tail to the command on macOS or Linux or in Git Bash. The following command returns the ten most recent tags, ordered by commit time:

```
git tag --sort=committerdate | tail -10
```

Together with the -l option, you can pass a search pattern. For example, git tag -l '2nd*' returns all tags whose name starts with "2nd."

If you run git tag without any other options or arguments, git tag --list will be implicitly applied.

- -m <txt> or --message=<txt> provides a tag with a message. If you use this option without -a, -s, or -u <keyid>, -a will be applied implicitly (i.e., an annotated tag will be created).

- -s or --sign creates a GNU Privacy Guard (GnuPG)-signed tag using the key matching the email address (user.email).

- --sort=<sortorder> specifies the order in which the tags should be output. The permitted settings are authordate, committerdate, creatordate, and taggerdate. Other permitted keywords are provided by git-for-each-ref. A hyphen inverts the sort order (e.g., --sort=-taggerdate). By default, the tags are sorted alphabetically.

- -u <key> or --local-user=<key> creates a GnuPG-signed tag using the specified key.

12.2   Revision Syntax

In Chapter 3, Section 3.12, we introduced you to some variants of the revision syntax. With these notations, you can guide `git` commands to refer to specific commits or other objects. Table 12.2 summarizes the most important variants, with examples.

Note that the notation @{xxx} refers to the local reflog with the last actions performed. This type of syntax can therefore only be used if that log is available. In a freshly cloned repository, the reflog is empty.

Example	Meaning
HEAD	Head of the current branch
@	Head of the current branch (short notation)
develop	Head of different branch
develop:readme.txt	README file at the head of another branch
refs/remotes/origin/feature	Head of a remote branch
v1.3	Commit with tag v1.3
HEAD@{2 days ago}	Commit in current branch 2 days ago (reflog)
main@{7}	Commit in main branch prior to 7 subsequent actions (reflog)
HEAD~	Predecessor (parent) of the last commit
HEAD~3	Predecessor of the pre-predecessor
v1.3~3	Predecessor of the pre-predecessor of the commit with tag v1.3
234ae33^	First parent of merge commit 234ae33
234ae33^^	Second parent of merge commit 234ae33

Table 12.2 Revision Syntax

12.2.1   Commit Ranges (rev1..rev2 versus rev1...rev2)

With some commands, you can pass revision ranges in the form `rev1..rev2` or `rev1...rev2`, where the revisions are often simply the names of two branches. Unfortunately, no consistent interpretation of these two notations exists in Git. Rather, processing depends on the particular command. See Chapter 4, Section 4.1 and Section 4.2, for usage examples.

12.3   git Configuration

In the final section of this book, we'll provide a brief overview of Git's most important configuration files. A central role is of course played by *.git/config*, where most repository-specific settings are stored. Moreover, *.gitignore*, *.gitattribute*, and *.gitmodules* are added.

> **Why the Period?**
>
> The names of most configuration files start with a period. On Linux and macOS, such files and directories are considered hidden. The `ls` command shows such files only with the additional option -a, the file manager only after a shortcut key.
>
> On Windows, filenames beginning with a period are allowed, but they're treated like any other files.

12.3.1   Configuration File .git/config

Basic Git settings are stored at three levels:

- *System-wide settings* apply to all Git users on a machine. They're stored in the following locations depending on the operating system:
  - Windows: *C:\Program Files\Git\etc\gitconfig*
  - Linux: */etc/gitconfig*
  - macOS: */etc/gitconfig*

  In practice, system-wide settings are common only on Windows, while the */etc/gitconfig* file mostly doesn't exist or is empty on macOS and Linux.

- *Personal settings* apply across repositories. These settings are located in the *.gitconfig* file in the personal directory (home directory). The user's name and email address are usually stored there, often also his or her favorite editor, as well as some other basic settings (e.g., for authentication or for handling line endings).

- *Local settings* apply only to the repository. These settings are stored in the *.git/config* file within the repository.

In case of contradictions, local settings take precedence over personal or system-wide settings. The `git config --list --show-origin` command provides a summary of all the settings that apply in the current directory, while also specifying which configuration file is taken into account:

```
git config --list --show-origin
    file:/home/kofler/.gitconfig        user.name=Michael Kofler
    file:/home/kofler/.gitconfig        user.email=MichaelKofler@u...
    file:/home/kofler/.gitconfig        core.editor=/usr/bin/jmacs
    file:/home/kofler/.gitconfig        core.pager=less --raw-cont...
```

```
file:.git/config    core.repositoryformatversion=0
file:.git/config    core.filemode=true
file:.git/config    core.bare=false
file:.git/config    core.logallrefupdates=true
file:.git/config    pull.rebase=true
file:.git/config    remote.origin.url=git@github.com:MichaelK...
file:.git/config    remote.origin.fetch=+refs/heads/*:refs/re...
...
```

A quick look into the respective configuration file shows the simple syntax structure. Most of the basic settings are located in the [core] group. In addition, other groups of settings exist for specific subcommands, for instance, [pull] with options for git pull. Detailed settings for individual branches are introduced with [branch "name"], settings for external repositories with [remote "name"].

```
# .git/config file
[core]
    repositoryformatversion = 0
    filemode                = true
    bare                    = false
    logallrefupdates        = true
[pull]
    rebase = true
[remote "origin"]
    url   = git@github.com:MichaelKofler/git-buch.git
    fetch = +refs/heads/*:refs/remotes/origin/*
...
```

You can make changes directly in the file in question or using the git config <option> <value> command. If a personal setting must be modified, you can additionally use the --global option; for system-wide settings, you would use the --system option.

Note that other commands besides git config can make changes to *.git/config*. These commands include git branch --set-upstream-to git checkout --track, git remote, and git push --set-upstream.

12.3.2   Basic Settings

We can't provide references for all the options in *.git/config* in this book, as far too many keywords exist. The vast majority of them you'll never need in everyday Git use.

Let's summarize some of the most basic settings:

■ **Name and email address**
  user.name and user.email determine the name and email address that will be stored for commits (see Chapter 2, Section 2.3).

- **Editor**
  core.editor specifies which editor is started by Git when a commit message or other text is to be entered or modified (see Chapter 2, Section 2.1).

- **Pager**
  The *pager* is the program that allows you to scroll through a multi-page git command output using the cursor keys. By default, the less command is used. If international characters or emojis are displayed incorrectly, running less with the --raw-control-chars option may help (see Chapter 4, Section 4.1):

  ```
  git config --global core.pager 'less --raw-control-chars'
  ```

- **Line break**
  Windows expects the carriage return (CR) and line feed (LF) characters at the end of each line, while Linux and macOS make do with LFs only. Via core.autocrlf = true, Git takes care of keeping text files compatible with the operating system in use (see Chapter 2, Section 2.1).

- **Authentication**
  Git can use an operating system utility for authentication, such as Windows Credential Manager or macOS Keychain. The required credential.helper option is often set during installation (see Chapter 2, Section 2.4). Common settings are manager-core (Windows), osxchain (macOS), and libsecret (Linux, only if libsecret has already been installed).

- **Master or main**
  Using init.defaultBranch = main, you can specify that main is used as the default branch when initializing new repositories.

- **Pull behavior**
  If multiple developers work on the same branch and want the commit sequence to be as tidy as possible, automatically rebasing on each git pull may be appropriate. We explained the advantages and disadvantages of pull.rebasing = true in Chapter 3, Section 3.10.

  Conversely, using pull.rebasing = false will cause git pull to attempt to process the changes as a fast-forward merge. If that approach isn't possible, a "real" merge process, including a commit, will take place. This behavior is the default behavior of git pull.

  Another option is pull.ff = only. Again, git pull tries a fast-forward merge. If that doesn't succeed, git pull will terminate with an error message.

- **Automatically transfer annotated tags with push**
  git push typically ignores tags unless you use the --follow-tags option. In that case, annotated tags (and only those tags) will be automatically transmitted as well. push.followTags = true enables this option by default (see Chapter 3, Section 3.11).

- **Abbreviations**
  Git aliases can save you a lot of typing effort (see Chapter 9, Section 9.4). The abbreviations are stored in the [alias] section of the configuration file in the form <myalias> = <subcmd options>.

- **Template for the commit message**
  You can use `commit.template = <filename>` to reference a text file to be used as a template for commit messages. This template is used whenever Git starts an editor, but not when you specify the message directly via `git commit -m '<message>'`.

- **Colors**
  The commands `git log`, `git blame`, and others highlight certain details in color. If you don't like the default colors, get some inspiration from the following tutorials on Stack Overflow:

  - *https://stackoverflow.com/questions/10998792*
  - *https://stackoverflow.com/questions/5889878*
  - *https://stackoverflow.com/questions/3958977*

12.3.3   Configuration File .gitignore

As the name implies, *.gitignore* contains instructions about which files from the project directory Git should ignore and should therefore *not* include in the repository. The syntax is easy to understand using the examples provided in Table 12.3. You can read about additional variants at the following link:

https://git-scm.com/docs/gitignore

Example	Meaning
`# Comment`	Comment line
`mysecret`	Ignore the `mysecret` file
`*.o`	Ignore `*.o` files
`*~`	Ignore backup files of the form `*~`
`\#*#`	Ignore backup files of the form `#*#`
`tmp/`	Ignore the entire `tmp` directory
`!tmp/important`	Deviate from the other rules and do include `tmp/important`

Table 12.3 Syntax Examples for ".gitignore"

You can set up an individual *.gitignore* file in each directory, whose rules will then apply only to that directory. In general, *.gitignore* has no effect on files that have already been versioned. The configuration file applies only to future Git operations.

12.3.4   Configuration File .gitmodules

If you use `git submodules` to nest Git repositories, *.gitmodules* contains the appropriate settings. The syntax of the file looks like the following example:

```
# Example of .gitmodules
[submodule "hello-world-node"]
        path = hello-world-node
        url = https://github.com/docbuc/hello-world-node
[submodule "grafana"]
        path = grafana
        url = https://github.com/docbuc/grafana.git
```

12.3.5   Configuration File .gitattributes

In the *.gitattributes* file, attributes can be assigned to specific filenames or filename patterns. These attributes specify, for example, that a file should be considered a text file, what language-specific rules `git diff` should apply when comparing such files, and more.

```
# Example for .gitattributes
# *.c and *.h files
*.c     diff=cpp
*.h     diff=cpp
# View *.md files as text files
*.md    text
```

As a rule, setting up *.gitattributes* at all isn't necessary. If you do, however, additional detailed information is available at the following link:

https://git-scm.com/docs/gitattributes

12

The Authors

 **Bernd Öggl** is an experienced system administrator and web developer. Since 2001 he has been creating websites for customers, implementing individual development projects, and passing on his knowledge at conferences and in publications.

 **Michael Kofler** studied telematics at Graz University of Technology and is one of the most successful German-language IT specialist authors. In addition to Linux, his areas of expertise include IT security, Python, Swift, Java, and the Raspberry Pi. He is a developer, advises companies, and works as a lecturer.

Index